LOUD HAWK

LOUD HAWK

THE UNITED STATES
VERSUS THE AMERICAN INDIAN MOVEMENT

BY KENNETH S. STERN

UNIVERSITY OF OKLAHOMA PRESS

Norman

Someday, someone, who may not yet be born, will have a mission: to change all the history texts to read that "Columbus was the first European to land on American shores."

If that person is truly successful, the sentence will be followed by another: "It was a sad day for Indian people."

To that young man or woman, I dedicate this book.

Library of Congress Cataloging-in-Publication Data

Stern, Kenneth S. (Kenneth Saul), 1953–
    Loud Hawk : the United States versus the American Indian Movement / by Kenneth S. Stern.
        p.   cm.
    Includes index.
    ISBN 0-8061-2587-X (cloth)
    ISBN 0-8061-3439-9 (paper)
    1. Banks, Dennis—Trials, litigation, etc.   2. Firearms—Law and legislation—Oregon—Criminal provisions. 3. Malicious prosecution—Oregon.   4. Indians of North America—Government relations—1934–   5. American Indian Movement.   I Title.
KF224.B36S74   1994   93-6175
                                                                      CIP

The paper in this book meets the guidelines for permanence and durability of the Committee on Production Guidelines for Book Longevity of the Council on Library Resources, Inc. ∞

2   3   4   5   6   7   8   9   10

CONTENTS

v

PREFACE

THERE are only a handful of people in each generation who forge real change. There are fewer still whose changes make things better. Dennis James Banks, the charismatic founder of the American Indian Movement, is one of those very few.

Twenty years ago Indian people suffered from racism, poor health care, malnutrition, inferior education, and high alcohol and suicide rates. Unemployment frequently exceeded 90 percent. These problems still exist.

What did Dennis Banks do? He patrolled Minneapolis streets to protect Indian people from police brutality. He insisted the government prosecute those who killed Indians. He demanded respect for Indian peoples' rights, their customs, their land, and their heritage. Most important, he helped an entire generation feel that it is "okay" to be an Indian. Now, with that pride, there is hope where there was little before.

Today, Dennis Banks is a diplomat of sorts. The U.S. Congress, state governments, and Indian leaders seek him out for advice on Indian health and education, on laws to stop the black market in artifacts and body parts stolen from Indian graves, on corruption in the Bureau of Indian Affairs, on how Indian nations can become self-sufficient and self-governing again.

He said the same things twenty years ago. Only then, the government was not listening.

So he spoke louder.

And the government went after him.

In the summer of 1975, Dennis Banks was afraid for his life.

Someday, someone will write *The Dennis Banks Story*. This is not that book. Rather, this is the story of a criminal case that began in Portland, Oregon, in 1975. Dennis Banks was one of the defendants. The case never went to trial. It ended in 1988, after thirteen years of pretrial litigation. It is the longest pretrial criminal case in U.S. history.

Five years before the legal battle ended, Dennis poured a cup of coffee for me at his kitchen table and asked, "When this case is over, will you write about it? It's important that people know."

What Dennis had in mind, I think, was a book more about the novel legal twists than about the people and the times. After all, this case was dismissed for constitutional violations four times, then resurrected. It was even argued before the U.S. Supreme Court.

Many of the legal twists are here—to give flavor and structure to the story. But for every motion or argument, twenty or thirty were neglected. Those who are interested can find them in law books and court papers.[1]

The real story of this case is in how it evolved historically. The government's allegations and the defendants' countercharges had their roots in a war. It was a war between Indian activists and the government. It took place on the Pine Ridge Indian Reservation in South Dakota in the summer of 1975. Many people died. Little has been written about it.

The story I tell here is true. Sometimes, to protect innocent and guilty alike, I have changed people's identities. In those few cases, I have noted the false names. In a few places, I have condensed events, or changed backgrounds, to avoid making the story too disjointed or confusing. (In chapter 14, for example, there were two investigatory trips into eastern Oregon; I combined the more important events into one.)

Many quotes (especially in the earlier part of the book, before

---

1. *United States v. Loud Hawk et al.*, 816 F.2d 1323 (9th Cir., 1987); *United States v. Loud Hawk et al.*, 474 U.S. 302, 88 L.Ed.2d 640, 106 S.Ct. 648, rehearing denied 475 U.S. 1061, 89 L.Ed2d 596, 106 S.Ct 1289 (1986); *United States v. Loud Hawk et al.*, 741 F.2d 1184 (9th Cir., 1984); *United States v. Banks et al.*, 682 F.2d 841 (9th Cir., 1982), cert. denied, 459 U.S. 1117, 103 S.Ct. 755, 74 L.Ed.2d 972 (1983); *United States v. Loud Hawk et al.*, 628 F. 2d 1139 (9th Cir., 1979) (en banc), cert. denied, 445 U.S. 917, 100 S.Ct 1279, 63 L.Ed.2d 602 (1980); *United States v. Loud Hawk et al.*, withdrawn panel decision of July 26, 1977 (9th Cir., 1977); *United States v. Loud Hawk et al.*, 564 F. Supp. 691 (D.C., Or. 1983); record of *United States v. Loud Hawk et al.*, 75-CR-296-RE, United States District Court for the District of Oregon.

the cup of coffee that started my avid note-taking) are from memory or are reconstructions based on FBI documents, transcripts, letters, and interviews. Some of the quotes have been edited for easier reading, without altering their meaning.

I have tried to tell everything the way it happened. I am sure I have made mistakes. In a work covering so many years and people, that is inevitable. I apologize in advance. But the reader should know that the story told here is true.

For this I thank Dennis Banks. He never asked to see the manuscript, nor did he suggest that I leave things out or put things in.

KENNETH S. STERN

Brooklyn, New York

LOUD HAWK

CHAPTER 1

✝ ✝ ✝

MILEPOST 371

"HEY, Ken, how's the baby?" dispatcher T. J. Botner asked, as Ken Griffiths rushed through the Oregon State Police barracks, shedding his heavy overcoat.

"Pretty as can be," he answered, moving past the outer office into the squad room.

Ten minutes later, roll call was over. It had been the same as always. Boring.

Griffiths, an ordinary looking fellow despite his blue uniform and shiny trooper's badge, swallowed the last of his coffee and retrieved his winter coat. With his radar device in hand, he headed to his assigned car—and another shift at milepost 371, ready to catch speeders who thought they could make it through the desert on a cold moonless night a little faster than the law allowed.

On his way out of the barracks, Botner stopped him. "Hey, Ken, take a look at this, will ya?" he asked.

The dispatcher shoved a piece of paper at Griffiths. It was a fresh teletype from the Federal Bureau of Investigation in Portland. Another thing to remember. "Be on the lookout—a 1969 Dodge Explorer motor home, license . . . , and a white station wagon . . . possible federal fugitives . . . might be traveling . . . Pacific Northwest."

Griffiths handed the paper back. Sure. Nobody ever went through tiny, dusty Ontario, Oregon.

Griffiths took the second exit off the interstate, crossed the Chester overpass, drove down the entrance ramp, and nestled his patrol car into its sheltered hiding place. Catching speeders took little attention; he could daydream at the same time. First, he would notice the glimmer of headlights in the mirror. Then he would aim the radar gun and read the number. Once Griffiths let a vehicle pass, so did the distraction from his daydreams.

He noticed a car in the distance. It was not a speeding vehicle.

But it was a motor home, and that triggered an association in Griffiths's mind. Botner's teletype had mentioned a motor home. But this one was newer, it was not a Dodge, and it had Oregon plates. He was sure the motor home in the all points bulletin (APB) had out-of-state plates.

Griffiths was about to return to his daydreams when another large set of headlights appeared in the distance. Two sets. The radar gun did not indicate the vehicles were speeding, but as they passed, his heart began to pound: a white motor home, with out-of-state plates, and a station wagon.

Griffiths put the radar gun down and got his patrol car onto the highway in an instant. He radioed to the barracks. "T. J. I just made contact with a motor home and a station wagon," he said. "Both white. Both out-of-state plates. I'm going to pull close to them. Read me the descriptions from the APB. Over."

As Griffiths overtook the station wagon near milepost 374, he edged his way to the motor home. Botner radioed back. The license plates and descriptions matched. "Careful, Ken," he advised. "The APB says they're dangerous federal fugitives."

The motor home, the patrol car, and the station wagon cruised past milepost 375, three minutes from the Idaho border. Botner had already radioed Trooper Clayton Kramer to drop everything and help Griffiths. Kramer was lodging a drunk at the Ontario city jail. He left the man with the city police and ran to his patrol car. Jumping into the driver's seat and starting the ignition in one motion, he barreled down the empty streets toward the interstate entrance. There were two street lights in Ontario. Both were green.

As Kramer approached the interstate, Griffiths decided to stop the motor home. The Snake River—the border with Idaho—was only two miles away. On came the overhead lights, up went the high beams, and on drove the motor home. "He isn't going to stop!" Griffiths radioed Botner. "Pull over, goddamn it!" he shouted, more to himself than to the motor home, whose occupants could not possibly hear.

Just as Griffiths started to radio Kramer in a panic, the motor home slowed. Its right directional signal flashed, and it decelerated as it veered onto the shoulder. As it came to a stop, Griffiths glanced at his rearview mirror. He saw the station wagon one hundred yards behind, on the shoulder. The driver had stopped of his own accord. Finally, he saw Kramer's rotating lights. Kramer was pulling behind the motionless wagon.

Griffiths silently talked himself through the steps. "Careful now, Ken. Everything has to be slow, by the book. Methodical. Quick radio check with Kramer. Okay, he'll get the people out of the station wagon. Here goes."

The police shotgun was shaking in his hands as Griffiths opened the door of his squad car. The cold, fresh, desert air slapped him alert.

He walked slowly around the back of the large motor home, inching up to the front door. With the butt of the gun, he banged on the metal. He tried matching the authority of that sound with his voice, hiding his fear. Whoever was inside had to know he was in charge. "Everyone out now," he demanded. "Come on, everyone get out of the vehicle."

It took only five seconds for the door of the motor home to open, but it seemed longer to the cold police officer. Federal fugitives!

Prepared for the worst, Griffiths clutched his shotgun. He expected the occupants to resemble Jesse and Frank James. To his surprise, out walked a Mexican fellow, sort of stocky, with curly hair, not particularly scary looking.

"Stand off by the shoulder. Over there. Anyone else inside?" he asked.

"Only women and children," the man answered.

Down the motor home steps came an Indian child in diapers, her big brown eyes just awakening. Her tiny hands were held by two attractive young Indian women, one very pregnant.

All four occupants were dressed for the warm motor home, not for the cold eastern Oregon night. They stood, arms folded, moving side to side as they stomped their feet for warmth, while Griffiths tried to maintain the safest position for himself. Even though these people did not look dangerous, he was no fool. Someone could still be in the motor home—armed. He was the only cop there.

"Anyone still inside?" Griffiths kept asking, again and again. The man and women and baby were shivering in the cold, and Griffiths's nervousness, coupled with an almost instinctual response to the trembling of his captives, put a quiver in his voice.

"Anyone still in there?" he demanded, while fixing his eyes on the "fugitives" as best he could in the dark, his shotgun nervously moving with each breath, up and down, up and down.

"Answer me, goddamn it! Anyone else inside? Is that it? Anyone else in there?"

A quick, firm answer finally came from the Mexican. "*No.*" Within a millisecond, five separate actions took place. Each, in succession, took only an instant. But they seemed to occur in slow motion.

The Mexican bolted toward the roadway fence.

The motor home's backup lights came on.

Griffiths thought he heard a shot fired in his direction.

The motor home sped forward.

Griffiths emptied both barrels at the fleeing Mexican.

As Griffiths's gun went off, the two women dived for the ground, pulling the baby with them. Then they scrambled down the shoulder, toward the station wagon. Were they going to try to escape too? Griffiths thought not, not with a baby and one so pregnant she could not run.

"Walk to the station wagon with your hands up!" he shouted to them.

Watching their progress, he radioed Kramer to guard them. Griffiths weighed what to do. The Mexican might have been hit, but he was not stopped. It was too dark and dangerous to go after him alone. According to Botner, the Ontario police were on their way, and word was already over the air: "Officer under fire!" Every law enforcement officer within a thirty-mile radius would be speeding to Ontario.

In less than a minute, two Ontario city police officers arrived, and Griffiths took off after the motor home. A half mile down the road, a literal stone's throw from the Snake River and Idaho, the motor home rested in the highway's depressed median strip.

Griffiths got out and looked around from a distance, keeping his eyes on the windows of the motor home, watching for any movement. The engine was still running, the lights were on, and the door was shut. Unless someone inside tried something, that is how it would remain. Griffiths, shivering from the thought that the son of a bitch Mexican could have killed him, climbed back into his warm patrol car and waited. This time he was not going to do anything until help arrived.

CHAPTER 2

✛ ✛ ✛

MIGHTY MIDGETS

"WALK faster and get your hands up!" Kramer yelled as the women came toward him.

Frightened and cold, pregnant KaMook Banks, her eighteen-month-old daughter, Tasina (nicknamed "Tosh"), and Anna Mae Aquash walked the highway's shoulder, into the corridor cut by the station wagon's headlights.

"Think they got away?" Anna Mae whispered to KaMook, her lips barely moving, her head pointed forward.

"Don't know," KaMook replied, staring straight ahead. "I think I heard Leonard groan. He might have been hit."

"C'mon!" Kramer yelled, "get back here *now*, and keep your hands up!"

The woman saw Kramer's silhouette, beefy and erect from his Smokey the Bear hat down to his high black leather boots, backlit in the stray beams.

"We're holding a baby," Anna Mae yelled. "Coming fast as we can."

"Just get back here, keep your hands in sight and your mouths shut, and lie down on the ground, next to these two Indian jokers," Kramer shouted.

Russ Redner and Kenny Loud Hawk, Indian men in their twenties, were lying face down on the frozen asphalt, perpendicular to the highway. Each was awash in the patrol car's beacon. Each had his hands bound behind his back.

Kramer and the two city officers who had joined him watched while the Indian women leaned on their knees, then lay face down beside their friends. Nylon handcuffs were yanked around the women's hands, then tightened with a jerk. As the women's wrists were snapped up behind their backs, they moaned. The upward motion of their arms crushed their faces into the ground.

"I'm pregnant," KaMook pleaded. "Officer, I can't lie on my stomach."

"Just stay the fuck where you are, Indian," one of the city officers shouted, while the other drove his boot into her back.

"Hey, you sure she doesn't have a shotgun inside her?" the second officer asked, laughing, twisting his heel down harder.

"If she does, it'll be her last one."

Redner lifted his head, turned toward the officers, and yelled, "Show the women a little respect!"

A shotgun was put against his skull. One of the officers, in a mocking voice, as if making a request, said, "Indian, you don't shut up, I'm gonna fuckin' blow your head off!"

Redner was about to say something. The officer cocked his gun. Redner lowered his head to the road.

After a minute when no one spoke, Kramer stepped forward and removed KaMook's cuffs. She sat up slowly and held her child, rocking back and forth.

When the baby stirred, KaMook whispered to her. "Shoosh, Tosh," she said, "everything will be okay."

"Don't talk, Indian!" one of the officers screamed at her, his gun pointed. The baby cried.

They waited, shivering, for thirty minutes. There was no moonlight. The asphalt was chilling. While the Indians lay prone, pickup trucks with rifles on their rear cab windows drove by. Most slowed down. A few stopped.

"See you got some Indians. Need any help?" one beer-bellied local asked, his right hand resting on his rifle rack.

"No thanks, we've got 'em where we want 'em," one of the officers replied.

A caravan of state police cars whizzed by, going east, toward the motor home. Kramer joined them. "Gonna see how Griffiths's doing," he said, leaving the Indians guarded by the two city patrolmen.

Within minutes, the Indians heard gunshots down the road. First there were single shots. Then there was a barrage. It sounded like a battle. The desert grew silent for a while. Then, now and again, they heard a booming, single, high-caliber shot cutting through the night air. Then silence.

An *Idaho Statesman* reporter arrived with a photographer. Snapping fast, the photographer moved directly above the prostrate prisoners.

"Get the fuck out of here, or you're going to be arrested too!" one of the Ontario officers yelled. When he started moving toward the photographer, his rifle in hand, the news people left.

Ten minutes after the reporter departed, Griffiths returned, with a half-dozen state police officers.

"Get moving!" one blue-uniformed officer shouted at a numb Kenny Loud Hawk as he yanked him off the ground and shoved him into the back of a patrol car.

On the ride to the Oregon State Police (OSP) barracks, the Indians peered down the roadway. The desert was flooded with car headlights, beacons, and rotating red and blue police lights. Off to the east they could see high-powered searchlights slowly panning the ground. The gunfire had stopped.

Dispatchers in Nyssa, Weiser, Fruitland, and Vale—tiny desert towns straddling the Snake River—repeated the call: "OSP officer under fire, near the interstate bridge in Ontario!"

Dozens of peace officers grabbed their guns, jumped into their cars, and sped toward the river. The Idaho officers erected a roadblock across their side of the bridge. The Oregon officers, including off-duty state troopers and Ontario police, searched the river's west bank. At least two fugitives were on the loose.

While KaMook Banks, Anna Mae Aquash, Russ Redner, and Kenny Loud Hawk had been lying on the ground, Ken Griffiths had been waiting by the motor home. He watched. Nothing moved.

"You okay?" Sgt. Joseph Ammirati, his superior, asked a half hour later. He had led a caravan of police cars to the scene, each blazing a mosaic of red and blue lights. Troopers Kramer and Rodney Schmeer and more Ontario city police had come with him.

Griffiths nodded, "Yes."

"See any movement?"

"Nope."

"Okay. We'll make sure."

Ammirati walked to his patrol car. "Come out with your hands up!" he yelled through its P.A. system. He repeated the command fifteen seconds later, punctuated with a warning shot over the motor home. No response. Another command. Another shot into the air. Another silence.

Ammirati, his jowls drooping from disappointment, stood with legs apart, aimed his shotgun, then fired into the rear windshield. He fired two more blasts through the motor home, then put the gun down. Tear gas was a better idea. He radioed Botner. The state police did not have any. A city officer volunteered his agency's supply.

Five minutes later, Ammirati, Trooper Schmeer, and Officer Randy Cook of the Ontario police stood in the cold, studying the city's equipment. It came in two parts: a .37mm gas gun, and a single piercing gas grenade. It was the only such grenade allocated to all the police agencies in a county the size of Massachusetts. No one had ever practiced with it.

Schmeer and Cook handed the parts back and forth. They squinted into the spotlights, rotating the grenade and the gun, trying to locate any finely printed instructions.

Schmeer finally said, "I think I've figured it out."

Ammirati ordered him to stand by, while the sergeant tried one last time. Just like on television. "Come on out with your hands up!" he yelled. The amplified sound squawked whenever he raised his voice for emphasis. "This is your last chance!"

Ammirati nodded to Schmeer. The trooper aimed at the rear window of the motor home. The .37mm gas gun went off with a burst, followed by the sound of breaking glass.

It took a moment to realize that the gas gun worked too well. The projectile easily sliced through the rear windshield and emerged through the front windshield. Some eastern Oregon prairie dog or rabbit down the road was getting gassed—not anyone who still happened to be in the motor home.

Ammirati asked if the Ontario police had any other rounds.

"No," said Randy Cook. Then he added, "We have something called a Mighty Midget Pistol Launcher, but it's not penetrating."

"Try it," Ammirati ordered.

"Sarge," Cook said, "this is for outdoor use."

Ammirati inspected it with a blank stare, handed it back to Cook, and pointed at the motor home.

Cook shrugged, approached the motor home's pockmarked

rear window, raised the pistol launcher, aimed for the spot that the previous gas round had gone through, and fired.

The projectile bounded off the glass and landed at Ammirati's feet. A minute later, Ammirati, still coughing from the gas, ordered a barrage of bullets and buckshot. The gunfire was so loud it was heard back at the station wagon and for miles beyond. The mirrors were shot out first, so that no one inside could watch. Then the windshields were fired at until they looked like Swiss cheese. The Mighty Midgets now did their work unimpeded.

Ammirati ordered Schmeer into the motor home. Fighting the tear gas, the trooper glanced around. Whoever had been inside was no longer there. Schmeer was both relieved and angry; relieved that he did not have to discover bloody body parts and angry that he and the other officers had wasted a half hour shooting at an inanimate object—and themselves—while they could have been searching for the fugitives.

One city officer was left guarding the motor home. Griffiths and the rest returned to the station wagon, picked up the Indians, and took them to the OSP barracks.

It was a short ride. The captives were led into the building and seated roughly on wooden chairs in a back room illuminated by incandescent lights. Their hands were bound firmly behind them. KaMook's, too. Baby Tosh had been taken away. Griffiths read each his or her *Miranda* rights. The prisoners said nothing.

As the prisoners were being booked, agents of the FBI were heading toward eastern Oregon. They had already talked with Ammirati on the telephone. "Don't you idiots know how to read?" one agent yelled.

Their APB had been explicit. The first paragraph described the vehicles. The second paragraph, although short, was emphatically worded: "If vehicles sighted, *do not stop*, but advise FBI, Portland, immediately for more details."

Ken Griffiths had not noticed that part.

Two eager FBI agents, Daniel Bond and Keith Jacobs, arrived in Ontario by 2:00 A.M., after a 150-mile dash down the interstate from Pendleton, Oregon.

"These guys are finally doing something right," Bond said to his partner, after Ammirati briefed them.

The state and local officers were searching the railroad tracks, riverbanks, restaurants, motels, bus depots—every logical area to spot any out-of-place person.

Now, however, the FBI was in charge. Bond and Jacobs gave their first order—to Ammirati. "Call off the search until morning."

At 3:00 A.M., the two agents stood at the front of the OSP squad room. Sitting attentively, like students, were OSP Lt. Don Kleinsmith, OSP Sgt. Ammirati, OSP Investigator Ed Hanson, and Deputy District Attorney Byron Chatfield. Jacobs strolled to the room's green door and closed it, firmly. He returned to the front of the room and sat on the edge of an old gray metal desk. One of Jacobs's legs dangled in the air; the other touched the linoleum floor.

"We have informants," he said. "The people we're looking for are two American Indian Movement leaders, Leonard Peltier and Dennis Banks."

The state police nodded. The names were familiar, but that was all.

While Bond and Jacobs were briefing the local authorities, their boss, John O'Rourke, the top FBI agent in Oregon, had assembled forty FBI agents at the Portland airport. They were to fly to Boise, Idaho, where they would meet agents flying in from South Dakota, rent cars, and drive fifty-three miles to Ontario.

As their jet gained altitude, O'Rourke checked with two of his most trusted agents, Dave Milam and Steve Hancock.

"Got pictures of Banks and Peltier with you?"

"Yeah," Milam answered.

Another agent said, angrily, "I hope we get those sons of bitches."

A third added, "It's about time. I promise you. Peltier's not going to knock off any of us this time!"

The manhunt that began anew as the sun rose in the Oregon desert on November 15 was under firm FBI control. FBI agents were scattered around the desert, looking in places they did not want the local officers to know about. The FBI had informants.

"You guys search the vehicles. We'll hunt for the Indians, then do our own search later," O'Rourke instructed the state police as soon as he arrived at the Ontario barracks. The vehicles had been towed to a red and white hut known as Art's Garage and were waiting to be picked apart. At 3:30 P.M., Ontario's justice of the peace, Nita Bellows, signed a search warrant.

Sgt. Bill Zeller, an OSP fingerprint expert, entered the vehicles first. He dusted every surface and lifted every print. Investigator Hanson photographed the vehicle exteriors and the more important items Zeller brought out. Agents Milam and Hancock watched and took notes on long sheets of white paper.

The motor home was enormous. Zeller's search could take days. Everything was dusted, examined, and cataloged. Some items were photographed. There were cigarette packs. Pieces of scrap paper. Empty pickle jars. Cans of evaporated milk. Pots and pans. Diapers. Peanuts. A Kellogg's Corn Flakes box with a picture of Santa Claus. *People* magazines. A box of ninety-six ice cream cones. A copy of the screenplay for *Missouri Breaks*.

"Hey, Bill," one of the FBI agents said, "why don't you stop searching the motor home and take a quick run through the station wagon?"

Zeller grumbled, collected his tools, and went over to the smaller vehicle. Under the passenger seat he found a .44 Magnum—a legal pistol, nothing unusual in the Oregon desert.

Of more interest than the weapon or the clothes scattered throughout were seven cardboard boxes in the back, buried under clothes and blankets. Each was in a green plastic garbage bag. As Zeller moved the plastic aside, he saw the words EXPLOSIVE and DuPONT in big, bright, orange letters. He crawled out of the vehicle and walked away, slowly.

"Shit," he said, "take a look at this!"

There were seven fifty-pound cases of dynamite in the station wagon. If they should detonate at once, the Snake River would have a new bend.

CHAPTER 3

✝ ✝ ✝

BOMBER BILL

THE explosives were discovered too late to make the evening news. But the other events of the preceding night, as told by the FBI, made up the lead item on the news programs, beating out the residual ripples from the week's top stories—Justice William O. Douglas's resignation from the U.S. Supreme Court, the UN's equating of Zionism with racism, and pretrial skirmishing in the prosecution of Symbionese Liberation Army captive-turned-soldier Patty Hearst.

The television news contorted events into shorthand. Four Indian adults were arrested. At least two people escaped. The FBI thought the two were Indian activists Dennis Banks and Leonard Peltier. But the central "fact," emphasized by the FBI, and repeated over and over by the reporters that night, was a "shootout."

Even if the escaping person had fired the one round Griffiths alleged, that would hardly constitute a shootout. The OK Corral was a shootout; this was just one shot. Nonetheless, based on the FBI's information, the story was reported as a classic cowboys and Indians affair, bad guys and good guys shooting at each other. One print headline even announced, FIVE APPREHENDED IN SHOOTOUT, as if 18-month-old Tasina had fired off more than burps and scared, cold sobs.

The FBI's overemphasis on the gunplay was calculated. It hoped to impress would-be jurors who would sit in judgment on yet-to-be-charged crimes. The FBI was out to "get those sons of bitches." Bad Indians. Bad Indians with guns. Bad Indians shooting guns. Bad Indians shooting guns at whites. Bad Indians shooting guns at white cops.

In Salem, Oregon, on November 15, 1975, I managed to survive yet another long day as a first-year law student at Willamette

University. "I hate this shit!" I had mumbled to no one in particular, leaving the school building well after sunset.

Any hope that law school would be interesting was long abandoned, ten weeks into the semester. Now, school was but a means to an end—the license. I believed in social justice. I wanted to use law to help people change the system. The activists I had admired growing up—the draft resisters, the antiwar protesters, the civil rights workers—were the ones I wanted to represent.

People who fought the status quo and challenged society to let go of archaic and dangerous notions frequently needed a lawyer's help. People who resisted segregation ended up in southern jails. People who fought to end the war in Vietnam were arrested everywhere. Minorities and women victimized by discrimination needed attorneys. The seventies were the end of an era of activism, and I, Ken Stern, wanted to serve the remaining activists, to help those in trouble stay on the streets and to use the theater of criminal trials to educate all who would listen. That would be my contribution, my way of helping to remake society, to make life better and fairer, to create fundamental change.

I knew that as soon as I finished law school, I would not join a firm, strive to become a partner, and plan away the rest of my life as a functionary, transferring rich peoples' money, taking a cut as it passed by. I would be my own boss. I would work for the clients I chose and find cases where I could make a difference. I was young (twenty-two), eager, motivated, idealistic, and passionately political. If there was to be a new Rosenberg case, I wanted to be part of it. If there was to be a new Chicago Conspiracy trial, I wanted to help. I needed to make a mark, to be in the fray, challenging the legal system.

For a student with such goals, law school was torture. Worse, it was irrelevant.

No one taught how to be a lawyer; everyone proffered disembodied rules so that a future bar exam could be passed. Law school worked from the back forward. If as many students as possible passed the bar exam, the school would have an enhanced reputation and attract better students, who would have a higher pass rate. It was a vicious cycle but one that could only be kept in its own insular rotation if the point was to teach how to pass a bar exam, rather than how to be a lawyer. I wanted the second course, the one not offered.

On the night of November 15, 1975, I was distressed. Law school was wearing on my soul more than I could admit. Four weeks before I had embarked on the slippery slope of skipping classes. Torts was the first to go. Torts is the study of civil wrongs—negligence, assault, product liability. The most uncivil wrong of all was that I was expected to be in class at 8:00 A.M. sharp and listen to the professor read back what I had read the night before in the casebook. I would read the night before; he would read in the morning. Strong coffee was no antidote.

After a few weeks, I came to the conclusion that I could read as well as the teacher. A dangerous thought. With that realization, the decision to be anywhere other than in bed at 8:00 A.M. seemed foolish. But the decision to refrain from an inane class was a determination capable of expansion. The other classes were no better—just later. The evening of November 15 was when it all hit me. Was it worth it? Would I be able to go through law school without attending class? Would I flunk out? Disgrace myself? Embarrass my parents? Waste money? The anxiety was so potent that I did something sinful for a book lover. I walked over to a law book lying on the floor, one of those meaty, 1,500-page, granitelike tomes, and gave it my best soccer kick into the white plasterboard wall.

I knew I needed an outlet. But for that evening, I decided to let it go. I poured a Jack Daniels, pitched two ice cubes into the glass, and turned on the news.

That night I watched a report of Indians arrested in eastern Oregon. Something bothered me. The way the officials and the news people reported it, a shootout made little sense. The story had Trooper Griffiths stopping the motor home. Then two women, a baby, and a man emerged. The officer and the occupants must have been close together. Then the man dashed for the highway fence and in the process of jumping over it, shot at the cop. The shootout started. In Ontario.

I could picture it all. Less than three months before, I had driven cross country and spent my first Oregon night in Ontario. The Fireside Motel bordered the freeway fence. It was right by the exit, less than a mile from the Snake River. I knew exactly where the alleged shootout had taken place. I had stood there in the cool desert night, bright with moonlight, leaning against that same roadside fence, marveling at this new land, so distant from my native New York, so full of open spaces and fresh air laced with the sweet smell of desert sage.

Sipping my bourbon, I remembered that Ontario highway well. What the reporter and FBI officials said was perplexing. They claimed the man was shooting as he was going over the fence. Unlikely. The fence was too high. I had stood there. He could not climb it and aim while trying to escape on a moonless night. If he had shot, the man must have had no regard for the women and child. How could he be sure he would hit the officer but miss his nearby friends? The way the news people created the image, it was as if the escapee would have had to shoot through the women to get to the cop. Something was wrong.

I turned off my black and white television and went to sleep intrigued—for the first time since law school had begun.

No one ever felt ambivalent about Bomber Bill Fettig. He was pleasant to those who left him alone, an irritant to those who cramped his independence. But if you wanted things to go BOOM, there was no better person in the west. The man had gusto.

Fettig had started blowing up things professionally during World War II. In the army he was an explosive ordnance disposal specialist. He spent twenty-five years in the military, getting paid to destroy the military's destructive devices.

After World War II, when land used for practice bombing ranges was returned to the people who had donated it, the ground was combed for unexploded bombs. The seeming duds had to be blown up. Bomber Bill Fettig was the man who did it.

The president's life could be endangered by an explosive device. The Secret Service had a special bomb disposal unit. Bomber Bill Fettig taught them how.

Fettig knew how to detonate everything from a firecracker to a nuclear weapon. When he retired from the military in 1968, he was hired by the Oregon State Police. He now spent his days driving around the state and getting rid of old explosives found at mining camps, in the woods, or any other place they happened to turn up. This was retirement as it should be. Fettig was getting paid to have fun.

Fettig got a call from his superior, OSP Lt. William McCollum on Saturday night, November 15. By 5:00 A.M. on the 16th, he was on the road, headlights and heater on, heading for Ontario, eight hours away.

It was midafternoon when he arrived at Art's Garage. Four police cars, two of them unmarked, were parked outside. Inside, Sgt. Zeller was fingerprinting the station wagon, applying his magic dust slowly, in swirls, careful to stay away from the dynamite. While collecting ridges and whirls left by oily fingers, he had uncovered a dozen weapons—rifles and handguns, some semiautomatic—hidden in the vehicles. Some had obliterated serial numbers. Zeller had accomplished enough to satisfy the FBI for one day. Putting his brush, powder, tape, and glass slides aside, Zeller motioned to Fettig with a wink and a "thumbs up." He stood aside.

Fettig removed one of the plastic garbage bags covering a cardboard box in the back of the white station wagon. Inside was a full case of DuPont Gelex #2—70 percent strength, dated 1973. "Good stuff," Fettig mumbled to Zeller, who was watching from a distance, next to two FBI men.

Fettig opened the bags covering each of the other six cases. Each case, in turn, was removed and photographed by the FBI agents and OSP Officer Hanson. One of the boxes was discolored and very wet. It fell apart. The rest held together. Fettig carefully put all seven cases into the trunk of his patrol car. They were piled high. The trunk lid would not close. Fettig tied it down with an old piece of rope that had once been white but was now a grease-smudged gray.

He drove his white OSP patrol car out of Art's, motioned for the others to follow, and turned onto the main road, heading to a pistol range west of town. Cars with FBI and state police followed, in procession.

Fettig's car bounced and bumped down a dirt road. He made a wide turn into the range, throwing gravel from the road with his right-side wheels, and stopped. He rolled down his window and stuck his arm out, motioning for the others to stop too. Acknowledged, he wound the window back up, then opened his door and stepped outside into the desert's bright afternoon sunshine.

He looked down. He looked left. He looked right. He looked behind. He was surveying his outdoor theater. His audience should be far enough away to be safe but close enough for a good view.

Fettig took two sticks of dynamite from each of the cases at random, as if he were drawing tickets at a raffle. Then he reached into his pocket and retrieved a knife. As he held each selected stick, in turn, he cut open the red wax wrapper and scraped the inside clean. One wrapper from each case was given as evidence to the FBI agent, Milam, another duplicate set of seven to OSP criminalist Hanson.

Having built up the tension with his slow, methodical scraping, he now spoke quietly but with authority, "Move back, please." No one argued. Now was the time for the real show to begin.

Fettig took a dynamite stick from one of the boxes and held it naturally, comfortably, like a chef would hold a knife or a baseball player a bat. He knew that the assembled law enforcement audience would be impressed with his apparent disdain for danger. They always were. People mistook his calm expertise for either machismo or stupidity. He did not care. It helped set the atmosphere.

Fettig always carried explosive cord and blasting caps in his car. He sliced a piece off the cord with a quick flash of his knife and then joined it and a blasting cap to the stick of dynamite. With great panache he pulled a silvery matchbook from the breast pocket of his blue windbreaker.

Holding the bomb under his left armpit, he cupped his hands around his mouth and yelled to his enthralled audience, "Get ready!"

The match, lit, then sheltered protectively between his hands against the desert breeze, ignited the fuse and was extinguished with a quick shake. Fettig set the bomb on the gravel. After watching the fuse burn six inches, he strolled back a comfortable distance, seemingly indifferent. The stick sat on the desert floor for 30 seconds while the tension built, the fuse sizzling. Agent Milam had his camera ready. It almost seemed too long, as if something had gone wrong. Fettig liked it that way. Then, all of a sudden, a flash. *Poof!* The stick was gone, destroyed. Fettig suppressed a smile.

He had enjoyed that. He walked to the huddle of police officers, accepting congratulations. Then, almost as an afterthought, he said, "Better make sure you guys got pictures. I'll do another one." This was fun, and the toys were free.

Fettig repeated his act. This time, for greater effect, he picked three sticks. Three sticks, the cord binding them together, look more like bombs on television.

The agent and Trooper Hanson stared through their cameras again. Waiting, a flash, *poof,* shutters clicking, and that was that. Fettig could have played with the explosives all afternoon. But he had other responsibilities. He had to appear professional. Having put on his show, he prepared a mellower finale.

He lifted all the cartons, plastic bags, and the remainder of the 350 pounds of sticks and arranged four separate mounds. He poured oil on each. He lit each pile with a match.

Four big bonfires burned everything, the dark smoke spiraling into the crisp desert air. Every molecule of evidence burned completely. Fettig had driven four hundred miles to dispose of this material thoroughly. Only ashes remained.

Fettig watched his final scene silently. He walked over to the smoldering residue. He did not quite kick it. He used his shoe as a shovel, digging under the top layer to expose and inspect the material below.

Satisfied, he waved his arm. On cue, a crew from the State Highway Department drove its heavy equipment onto his stage and buried the ashes in the desert.

His performance ended, Fettig drove west, into the sunset. Three hundred fifty pounds of what appeared to have been dynamite was now a mass of carbon molecules, permanently blended into the eastern Oregon landscape.

While FBI agents were swarming the countryside, while officers were inspecting every inch of the vehicles inside Art's Garage, Russ Redner, Kenny Loud Hawk, Anna Mae Aquash, and Ka-Mook Banks were prisoners in the county jail in Vale, Oregon, twenty minutes from Ontario. The cells were tiny, almost airless, and painted drab green. The bars had spots of rust. The jail was in a dark, damp area in the basement of the county courthouse, in the middle of nowhere.

The Indians were frightened.

KaMook was suffering from chills and nausea. She needed the medication her doctor had prescribed. She was in her eighth month, and this baby, like the last one, would be delivered by cesarean. She was insistent, asking the matron, "Please! I gotta find out if my baby is okay. I need my medication."

The matron stood, silently, her hands folded against her chest.

"I'm sick," KaMook pleaded. "I was lying on my stomach in the cold, and an officer pushed down hard on my back. Please. I need to see a doctor. He might have hurt my baby."

The matron was not unkind. But nothing happened. It would be a week before she saw either a doctor or her pills.

She had more success making arrangements for her daughter, Tasina. KaMook had been allowed one telephone call.

"Margaret," she said, "I'm in jail in Vale, Oregon. It's not far from Boise, they tell me. I don't know what's gonna happen. Can you come get Tosh?"

Her sister, Margaret Bird, arrived the next day from Oklahoma. Tosh was okay. One less worry.

KaMook waited in her cell, taking it all in. She knew that soon she would be moved, either to Portland, the site of the U.S. Courthouse, where she had heard federal charges were going to be brought, or to Kansas, where she had been released pending trial on other federal charges. She had been arrested in Wichita. She had been traveling in a car with other Indian people. The car had made a funny noise. They pulled to the shoulder. Everyone got out. The noise continued. The car exploded.

No one was badly hurt. But KaMook Banks, at the tender age of 19, a pregnant Sioux Indian from the Pine Ridge reservation in South Dakota, was arrested, led away in handcuffs, and indicted by a federal grand jury for possessing illegal firearms found charred in the residue. That was only eight weeks ago, in September. Now, in November, this was a repeat performance. Jails were no fun. Every decision was controlled. Waking. Walking. Speaking. Eating. Urinating. Nothing went unregulated. No shred of personal power or judgment remained.

As bad as jail in Kansas had been, Vale was worse. It smelled of urine and staleness. There was nothing to do. It was redneck. She could hear the jailers down the hall. "Hey, you, wetback, stop speaking Spanish!" "Hey, wetback, where'd you get that ugly face!" "Wetback, you'd better watch your ass when you get out of here!"

Irrigation made it possible to grow crops in the desert, and the crops drew migrant farm workers. Some must have had too much to drink, or no place to sleep, or committed some crime that landed them in jail. KaMook felt for them. But once behind bars, their real crime became clear. She heard it in every sentence the jailers spoke. Their crime was their heritage. KaMook could relate.

Anna Mae was the older of the two women. She was focused, in charge. She knew what they needed. A damn good lawyer.

Anna Mae knew some people in Boise. She called carefully. She knew her one telephone call would be monitored.

"Hey, man. Listen, sorry to disturb you in the middle of the night," she said. "But we've had a change of plans. We've been busted. Yeah, we're in someplace called Vale, Oregon. Don't know exactly where that is. Can you organize some legal help? Like, right away?"

"Time's up," a gravel-voiced jailer said. The phone went dead.

CHAPTER 4

RANK AND SERIAL NUMBER

THE Pine Ridge Indian Reservation in South Dakota was a desolate place. Like most Indian reservations, the land was barren. It fit peoples' lives.

Dennis Banks, a thirty-eight-year-old Chippewa, was Ka-Mook's husband and Tasina's father. He was a founder of the American Indian Movement (AIM). He had spoken about his people's desperation for many years.

"Indians have a life expectancy of forty-four years," he told any audience that would listen. "On many reservations, there are no jobs. Unemployment on Pine Ridge is 87 percent. Indians have no hope. Our suicide rate is second only to psychiatrists'. We live in rotten conditions, many in tarpaper huts, without water or heat. We have little health care, and what we have is terrible. Our infant mortality rate is the highest."

There was too much to tell, and he had been telling it for too long. To church groups. To government officials. To international organizations. To schoolchildren.

"Our ancestors treatied with the U.S. government," he would say. "In return for peace, we were guaranteed our rights over small parts of the land our peoples had inhabited for generations, so that we could continue our way of life. Then the lands were stolen. Some for gold. Others for water or coal or uranium for the energy companies or for grazing land for white cattle ranchers. The government violated every treaty. Our way of life was stolen, too.

"The missionaries came. Our religion was stolen. The Bureau of Indian Affairs came. Our way of governing ourselves, thousands of years old, was stolen. We are still a conquered people. Our children are taken away from us, stolen, sent to boarding schools hundreds of miles away. They're punished for practicing their native religions, hit when they speak their native tongues."

"Aren't you just a militant?" someone from the audience would invariably ask.

"I just want my people to survive," he would say. "No one listened when we spoke politely about injustice. Only when we raised our voices did people begin to listen."

KaMook Banks, born Darlene Pearl Nichols, was an Oglala Sioux, from the Pine Ridge Indian Reservation. She had been only sixteen when she met Dennis in 1973, at the time when Indian voices were raised the loudest.

"It was just kind of a normal thing," she had told one of her Kansas lawyers, in jail after her September 1975 arrest. "A white could kill an Indian. It always happened. What could we do?

"Wesley Bad Heart Bull was shot just because he was an Indian. The authorities didn't care. After that was when the elders called in Dennis and them. We took over Wounded Knee as a protest, like the college students had taken over buildings as a protest. This was our own Indian land. But the army was called in to attack us. For seventy-one days, the army and the FBI shot at us. My uncle, Buddy, was killed."

"You were sixteen then?" the lawyer asked, taking notes.

"Right. And then, after Wounded Knee, they tried to imprison everybody. They had Dennis on trial for nine months until the judge threw out the case because the government had lied, planted evidence, wiretapped, used perjury. And then there were the murders."

KaMook paused. The lawyer noticed her downcast brown eyes.

"After Wounded Knee," she continued, "the FBI attacked us. They armed Dick Wilson's Goon squad, let his people get away with murder.[1] Wounded Knee was in '73. Since then two hundred AIM members have been killed or attacked. Pine Ridge has a murder rate six times that of Chicago and Detroit. No one cares. We asked the government to investigate. No one did, until June."

---

1. Dick Wilson was the Oglala Sioux tribal chairman, head of the tribal government organized under the Bureau of Indian Affairs (BIA). He had a personal army, which called itself the Goon squad, for "Guardians Of the Oglala Nation."

"That was when the FBI agents got killed on the reservation?" the lawyer asked.

"Joe Stuntz, too. Everyone talks about the agents. No one remembers that an Indian was killed, too. And it was the feds who came in shooting."

"Couldn't there be just a little justice in there with the law?" Rose Weasel Bear, an Oglala Sioux, had asked. Her brother and nephew had been found dead. "Accidental," the authorities ruled, refusing to investigate further. One had been hanged, the other axed.

South Dakota-based FBI agents Dean Howard Hughes and Owen Victor Harvey were veterans of this war just as much as the Indians. On November 15, 1975, they were not investigating Ms. Weasel Bear's complaints. They were jetting to Ontario, Oregon.

"Can't wait to take another crack at Anna Mae," Hughes said to Harvey, as their plane approached Boise. "Maybe this time she'll tell us which of her friends killed our guys."

Harvey nodded. Anna Mae knew everyone who had been staying at the tent city where the agents had been gunned down five months before.

"The agents were serving an arrest warrant," an FBI spokesman had said.

"They came in shooting," AIM witnesses swore.

After the shooting stopped on June 26, 1975, Agents Jack Coler and Ronald Williams, and one young Indian, Joe Stuntz, were dead. This time, the FBI decided to investigate a reservation death.

"The agents came in like Vietnam," KaMook had told her Kansas lawyer. "Armored personnel carriers. Attack helicopters. Combat gear. M-16s. They terrorized the children, pointing guns at them."

The U.S. Commission on Civil Rights agreed. They condemned the FBI's "full-scale military-style invasion" of the reservation.

Anna Mae Aquash had also lived there that terrible summer. She, too, was arrested in September—but at a place called Crow Dog's Paradise, in South Dakota. She told friends, "They came in. There were at least fifty of them, armed to the teeth. They pulled people out of tents, out of our beds, some of us naked, and lined us up, pointing M-16s. They pointed guns and asked, 'Okay, motherfucker, who killed the agents?' A lot of us were punched. Some in the stomach. Some in the back. Some had their hair yanked. No one cooperated.

"The agents, commando style, rushed through the buildings and the tents at Crow Dog's, tearing everything apart. Weapons were found, some without serial numbers. Almost everyone was arrested and charged. Me, too."

She was questioned by FBI Agent David Price after that summer arrest. She was repeatedly asked about the killing of the agents.

"Price told me, 'Cooperate, or I'll see you dead within a year,'" Anna Mae told friends.

Harvey and Hughes were softer than Price, but their interest in Anna Mae was clear. She was brought into a small but well-lit Oregon jail room. The matron sat her down in a wooden chair with a curved, slotted back.

"I'm not talking to you pigs," was all she said, no matter the question.

The agents gave up. Anna Mae was returned to her cell.

KaMook Banks was next. Brought in in chains, she sat silently, while the agents spoke.

"You're Dennis Banks's wife, right?" one asked.

"The baby is Dennis's too—both of them, right?" the other asked, pointing.

"Have any ideas where your husband might go? We know he was with you."

"I need to see a doctor," KaMook replied. "I have to get my pills. I don't know about anything else."

"But, . . ." the agent started.

"I'm not talking to you guys, and I need my medicine!" she yelled. She was led back to her cell.

Hughes and Harvey checked the reports on AIM. Kenny Loud Hawk and Russ Redner were relatively unknown. Both had clean records. Loud Hawk was twenty-one. His face was round and pockmarked. His hair was long, dark, and in braids. He was from the town of Oglala, where the most traditional people on the Pine Ridge reservation lived. He looked as if he belonged in a nineteenth-century black and white photograph of a Sioux warrior. He also sounded the part. He was appropriately stoic. He rarely spoke.

Loud Hawk was seated in the small room, his hands, like the women's, shackled in front, the metal links drooping down his legs to his ankles, which were also bound. He had to walk with a shuffle.

Hughes asked, "Kenny, we know that Dennis Banks and Leonard Peltier were with you. Why don't you just tell us about it? It'll go easier that way."

Loud Hawk's eyes were wide and fixed. He was scared, as if he had been plucked up by a spaceship and interrogated by Martians. He had never been off the reservation before. He had never spoken with white people before. He sat nervously, quietly.

"Kenny," Hughes began again, "you know that you were there last June, after our two agents had been shot."

Loud Hawk said nothing, but he remembered. He remembered how the FBI had surrounded the Indian compound and bombarded it with bullets. The sounds, heard throughout Oglala, were those of combat: large-caliber bullets, automatic fire, helicopters. Sounds of real war, like the descriptions he had heard in stories as a child, except that those had been about Gatling guns against his people, instead of helicopters. Kenny thought of his great-uncle, who had distinguished himself in battle against Custer, saving Indian lives and killing the enemy. The whites called it "Little Big Horn."

"C'mon, Kenny," one of the agents persisted. "We know what you did."

When the agents swarmed onto the reservation on June 26, they had surrounded the Indian encampment. There was a firefight between the Indians inside and the agents who had encircled them. When the shooting stopped and the agents searched the compound, everyone except the three dead bodies had disappeared. The agents were dumbfounded and determined to know how the Indians had escaped.

"Kenny Loud Hawk snuck horses into the tent city and led Leonard Peltier and the rest of the people out right under your noses!" more than one informant had told the FBI.

"Kenny," Harvey said, "we know you helped them escape. Tell us about it. Who was there?"

Loud Hawk shook his head nervously, side to side. "No," he gestured.

"Kenny, you know explosives and gun charges are very serious. You're going to be an old man before you get out of jail. Why not cooperate? Tell us about June 26 and the dead agents. You have a life to lead. Help us out. If you cooperate, we'll do our best to keep you out of jail."

Sweating, Loud Hawk looked at the agents. Slowly he shook his head again. He shook it faster and faster, until he stopped abruptly and let his chin fall against his chest. He stared at his hands, chained against his lap. The agents continued to talk. He blocked the words, ignoring them. The jailer led him back to his cell.

Redner was last. At twenty-eight, he was the oldest of the group, and the tallest. "Redner's also a Wounded Knee veteran," one agent noted. They did not know much more.

Redner was new to the other Indians, too He had joined Kenny and KaMook and Anna Mae a week before their arrest. He was just a familiar face from Wounded Knee. His first real conversation with Kenny had been in the station wagon.

"I'm a Western Shoshone, from California," Redner had explained, looking over to Loud Hawk, who was stretched out in the passenger seat. "I was taken from my family as a kid," he said, "and sent to live with a white family. I was raised by a white cop in Eureka. They tried to raise me white, tried to make me think I was white. I'd almost believe it, then something would happen. You know, some remark. Some kid would say 'Hey Cochise,' or something like that. 'Indian, who ya gonna scalp today?'

"You know, I never really thought about how much it disturbed me. To live in the white world, I thought you had to believe Indian people didn't exist.

"Then I went to 'Nam. Volunteered. After a while, I couldn't figure out why I was shooting at those people. I started thinking I had more in common with them than with my side, who treated me like shit because I'm a Skin.

"The funny thing," he continued, "was after I got back. I got three Purple Hearts in 'Nam. Still have shrapnel in me. But the firefights at Knee were the worst I ever went through. Remember how they were, Kenny? Man, I couldn't believe that there I was, pointing a .22 across a ridge. You know who was on the other side, directing M-16s back at me? My old commander!"

Redner had remained silent for a few minutes, contemplating this contradiction in his life, as the motor home and station wagon cut through the empty Oregon desert. He began again, explaining why he joined what he called "the mission."

"This is a war, Kenny, just like 'Nam was," he said. "You were raised on the res, in the culture. For me it's harder. Shit, I won't ever be able to drum as well as my daughter will by the time she's five. But I'm a warrior now, too, protecting my people. At least now I know what I'm fighting for. The training they gave me I'll put to good use. That's why I came along."

It was at that point that Redner noticed a police car passing them, pulling behind the motor home, a few miles from Ontario. Now, less than two days later, he was chained and seated before two FBI agents in a cold room.

"My name is Russ Redner. I don't have a rank or serial number anymore. I'm a warrior for my Indian people," was all he would say.

"The FBI reports that the Indians' vehicles were full of dynamite and firearms," the television reporter said, the night of November 16, 1975.

The story continued. "The FBI claims that one of the vehicles—a motor home—belongs to actor Marlon Brando. Brando is a known supporter of radical Indian causes. Two years ago, he turned down an Academy Award for his role in *The Godfather* as a protest against the portrayal of Indians in movies and on television. Asked about the arrests in eastern Oregon, the actor has refused any comment."

✝ ✝ ✝

CHAPTER 5

OFFENSE/DEFENSE

REDNER and Loud Hawk shuffled into the narrow corridor outside Ontario Justice Court. The chains that bound them rattled while they walked. Guards surrounded them. Television crews stood on chairs against the walls, aiming cameras and lights downward.

The guards opened the wooden double door to the small courtroom and lowered the Indians onto brown metal folding chairs in the first row. Beverly Axelrod, a curly-haired WKLDOC attorney,[1] was waiting. She had just arrived from San Francisco.

"What's this bullshit about us 'possessing dangerous weapons with intent to use'?" Redner asked her, as he read the state charges. "They know we surrendered and never threatened no one."

Redner had had a legal buck knife in a black leather sheath on his belt. Zeller had found a .44 caliber pistol under Loud Hawk's station wagon seat.

"Don't worry," Axelrod said. "They have hooks—underlying legal charges—to keep Anna Mae and KaMook in jail. They're indicted in South Dakota and Kansas, and technically, they weren't supposed to leave those states. But there's nothing to hold you guys. The feds can't seem to produce a simple, one-page complaint form, even though they've had more than two days to do it. So the local yokel D.A. drew up these charges. They're just to keep you guys in jail until the feds in Portland get their act together. You'll never go to trial on them."

It was a short appearance in the cramped, dirt green, dimly lit room. In an excited voice, Justice of the Peace Nita Bellows told

---

1. The Wounded Knee Legal Defense/Offense Committee (pronounced "*Wick*-el-doc.") had been established to defend the scores of Indians charged with criminal offenses after the takeover of Wounded Knee in 1973.

the defendants what their rights were. They said nothing. She read the charges. They said nothing. Axelrod spoke a few words. Redner and Loud Hawk were led out, shuffling again in their manacles, past the television cameras, back to their cells.

The federal prosecutors filed a complaint that afternoon. Within hours, all four prisoners were driven to the Boise airport for a flight to Portland. There were cars ahead and cars behind: three FBI agents in each one that had a defendant, one agent in each of those cars holding a loaded M-16. From time to time the guns were pointed at the Indians. Anna Mae's guard looked her directly in the eyes. "The safety is off," he noted.

"You're due in court," the guards at the Vancouver, Washington, city jail told Redner and Loud Hawk the next morning, November 18. After a night in this larger, smellier, noisier, more crowded prison, they were eager to go.

Twenty minutes later, after a heavily armed ride across the Columbia River, they were guided through a brass door. This was Portland's federal courthouse, a square, granite, Depression era structure, shaped and sculpted like a prison. The marshal who pushed and prodded them fit his surroundings. He was white, middle-aged, overweight, almost round, and had a fat, soggy cigar drooping from his lower lip.

KaMook and Anna Mae were minutes behind. They had spent the night at the women's prison, Clare Argow, in Portland. They were lifted out of a van fitted with metal mesh on the windows, then shoved forward and pushed through the courthouse door. KaMook's chained hands were folded low, almost arched, tucked under her round belly.

All four were taken up a small elevator to the fourth-floor marshal's office. They were buzzed into a well-lit room. The floor was white linoleum. There were no seats.

"Stand over there!" one of the marshals commanded, pointing to a corner. One at a time, the Indians were escorted to a table, fingerprinted, then returned to the corner. They said nothing.

The men were put in one cell, the women in another. Each lockup had its own toilet, a white porcelain bowl without a seat that was positioned so that the marshals could watch from their desks on the other side of the bars.

Ed Jones walked into the courthouse lobby, looked around, walked out, and walked in again. His palms were wet.

Jones had graduated from law school the spring before, passed the bar exam, then been sworn into the bar in September. Federal court was where experienced attorneys belonged, in tailored suits and manicured fingernails, members of the "good old boys" network. His long, thin, red hair trailing well below the shoulder of his one bargain-basement suit, Jones felt out of place.

Jones had a red mustache below his angular nose. His manner was that of a games player. He did not look; he squinted. He had a flare for cleverness and a quick sense of humor, like a riverboat gambler. He enjoyed life. Had Groucho Marx been a WASP, he could have been Ed Jones.

Jones walked up to and turned away from three people in the courthouse lobby before he had the courage to ask, "What floor do they keep prisoners on?"

His hands were almost dripping when, finally in the right place, he waited for his clients to be brought to him.

The cigar-sucking marshal led the Indians into the lawyer interview room. Their chains were taken off. The marshal closed the door and locked Jones inside with the Indians.

Everyone stood. Everyone was silent. Jones looked around, then made eye contact with Anna Mae. He walked over to the young Indian and shook the "radical" handshake, fist around fist, thumbs interlocking. Then he looked to Loud Hawk and then KaMook Banks, who both nodded to him distantly, without coming forward or offering their hands. They would have to judge him first.

Jones turned around. Russ stuck his hand out, grabbed Jones's thumb to thumb, then switching quickly to a "normal" handshake, then four fingers interlocking, then back to thumb to thumb, completing the circuit. This was the latest movement handshake. Jones was one-half step behind throughout. He worried that his clammy hand would give him away. The maneuver completed, he rubbed his palm surreptitiously on his pant leg, watching Redner, relieved that the Indian had not done the same.

No one spoke. Jones looked around. The small room had a full glass window, at least an inch thick, to the front. Everything was brilliantly lit by two panels of flourescent lights in a dropped ceiling. He noticed Anna Mae staring, straight up. She obviously thought the room was wired.

"They're not supposed to bug attorney-client conversations," Jones said, trying to be reassuring.

Anna Mae's eyes jumped to his. Her expression was a mixture of skepticism and anger. Quickly, Jones added, "But I wouldn't bet against it."

They all sat around the wooden table. In the middle was the bottom half of a tin can, the sides pressed down. Inside were a dozen cigarette butts, some with filters but most straights or hand rolled. Bits of old, charred tobacco clung to the seams and corners of the can. The table around it was pockmarked with burns, some circular, some oblong.

"You know that Beverly Axelrod called my partner, Ron, asking us to help you guys?" Jones asked. KaMook and Anna Mae nodded.

"Ron's out of town," Jones continued. "He told me to tell you not to worry. He's cutting his trip short. He'll see you tomorrow."

"Is there any news?" KaMook asked. "Anyone else been arrested?" She was eager to know if the Mexican-looking fellow and the person who drove the motor home away had been identified.

"As far as I know, no," Jones said, "although I read in the morning paper that a farm was burglarized outside Ontario. Apparently a gun and a car were stolen. They say it was Leonard Peltier. From fingerprints."

The Indians sat motionless, silent, waiting for the subject to change. They did not want anything they said or did to indicate whether Peltier had been with them. Peltier was a fugitive— wanted for the June 1975 murder of two FBI agents on the Pine Ridge Indian Reservation.

"How's it look?" Redner asked, harshly, impatient with the quiet.

"Hard to tell," Jones said, his voice cracking from nervousness. "I'm sure Ron will get some police reports soon, and we'll find some other lawyers to help us out. Then we'll see where we are."

"Can you get them to give me my medicine?" KaMook asked, plaintively.

"How about getting our clothes?" Anna Mae added.

Jones did not know if he could. "I'll try," he said, attempting to hide his uncertainty. He took a legal pad from his brightly colored, beaded shoulder bag and wrote notes.

Anna Mae looked to KaMook. KaMook nodded.

"There are some people you should call, who might be able to help," Anna Mae said.

"Sure," Jones replied, writing the names, some with addresses, some with telephone numbers, whatever the women could remember.

The marshal with the cigar knocked on the door, turned the key, and poked his head in. "Time to go!" he ordered, motioning with his index finger for Jones to leave first. As Jones picked up his briefcase and walked out, he looked back. The Indians, heads down, were offering their hands, forward, to be chained.

I rushed home from the one law class I had beaten myself into attending, expecting the Indians' arraignment to be one of the first stories on the 5 o'clock television news. I dropped my books on the floor, adjusted the reception with my coat hanger antennae, and spread out on my lumpy, rented couch.

"The Indians arrested in last week's shootout in eastern Oregon were in federal court in Portland today," the story began, a reporter talking into the camera, with a graphic silhouette of an Indian male, the logo of the American Indian Movement, behind her head. "The two women were sent to other states where they have charges pending. They'll face trial here later, prosecutors say. The two men—Kenneth Moses Loud Hawk and Russ James Redner—were arraigned on a complaint charging them with harboring fugitive Indian leader Dennis Banks and with possessing explosives. They'll be back in court on November 26th for a hearing. Bail was set at $55,000 each."

The image changed. There was a man, in his early fifties, graying hair, wearing an oversized bowtie. He was standing outdoors, smiling, answering questions. The letters underneath identified him: "SIDNEY I. LEZAK, United States Attorney."

"The search for the fugitives is still on. . . . Yes, a small arsenal was found. . . . I'm sure Mr. Brando will be questioned. . . . Yes, there will be charges against others brought soon."

Lezak looked self-assured as he answered a reporter's question about the dynamite.

"This is a very serious case," he said. "Our experts tell us the explosives could have blown up a ten-story office building."

I sat up. Was there evidence that the Indians were going to destroy an office building? Is that what this case was about?

The U.S. attorney continued. "The explosives were so volatile that the government had to destroy them on Sunday. They were too hot to handle."

The story ended, and a Rainier beer commercial came on. While I flipped to other channels, eager for more details, I was puzzled. Finding commercials on the other stations as well, I waited, lit my pipe, and pondered.

The government claimed that the Indians had traveled far before they got to Ontario. If the dynamite was too dangerous to keep, even for a few days under guard, then why hadn't the vehicles, bouncing over hundreds of miles of road, exploded?

Could the government just destroy evidence like that? I hadn't heard anything about that in law school. I picked through my first-year law books. Nothing.

I opened my legal ethics casebook. It said that prosecutors could talk about arrests and indictments, but they could not make public comments about evidence in pending cases. I had just listened to the U.S. attorney tell television viewers and newspaper readers—potential jurors—that there was frightening physical evidence, which he couldn't actually produce any longer. Was there some exception I had missed?

This was interesting law, three-dimensional law, unfolding before me. There was, of course, the unsettling question of how these alleged explosives were going to be used. Was that why Lezak had mentioned the "ten-story office building"? Maybe he wanted to divert attention from the destruction of the evidence? Maybe there was no "ten-story office building" after all? Maybe the dynamite never existed? Maybe it was planted? John Trudell, a leader of AIM, had been quoted in the newspaper, saying just that.

I had grown up in the '60s and '70s. The Gulf of Tonkin. Watergate. The government sometimes lied. Was this one of those times? Something was wrong here. This case was fantastic!

I *had* to get involved.

I was sweating. I picked up and put down my telephone receiver half a dozen times. I refilled my pipe. I grabbed an extra handful of nuts from my refrigerator.

I picked up the telephone again, dialed half a number from a business card, and hung up. The Indians would be *crazy* to give me anything important to do. The FBI had, for years, put informants into political groups. If I volunteered, pushed my way in, would they suspect me? I knew I would suspect someone, new in town, who offered help. It had not been long since FBI documents about Fred Hampton had been released. He had been a black political activist. The FBI had asked an informant to diagram Hampton's apartment, pinpointing where he slept. Within weeks, Hampton was assassinated in his bed, in the exact spot the informant had drawn. Everyone in progressive circles was being extra careful. Finally, I let the telephone ring.

The bookstore was in the basement of a small, blue, one-family house in Portland, Oregon. Inside, behind a coffee-stained bridge table, sat a woman with long black hair. She was alone, in the middle of the room. Around her were three double-sided, sloping wooden bookshelves, a magazine rack with a wide selection of socialist and Marxist periodicals, a sofa with stuffing creeping out of each arm, and a stack of thirty gray metal folding chairs leaning against a wall.

The first meeting of the Loud Hawk/Redner defense committee had been called for 7:00 P.M., November 20, 1975. Fortunately, the one law firm I knew in Portland—Steenson, Parkinson and Lea—had been recruited (by Ron Schiffman) to represent Russ Redner. When I had called them, two days earlier, Tom Steenson invited me to attend. I was ecstatic, the first to arrive.

An hour later, two Indian women, one holding a young child, walked in. They were guided by S. Lynn Parkinson. Lynn, as he was called, was in his early thirties. His beard was wispy, and his thin black hair was slicked back with a pint of grease. Lynn was to Sha Na Na what Ed Jones was to Groucho Marx. Twenty impatient white people watched as the newcomers shed their coats, without apology for being late.

"Hey, everybody," Lynn began, as he sat in one of the folding chairs now arranged in a circle, "this is Lena Redner, Russ Redner's wife. And this is Susana Gren, an AIM organizer from Denver. And the baby is, ah . . ."

"Tsi-Am-Utza," Lena said.

"Tsi-Am-Utza, thanks," Lynn continued, "Russ and Lena's daughter. They all just hit town. They're staying in a motel. One of the things this defense committee is going to have to do is raise money to house the people who'll be coming in before trial."

Lynn listed the things he wanted the committee to do: raise money, collect food and clothing and bedding, write and distribute leaflets, talk about the case at every chance—on the bus, to fellow office workers, to anyone who might end up a juror.

Lynn spat out suggestions, and then they died. No one volunteered or discussed.

Of the twenty people in the room, sixteen were women. Some glared at Lynn. A few whispered to each other. Some only half-whispered. "Sexist pig," one woman said, "telling us what to do, monopolizing this meeting!" Lynn could not talk through their angry stares. He stopped.

The next hour's awkward silences were punctuated with disjointed comments. "Indian people are probably more oppressed than prisoners," someone offered. "Even more oppressed than blacks," someone else replied. Silence. "They're a people colonized by the imperialists," a third person said. "Yeah," she continued, "it's important to support Indian struggles, because in the struggle against capitalism, the Indians are truly in the belly of the beast." "Um hum," many people mumbled. Then silence. "Hey, I have a friend who knows someone at the *Oregonian* who might do a story about the case," one woman with short, graying hair said.

"Wonderful," someone else commented. More silence, no one suggesting anything specific that might be written.

"I can do a flyer," a man with floppy long blond hair proposed.

"Okay," a woman with straight short blond hair said.

No one said what a flyer might be used for, or where it could be posted.

"What'll we call this group?" someone asked.

"How 'bout the 'Lowd Hock'/Redner Defense Committee?" a tall, thin woman with a Brooklyn accent said.

Finally one of the Indian women spoke. "I appreciate everyone coming here," Susana said. "But you have to learn some things about us Indian people." No one interrupted her long pause.

"First," she began again, "since Wounded Knee, we've been hunted, killed, by the Goon squad and the FBI. No one knows about it. Some church people and some members of Congress have talked about it, but the mass media won't print it. There's a news blackout.

"There's a real war going on against us Indian people. This case is part of it. We're not talking just about defending these two guys. This case is an attack on all of us. We're defending all Indian people. We don't expect Indian people to be treated fairly." She looked at Lena Redner and stopped.

Lynn spoke again. "Russ Redner is a Vietnam vet with no record and four years of college. He has three Purple Hearts. He's held on outrageous bail. So is Kenny Loud Hawk. If they were white, they'd be released on their own recognizance, or at least have reasonable bail."

"Right on!" the woman with the Brooklyn accent said.

"Our first job is to get Russ and Kenny out," Lynn continued. "Their bail—combined, its $110,000—might as well be $10 million. Our only chance is to pack the courtroom every hearing, let the judge know we're watching him, that there's a community demanding he release Kenny and Russ."

"Exactly," Susana said. "So, we have to get our boys out and get them a fair trial. But we also have to take the offensive against the government, fight back, use the media to educate people about all the deaths and terror in South Dakota. We have to use this as an opportunity, be on the offensive. We should call this the 'Loud Hawk/Redner Offense/Defense Committee.'"

I sat and listened. An "offense/defense" committee? Another thing not mentioned in law school. The nexus between community work and legal work was not even a concept there. Could work in the community make a fairer trial? What could be done to counteract the prejudicial statements the U.S. attorney and the FBI were telling a trusting press? Could this case be used as something positive, something beyond its own narrow legal issues, to *help* people? What were the problems of Indian people, anyway? I had never met an Indian before. Did their troubles justify the possession of guns and explosives? Most of the people in the bookstore apparently thought so. Were these Indians terrorists? Were they guerrillas? Were they just poor people trying to survive? Or were they some strange combination of these things?

These were fascinating questions. It was interesting history and politics and law that law school did not teach. Court as theater. Court as power. The audience as a passive but active participant, just by being there.

On the way out I cornered Parkinson, offering to research legal issues. "Come to court on the 26th if you can. We may know what we need by then," he said.

I walked up to Lena and Susana, shook their hands, said good night, and drove home to Salem, Oregon. My mind was racing the entire fifty miles. The meeting had been strained, disorganized, at times doctrinaire, rhetorical, and freaky, but invigorating. When Susana spoke from the heart about this case as part of a war against the entire Indian community, she meant it. That perspective could explain the bizarre, overzealous attitude of the government. Destroying evidence. Distorting facts. Using hyperbole to scare Oregonians. But Susana's statement also raised questions. Who were these people? Why was the government after them?

CHAPTER 6

✛ ✛ ✛

NITS MAKE LICE

EVERYONE knows something about Indians. I did, too. Indians helped the Pilgrims survive the first, horrid, winter in the New World. They sold Manhattan Island to the Dutch for a few trinkets. There was something called the French and Indian War. In the last century, Indians would not let western homesteaders live in peace. Those Indians we did not kill in war we rounded up and put on reservations. After that, there were only a few "renegades" to deal with. Certain Comanches and Sioux and Nez Perces and Cheyennes. Geronimo. Cochise. Crazy Horse. Chief Joseph.

If I was going to work on this *Loud Hawk* case, as Parkinson called it, I had to learn, then imagine, so I could understand our clients. What if I were Indian? What would I feel? What would I feel one hundred years after my great-grandparents' way of life ended? What would I feel about the poverty of my relatives on the reservation? What would I feel about white people? What would I feel about this war Susana spoke of? Would I see myself as a soldier? A peacemaker? Someone who wanted to be left alone? Someone who wanted to blend into the white world? How would what I felt as this imaginary Indian correlate with what I thought as a real Jewish, white, middle-class male with progressive political ideals?

I put aside my law books and read everything the Salem, Oregon, library had on Indians. I learned and imagined.

Indian people were here thousands of years before Columbus arrived, misdirected as he was on his search for a shorter route to India. They lived in different nations—each with its own name and culture and language and laws. Lakota. Onondaga. Siletz. Willamette. Shoshone. Comanche. Hopi. Navaho.

There was a subtext to the elementary school story I learned about the purchase of Manhattan Island: Indians were dumb, selling such an important property for next to nothing. But as I read, for the first time, I understood the other side of the transaction. The Indians must have thought the Europeans were crazy. How can one actually "own" land? Land is. The Great Spirit made land. People and animals and birds and insects used it. People and animals and birds and insects died. The land continued. To own land made no more sense than to own the air or the water or the clouds or the birds or the trees or the sky or the stars. So if some white people insisted on giving something of value for something that could not be sold, why not humor them and take it?

I'm Jewish, and I learned Indian history as a Jew. Indian history is a history of genocide. I know about genocide. Early in this century, my cousins were killed in a pogrom in Russia—toddlers three and four years old sliced in two by sharp, shiny, swooshing Cossack swords. My maternal great-grandfather was hung by his beard from a tree in the village square and rescued by the village priest. I had relatives among the six million thirty-five years later—taken in cattle cars from towns named Munkacs and Polena to places called Auschwitz and Bergen-Belsen. They were starved. Gassed. Burned. I thought of them, desperate, in their trains when I read about the trains heading to the American West, the golden spike, the whites shooting Indians out of the window for sport, just as they shot buffalo. Most times they would let the carcasses rot. Sometimes they took souvenirs.

Trinkets in New York? What ever happened to the indigenous population? My elementary school never taught about the Raritan Indians. They lived on what is now Staten Island. In 1641, Dutch soldiers attacked the Raritans, in revenge for acts actually committed by white settlers. The Raritans resisted. Four of them were killed. The Indians killed four attacking soldiers. The Dutch sent more soldiers. They massacred the entire village while the Indians slept. Men, women, and children were bayoneted. Then they were hacked to pieces like raw meat and left. Presumably the Dutch soldiers returned to their homes in what is now the Wall Street area of New York City and pleased with their work, kissed their own wives and children good night.

In 1838, our army, Gen. Winfield Scott in command, rounded up thousands of Cherokees from the Southeast, tearing them from their ancestral home. First he concentrated them in camps. Then he marched them to Oklahoma in the dead of winter. One out of four Cherokees died during that march. The Indians call it the Trail of Tears.

If I were Indian, how could I not resent a society that slaughtered my people and then did not care enough to teach about it?

I wondered. If I were Indian, would I compare a horror such as the Trail of Tears to the My Lai massacre in Vietnam? Soldiers killed civilians. But Lt. Calley's horrible acts did not jettison him into public office. Cherokees, Seminoles, Chickasaws, Choctaws, and Creeks remember a soldier they called Sharp Knife. Sharp Knife murdered thousands of Indian people. The whites, who called him Andrew Jackson, elected him president of the United States in 1828.

If I were Indian, how could I not see my relationship with the U.S. government as one of treachery and genocide? All the treaties signed with the Indians—368 of them—were abrogated or violated by the U.S. government. If I were an Indian, I would laugh every time an American administration accused some foreign government of not living up to its word.

I would remember Sand Creek, in 1864. Six hundred Cheyennes were camped there, four hundred of them women and children. Most of the men were away hunting. They had been promised safety by an American major. He had given them an American flag to hang, to show they were peaceful. The flag was hung. Soldiers attacked. Women and children were sleeping. They heard shouts and hoofs and people running. The Indians still thought their friends, the soldiers, would not hurt them. The soldiers opened fire from two sides. They lofted artillery into the camp. The women and children huddled near the American flag. A white flag was also raised. Old men walked toward the soldiers, begging and pleading. They were shot down. Others ran to the soldiers, pleading for the women and children. They were shot down.

One white eyewitness wrote,

There were some thirty or forty squaws collected in a hole for protection; they sent out a little girl about six years old with a white flag on a stick; she had not proceeded but a few steps when she was shot and killed. All the squaws in that hole were afterwards killed, and four or five bucks outside. . . . Every one I saw dead was scalped. I saw one squaw cut open with an unborn child . . . lying by her side. I saw the body of White Antelope with the privates cut off, and I heard a soldier say he was going to make a tobacco pouch out of them. . . . I saw a little girl about five years of age who had been hid in the sand; two soldiers discovered her, drew their pistols and shot her, and then pulled her out of the sand by the arm. I saw quite a number of infants in arms killed with their mothers.[1]

If I were an Indian, I would have a thought familiar to every Jew: How could so-called civilized people act like this? Could I, as an Indian, trust a government that had not only carried out this genocide but coolly advocated it? A government that has never bothered to admit the scope of the horror of its deeds since?

In the last century, government officials, speaking at public forums, advocated killing Indian babies. "Nits make lice," Col. John M. Chivington declared in Denver. How could I deal with a society that saw me as subhuman and still teaches that in its schools, in its movies, in its folklore?

Did not that legacy have a lot to do with the destroyed, directionless lives many of my people lived today, without hope, whether on or off reservations? Would not my modern history be just as painful? If I were an Indian, I would probably have been taken away from my family, sent to boarding school, punished for who I was. The land where my parents lived would have been deemed worthless by the whites a hundred years ago. Now, if something previously unknown or overlooked made the land newly attractive—coal, oil, uranium, water—it would be taken away again. If I were a Colville or a Navaho, I might have grown up playing on the tailings from uranium mines. On other reservations, my land might have been torn bare by the energy companies, strip-mined, poisoning my children's water.

On the Pine Ridge Indian Reservation in South Dakota, if I were a supporter of the American Indian Movement, I would

1. Robert Bent, from U.S. Congress. 39th. 2d Sess., Senate Report 156, quoted in Dee Brown, *Bury My Heart at Wounded Knee* (New York: Henry Holt, 1970):90.

have more basic worries. The Goon squad, run by the tribal chairman and supported by the FBI, would be trying to kill me.

Ed Jones, Ron Schiffman, Sheila Lea, Tom Steenson, and Lynn Parkinson had a busy week. First, they decided who should represent each defendant. There was no overriding reason for the choice. Most legal motions would be filed on behalf of both Indians by either firm, a joint enterprise. Both firms were actively political, representing protestors and prisoners and migrant farm workers and blacks beaten up by the police. But this was a major case, and the firm with more criminal experience, Schiffman and Jones, should handle the "lead" defendant, Loud Hawk. Loud Hawk's name came first in the court file. His lawyers would go before Redner's in most things—opening and closing statements, cross-examination of witnesses. Schiffman was the only lawyer who had been in practice more than a few months.

The day after the last court appearance, the government filed an affidavit from Agent Robert Little, along with an inventory of items seized from the vehicles. When Redner saw the papers, he exploded.

"Shit!" he said to the five lawyers in the jail's attorney conference room. "You mean they planted two *snitches* with us?"

Little had sworn that two "Confidential Reliable Informants," identified only as "A" and "B," had told the FBI on November 13, 1975, the day before the vehicles were stopped in Ontario, Oregon, that Dennis Banks "might be planning to travel in [a motor home and station wagon] along with other federal fugitives." Informant "A" had given reliable information to the FBI "on at least 100 occasions." Informant "B" had "provided information on at least 20 occasions." And, according to Agent Little, the FBI in the Seattle area "had been conducting surveillance in their area since November 8, 1975, on a Dodge Explorer motor home, New Mexico License A8969, and a white station wagon. . . . [On November 13, 1975] said motor home and station wagon could not again be located in the area of the Port Madison Indian Reservations, Kitsap County, Washington, where it had been previously located."

"Who the fuck could it have been?" Redner asked, banging the table. Loud Hawk shrugged. He had no idea. The thought was frightening. Someone they had eaten with, talked to, let their children play with, may have at the same time told the FBI about their mission.

"We gotta figure out who they are," Russ said. "They must be out there, snitching now. And what did they tell the other 120 times?"

Schiffman, in his early thirties, with long, curly, brown hair, and a full, rounded beard, spoke in a calm voice. "Russ, man," he said, "first things first. We may never know who the snitches are, although, guaranteed, we'll try to find out. There may have been no snitches at all. The FBI might be making this up to justify the stop of the vehicle. Or the snitches might have been following you, and maybe that's why they didn't bother pulling you over sooner. Who knows? It's too early to tell."

Redner interrupted, "But the fuckers had a goddamn *snitch*— two of them out there, and . . ."

"That's right," Schiffman interrupted, his hand on Redner's shoulder, "they're out there. You're in here. And you may be in here until you're a fucking grandfather, they got you by the balls with so much shit, so listen to me!"

Redner took a breath and turned to meet Schiffman's eyes.

"First," Schiffman said, "we've got to come up with a plan to get you out of jail. If you stay in here until trial, you guys are cooked. Released people walk into courtrooms freer than those brought in in chains. The jury may never see the actual chains, but they see a chained person.

"Second, if you guys get convicted, as I think you will, it'll be harder for a judge to give you a shitload of time if you've been out on the streets and behaving yourselves. Putting you back behind bars is a change in the status quo."

"How long do you think it'll take to get us out of here?" Redner asked.

"Don't know," Schiffman replied.

"Can I visit Tsi-Am-Utza?" Redner asked nervously. "I don't want her to forget her old man."

"We'll see if we can arrange contact visits, but don't hold your breath."

"Fuck!" Redner shouted, standing up, pounding his fist on the table, then turning his back to Loud Hawk and the lawyers.

Lena Redner and Tsi-Am-Utza watched from the front row of the huge, ornate courtroom, as the two Indian men were brought into the room in jail clothes and chains, sandwiched between two U.S. marshals. Russ Redner and Kenny Loud Hawk were unshackled with the same air of detachment that one unchains a bicycle and deposited next to their lawyers.

"There's daddy," Lena whispered to Tsi-Am-Utza, pointing to the taller, thinner, older Indian. Redner was whispering something to Lea. When he heard his daughter, he sprang up and walked toward the spectator section.

The marshals moved to block him. Redner jerked his arm from their grasp. "Take your hands off me, man!" Redner yelled. "All I was doin' was going to say hello to my wife and baby. They're right there," he said, pointing.

Schiffman was now at Redner's side. He whispered something. "Shit, man," Redner said, in a resigned tone, "you mean I can't even say hello to them here. It has to be in jail?"

Shiffman nodded.

Redner sat and turned his chair around so that the back faced forward. He stared straight at Lena and Tsi-Am-Utza, waved and smiled, ignoring the other two hundred people who filled the courtroom's long, polished oak benches.

A prosecutor entered through the side door, greeted Schiffman, then moved to the far counsel table. Schiffman walked back to the spectator section. He came to Lena, bent over, and said, "You won't believe this. Guess what the prosecutor's name is."

Lena looked blank.

"His given name is Thomas Hawk," Schiffman said. "But he goes by Tommy!"

"Tommy Hawk?" Lena asked. "He isn't Indian, is he?"

"No," Schiffman said, "he's just a right-wing white asshole who won an award for prosecuting draft protestors. His name fits. Expect a hatchet job."

At exactly 9:30 A.M., Judge George Juba entered the courtroom. His features were lost behind his ornate oak bench, fifty feet from the spectators.

The clerk pounded a gavel. Tommy Hawk stood. "Mr. Redner

and Mr. Loud Hawk were indicted by the federal grand jury yesterday in nine counts of the ten-count indictment," he said.

The judge read the indictment of Kenneth Moses Loud Hawk, Russ James Redner, Anna Mae Aquash, KaMook Banks, Dennis James Banks, and Leonard Peltier out loud: ". . . possessing a destructive device consisting of various parts, pocket watches, holes drilled in the face, a screw inserted to make contact with the moving hands, with a soldered battery connector and ground wire, flashbulbs, four batteries, timing devices and several cases of dynamite." The eight other counts charged them with possessing guns with obliterated serial numbers. The claim from the initial complaint that Loud Hawk and Redner had harbored Dennis Banks was gone.

Since the defendants had no money, they were entitled to court-appointed counsel. They wanted Schiffman and Jones and Steenson and Parkinson and Lea, attorneys who understood and were sympathetic with their cause.

"We have a very strict policy," Juba growled. "We don't permit defendants to choose their own appointed lawyers."

"In that case we'll represent Mr. Loud Hawk and Mr. Redner without fee," Schiffman said.

After a surprisingly productive offense/defense committee meeting that night—people had assigned themselves specific tasks: telephone trees, calling bands to play benefits, getting Lena on the local public radio station, renting a house for a permanent defense committee—Lynn and I drove crosstown to Pretty Boy Floyds, a wood-paneled bar with imported beers. I felt honored, a mere law student being invited out with one of the attorneys.

Parkinson dressed casually. His style was 1950s. Like Steenson and Lea, he had recently graduated from law school. And, like Lea, he had started late. Lea had been married. Her daughter was a teenager before she went back to school. Parkinson had been a grass roots political organizer and a bass player in raunchy rock bands before deciding on law. His wife, Kitsy, was a teacher, and they had a baby, Megan. They lived in Redland, a small community half an hour from Portland, on a barren piece of land. Lynn was building a cabin. They had just moved into it from their trailer. They could not afford running water yet.

"How can you be so upbeat?" I asked him. "The judge made an outrageous ruling. Rich people can choose their own lawyers, but poor people can't? How are you guys going to manage a case like this without getting paid?"

"You're learning," he said, with a smile. "The judge would rather appoint someone from the official list who would have these guys pled guilty in a week. I don't know what we're going to do about money. Shit, we just started out."

His eyes, the fascination in them, explained why he and the others were willing to take the case without fee. The decision had been unambivalent.

"You gotta understand," he said, "cases like this come along once in a lifetime, if you're lucky. These guys aren't criminals. They're activists. If they committed any violation of the law, it wasn't for their own benefit but to help people who are suffering. And the government is clearly the enemy in this. It's being vindictive. Aside from all the crap in the press, look how they put the indictment together. The guns weren't illegal per se, only because the serial numbers were rubbed out. They could have put all eight guns in one count. These weren't separate crimes. But because they plead each one separately, these guys face eighty years on the gun charges instead of ten. The fuckers! I'd *pay* to work on a case like this one."

Parkinson poured each of us another glass of beer. "Let me tell you something," he continued. "I just spent I don't know how many hours working on a case from the 'joint.'[2] A prisoner had to sue to get a set of false teeth. I busted my ass for him. Got him the teeth. Then, the other week, he calls me, collect. 'Hey Lynn,' he says like he's my best friend in the world, 'this is Gary Gilmore. I got pissed off at some faggot here and stomped on my choppers. Come down here and get me another set right away, would ya?' I wanted to kill that guy!

"But a case like Redner's!" Parkinson's face was pure joy.

---

2. Oregon State Penitentiary.

CHAPTER 7

✛ ✛ ✛

IRON DOOR WOMAN

FREE LOUD HAWK AND REDNER. STOP KILLING IN-DIAN PEOPLE. STOP THE LONGEST WAR. JUSTICE FOR THE FIRST AMERICANS. FBI GO HOME. U.S. OUT OF U.S.

The slogans were neatly printed in broad Magic Marker blues and yellows and reds and greens on white, square, oak tag. The signs had been staple-gunned onto scrap wood the night before. The picketers, mostly long-haired young women and men, marched around the courthouse, up Broadway, down Taylor Street, down Sixth Avenue, up Main Street, around and around, chanting, "Free Loud Hawk and Redner!" and "Justice for Indian People!" In single file, the group encircled the building.

Redner and Loud Hawk had been incarcerated for almost a month. It was now December 8, 1975.

"Let this building do something useful," a young hippie said as he propped a dozen signs against the granite courthouse and joined a large group heading inside. He left the signs near an Indian with long braided hair, one of six young Indian males pounding a bass drum that reverberated throughout downtown Portland.

In the courtroom, Steenson stood at the counsel table, ready to argue for Russ and Kenny's release.

To prove what good risks they were, Steenson called a witness, Gregory Lynch, an attorney expert in pretrial release decisions.

"Mr. Redner's married," Lynch said. "His wife is here. They have a child. He's got a B.A. from Evergreen State College. He's gone to college on the G.I. bill. He maintained a three-point average. He was a letter man in athletics. He spent four years in the service, a Vietnam veteran, honorable discharge. He's a deco-rated soldier with twelve medals, including the Bronze Star, three

Purple Hearts, a medal for valor. He's worked full time for the Indian community with the Department of Human Resources in California.

"I recommend release to the Urban Indian League," Lynch continued. "The Urban Indian League has never lost a defendant. Also, these defendants intend to stay for trial. . . . I asked them how they could better serve their movement—if they would leave at the first chance and serve in an underground capacity, or stay and use the court as a platform to project their point of view. Both were adamant about staying and showing that the Indians respect their word. They both recognize that there's going to be a lot of attention given to this trial, and they want to make use of that."

Judge Juba said "Thank you," and walked off the bench, having taken the matter "under advisement."

As the lawyers packed up their briefcases, their clients already back in jail, I inched up to the bar and seeing no one jumping to stop me, walked to the counsel table.

"What do you think the chances are, Lynn?" I asked.

"Hell if I know," he said, putting his yellow note pad away. "Since they have no records, and Russ is a war hero, they should be let out. But did you catch what Hawk snuck through on the last indictment?"

"What do you mean?"

"Well, Juba had set the bail at $55,000 each. Then Hawk got the grand jury to indict. That, in effect, started the case over again. Hawk has the power to set initial bail. The asshole doubled it! As it stands now, they have to raise $100,000 each."

"Why'd he do that?" I asked. "It wasn't as if these guys could've raised the $55,000."

"Just pure vindictiveness," Lynn grumbled, walking out of the courtroom.

Northwest Portland was a civilized neighborhood with a Berkeley/Haight-Ashbury flair. The two main north-south thoroughfares—21st and 23rd avenues—were lined with high wooden electric poles, carrying a dozen or more wires. Each avenue had a discount movie theater, taverns with pool tables, late night grocery stores, and hippie restaurants. Twenty-first Avenue had an old orange brick gas station now run as a taco stand. On 23rd, a religious butcher sold meat and spiritual items at Better Beef and Bible.

The rich and the pensioners, the "freaks" and the working-class people mixed on these two avenues and in the many neighborhood parks, some nestled between side streets, others touching the pristine forests bordering the northwestern edge of Northwest Portland.

Glisan Street ran east to west, two lanes between two curbs of parked cars. After the court appearance, I drove west on Glisan, heading to 21st Avenue to attach the newest black and red Loud Hawk/Redner Offense/Defense Committee leaflet to the wooden poles. It announced two benefit dinners and the next court appearance. Four staples, one for each corner, usually held a flyer to a pole. More staples were required at major intersections, where pitted wood and rusted staples were covered with layers of posters announcing concerts, singing lessons, movies, flea markets, lost animals, redemption.

As I passed 18th Avenue, I noticed a green, clean, full-sized new Plymouth. It had almost no chrome. I remembered that car near the courthouse, ten minutes before.

I slowed down. I sped up. I circled the same block, twice. The car was still there, a quarter block behind.

"Fuck!" I said to myself. "The assholes are following me!"

I felt satisfaction and outrage. My defense committee work had interested the government enough to have me followed. It was like receiving a good report card. But, my god, the government was following me!

When they were still behind me after four more turns, I became angry. "Fuck 'em!" I said out loud. If they wanted to waste time following me, at least I could make it interesting.

I circled back to Glisan Street. When I was half a block from 21st Avenue, I stopped. I double parked near a school. The tail car slowed, lingered, then passed. It stopped ahead, at the corner of 21st and Glisan. The light changed to green. The car stayed. The light turned red again. I pulled alongside. It was in the left lane. I was in the right. When I was level with its front seat, I turned my head and looked. There were two short-haired, suited FBI agents.

I smiled at them. They turned their heads, pretending to ignore me.

The light changed to green. I turned my flashers on and stared at them. The younger agent, in the passenger seat, looked back. I folded my arms across my chest and smiled.

Cars behind us honked. I nodded to the FBI car, folded my arms behind my head, and yawned. The FBI passenger said something to the FBI driver. The green car drove across the intersection. When another car followed, so the FBI car could not back up, I turned a sharp right onto 21st and took a quick, circuitous route back to the interstate, toward Salem. I memorized every car. Fifteen miles out of town, I was sure I had lost them.

The offices of Steenson, Parkinson and Lea were decorated in gray. The floor was gray linoleum squares with specks of black. Some tiles were missing; others were chipped. The desks were gray metal with chrome strips and formica tops, which were a gray with white specks. The chairs were gray. The walls were gray. The only colors were in the political posters, thumbtacked to the walls. Farm workers. North Vietnamese women with hoes. Prisoners behind bars. Indians behind bars. Puerto Rican nationalists. African National Congress members, posing with guns. Karl Marx. Ho Chi Minh. Joe Hill. Posters from the Weather Underground.

I opened their office door. Sheila Lea, skinny, gray-haired, in her late thirties, was sitting on a desk, opening the morning mail.

"Sheila!" I said as soon as I walked in. "You won't believe it!"

"What?" she asked.

"Well, first, the FBI followed me yesterday after court. I lost them. But when I got home and tried calling you guys for over an hour, my phone went crazy. I'd dial the first three or four digits, and then . . ."

"Let me guess," she interrupted. "You either got a new dial tone, or just static, or heard strange clicks."

"How did you know?" I asked. My telephone had all three symptoms.

"Try ours," she said. "It must be a contagious phone virus. Really, this is serious shit. From now on, we have to assume everyone is being followed, and everyone's phone is bugged. Lena was followed by *two* cars the other day. And you're the fourth person to complain about their phones so far this morning."

As we talked about phone security, Lea opened a white envelope from the court. "I don't believe it!" she said, then laughed, then walked around the office in a circle, faster and faster, fanning herself with the white, typewritten document.

"Tom!" she yelled.

Steenson opened the door from his cubicle. Lea handed him the paper and watched, awaiting a reaction. "What is it?" I asked, curious as hell.

"Juba's bail decision," Lea said. "He cut the baby in half, reducing the bail from $100,000 each to $50,000 each."

"That's where we were a few weeks ago!" I said.

"Exactly," she said.

"And get this," Steenson added, reading while he talked. "Although he says he has no 'negative information' about these guys, he says that $50,000 bail is justified because of their 'attempt to escape from apprehension in this matter.' Is he hallucinating, or just getting back door lies from the FBI? These guys pulled the station wagon over before the second trooper, Kramer, was even on the scene!

"And there's another order here that Russ is going to hate even more," he continued. "The great humanitarian, Justice George Cardozo Juba, won't even let Redner hold his baby! Contact visits would be—get this—*inconvenient* for the marshals. Fuck him!"

Steenson showed Lea the rest of the document, then grabbed it back. He was already holding two legal pads, four pens, an expanding file folder, a thick sweater, and a woolen cap.

He grabbed my coat, tossed it to me, and said, "C'mon!" We spent the next four hours in the law library. "We're going to find every recent case about federal bail statutes," he said. "Juba *can't* get away with *this*!"

We collected fifty relevant cases, three law review articles, and two treatises. We photocopied the relevant parts, brought them back to the empty office, and spread them on the floor. Bail decisions were rarely reversed when challenged. But there was a procedure that had to be gone through, and Juba had not bothered.

Steenson's office had no secretary, even during regular office hours. They could not afford one. Steenson typed the early drafts. I typed the revisions. By late that night, we had an eleven-page memorandum. The law was hierarchical. Juba had to start with the least severe release restriction—"personal recognizance," a defendant's promise to appear. He had to explain why he rejected that option, then work his way through the others—third-party release, low bail, reasonable bail—until the severest release restriction—unachievable bail. The rejection of each alternative had to be supported with facts.

Steenson's memorandum dissected Juba's ruling point by point with cases. Then he wrote, "The Court made an outrageous and completely unsubstantiated statement. . . . Nowhere in any statements, testimony, or evidence submitted to the Court . . . was there even the slightest allusion that either defendant attempted to escape. . . . Defendants emphatically deny that there is any truth whatsoever in this statement. This kind of 'Finding in Fact' based on thin air has created a fear in the minds of the defendants that it will be impossible for them to get a fair hearing on any subject in this Court."

Tom signed the memorandum with an angry gesture, pounded upside-down American flag stamps onto the envelope, and dropped it into the mail chute outside the office door.

It had an unintended, positive, effect. A week later, Robert C. Belloni, chief judge of the U.S. District Court for the District of Oregon, took Judge Juba off the case and assigned it to himself.

Slender, in his late fifties, soft spoken, Belloni was not an egomaniac like many other federal judges. Most Oregonians had never heard of him, although there were still cars on the Oregon coast with faded orange and black bumper stickers that read, CAN BELLONI. The judge's most noted ruling had interpreted treaties with Oregon's Indians. The treaties had promised respect for Indian fishing rights "as long as the river shall run." Belloni held the tribes were entitled to half the ocean salmon harvest. Belloni was also the only Oregon federal judge not secretly dressed in prosecutor's clothing. We had a chance.

KaMook Banks was in a hospital room, under guard, in Wichita, Kansas, on December 30, 1975.

"Take the handcuffs off her!" a doctor ordered again, this time successfully, when it was only an hour before KaMook's cesarean section.

The government agents had her handcuffed to her bed. They had orders to watch her during delivery.

A picture of her fugitive husband, Dennis Banks, was taped to the wall. She had not put it there. The FBI had, so that the guards and hospital personnel might recognize him if he was stupid enough to visit.

When KaMook had been brought back to Kansas from Portland five weeks before, her bail had been increased to $20,000. Her motions for release had failed, like Russ and Kenny's. Judge Frank Theis of Kansas would not even allow her out, temporarily, to give birth.

"She might flee with her husband," the Kansas prosecutor argued.

"Nonsense," her attorney responded. "Where is she going to run to, right after giving birth by cesarean section? She'll turn herself in after she's recovered from childbirth, in just a few days. She's never missed a court appearance yet."

"Well, she was traveling with fugitives out of state," the prosecutor responded. "Her husband's a fugitive. And one of the people she was with is Anna Mae Aquash. When Aquash was returned to face charges in South Dakota, the judge there released her, because she, technically, hadn't missed a court appearance either. She went underground the next day, Your Honor, and hasn't been seen since."

When KaMook woke up in her hospital jail bed, she was handed her new baby girl to breast-feed. Soon, the doctor entered the room and pushed past the two FBI agents. He examined his patients. "You're both doing great," he said, with a smile.

"By the way," he whispered, so the agents could not hear, "have you a name picked out, dear?"

"Yes, we do," KaMook responded. "Her name was already decided by the spirits at a ceremony my relations held in Pine Ridge before I was arrested. She'll be TaTiopa Maza Win."

"That's pretty," the doctor said. "Is that Indian?"

"It's Lakota," KaMook explained. "In English, it means Iron Door Woman."

CHAPTER 8

✜ ✜ ✜

PREJUDICE AND INFORMANTS

BY New Year's 1976, the offense/defense committee had Portland saturated with the *Loud Hawk* case. Nancy Sanders, Susanne Santos, and a dozen others stapled leaflets onto nearly every light pole and bulletin board. Laurel Winterscheid, Jerry Sheehan, and other student offense/defense committee members wrote weekly updates for their college newspapers. Members who worked at KBOO, the local public radio station, aired something every day.

Oregon Times, a statewide magazine, had a cover story. Ed Jones, Ron Schiffman, Sheila Lea, Tom Steenson, Lynn Parkinson, Lena Redner, Susana Gren, and visiting AIM leaders Vernon Bellecourt and John Trudell were interviewed on radio and television stations. Colleges as far away as Seattle and San Francisco requested speakers. Local musicians competed for the honor of performing benefits.

Linda Coelho was an active committee member. At fifteen, she was an independent, slight, short Indian girl who looked even younger. She weighed less than ninety pounds. She lived with her mother, Anna, and two sisters in a tiny house in Northeast Portland's ghetto, on Tillamook Street. The broken tables and chairs and the yellow, stained, living room carpet were covered with *Loud Hawk* paraphernalia. Stacks of white T-shirts with Indians behind black bars, protesting "Two Hundred Years of Your GODDAMN GLORY." Red, blue, yellow, and black posters decrying "Five Hundred Years of Genocide—Free Loud Hawk and Redner." Buttons of white and red and black with Indians behind bars demanding "Support Indian Resistance." Bumper stickers with red capital letters, "FREE LOUD HAWK AND REDNER."

Late one rainy winter evening, Linda was home alone. She heard a knock on the door and opened it. There were two white men, in their twenties, dressed in jackets and ties and shiny black shoes. They looked like FBI agents.

"Is your mother home?" one of them asked.

"No," Linda said.

"Do you expect her or Lena Redner back soon?" the man inquired.

Linda noticed a handgun under the second man's jacket. She slammed the door. Before it closed, she felt pressure from the other side. She leaned against the door and the latch barely snapped shut. She slipped the metal chain on.

The men banged on the door and then on a nearby window. Linda stood still, to the side, away from the door, by a couch in the corner of the living room.

The pounding continued, then let up. One man yelled through the door, "Tell your mother that we just stopped by to see how you and your family want to be buried!"

Anna Coelho found Linda in a corner, crying, a half hour later.

Now that defense work was going so well, I concentrated on *Loud Hawk*'s legal problems. The issues were not like the boring exercises of first year law school: property transfers, contract interpretation, zoning variances. *Loud Hawk*'s issues were novel, exciting, sparkling: FBI harassment, informants, pretrial release, destruction of evidence, FBI intrusion into the defense camp. Every day something new would happen—and would produce a legal issue.

One day Parkinson's wife, Kitsy, drove home an hour earlier than usual. She saw a man on her property, a foot from the top of a telephone pole, fiddling with something. He was not wearing a telephone company uniform. She had not passed a telephone company truck. When she surprised him, he ran into the woods. "Motion to Disclose Electronic Surveillance" was added to the list of legal pleadings.

"Might as well, but it's a waste of paper," Schiffman said. "Unless you catch the guy with the bug in his hand, they're just gonna deny it."

I concentrated on two issues. First, what, exactly, were Redner and Loud Hawk and the others charged with doing? Was merely possessing dynamite illegal? If so, why weren't farmers who blew up stumps or beaver dams prosecuted? If there was some required registration regulation, what was it? What, specifically, would the government have to prove to convict them?

I pored through the books at Willamette University's law library, every evening reshelving the dozens of books I had piled on my table so that no curious FBI agent could see on what I was working.

Second, this was a federal crime, but what gave the federal government the power to regulate explosives? I checked. The answer was, "Nothing." The federal government could only regulate things that concerned the federal government, like border issues or tax issues or commerce issues, things that affect international or interstate interests.

The cases, confusing individually, made sense collectively. Congress had created a myth using its power to raise revenue through taxes. Redner could possess explosives legally. However, if he had a "nefarious intent," a nasty thought like, "I'll use this stuff to blow up bridges and roads so that the Goon squad has a harder time terrorizing traditional Indians in Pine Ridge," something magical happened. Then, the law required Redner to run to his local Internal Revenue Service office, register his explosives, pay $200 in taxes, and obtain a serial number. His failure to do that could send him to jail for thirty years.

That the government could create a crime through a sham tax was one thing. But what about the Fifth Amendment, which says the government cannot make a person incriminate himself or herself? Imagine if Redner walked into an IRS office carrying 350 pounds of dynamite, fuses, caps, and pocket watches with holes drilled into their faces and screws inserted into the holes so that when they made contact with the watch hands an electrical circuit was completed, and said, "Excuse me, sir, I have these nice bombs here that I plan to use to blow up public property; what line do I stand in to register them, get a serial number, and pay my taxes, please?" Surely the IRS would call the FBI.

"No," reasoned the courts. "The IRS has an obligation of confidentiality. It is required, by law, to register the bomb and not tell anyone, even the FBI or police."

I remembered the Nixon administration's use of the IRS to

harass its "enemies." Didn't that disprove the "obligation of confidentiality?" Two recent cases raised the same theory. Both lost.

A challenge to the law seemed useless. I was ecstatic nonetheless. While my Willamette classmates were writing pretend memorandums for pretend future bosses, I was working on something real, developing ideas that were logical enough to have been presented by other, seasoned, real life lawyers in other real cases.

The relevance was what excited me. That was why I was consumed by my other *Loud Hawk* research project. Although it seemed less logical, it had more potential. Rather than focusing on a narrow legal problem, like the tax fantasy, it was expansive. "What can we do about the destruction of the dynamite?" was the question the lawyers and I kept asking ourselves. This was an irregular occurrence. It seemed natural to exploit. But how? We did not know why an Oregon State Police bomb disposal person named William Fettig had destroyed the alleged dynamite. Tommy Hawk said the stuff was just too volatile to keep. Maybe it was. Then again, maybe it was not? The government rarely burns evidence it wants a jury to believe a defendant possessed. Maybe it was never there?

I found cases about destruction of evidence. I read them, copied them, reshelved the books, reread them. Most were drug cases. The Drug Enforcement Agency (DEA) would catch someone at the border with 500 pounds of marijuana. The DEA would burn 490 pounds. Some clerk would "lose" the remaining 10 pounds. The defense would file a motion seeking dismissal or suppression—a ruling prohibiting the prosecution from proving the existence of the marijuana through "secondary" evidence, such as testimony and photographs. The law was clear. A person charged with a crime had an absolute right to inspect anything taken from him, for use in his defense. The government had an absolute obligation to hold onto material seized from a defendant.

The courts would say something like, "Well, this defendant before us wasn't really hurt, and there was other, overwhelming evidence of guilt, so we'll let this prosecution continue. But, prosecutor, don't dare do it again!"

I stacked the cases chronologically. The warnings had started in the early 1970s, then escalated into threats, as the judges' words went unheeded. "Prosecutors are flirting with dismissal," the most recent case said.

For Redner and Loud Hawk, we could point to those strong warnings. But that was all the courts seemed to do—warn. They had never dismissed for destruction of evidence.

We had another problem, something called "prejudice." The court would say, "So what if Loud Hawk and Redner and their lawyers couldn't see the 350 pounds of explosives? The jury would hear testimony and see pictures. They weren't going to have the actual explosives before them in the courtroom anyway."

I was so absorbed in the problem of prejudice I was dreaming about it. If only our case were damaged in some way, we would have a better argument for dismissal. Ron Schiffman and Ed Jones were fixated on this issue, too. We all had creative ideas, but every in-depth discussion came back to the question of how were *we* hurt by not being able to see the alleged dynamite in *this* case? None of us had an answer.

One rainy January afternoon, Schiffman gathered all the lawyers in his office on 25th Avenue in Northwest Portland. It was a converted garage attached to an old, three-story white house with blue trim. The floors were carpeted, and some of the chairs were upholstered. The meeting had already started when I walked in with a hundred pages of xeroxed cases folded into the back of a legal pad.

"Nobody's leaving here 'til we get a theory!" Schiffman yelled as I sat down.

"The problem is, Ron, that we don't have any real prejudice," Ed Jones said. "It's hard enough to conjure up any imagined prejudice, for that matter!" he added.

While Jones was speaking, he was sitting on the floor, cleaning marijuana seeds from a half-inch-high pile of pot on the cardboard back of a legal pad. The room already smelled, and Sheila was taking a hit off the tip of a joint held by a silver alligator clip connected to a key chain. When she could get no more smoke, she ate the end of the roach.

The converted garage had no windows. The ceiling was low. Smoke congregated near the incandescent lights overhead as everyone freely associated. The light bulbs were absorbing a bluish tinge. Jones kept rolling joints.

"Prejudice?" Jones said, then repeated, "Prejudice! Let's see. How were we hurt? I guess we could say that the stuff couldn't explode?"

"We could, Ed," I volunteered, "but the cases require us to make a showing. How could we prove that?"

"Why do we have to prove anything?" Steenson asked. "They're the ones who destroyed the stuff. Shouldn't they have to prove that it *could* explode?"

"I agree," I said. "I think that's how the law should be. But I'll show you the cases. All the courts say that the burden of proof in a pretrial motion is on the defendant. It's fucked."

"And, anyway," Lea said, "they have pictures the FBI took of the stuff exploding."

"Right," Schiffman grunted.

"Maybe prejudice just isn't there, Ron?" Jones asked.

Another joint was coming my way. I debated whether to take a full hit or a short hit, or to pretend that I was smoking it—keep the smoke in my mouth without inhaling—then let it out my nose so it seemed as if I had inhaled, or just to pass it on. I started speaking, then passed the roach to my left as if I were too involved with a good thought to distract myself with a toke.

"You're right, Ron," I said, "something *has* to be here. The law's so *good*! Maybe we can find something else in it to make up for our lack of a good fact."

Everyone was silent, seemingly in deep thought. I continued, out loud, now too stoned to keep ideas to myself, afraid that if any were good I'd forget what they were before I could voice them.

"The problem," I mumbled, "is that the legal standard makes no sense. The law requires us to show how we're hurt. But the evidence we need to show how we're hurt was destroyed by the government. That's a tautology. The law makes us prove what the government has prohibited us from proving."

"Man, that's it!" Schiffman said, slapping his hands together. "We need to argue as follows: When the government destroys evidence that makes it impossible for us to show how we've been hurt, the burden to show that we haven't been hurt must be on the government. That only seems fair. *They're* the ones who destroyed it. *They* should have to show that there is *no* prejudice.

We should argue that there is a legal *presumption* of prejudice, that the government must rebut."

I was excited but had to see if the argument withheld attack. "Ron, again, I agree," I started, "but that's not what the cases say. They say that a *defendant* has the burden. And in many of the destruction cases, the difficulty in proving the harm is a by-product of the destruction just as much as in our case."

"Let's see," Schiffman said, standing up. "Maybe there's some room to maneuver in those cases."

He sat on the carpet, his knees folded, and motioned to me. I joined him and spread out the copies. The other lawyers talked among themselves and smoked as I showed Schiffman each case.

"I see what you mean," he said, "but we need to find some distinction to make a 'presumption of prejudice' argument. Let's start over again and map out the key facts."

"In this case," I said, "the evidence was intentionally destroyed because the government thought it couldn't prosecute. Then, a totally unexpected witness popped up."

"Um hum," Schiffman said.

"And in this one," I continued, "some drugs got mixed up in the evidence locker. It was a mistake. And in this one, they didn't realize that the evidence was important, and they just lost it."

"The difference in our case," Schiffman said, getting excited, "was that they *intentionally* destroyed the evidence."

"That's true, but I'm sure I saw another case like that," I said, thumbing through the pile. "Yeah, here, this California case. Let's see. They seized a lot of marijuana and had a policy to destroy it. But they saved a sample. You know, Ron, we *may* be able to craft a distinction."

"It's the level of intent!" Schiffman said. "Some cases, they lost the shit, in others the destruction was negligent, and even when it was intentional, either the evidence was not really important or they kept a sample."

"That's right!" I said. "In our case, the destruction was intentional and complete, and the evidence was central, charged in the indictment. *Loud Hawk's* destruction was the most deliberate and purposeful and willful, especially in the face of the warning from the courts."

"That's our distinction!" Schiffman yelled, standing up, waving the pile of cases like a winning lottery ticket. Parkinson and Lea and Jones and Steenson all focused on him.

"It's like a scale," Schiffman explained. "The greater the government's culpability in the destruction, the more reason to give it the burden of proving lack of prejudice to the defense!"

Another joint was passed around.

On January 23, I walked into the courtroom with the defense lawyers for the first time. And for the first time, Schiffman invited me to the lawyer's side of the oak bar.

"We're arguing the destruction of evidence question today, and I want you nearby. You know the cases," he said, his arm around me. Even though I was sitting against the bar rather than at the counsel table, I was elated. The lawyers had accepted me and found my novice legal work worthwhile.

"Come here for a second," Parkinson said, before Judge Belloni took the bench. I walked the fifteen feet to the counsel table. Redner and Loud Hawk were being unshackled by the marshals.

"Russ, Kenny," he said, "I want you guys to meet Ken Stern. He's a law student and has been doing good work on the case."

"Hi," was all I managed to say, shaking their hands, feeling stupid. A law student should be able to say something clever. Nothing came to me. They nodded a greeting. Russ said, "Thanks."

I was nervous. Schiffman had created something marvelous with his presumption of prejudice argument. But even though it made some sense intellectually, it was a legal argument built with smoke and mirrors. Tommy Hawk seemed intelligent. I knew what I would argue if I were the prosecutor. "Your Honor," I would say, "Mr. Schiffman's 'presumption of prejudice' may be well and good, but there's a reason he has cited no case using that language or that concept. The cases are unanimous. A defendant has to *show* prejudice. In this case, there *is* no prejudice. How could there be? That's why the defense has concocted this nonexistent 'presumption.' It's pure fantasy, Your Honor, without legal authority, born from desperation."

Belloni took the bench. Schiffman stood and argued his motion. I absorbed every word, reviewing his performance instantaneously, with each passing phrase. It was either "I'm glad he said that," or "I'd say that a bit differently, but it was okay" or "I hope he remembers to say . . . ," or, most frequently, "I wish I were up there arguing this!"

"Your Honor" he said, with authority, his hands placed straight down on the counsel table before him, "we're faced with what the Supreme Court has labeled a denial of due process, where the prosecution sets out to intentionally and willfully destroy evidence. . . . Now, the government is saying, 'Well, this dynamite was so dangerous, we couldn't put it in boxes and store it someplace.' That's patently absurd! Dynamite is stored all the time. That's how commercial dynamite is sold, that's how it's distributed, that's how it's transported."

Hawk responded, "Your Honor, what distinguishes this case is that the substance destroyed was a volatile, dangerous explosive. Now, the government intends to prove at trial that found in the vehicle that Mr. Redner and Mr. Loud Hawk were occupying were seven cases of dynamite. That dynamite was photographed in place in the vehicle. It was removed and photographed again. An Oregon State Police bomb expert removed portions of dynamite from each box, removed representative wrappers, then transported the dynamite to a safe location."

I was excited, hopeful. Apparently, Hawk had not bothered to read the case law to refute Schiffman's cockamamy theory. Hawk was resting his entire argument on a single idea—that the dynamite was too dangerous to keep. He conceded everything else.

"Well," Judge Belloni asked, "did any representative of the defendants have an opportunity to witness that procedure?"

"At that time, Your Honor, there weren't any representatives of the defendants," Hawk answered. "They had not been appointed counsel." ("He's wrong!" I thought. He forgot about Axelrod. I scribbled a note, shuffled to the counsel table, and handed it to Schiffman.)

Hawk continued, "Your Honor, sticks were taken from the boxes. They were constructed into bombs and exploded by the Oregon State Police bomb expert. That expert will testify at trial that dynamite is a highly dangerous, volatile substance and has to be stored in certain locations. . . . Your Honor, it's the same as if we had nitroglycerin. We wouldn't expect to bring that nitroglycerin into this courtroom."

Hawk sat. Schiffman stood. He claimed that his presumption of prejudice argument was so strong Hawk had not bothered to respond to it and that Judge Belloni was right, the defense should have been contacted before the dynamite was destroyed. "And counsel was there," he added. "They could have notified Beverly Axelrod."

Our weak argument went over well. Schiffman had sparked Belloni's interest, while Hawk had hung onto his "it was too dangerous" argument too tenaciously.

Schiffman and I walked out of the courtroom together at a break. "You know," he said, surprised at what he was about to say, "Belloni could just give us this one! Those joints were worth their weight in gold."

Fifteen minutes later, Judge Belloni was back on the bench. He had a long list of motions. I felt alternatively excited and disappointed at every point in every argument. Mostly, I yearned to be making the arguments myself.

"Let's go on to the next motion," he said, after Tommy Hawk responded to our charge that the government had put spies in the defense camp.

Hawk had said, "There are no such informants." Judge Belloni had been satisfied. Russ Redner had become agitated. I watched as he leaned over to Sheila Lea four or five times and whispered into her ear, each time more aggressively.

Ed Jones was standing, arguing, "Mr. Hawk might not be aware of FBI agents in the defense camp, Your Honor."

"Let's move on to the next motion," the judge said again.

Jones sat. Lea stood. Leaning forward on the counsel table, she asked, "Your Honor, may the defendant Mr. Redner make a statement?"

"Oh, he's represented by counsel," Belloni replied.

Lea remained standing. "I think he could speak better for himself, Your Honor, if you would," she said.

Belloni was on the edge of anger. "All right!" he said. "Let's take the next motion, now!"

Her hands on her hips, Lea confronted the judge. "May Mr. Redner make a statement, Your Honor?" she challenged.

"No!" Belloni bellowed.

Redner was visibly upset. As he stood, his arms flailed. The marshals were ready to pounce. Before they could, Redner was standing still, yelling at the judge.

"How come I can't speak for myself, Your Honor?" he screamed. "Indian people are on trial for their lives in this country, and the fact is that prosecutors aren't always told about FBI informants. That came out in a case in Minnesota . . ."

Belloni's tone was intentionally calmer than it had just been. "You're represented by counsel," he explained.

"Well," Redner said in an excited voice, "I'm also represented by myself, because I can show this Court how the government goes out of its way to plant informers, to harass witnesses . . ."

"Well, let's make it clear . . . ," Belloni interrupted, less reserved.

There was no stopping Redner.

"My attorneys have virtually no experience with Indian cases," Redner said. "I have very limited experience. And the prosecutor over here has no experience with Indians at all. In other cases, the defendants were allowed to speak for themselves . . ."

"Well, Mr. . . . ," was all Belloni could edge in.

"And there've been so many outrages by the government that Indian people have had to go to jail just to prove their point. I'd like to have a voice in my own behalf. I'm the one facing forty years or whatever it is."

Redner was slowing down. Belloni took the opportunity. "If you're being represented by Ms. Lea, she'll have to speak for you."

"Your Honor," Lea said, in an angry voice that still held onto decorum, "I'm obviously a *white* attorney. I don't have some of the awareness that my client as an *Indian* has. We have no *Indian* attorneys to represent these people. It's only fair that he be allowed to speak when we're in areas where we cannot represent him."

"Ms. Lea," the judge said, realizing that he had regained control, "I ruled on that matter. Let's get on to the next motion now. Defendants' motion for search and disclosure of electronic or other surveillance."

As Ed Jones and Tommy Hawk debated the legal procedure by which the government was to determine if the same government was illegally surveilling the defense, Redner squirmed in his chair.

His agitation did not correlate with the point and counterpoint of the legal argument. He was engaged in some ferocious internal debate.

Jones was in midsentence when Redner burst from his seat in a motion that panicked the marshals. They were ready to leap and then stopped as they heard him speak. Screaming, Redner said, "Your Honor, I'm going to go ahead and say what I have to say, and you can drag me out of here . . ."

"Mr. Redner!" the judge tried, to no avail.

". . . if you want to because . . . when we were first arrested . . ."

"Mr. Redner," Belloni shouted, in a fatherly tone, "*please*, let me say something."

"No!" Redner bellowed. "I have something to say about these informer cases, and you're not dealing with it. So you're denying me the right to speak for my own freedom."

"I cannot . . . ," the judge started to explain.

Redner would not stop. "And if you're not going to deal with it, then I'll have to take it in my own hands. This guy," he said, pointing at Tommy Hawk, "is going to railroad us into jail, and *you're* not going to listen to me, *you're* not going to allow me or my representative to speak or . . ." Redner was slowing, groping for direction.

"Mr. Redner," Belloni said, calmly, "I have in mind allowing you to speak a little later. If you'll just keep your shirt on and sit down."

"What about the issue right now?" Redner argued.

"Mr. Redner," the judge lectured, his voice rising again, "*I'm* running this courtroom, and I will not . . ."

"I'm the one facing trial, Your Honor, facing forty years or whatever it is, not you!"

"I will not conduct it in a circus atmosphere!" Belloni said. "I will allow you to speak after a while. First I want to go through this in an orderly manner."

Redner thought for a second, then said, "Well, okay. But I'll tell you this. If I'm going to be taken out of here by the marshals, I'm just going to jump up and say it anyway, because I don't like the way the government has been treating me for 200 years and the way they handled that nine-month trial of Dennis Banks in Minnesota. There were informers everywhere, electronic surveillance, harassment, you name it."

"Mr. Redner," Judge Belloni said, exasperated, "I intend to let you talk. Defendants' first motion for disclosure and inspection is what I have down here next."

For the next half hour arguments on the lesser motions gripped me—questions about how the grand jury had been selected, about recording any future grand jury session, about selection of the trial jury, about technical language in the indictment, about handwriting exemplars.[1] Throughout, I kept thinking about the intensity of Redner's confrontation with the judge. In jail for over two months despite being a war hero with no previous record, he was fed up and had nothing to lose. Yet his explosion was controlled; he referred to the judge as "Your Honor" in mid-yell. Belloni, for his part, went with the ebb and flow and finally regained control without looking like he had backed down. Fascinating as they were, the legal arguments presented by my new friends, using some of my own, first legal work, were still an anticlimax. Belloni had promised Redner time to speak. He would talk about informants—a legal issue to the judge, a question of war to Russ Redner.

Finally, Belloni finished his list. The last item was the trial date, which he changed from February 8, 1976, to March 8, 1976. "The defense has had problems with its investigation and needs another month to prepare," it was explained.

Belloni looked at Redner, nodded, and said, "You may make your statement."

Redner stood, stretched from side to side, and started slowly. "I'd like to bring up a case that happened in Minnesota with the field director of the American Indian Movement, Dennis Banks," he began. "Judge Nichol was the presiding judge. The case lasted nine months. Judge Nichol said he found it difficult to believe what the government had done. For example, a defense lawyer, William Kunstler, went to a side door—a door to the judge's own chambers—and suggested that the FBI might be listening illegally through the cracks. He opened the door, and guess what rolled out? Two FBI agents. Later it was found out that an FBI

---

1. The government wanted Redner and Loud Hawk to provide handwriting samples for comparison to documents found in the vehicles. The defendants refused. The government wanted them held in contempt.

and CIA plant named Douglas Durham had infiltrated the Amercan Indian Movement; he was Dennis Banks's right arm throughout the trial. And meanwhile, the judge was unaware of it, and the prosecutor was unaware of it.

"This is why we want to find out who my accusers are. The FBI says it has two snitches who snitched 120 times, and that's how we got busted. We were just minding our own business, not doing anything."

Redner's speech was getting less intense, quicker, more rambling. Everyone in the courtroom was riveted.

Ron Schiffman and Tom Steenson squirmed. I presumed they were concerned, as was I, that Redner might ramble on and say things that could be used against him at trial. But he moved away from what he privately termed "the mission."

Looking directly at the judge, almost pleading, Redner said, "You suggested that a probation officer, Mr. Greathouse, work with the Urban Indian Council to plan for our release. What happened is so bizarre I can't believe it. He suggested that Indians were warlike because they fought each other, so it was all right for whites to kill Indians because it was a society where the strongest survived. He didn't ask for information about us or our backgrounds. He kept asking only about our case. I had to say, 'I don't want to talk to you unless I have my attorney here.' So this man, posing as a guise for freedom, came in with ulterior motives, maybe to get information for the government."

Redner paused for a moment, thinking. "He got to me," he said, apologetically, softly. Then more quickly, his volume raising, "I don't like being locked up. *We're* the ones who are displaced people. We got all this land from the East Coast to the West Coast ripped off. Twenty-nine Indian people are dead. Two hundred back in Pine Ridge have been murdered."

A spectator shouted, "Talk about it, Bud."

A marshal stirred, looking into the packed rows, but the moment passed, as Redner, now in full stride, continued, his arms moving in rhythm with his words.

"They're raiding houses, they're picking little kids out of their cars. This happened right up here in Olympia. Soon after we were busted, they went up to Frank's Landing, 75 of these people, and just marched in there and arrested three women.[2] Three women! They didn't deal with the men. This is what this case is going to be about: the fact that I'm Shoshone, and I stand on the treaties of 1868 and 1863. And this land is still ours!

"Now, I want you to *deal* with some of this. We haven't threatened anybody. We were shot at. We're chained up. My wife was harassed, followed. People knock at the door at midnight and say, 'How do you want to be buried?' People have been shooting at us. This is what Indian people are going through, and I'm an Indian person. But I have some heart in here. I'm human. My people are human. And we want this Court, we want this prosecutor, we want these marshals, we want all these people, all you people, you aliens, we want you to deal with us, deal with our treaties, deal with us as human beings and start looking at our side of the case.

"This is not an ordinary criminal case. The FBI was in on this from Day One. I want to know who their informants are. I want to have somebody tell me why I can't get out of jail so I can prepare my defense adequately with my counsel. I want to get out on the street. I want my counsel to prove that I'm innocent and that the guilt lies with the government!"

2. Frank's Landing is a small reservation in southwestern Washington, where Indian fishing rights had first been asserted in the late 1950s.

CHAPTER 9

REKINDLING THE DREAM

IN the 1860s, Red Cloud and the warriors of the Oglala band of the Sioux won battle after battle. The government was frantic. There was no way to defend endless miles of railroad track.

The Treaty of 1868, called the Fort Laramie Treaty, protected the railroads. The government promised to withdraw from parts of Indian territory—to close its forts along the Bozeman trail, and the trail itself—forever. In return the Indians agreed, for the first time, to boundaries on their lands. These "unceded Indian territories" extended from the Missouri River west to the Big Horn Mountains in Wyoming and from just below the Canadian border south into Nebraska. They encompassed all of present-day South Dakota west of the Missouri River, more than half of Nebraska, a third of Wyoming, a quarter of North Dakota, and a significant chunk of Montana.

The government promised to keep white settlers and fortune hunters out of Indian territory. The settlers and fortune hunters came anyway. They harassed and killed Indians and their animals. The government did nothing to stop them.

In 1874, Gen. George Armstrong Custer confirmed a report of gold in the Black Hills, "from the grass roots down." The government tried to buy the Black Hills. The Sioux were not interested. The Black Hills were the most sacred spot on earth; Paha Sapa, they called it. Paha Sapa was Mother, the center of the Universe. Gods lived there. Warriors came there to seek visions, to commune with the Great Spirit.

The U.S. government violated its pledge of peace and went to war against the Indians. Despite the Indian victory at Little Big Horn, by 1876, the sacred Black Hills were taken—and along with them, the bulk of the unceded Indian territories. What was left of the "Great Sioux Reservation" was almost entirely within western

South Dakota. Indians found outside—on land where their ancestors had gone unmolested, land that their folklore told about, land legally belonging to them—were considered "hostile."

In 1889, after the state of South Dakota was proclaimed, the government unilaterally broke the Sioux reservation into smaller units for the various Sioux bands, taking the land in between. All continuity was gone. Conditions were intolerable. Unable to roam and hunt, the Indians had to rely on the government's treatied promise of provisions. Crooked brokers and insensitive bureaucrats let people starve to death.

A new religious movement, the Ghost Dance, spread across Indian country in 1890. Its champion, an elder named Big Foot, preached a messianic message that blended Indian spirituality and Christian proselytizing. The Ghost Dance was guaranteed to resurrect dead warriors. Dancing, singing, and praying was all the dancers need do; the Messiah would do the rest and make the Indian people whole again.

But churches had invaded the reservation, and Indian religion became illegal. Government agents alerted the military.

On December 28, 1890, Big Foot had pneumonia, was hemorrhaging, and could no longer walk. Confined to a wagon, he was surrounded by his followers, 120 men and 230 women and children. Four units of cavalry approached. Everyone was taken prisoner. Hotchkiss guns were aimed at them. They were impounded at a hamlet called Wounded Knee.

The rest of the Seventh Regiment arrived, with more Hotchkiss guns. They had orders to ship Big Foot and his followers by Union Pacific Railroad to a concentration camp in Omaha.

A bugle sounded. Soldiers on horseback surrounded the Indians who were ordered to give up their weapons. The guns were stacked. But the soldiers were not satisfied. They marched into tepees. They grabbed bundles and tore them apart. Tent stakes, axes, and knives were piled beside the guns.

The soldiers still were not satisfied. Although it was winter, the soldiers ordered the Indians to remove their blankets and be searched. Demeaned and angry, the Indians nonetheless submitted. Only Yellow Bird, a medicine man, complained. He danced the Ghost Dance and sang a song, telling the warriors that no bullet could pass through their sacred ribbon shirts.

The soldiers found two rifles. One was a new Winchester. A youngster named Black Coyote held the gun above his head, protesting that he had just spent a fortune to buy it. He had not pointed it at anyone. Soldiers grabbed him, spun him around, and seized the gun. Right then, a shot went off. No one was sure where it came from. The soldiers opened fire on the defenseless Indians. Within seconds, the air was putrid with gun smoke. The gunfire thundered. The shrapnel from the Hotchkiss guns tore apart tepees and Indians. Those who were running away were shot in the back.

"We tried to run," Louise Weasel Bear said, "but they shot us like we were buffalo. I know there are some good white people, but the soldiers must be mean to shoot children and women."

Nearly 300 of Big Foot's band of 350 were killed. Those found alive, including the wounded, were put in wagons and taken to Pine Ridge, where they were left outside in the bitter cold. The dead Indians at Wounded Knee froze overnight, transformed into gnarled and hideous shapes.

Many years later, as an old man, Indian spiritual leader Black Elk said,

I did not know then how much was ended. When I look back now from this high hill of my old age, I can still see the butchered women and children lying heaped and scattered all along the crooked gulch as plain as when I saw them with eyes still young. And I can see that something else died there in the bloody mud, and was buried in the blizzard. A people's dream died there. It was a beautiful dream. . . . The nation's hoop is broken and scattered. There is no center any longer and the sacred tree is dead.[1]

"We are rekindling the dream," Dennis Banks said, in a speech in Nebraska, only weeks before he went underground in the summer of 1975. "We want recognition of our sovereignty, the rebuilding of our nation's hoop. We need to reclaim our spirituality. We need the government to end this longest war."

1. This account is based on Brown, *Bury My Heart at Wounded Knee*, 439–45. Black Elk's quote is from John G. Neihardt, *Black Elk Speaks* (Lincoln: University Nebraska Press, 1961), 276.

✛ ✛ ✛

FROM THE CELL OF D. BANKS SATURDAY NIGHT,
JANUARY 24, 1976.
FOR MY ATTORNEYS' EYES ONLY.

What a way for a day to begin! The first thing I remember was Trudy Brightman standing in the bedroom doorway telling me that the FBI had surrounded the house. I got out of bed wondering if this was it. Would they come in shooting? Tear gas and shoot us as we ran out? I had seen them do away with that group in Los Angeles,[2] and I remember how they went in after those Black Panthers.

I looked out the bedroom window and couldn't see a damn thing. Was Trudy mistaken? And then I walked into Lee's bedroom, where I saw she wasn't mistaken at all. There they stood, about 10 to 15 of them. All with guns drawn. 38s. 357s. AR-15s. This was the real thing alright.

I could hear them hollering, "Come on out, Banks. We've got you surrounded!"

I never really planned anything or ever thought of this happening, and so when it did I was worried about Lee and Trudy and the kids getting hurt. But Trudy already had the kids out of danger. She had sent them over to the neighbors.

More hollering. "You have 30 seconds, Banks, to come out or we're coming in!" It was an agent who identified himself as Stephen Brown.

And then a thought struck me. It would end with me killed or in cuffs. If they were going to come in, shooting, or shoot me or us after we came out, then that's the way it would be. I was in no rush to be shot. Once it happens, that's it. And I thought if I end up being cuffed and arrested, then I might as well just take my sweet time. So I calmly put my clothes on and walked through the house trying to locate a book by Josephy. Hell, no sense doing time without a good book, I thought. Lee was getting dressed and hollering back, "We're coming, damn it, we're just getting dressed." The agent

2. A house in which the Symbionese Liberation Army (SLA) and Patty Hearst were supposedly hiding was attacked by the FBI. It burned, killing some members of the group.

*screamed until it was just one loud shrill. He was the one worried and
scared.*

*Finally with two books, my pipe, tobacco, and a coat I walked out
and said, "Good morning, can I help you?"*

That's how my morning started on January 24, 1976.

*After I was brought in I refused to get fingerprinted and mugged.
Hell, they have hundreds of shots of me and my fingerprints. They
threw me in a cell with four bunks, all empty with a bare mattress on
each.*

*A half hour later, two FBI agents came to the cell and wanted me to
go with them. I refused. They said they just wanted to get a physical
description of me. I told them to measure me lying down. The agents'
names were Duke Dietrich and Stephen Brown.*

*Dietrich did most of the talking. Five times I said I wanted to remain
silent and wouldn't talk to anyone unless my attorney was present.
They persisted. They were there about 4 or 5 minutes. I said if they
wanted to talk about the crimes in this country, then I would gladly talk
for several hours about the FBI's criminal record, not mine. With that
they left. As Brown was leaving he told me, "You're not ever going to
get a lawyer!"*

*Meantime, Trudy was beginning to call around the country. Within
an hour after I was arrested, calls began coming in from Washington State, New York, Minnesota, Oregon, Oklahoma, southern
California, South Dakota. Trudy sure was strong today. Lee is lucky
that she didn't panic during those critical early minutes. I guess we all
are.*

*About two hours after I was in jail I got a call from Beverly
Axelrod. She, Sam Gross, and Melinda came while Lee was visiting
with Aubrey Grossman, then we all joined in the lawyers room. We
decided to let Beverly and Aubrey begin a defense committee on my
behalf.*

*While we were all visiting, an FBI agent came in and told Lee that
he was free to go. I watched as a sigh of relief came over Lee. He is a
great man.*

7:15 P.M.—Kunstler called. Said he was coming in.

7:20 P.M.—Another call from N.Y. Council of Churches.

8:15 P.M.—The Lt. came back and told me that the calls are still coming in. Seminary students as well. He brought in more tobacco. My brother-in-law Hawkins left it. Hawkins left me some clothes also. I have the three books to read that Lee left: Patriot Chiefs, History of Indians in the U.S., *and* Victories of the Apache Tribe.

The phone here has a strange whirling sound and clicks about every 15 to 20 seconds. I suspect all my calls are monitored.

8 A.M., SATURDAY, JANUARY 25, 1976—THE FIRST MORNING, DAY 2

8:30 A.M.—The jailer is standing by the cell door. I just got a call from an attorney in Milwaukee, Sheldon, who wants to know if I need help. I told him I would call him later. He asked, "How did the night go?"

My damn back is killing me. Not hard pain but the kind after you've slept on boards all night. I started doing situps to get the kinks out of my bones. My spirits are OK. My thoughts right now are of KaMook, Tosh, and the new baby. I love them so. I wonder if I will ever see them again.

"How's your back today, Dennis?" a tall, skinny, curly-haired lawyer in a tailored gray suit asked, as he slowly lowered himself onto an orange plastic chair in the San Francisco jail's interview room.

"Better," Dennis Banks replied, "how's yours?"

"Oy," the lawyer said, taking a yellow legal pad from his red leather briefcase, "don't ask."

Within hours of his arrest, noted movement attorneys had lined up, offering themselves. Banks had chosen Dennis Roberts, from Oakland. Roberts was sharp and smooth, an expert in criminal defense. He was bearded, in his late thirties, over six feet tall, and wore a California tan and a Brooklyn accent.

"I've decided on Roberts," Banks had told Trudy. "I like his style. He worked on the Chicago Conspiracy case, defended

Huey Newton and Angela Davis, and, Kunstler tells me, as a law student, Roberts was one of the first to go South to defend the civil rights workers. I like that. Everyone says he's a brilliant tactician."

Roberts folded his legs at the knees, put the legal pad on his right thigh, and announced, "The way I see it, you've got two pulls on ya. South Dakota wants you for the sentencing you skipped this past summer,[3] and the feds want you in Portland for all that bomb and gun shit."

"I want to avoid South Dakota if I can," Banks interrupted.

"Put the danger of South Dakota aside for the moment," Roberts ordered. "They got you by the balls."

Banks nodded.

"Okay," Roberts said, "I think they'll want you in Portland first, to fuck with ya."

"How?" Banks asked.

"They'll get the most flesh out of you that way. It'll be dead time. You won't be sentenced in South Dakota until after the Portland case is over. That could take months, maybe a year or more. The time you spend in jail waiting in Oregon won't count on the sentence you get later in South Dakota. We should get you to South Dakota first. That way, you'll be sentenced and start serving state time while you're waiting for your trial in Portland. You'd also be safer, because we'd get you moved to Oregon right away, so you can help prepare for trial."

"Um hum," Banks said, thinking the twists over. "I can serve the South Dakota time while waiting in Oregon, right?"

"Right," Roberts said. "And, in the meantime, we keep you here. There's no better place to pull a defense committee together than in the Bay Area. People here love ya."

I arrived late at Jack and Micki Scott's gray Victorian house on Monday evening, the 26th of January. The sun had already set, but its last glimmers reflected golden on the downtown buildings in the valley below Portland's Northwest hills.

I was nervous as I walked the half block from my car to their

---

3. Dennis Banks had been found guilty in 1975 for his part in a 1972 protest-turned-riot in Custer, South Dakota.

front door. Three weeks earlier I had met the Scotts at an offense/defense committee meeting.

"We came here tonight," Jack had said, "to offer our house for a fund raising dinner for Kenny and Russ."

The Scotts, both athletic and in their early thirties, were movement celebrities. I had not paid much attention to the details of the Patty Hearst affair—the millionaire heiress who was kidnapped by the Symbionese Liberation Army and then joined them in bank robberies—but Jack and Micki were mixed up in that.

When the FBI believed it had found Tania (as Patty called her revolutionary self) in a Los Angeles house, it ordered the occupants out. They refused. A shoot-out started. The FBI barraged the building with bullets and tear gas. The house burned, killing SLA members. Jack and Micki were supposed to have helped her hide from the FBI in a Pennsylvania farmhouse after that. They were subpoenaed to appear before a grand jury. They refused to testify. The government was threatening to jail them for contempt.[4]

Their house had a vestibule, and inside, past a lethargic old German Shepard named Sigmund, were two dozen shoes, lined up. One pair of sneakers, twice the size of the others, stood out. Bill Walton, star center of the Portland Trail Blazers, lived here, too.

I found myself staring when I first saw him. His gestures took up twice the expected space; his arms disturbed upper air previously protected by the high Victorian ceilings. When he walked through doorways, he ducked, unconsciously. He was almost seven feet tall.

An Indian man named Vernon Bellecourt was speaking in the living room. He had long, braided hair and was built solidly, like a football player. An AIM founder, he spoke with a sophistica-

4. Grand juries were established in common law as a way to protect people from overzealous prosecutors. Prosecutors had to prove to this group of citizens that there was reasonable cause to believe that a crime had been committed and that the person to be charged committed the crime. During the Nixon administration, the grand jury was used increasingly as a prosecutorial weapon. People who were called to testify were given only limited immunity from prosecution. If they refused to testify, they could be held in contempt and jailed.

tion lacking in the other AIM members I had met.

"I talked with Dennis Banks yesterday," he said, standing before a tile fireplace. Fifty white people sat before him, on the oak floor, looking up, legs crossed in yoga position. They had paid $25 a couple to listen.

"He sends his regards and his thanks for your help."

Bellecourt took a sip of water. "These are hard times for Indian people," he continued. "We're still subjugated. We're trying to improve our conditions by challenging the corruption in the Bureau of Indian Affairs. For that, we're attacked. There have been scores of murders on the Pine Ridge reservation by a Goon squad supported and armed by the FBI. The government has tried to jail our leadership—Russell Means and Dennis Banks. In jail, our leaders have been attacked, knifed, and threatened with death.

"Even our warriors, like Kenny Loud Hawk and Russ Redner, are targets for the government's courts and jails. The government just indicted three more of our boys, Dino Butler, Bob Robideau, and Leonard Peltier, charged them with killing two FBI agents on the Pine Ridge reservation last summer. No one's been charged with killing Joe Stuntz, an Indian who died there that day, too.

"We're not afraid of trials. We're concerned that juries won't be able to hear the real story, the terror and crimes by the FBI against our people. Your support—in demonstrations, by showing up for court hearings, by donating time and money—is essential."

Lynn Parkinson moved behind me, put his hand on my shoulder, and whispered, "I need a smoke, and these guys only allow tobacco in their basement. Coming?"

We edged our way past the bodies on the floor. Parkinson slid back a bolt lock and opened a wood door. We walked down rickety wooden stairs to an unfinished basement. Lynn had been here before. He pulled an invisible string for light.

At the bottom, standing on the dusty concrete floor, among cobwebs, I packed my pipe with Old Dominion blend. Parkinson rolled Drum tobacco into a cigarette paper with one hand.

"Got some bad news," he finally said, after flicking out a match and inhaling. "Belloni denied the suppression motion."

"Shit!" I said, feeling guilty. Maybe it was my fault? If I had stayed up another night digging deeper in the library, would it have made a difference?

"What did he say?" I asked.

"The order came today. Here," he said, pulling a creased copy from his back pocket.

I read the typewritten sheet. Belloni denied the motion but said that we could renew our objections at trial "if the government does not prove sufficient reasons for the dynamite's destruction."

"I don't understand," I said, handing the paper back.

"Well," Parkinson said, taking a long drag, then continuing, "he's requiring Hawk to explain why the stuff was destroyed. It's a good ruling for us, in theory. If Hawk can't explain it, we get the explosives counts thrown out at trial, or a mistrial, because the jury would have heard too much about it."

"That's not bad," I said.

"Well, it's hard for a judge to put a case into total chaos in midtrial, after a jury has been empaneled and after weeks of testimony."

"That's true," I said. "Is there any way we can push him on it harder now? Maybe we should suggest that it would be less chaotic to force Hawk to make that showing now than at trial?"

"That's what I've been thinking," Parkinson said, pulling out a baggie of marijuana and rolling a joint. "Ron's upstairs. Go find him."

Two hours later, the three of us emerged from the smoky basement with a plan. We would file a motion for reconsideration, asking Belloni for a pretrial evidentiary hearing on the destruction issue.

"There's nothing to lose," Schiffman said, "And even if we don't win, at least we get a peek at some of Hawk's witnesses. I'm dying to see that Fettig guy."

CHAPTER 10

+ + +

A BULLET IN A GUY'S HEAD

AFTER weeks of searching, Lena finally found a Portland land-lord who would rent to the AIM Indians.

The two-story building was an old frame home on SW Hood Street, fifty feet from the Interstate 5 cutout. It sat on a sloping corner lot and had a long front porch and a small stoop by the kitchen door. Inside, the floors and arches and moldings and banisters were hardwood, and someone had once started refinishing them, then given up or moved. Except for a few spots of uncovered wood, everything else, floor to ceiling, was painted in a hodgepodge of color—yellow, mustard, reds, blues, and greens. It was a poor person's house.

Furniture had been donated and an office set up downstairs. The desk had half its drawers, and the chairs were missing under-pinnings or backs. The living room's three large windows looked out to the front porch and a jungle of unattended bushes beyond, an illusionary buffer from the interstate. An old rust-colored couch, leaking stuffing, sat against one wall, across from two foul-smelling upholstered chairs. The chairs were camouflaged with torn blue and white tie-dyed sheets. A black and white television, missing knobs, balanced on a Day-Glo blue plastic milk box in the corner.

When the defense committee met (once a week now), every-one tried to squeeze into the living room. That space, the adjoin-ing office, and the kitchen were the "public" places. The back bedroom/office downstairs and the entire upstairs were off-limits except to known and trusted AIM members.

Between meetings, people socialized in the kitchen. It was the brightest room, with unobstructed southern windows.

"Look," Lena showed me, "sitting at the table here, you can see people coming up the side stairs or parking on Hood Street.

And see that brown trailer across the street there? That was a vacant lot when we moved in."

Everyone watched that trailer from the kitchen table in the weeks to come. Its windows were always dark. No one ever saw anyone going in or coming out. Mail was never delivered. Yet fresh footprints were always nearby: men's flat leather soles and standard issue Cat's Paw heels.

The AIM house's kitchen stove did not work well, just the two burners on the right. No one seemed disturbed. There was a large hole in the ceiling directly over the two burners on the left. If you bent over it just right, you could peer into the room above, the upstairs bathroom. "AIM means something else up there," one male Indian said, chuckling. The ten-inch hole was in front of the toilet bowl.

The house was a nerve center. Poor Indians from out of town stayed there. One of the first to arrive was Lena's mother, Ramona.

"She was the master chef of Wounded Knee," Lena said proudly. "There was no food. The FBI tried to starve us out, but Mom always found something to cook, and it always tasted great!" Ramona was a skinny, short woman who chain smoked Camel straights. She overheard her daughter and looked embarrassed. I watched from the kitchen table as she stood at the stove, boiled a gallon of water in a pitted aluminum pot, then dropped the last half of a coffee tin in.

"Want some coffee?" she asked, stirring, looking toward me but not at me.

I hesitated. If she made coffee that way, she must be expecting a lot of people soon. "No, thank you," I said, feeling appropriately polite.

She looked wounded, turned off the stove, and walked out of the room.

The next time I visited, Lena led me to the back bedroom and closed the door.

"I knew you didn't mean anything by it," she said, "but you hurt Mom when you didn't drink coffee the other day."

"I just wanted to make sure there was enough," I explained.

"Indian people don't worry about such things," she said. "It's considered impolite to refuse."

Thereafter, I was one of Ramona's favorite people. I ate everything she offered. Her specialty was donated food: rabbit, venison, salmon, spaghetti, sweet fry bread, the smelt that came by the bucketful in late winter.

Sitting Bull, the great Sioux chief, had nowhere to go. He would have been penned up or shot if he had remained in his ancestral land.

He fled to Canada in 1877 and lived there until 1881. Although the Canadians let him and his people stay, they refused him land on which to settle. In 1880, the Canadian winter was particularly harsh. Many people went hungry. Horses froze to death. Sitting Bull had no choice; he decided to surrender. The U.S. government promised him a pardon if he returned to the reservation. Instead, the government arrested him and confined him to a military prison for two years. He spent his last years on the Pine Ridge Indian Reservation, only to be assassinated days before the 1890 Wounded Knee massacre.

The Nez Perces (named by French trappers) were a nation that Lewis and Clark met on their 1805 journey to the Pacific. They welcomed the expedition, fed them, and looked after their horses while the company went on by canoe. For nearly seventy years, in the wild, beautiful, and unsettled Pacific Northwest, the whites and the Nez Perces lived in peace.

White hunger for land was insatiable, even though it was plentiful. Chief Joseph fought efforts to imprison his people on a small reservation in Lapwai, Idaho. His struggle was doomed after gold was discovered. In 1877, Chief Joseph tried to lead his followers to safety in Canada, where Sitting Bull had gone. Just miles before the border, he was trapped. After five days of fighting and negotiations, he surrendered, saying,

I am tired of fighting. Our chiefs are killed. Looking Glass is dead. Toohoolhoolzote is dead. The old men are all dead. It is the young men who say yes or no. He who led the young men is dead. It is cold and we have no blankets. The little children are freezing to death. My people, some of them, have run away to the hills, and have no blankets, no food; no one knows where they are perhaps freezing to death. I want to have time to look for my children and see how many of them I can find. Maybe I shall find them among the dead. Hear me, my chiefs! I am tired; my heart is sick and sad. From where the sun now stands I will fight no more forever.[1]

Chief Joseph was taken prisoner but was not sent to Lapwai, as promised at his surrender. Instead, he and his followers were kept as prisoners of war in Fort Leavenworth, Kansas. After nearly a hundred of them died, the remainder were taken to a barren part of Indian Territory, where they struggled to survive, homesick for Lapwai. It took years of work by clergy and other sympathizers before the Nez Perces were allowed to return home. There were only 287 of them left, and of these, over 150, including Chief Joseph, were declared "too dangerous" to be allowed back to their small, penned-in reservation.

Chief Joseph and the "too dangerous" others were dispatched to the Colville reservation, in Washington State. He died there in 1904, in exile. The reservation doctor gave the cause of death as "a broken heart." Today this proud man's travails are commemorated on the Colville reservation by a wooden, sun-faded sign at the side of a road. It is surrounded by unattended weeds, junked cars, and other signs of the legacy of poverty brought on by destruction of a way of life.

Like Sitting Bull, who had managed to escape to Canada, and Chief Joseph, who had come so close but did not, a wounded Leonard Peltier had made his way north. On February 6, 1976, Peltier was arrested in Canada, along with another AIM member, Frank Black Horse. In their possession was a .30-.30 rifle stolen during a burglary at an Ontario, Oregon, farmhouse on November 15, 1975.

Tommy Hawk paced. "I can't believe Belloni let them out of jail!" he said to himself, over and over.

Judge Belloni had held a hearing on February 2, 1976. KaMook Banks and Michael Bonds,[2] her lawyer, had appeared in court

---

1. Brown, *Bury My Heart at Wounded Knee*, 328–29.

2. Not his real name. Bonds was six feet tall, blond, and a former prosecutor. He was also respected as one of the best trial lawyers in Portland. And whereas Judge Juba had refused to let Loud Hawk and Redner choose their court-appointed attorneys, Judge Belloni had appointed Bonds—KaMook's chosen lawyer—without request. He thereafter appointed the firms of Steenson, Par-

with a release plan. Eugene Uphoff, a prominent Portland physi-
cian, had agreed to supervise her on behalf of the American
Friends Service Committee, a Quaker organization. She could
stay with him if need be. She would call him every day. He would
call the judge if she violated any condition. Belloni was "impressed."

The only impediment to KaMook's freedom was the $20,000
in bail needed for the Kansas court, something Belloni could do
nothing about. At KaMook Banks's hearing, Belloni had commented, "If Loud Hawk and Redner submit similar plans, I'd be
inclined to release them, too." They had. He did. Hawk was
livid.

As he paced around his office, his internal debate was intense.
On one side, he knew that he should take his defeats and get on
to the next phase. If he could convict these Indian terrorists,
they would go to jail for a long time. But that long view was
difficult. He walked down the hall to his secretary, pressing her
for his letter. He paced. When she finished typing, he grabbed it,
signed it, and had it delivered upstairs to the judge immediately,
with copies to defense counsel.

The next day, across town, Ron Schiffman opened his morning mail.

"Listen to this," Ron said to his partner, Ed Jones. "Hawk felt
compelled to express his 'great concern of the flight risk posed by
the release of these defendants, as well as their danger to the
community.' Belloni must be shitting bricks!"

Ed looked confused.

"I know Hawk," Ron explained. "He just couldn't take Belloni
releasing these guys. Hawk's loony on this one. He just couldn't
keep his mouth shut. What'd he expect? Belloni should have
Russ and Kenny picked up and jailed again just because Tommy
Hawk's pissed?

"You know," he continued, walking around his converted garage office, rereading the letter, "I'd expect Tommy to write this,
but to *mail* it is something else. He's lost the filter that separates
zeal from suicide. Ed, I think he's going to self-destruct!"

---

kinson and Lea to represent Redner and Schiffman and Jones to represent Loud
Hawk. Now, at least, the lawyers would be paid.

"Hey, boys!" Diane Ackerman, a teenage Indian woman yelled, as Redner and Loud Hawk were buzzed through the outside gate, the last obstacle at the Vancouver city jail. She and Lena ran toward them. As Russ and Lena hugged, long and tight, Diane embraced Kenny intensely. Their tongues explored.

After the two couples drove across the Columbia River Bridge into Portland, Kenny left the highway and at Diane's direction, cruised Interstate Avenue. Russ, necking with Lena in the back seat, did not notice.

"Take the car, man," Kenny told Russ, as he veered into a motel's parking lot and stopped short. "Don't expect to hear from us for a week." He and Diane walked into the motel, quickly, hands on each other's backsides.

When Russ and Lena arrived at the defense house on SW Hood Street ten minutes later, Ramona was waiting on the sidewalk, holding her granddaughter Tsi-Am-Utza's hand.

Russ bolted from the car and scooped up his daughter.

"That's daddy!" Lena said.

Russ hugged her. "You're such a big girl!" he whispered into her ear. Tsi-Am-Utza cried and squirmed and tried to get free. Russ, fighting tears, handed his daughter to Lena and stomped inside, past Ramona. Blasting through the kitchen, he hollered, "Shit, my own daughter doesn't even recognize me anymore!"

It had been nearly one hundred days.

The same day Russ Redner was reintroduced to his daughter and Kenny Loud Hawk to Diane, Dennis Banks was brought in chains to federal court in San Francisco. He walked out a free man.

"The magistrate allowed Mr. Banks to post a small cash bond, backed with the deed to a supporter's house," Dennis Roberts told the television cameras and the dozen hand-held microphones on the courthouse steps.

"Mr. Roberts," a reporter pressed, "South Dakota officials have been quoted as being 'mad as hell' about the judge's decision to release Mr. Banks before his extradition hearing."

"That's not surprising," Roberts said, "William Janklow, the attorney general of South Dakota, has said that the way to deal with AIM leaders, like Mr. Banks, is to 'put a bullet in their heads.' That's a direct quote. That's why Dennis Banks didn't stick around to go to jail on phony riot charges. He was going to be killed. We're going to ask Governor Brown to deny South Dakota's request for Mr. Banks's return."

The following morning, in Roberts's Grand Avenue office, Banks sat on his lawyer's leather couch and said, "Let's go over it again."

"Well, there are pros and cons," Roberts explained, sitting in his high-backed chair, sipping tea from a mug. "Looks like they're going to try Russ and Kenny and KaMook together next month in Portland," he continued. "There's no way we can get you in and out of South Dakota that fast, so they'd probably try you by yourself, later. We'd get a free view of the evidence, but it wouldn't be good for KaMook. There won't be as much attention on the case if you're not there. Anyway, going back to South Dakota now means you'd be sentenced and back in jail."

"Yeah," Banks said, "I *still* can't believe you got me out!"

"Just shows you the luck of the draw, my man," Roberts said, with a smug smile, leaning back in his imposing chair. "Some judges are better than others. And treating their docket clerks like human beings, well, it helps."

"What do we do about KaMook?" Banks asked.

"She has good lawyers, both in Kansas and Oregon. She's free on the Oregon case. The judge up there sounds okay, but Judge Theis, in Kansas, demands full cash bail. Face it. You're going to have to raise the money."

That afternoon, Banks met with a Bay Area church leader.

"Dennis," the charismatic reverend said, taking the Indian on a tour of his church, "I understand South Dakota and the FBI. Russell Means[3] was lucky he wasn't killed in jail last week."

"They tried," Banks said, as they walked. "The knife hit a rib. According to the doctors, if it had been a few centimeters up or down, it would have stuck in his heart."

The reverend stopped. "I'm scared for KaMook," he said. "As I'm sure you know, my congregation is poor. It's all working-class and unemployed people. Twenty thousand dollars is a lot of

3. An AIM leader.

money. But let me see what I can do."

The following Sunday, Banks sat in the church, to the side of the pulpit, listening intently, while the reverend gave an impassioned sermon.

"I know you don't have much to give," he said, "but there's a young Indian mother, KaMook Banks, whose life is at stake! Two hundred AIM members have been killed, many of them mutilated, bludgeoned, knifed, hung, run off roads, shot, slashed, axed, all in the last three years, since Wounded Knee. They just stabbed Russell Means in his jail cell. South Dakota wants this man here, Dennis Banks, dead. KaMook Banks is his wife. These racists will get her if they can't get him!"

Within a week, Jim Jones's parishioners, later of tragic Jonestown fame, donating their own spare change and sparse dollars and collecting funds in coffee tins door to door, raised KaMook's $20,000.

The defense house was more lively now. Russ and Lena Redner lived in an upstairs bedroom with Tsi-Am-Utza. KaMook was downstairs. Loud Hawk had just moved in. Diane Ackerman spent a lot of time there. Susana Gren, whose unspoken reason for coming to Portland was Kenny, had quietly left town.

Other AIM members were arriving. The older women were particularly interesting and strong.

Ellen Moves Camps, a Sioux woman in her fifties, was an AIM fixture. She was fifty pounds overweight. No one could figure out how. She was always expending energy going, moving, shaking things up. Her tongue was acerbic. She was one of the "women from the districts" KaMook often spoke of who had been thrown into the spotlight at Wounded Knee and needed to retain some residual brightness. All of the politics had not been glamour, though. Ellen's son had gone over to the other side, committing perjury at a Wounded Knee trial under the tutelage of two FBI agents. She had disowned him in open court.

Ten minutes after arriving at the defense house, Ellen was already shrieking.

"What's this empty beer can doing here?" she demanded of Redner. She didn't give him a chance to answer, as she opened the window and threw it outside.

"And what kind of crap is going on in this house anyway? What the hell do you think you're doing, Redner? You can't have alcohol or drugs here. Redner, go post a sign on the door saying, 'NO DRUGS OR ALCOHOL OR INFORMANTS ALLOWED.' Got it? What the hell have you been doing since you got out of jail anyway? Get your fat ass moving!" she yelled, as she actually shoved the six-foot, dumfounded Redner out of the room.

Before I met Ellen, I had been forewarned. She had berated the lawyers for two hours for not working more feverishly. "You're representing Indian people, goddamn it, get off your lily white asses!" she had screamed.

I worked hard and did not smoke marijuana or drink around Indian people, so I felt safe. Her attack on me was unforeseeable.

"You!" she screamed, two minutes after Lena introduced us. I had said "Hello," then excused myself to read cases in the office. She pulled me up from my chair by my shirt collar.

"You!" she hollered again, "You think Dennis Banks was there, don't you! You think he was in that motor home!"

I had never discussed the "facts of the case" with anyone. It was not my job to speculate. I did not need to know. Besides, whether Dennis Banks was or was not there did not matter. The others had been.

Shocked at her accusatory tone, I said, "No. I have no idea if Dennis Banks was there or not, nor do I particularly care."

She howled, "No, that's not good enough! He wasn't there! You have to believe that, or you can't work on this case!"

Lena watched from the corner of the next room, telegraphing her sympathy and her powerlessness to intervene. I chose my words carefully. If I gave in, Ellen might think I was an informant.

"Ms. Moves Camp," I said, "I don't know if he was there or not. It truly doesn't matter."

Her venom was now undistilled disdain. "Are you prejudiced against Indians? Are you? Tell me!" she shouted, moving closer. Spit landed on my cheek and on my glasses.

I thought for only a second. "Ellen," I said, "I don't think anyone can say they're entirely free of racism. At least, I can't say that. I try not to be racist, but I can't guarantee that I have no racism. I think we all do. We should just do our best to fight it."

That was sufficient. Ellen turned her back and walked out of the room. I was not accepted, but at least I was no longer a prime target. I felt as if I had survived a test. My second.

Two weeks earlier, I had driven Linda Coelho to her mother's home in Northeast Portland. Linda invited me in for a cup of coffee. I walked into her living room (all the curtains were drawn for security after the "Where do you want to be buried?" affair), where Linda's sisters, her mother, and two older Indian women sat. One was Dorothy Ackerman, Diane's mother. The other was an attractive woman in her late forties. She was alone on the couch. That was the only vacant seat.

"Hello," I said, as I sat down. She continued to talk, ignoring me.

This woman, Janet McCloud, looked to Dorothy, and said, "You know, I'm always sitting next to white men. I never understand it. I don't want to sit next to them. I don't understand them at all, what they want, what they do. Sometimes they sit next to me. I don't ask them to. If I never see another white man, I'd be happy. But I always seem to be sitting next to them."

It was a contest. How much abuse could I take without responding? I sat, sipping my coffee purposefully. I finished, got up, said "Good-bye" to everyone as if nothing had happened, and left.

The reason that Ellen and Janet had come to Portland was Dennis Banks's arrest. Even though he was not in Oregon yet, he was now part of the case. Banks was the leader. His impending arrival (Judge Belloni had pushed the trial date back to May 12 so that he could be included) generated excitement—and more work.

Banks had two cases to fight. Like the others, he had federal firearms charges: Hawk alleged that Banks drove the motor home away. And South Dakota would also file an extradition request, as it had in California. Banks had to convince the governors of both California and Oregon to refuse extradition. Only a few times had governors denied requests for prisoners wanted by other states. Those involved blacks wanted for racist reasons by southern states in the 1960s. Banks needed to prove that his claim paralleled theirs. Roberts had compiled affidavits, judicial rulings, articles, letters, and transcripts proving that South Dakota was racist toward Indians, that Banks's life was in danger there, and that his so-called riot conviction was a racist travesty of justice.

The Portland defense committee had speakers, educated with the facts, convincing people to sign petitions for the governor. We had already collected hundreds of signatures. The pitch was easy. Indian life was demonstrably cheap near the Pine Ridge reservation and throughout South Dakota.

Raymond Yellow Thunder, an older Indian man in neighboring Nebraska, had been kidnapped by American Legion members, stripped, and forced to dance naked for them. Then he was kicked, burned with cigarettes, and dumped into a car trunk, where he died.

Wesley Bad Heart Bull had been in a bar near Custer, South Dakota. A white man named Darold Schmidt had threatened to "get himself an Indian" that night. He knifed Bad Heart Bull to death, in front of eyewitnesses. He was only charged with manslaughter.

Banks had led a delegation to Custer to complain. A meeting with city officials had been scheduled, then called off at the last minute. Dennis was allowed in to discuss why. Wesley Bad Heart Bull's mother, Sarah Bad Heart Bull, also tried to enter the courthouse. A burly state cop shoved her down the granite steps. All hell broke loose.

Banks was in the city officials' office. A tear gas canister bounced in, and Banks picked up a stick, broke a window, and let the gas out. That was his "riot while armed" conviction. That was what South Dakota wanted to sentence him for.

The attorney general who prosecuted Dennis Banks was William Janklow. Janklow had been a legal services attorney on the Rosebud reservation years before. A young Indian girl named Jancita Eagle Deer had accused him of rape. Another time, two police officers said they had found Janklow driving through the reservation, drunk. Supposedly, he had no pants on, could not explain why, and screamed, "No son of a bitch Indian is going to arrest me!" when taken into custody.

The Rosebud Trial Court disbarred Janklow. He did not come to his own trial. The tribal attorney who prosecuted him was Dennis Banks.

Then Janklow ran for attorney general on an anti-AIM, anti-

Indian platform. A law student named John Gridley III attended a coffee for him. According to Gridley's sworn affidavit, Janklow said that in his opinion, the way to deal with AIM leaders (like Russell Means and Dennis Banks) was to put a bullet in their heads. He said, "Put a bullet in a guy's head, and he won't bother you any more." Janklow was elected.

South Dakota prison guards said Banks would not survive in jail. And that was just the beginning. According to AIM activists, nearly two hundred AIM members had been attacked or killed since Wounded Knee. Byron DeSersa, the latest victim, a legal worker, had been run off a road, where he bled to death. DeSersa was not even an AIM leader. Dennis Banks was. If he were returned to South Dakota, the extradition warrant would double as a death warrant.

✚ ✚ ✚

CHAPTER 11

A FAMILIAR SIGNATURE

ROGER Amiotte was a rancher of mixed blood whose land was in the northeast corner of the Pine Ridge Indian Reservation, near the town of Wamblee. On the afternoon of February 24, 1976, while checking his metal fencing, he found the body of a woman in a snow-covered ditch one hundred feet from the county road. She was wrapped in a blanket. The woman wore a maroon windbreaker, jeans, and blue canvas shoes. She had long fingernails. Her hands were adorned with fancy turquoise jewelry, including rings and a large bracelet.

The rancher rushed to his house and called the authorities. An unusually large entourage of officials responded. There were deputies, police, and four FBI agents. According to a BIA investigator, one was Special Agent David Price and another Special Agent William Wood.

The body was taken to the Pine Ridge hospital, where Dr. W. O. Brown performed an autopsy in the presence of FBI agents. The doctor said the unidentified Indian woman died of exposure. She had frozen to death. There was no sign of violence.

During the autopsy, an FBI agent asked Dr. Brown, "I need her hands. Sever them at the wrist, would ya, doc?"

As requested, Dr. Brown chopped them off. Rather than attempt fingerprint identification on the scene, the disembodied parts would be sent to Washington, D.C., for analysis.

Over the next days, the government agents approached mortuary after mortuary, asking to have the handless body buried. According to one undertaker, the FBI agents wanted the woman buried under a fictitious name. "Can't do it," he said. "You guys ought to know. That's illegal."

Finally, on March 3, the body was buried, nameless, in the Holy Rosary Mission on the reservation. That same day, the FBI notified its Rapid City office that the dead woman was Anna Mae Aquash. On March 5, the Halifax, Nova Scotia, police told Anna Mae's mother that her daughter had been found dead and that a piece of paper with her name and address had been on the body. On March 6, the FBI publicly announced that the body was that of Anna Mae Aquash.

We heard the news in Portland on the 7th. Everyone was in shock. Anna Mae had been underground. She was not the big catch, like Peltier or Banks. In all the excitement, she had almost been forgotten. These were the years when there were many fugitives around—people like Abbie Hoffman and Bernadine Dorhn, people from the Weather Underground, drafter resisters, antiwar activists. Anna Mae was just another.

"I just can't believe it," Russ, Kenny, and KaMook kept saying. It was hard enough to accept that Anna Mae was dead. But that she died of exposure was incredible, preposterous. She was a woman who thrived in the outdoors, who grew up in Canada, lived in Boston, survived Wounded Knee. She did not drink. No one who knew her believed she had frozen to death.

We needed more facts. Roberts's legal assistant, Karen Spelke, called everyone we could think of on the reservation. But the first thing, the obvious thing, was to get the body exhumed and autopsied by an independent examiner. As more information came in from South Dakota that day, a second autopsy became urgent. A doctor and a nurse at the hospital where the body had been taken had seen blood dripping from the back of Anna Mae's thawing head.

Russ and I wrote a press release. We had a rule: never speculate; always say only what you can back up. One error, and the defense committee would no longer be believed.

Russ was so certain, I had to demur. The original draft read, "The government says Anna Mae Aquash died of 'exposure.' We say it was exposure to an FBI bullet." I changed it. The version we released read, "We say it was exposure to a bullet, possibly from an FBI gun."

Either way, these were serious words. But Anna Mae was just the latest in a series of AIM member deaths. She certainly did not die the way the FBI said she had. If it had no complicity, why was it engaged in a cover-up? Why was it afraid of the truth?

On March 9, Bruce Ellison, a lawyer in Rapid City with WKLDOC, marched into the FBI office there and announced that he would petition the court to have the body exhumed. Before Ellison could get to the courthouse that afternoon, the FBI filed its own request for exhumation and reautopsy. The reasons its affidavit gave were that Anna Mae might have been killed in a hit-and-run accident or that she might have been murdered by AIM as a suspected informer. The signer of the affidavit was Special Agent Wood, who did not mention that he had been present at the first autopsy, where no sign of violence was allegedly found. Nor did the affidavit explain why the FBI had waited six days after it had allegedly "discovered" that the body was Aquash to request the exhumation. Wood, of course, did not offer any theory explaining how a person who might have been a victim of a hit-and-run accident could have been thrown one hundred feet from the highway, display no sign of contact with a vehicle, and end up in a ditch, neatly wrapped in a blanket.

The second autopsy was scheduled for March 11. Anna Mae's family, through WKLDOC attorney Ellison, hired Garry Peterson, an independent pathologist from St. Paul Hospital in Minnesota, to observe. When he arrived, Dr. Peterson was the only doctor there. The FBI had not bothered to have a pathologist at the autopsy it had requested. Peterson, who brought only the minimal equipment needed to observe, had to perform the procedure. It was not terribly complicated. An obvious bullet wound, surrounded by an even more obvious 5 cm x 5 cm discoloration, adorned the rear of Anna Mae's head, exactly where the hospital staff had seen the thawing body leak blood the week before. It did not require special tools or genius to find it. She died of exposure to a small-caliber bullet fired from a gun placed near the back of her head. She had been executed.

The FBI handling of this matter made no sense. If you have an unknown corpse in a community as homogeneous as the Pine Ridge reservation, the obvious thing to do is advertise that fact and bring in people who might be able to make an identification. In Anna Mae's case, just the opposite procedure was followed.

Gladys Bissonette, who knew Anna Mae Aquash from Wounded Knee, offered to see if she knew who the dead woman was. The mortician, Tom Chamberlain, refused. He had received orders from the FBI not to let any "unauthorized" person see the corpse.

Gladys would have been able to identify the body. First, there were the rings and bracelets that had been found on the hands. Anna Mae's trademark was large turquoise jewelry.

Second, Anna Mae was identifiable. The FBI maintained that the body was decomposed beyond recognition. Pictures were taken during the second autopsy. Friends of Anna Mae recognized her easily. And that fact, in turn, brings up an even stranger series of questions.

Price, who the BIA police say was one of the FBI agents who saw the body in Amiotte's ditch, knew Anna Mae well. He had been one of the agents who had arrested her on the South Dakota weapons charges in September 1975. Many people who witnessed the arrest remember when Price first spotted Anna Mae that day. "You!" he shouted in instant recognition. "I've been looking everywhere for you!"

That summer, after she was released pending trial, Anna Mae told many friends about Price. He had grilled her about the killing of the two FBI agents in June. He knew that Anna Mae had not been at the scene, but he also knew the circle in which she traveled. He thought she might have heard things.

Anna Mae refused to talk to Price or any other agent. A confidential FBI memorandum described how Anna Mae "put her head down on the desk and did not reply to the question. . . . [She said,] 'You can either shoot me or throw me in jail, as those are the two choices that I am taking.' She was asked specifically what she meant by this, to which she replied, 'That's what you're going to do to me anyway.'"

Anna Mae told her friends this story. She was worried. Price had told her that if she did not talk, he would "see [her] dead within a year."

Now, she was dead. And the agent who she said had threatened her was one of the first people to see her body but allegedly did not recognize it.

At the defense house, everyone was preoccupied with Anna Mae.

I noticed a deep sense of frustration among some of the AIM leaders who visited. Rumors had been circulating for months, from sources unknown, that Anna Mae had been an informant. Was she one of those who had supposedly tipped off the government about the trip in Marlon Brando's motor home? One question was, why had she been released from custody when she was returned to South Dakota after missing a court date? Some people speculated that it was because she was an informant, a snitch.

But those in the know knew that Anna Mae was not an informant. The question was whether the FBI had done to AIM what it had done to the Black Panthers, the Socialist Workers' Party, and many other unpopular organizations through a program known as COINTELPRO (short for counterintelligence program). Stories were starting to leak about how the FBI had spread rumors about and within these organizations, stirring things to the point where violence was the result. Had the FBI planned to create the impression that Anna Mae was an informant? It seemed possible, especially when, without being asked the question, the FBI issued a press release the day of the second autopsy denying that Anna Mae was an informant. The FBI never says who is or is not a snitch. The breaking of that ironclad rule in this case seemed designed to increase speculation on that point rather than diminish it. Perhaps, like the cutting off of her hands, the planted news story was also intended as a severance—an attempted break from the increasing speculation that the FBI was implicated in Anna Mae's murder.

When the initial shock of Anna Mae's death passed, one thing became clear to me. Whether she was killed by an FBI agent, an FBI informant, an AIM member believing stories, or some unknown party not connected to the incendiary political situation, the Indian community as a whole believed one thing in its heart, as much as it believed that the sun would come up tomorrow. Young and old, AIM activist or curious onlooker, the Indians' first reaction was that the FBI had murdered Anna Mae. They believed that if an agent had not actually pulled the trigger, the FBI was nonetheless involved with, and somehow responsible for, Anna Mae's death.

Even if this belief were unfounded, the fact that it was so widely shared made a powerful statement by itself. The unanimous indictment of the FBI could not happen in a vacuum. It was in accord with a long, experienced pattern.

The parallel for me was my great-grandfather. We knew it was the Cossacks who had strung him up by his beard in a Russian town square. But what if no one had actually seen them? Everyone would still have the same thought: "Cossack." Or in the South in the 1960s. If a young black man was swinging from an old magnolia, a cross burning nearby, everyone would suspect the Ku Klux Klan. This was its modus operandi, its trademark.

For Indian people, Anna Mae's death also bore a familiar signature.

CHAPTER 12

✛ ✛ ✛

DYNAMITE

THE government believed six adults had been in Brando's motor home on November 14, 1975. One was now dead. The other five were despondent. It could have been any of them.

KaMook and Kenny and Russ and Dennis were out of jail, but for how long? If they were convicted, the prosecution would seek long prison terms. Tommy Hawk had just filed papers labeling them "high-risk" defendants, a tag reserved by statute for people such as mass murderers and Mafia chieftains.

Of them all, Peltier was in the worst position. He had been on the FBI's "Ten Most Wanted" list. He was in solitary confinement in a Vancouver, British Columbia, jail. We read about his plight. Even though his cell was the most secure in a high security prison, he was constantly handcuffed. The guards did not unchain him to eat. He had to pull one hand up with the other. He refused to eat. Two weeks into a hunger strike, the authorities removed the restraints—during meals. Amnesty International blasted Peltier's condition of confinement as "unjustifiable."

There was, finally, some good news. In Portland, Judge Belloni agreed to hear the destruction of dynamite issue before trial. He scheduled a hearing for March 19, 1976. The day before, Hawk sent a detailed memorandum to the judge explaining why the evidence had been destroyed.

Representative samples of the wrappers . . . have been forwarded to the FBI lab for microscope and chemical examination. FBI experts are expected to testify that residual materials found on those wrappers identify the substance as dynamite. . . . An issue of destruction is not present here. What occurred was a destruction of the major dangerous portion of the substance with sufficient retention of residual samples, which coupled with the wrappers themselves, the photographs [of the dynamite], the observed and photographed detonation and the testi-

mony of witnesses at the scene, sufficiently establish the existence of
the dynamite.

If, as Hawk wrote, the scientific evidence showed that the
material scraped from the wrappers had all the components of
dynamite, how could we prove prejudice? Luckily, Belloni had
put the burden on Hawk to explain why *any* evidence had been
destroyed. Hawk wrote,

The dynamite contained nitroglycerin. The stability of that substance
is affected by exposure to extremes of heat and cold. . . . There was no
way for Trooper Fettig to determine what extremes of heat or cold this
dynamite had been exposed to. The fact that some of the boxes were
soaking wet indicated that it had been stored outdoors. If the dynamite
was unstable it was obviously extremely dangerous. [Furthermore] there
were no approved storage sites near the location of the dynamite.

On March 19, 1976, Hawk sat nervously at the counsel table.
This day, the courtroom was enemy territory. Indians and supporters and news people crammed into every seat. U.S. marshals
quieted the crowd of fifty people that waited, lined up in the
corridor, in case a seat became available. Celebrities sat inside, in
the first row: city officials, religious leaders, comedian Dick Gregory, activists Jack and Micki Scott, Andy Walton and his older
brother, Bill. Hawk remembered. Belloni, relaxed, in chambers,
had once said, "That Bill Walton is my favorite basketball player,
ever!" Walton was in the first row, ready to smile at the judge,
wearing a specially made extra-extra-large "Free Loud Hawk and
Redner" T-shirt.

Hawk watched as a court clerk slid an oak table and two chairs
from the judge's chambers. A quiet British couple sat down.
They were from Amnesty International. They had come to observe *United States v. Loud Hawk et al.* for possible human rights
abuses. Hawk felt—and was—surrounded.

Hawk's discomfort grew as Judge Belloni walked onto the
bench. Michael Bonds had been sitting next to the prosecutor.
As the judge's door opened, Bonds and Tom Steenson switched
seats. Two weeks before, Hawk had complained about Steenson's
light blue blazer, his only piece of courtroom attire.

"Doesn't he ever get it cleaned?" Hawk had asked Bonds. "The thing stinks!"

When Bonds told Steenson of Hawk's complaint, the last-minute chair switch was orchestrated. "About time we use germ warfare for Indians, instead of against 'em," Tom had said, determined to stink up his jacket even more. He elbowed Hawk "hello" as the first witness walked past the lawyers up to the stand.

James Key was our witness. He spoke with precision. He matched the government's explosives expert, William Fettig, degree for degree. Like Fettig, Key gave courses. Like Fettig, Key was an expert in the military. Like Fettig, Key knew how to detonate nuclear devices. Whereas Fettig left the military for law enforcement, Key had become a salesman for a powder company.

Wearing a tailored gray business suit and a red silk tie Windsor knotted around his neck, Key sat with his hands folded comfortably on his lap. His eyes looked forward, at ease. Ron Schiffman, seated thirty feet away at the counsel table, asked questions deliberately.

"Mr. Key," he began, "tell us, what is dynamite? Commercial dynamite?"

"Dynamite is primarily a commercial blasting agent," Key explained. "You have nitrate ethylene glycol, which is the main explosive ingredient. You also have ammonium nitrate pearls sensitized with diesel oil—it looks like fertilizer. Also, you have filler material, such as ground-up peach pits and apricot pits. You also have salts to act as a stabilizer and desensitizer for the nitrate ethylene glycol; and you have various gums and dopes mixed in. On the outside, you have a waxed paper covering."

"Mr. Key," Schiffman asked, "are you familiar with DuPont Gelex #2?"

"Yes. Gelex #2 is a semigelatin powder. They call it semigelatin because it's only good in water for about 12 hours in a bore hole. For example, if you loaded a bore hole with 40 gelatin dynamite, you can come back two years later and fire it. With semigelatin, if you waited overnight, in a water condition, it would not shoot."

"By not shooting, you mean it would *not* explode?"

"It would be doubtful."

"Now, who buys dynamite?"

"Anybody who wants to remove a stump, or a contractor building a road, a mining company like Anaconda, quarry operators . . ."

"Are farmers able to buy dynamite?"

"Farmers? Yes."

"Any special qualifications needed to buy it?"

"Only that you've not been convicted of a felony. You pay five dollars and are given a permit to buy explosives. It's good for life."

"Mr. Key, are you familiar with how dynamite is transported?"

"You just load it on trucks."

"Do you know how it's stored?"

"It's stored in magazines."

"Do you know whether there are any magazines in this area?"

"Well, when I was working for Atlas Powder Company, I traveled Oregon, southwestern Washington, and western Idaho. I serviced nine distributors that have adequate storage facilities. One is located in Clackamas, about twenty miles from Portland."

Schiffman's voice went up a notch. "Mr. Key," he asked, "are you familiar with the term 'leaching'?"

Key nodded. "Leaching or exuding," he said, "occurs after the cartridge has been in one position for a long time, subject to heat and humidity. The cartridge has salt, mixed with the nitrate ethylene glycol. When the nitrate ethylene glycol evaporates, it leaves behind a salty, crusty substance, somewhat dull in color."

"Now," Schiffman asked, "assume that you're confronted with a cartridge of dynamite that has leached. Would that cartridge be so volatile and unstable that it could not be transported or stored?"

"I don't see any reason why a cartridge that's encrusted with salt residue would present any hazard."

Schiffman smiled, turned a yellow page in his pad, and folded it firmly at the top, left to right, with his thumbnail.

"Now, tell me, what does the word 'crystallization' mean?" he asked.

"Frozen dynamite," Key said. "Dynamite that experiences temperatures of 26 degrees below zero or less. The nitrate ethylene glycol hardens, crystallizes. And then you have an extremely sensitive explosive."

"Is it possible to determine whether or not a cartridge of dynamite has crystallized?"

"Yes. There are field tests. The easiest is a taste test. You take exuded material and put it to your tongue. If there's a good deal of glycol present, you're going to find a very, very sweet taste. And I mean very sweet."

"Now assume," Schiffman asked, "that you found some of it in some state of crystallization. Would you have an opinion as to whether or not these cartridges would be so volatile that it would be unreasonable to transport or store them?"

"Yes, I would have an opinion," Key said, in a strong voice, "and the opinion would be no, it would not."

"No further questions."

Judge Belloni turned to Tommy Hawk. "Cross-examine," he said.

Hawk leaned to his left, away from Steenson, who had moved his chair even closer during Schiffman's questioning.

"Mr. Key," Hawk began, "I take it that you were in the navy in the 1960s, correct?"

"Yes, sir."

"Military dynamite is much different from commercial dynamite, isn't it?"

"It has an unlimited shelf life."

"Well, isn't the difference that military dynamite does not have nitroglycerine and some commercial dynamite does?"

"That's correct."

Hawk sat forward, ready to go in for the kill, the easy questions being a setup.

"If it doesn't have nitroglycerin, the sensitivity factors are entirely different than if it does have nitroglycerin, correct?"

"Well, let me clarify one thing for you," Key explained. "Hardly any manufacturer uses nitroglycerin anymore. It's nitrate ethylene glycol—antifreeze. They use that because it's less hazardous to manufacture."

"All right," Hawk said, pausing. The pause became awkward. Hawk, obviously lost for a question, left that line of attack.

"Now," he continued, "you've told us that dynamite is normally stored in magazines?

"That's correct."

"Why is that, sir?"

"Primarily to prevent theft."

"Are there any other reasons?"

"Safety purposes." Hawk's face hardened. That was not the answer he wanted.

"Now, assuming that you have a nice safe place like a desert where you weren't concerned about anyone stealing your dynamite, would you leave that dynamite out in the summer when the heat is 95 to 100 degrees?"

"Yeah, it's all right."

"The heat won't affect the sensitivity or stability of that dynamite?" Hawk sounded incredulous.

"Everything is relative," Key said, calmly, not biting at Hawk's tone. "I wouldn't say beyond being able to handle it, because I've left it out for a day on a rock job and handled it safely."

Hawk's voice became snivelly. "You mean you handled it and didn't get blown up?"

Schiffman was halfway to his feet, ready to object. Key did not need the help.

"I'm still here," the witness said, with a twang.

Belloni suppressed a snicker. Hawk, angered, became more deliberate, shouting his next question before the audience stopped laughing.

"Mr. Key, assume the following facts: that you came into contact with about seven cases of DuPont Gelex #2, 70 percent dynamite."

"Right."

"That you came in contact with it in late 1975."

"Okay."

"That you knew that the dynamite was manufactured sometime in 1973 from the date on the box. Therefore, that it was at least two years old."

"Okay."

"And you knew that that dynamite contained nitroglycerin, or believed that it did. Are you with me so far?"

"Uh-huh."

"You had no idea whatsoever where that dynamite had been for the past two years."

"Uh-huh."

"You did not know whether it had been exposed to extremes of heat. You did not know whether it had been exposed to extremes of cold. But you did know that at least two cases of the dynamite had been exposed to some elements because the boxes were literally soaking wet, so when you picked them up, they came apart in your hands."

"Uh-huh."

"You examined the sticks of dynamite, and there were no visible signs of deterioration, such as the leaching or exuding, crystallization, et cetera. Would you think that dynamite might be unsafe?"

Key paused for a second, considering his answer. "Well," he said, "from the way you described it, being two years old and the cartridges not indicating any leaching, and the boxes being water contaminated—no."

"All right," Hawk said, his voice nearly cracking. He was not about to give up.

"Now, assume one other thing in the hypothetical," he said. "Assume you wanted to store it someplace. Where would you store it?"

"I would store it in a magazine."

"Where is the nearest approved storage facility to Ontario, Oregon?" Hawk was taking chances.

"Probably in Boise, Idaho," Key answered.

Hawk was shaken. He thought the answer would be Clackamas, four hundred miles from Ontario.

"You know that for a fact?" Hawk asked.

"Yes."

"That there's one in Boise?"

"Yes, definitely. I used it."

"How long ago?" Hawk groped.

"1973. Come to think of it, there's also one in Pendleton."

"You sure of that?"

"Yes, the county has one. Let's see. Baker also has one. The county has one in Baker."

"All right. Baker—"

"Also there's one —"

"Baker is about 60, 70, or so miles north of Ontario, right?"

"Right. Also, there's a magazine at the Portland Cement Company south of Baker."

"Where's that?"

"That's the Granite Rock Quarry. About 30 miles south of Baker."

"That's all I have," he concluded, after another awkward pause. Schiffman jumped in.

"Mr. Key," he began, speaking quickly, in contrast to the slower pace Hawk's questions had faded into, "assume that you came into contact with seven cases of DuPont Gelex #2, 70 percent dynamite late in 1975. You determined that it was manufactured sometime in 1973. You knew that the dynamite contained nitrate ethylene glycol. You have no idea where the dynamite had been for two years. Two cases are so soaking wet that the bottoms were falling out. You examined the individual dynamite cartridges and determined that there was no visible evidence of deterioration. Would you have an opinion as to whether or not that dynamite could be reasonably stored and transferred?"

"Yes. It would be very easily done."

"In your opinion, it is an inordinately long distance to transport dynamite 50 to 100 miles?"

"No."

"How large is an average magazine?"

"It holds about 40,000 pounds."

"Does 350 pounds of dynamite, Gelex #2, sound like a tremendous amount of dynamite?"

"No. Not at all."

"No further questions!"

In the late 1960s, a group of Black Panthers had been tried in New York for conspiracy to bomb department stores. They had been acquitted. I wondered about that case. A government informant had replaced the Panther's real dynamite with fake dynamite. That fact was unimportant to the outcome in that case; if the same thing had happened in our case, it would be crucial. But even if the government had planted phony dynamite in the station wagon, how could I prove it? Impossible.

I looked at the issue the other way: what could Hawk do when court resumed after the weekend? Other than have a chemist testify that he found traces of nitrate ethylene glycol, or discover his best argument, that the law placed the onus of proof on the defense, nothing. Nevertheless, I spent twenty hours in the law library that weekend. In one pile I laid cases that cited *Brady v. Maryland*, a U.S. Supreme Court decision defining the government's duty to disclose evidence that might help the defense. In another pile I put cases that relied on *United States v. Bryant*, which stated that the government's duty to disclose favorable evidence necessarily implied a duty to preserve it before trial. As thick as these piles were, they had nothing to do with the trial itself.

What, it finally occurred to me, were Russ, Kenny, KaMook, and Dennis actually going to do at trial? I had not heard the lawyers discuss that. All their efforts were on pretrial motions. Perhaps we would argue technical problems with the charges? Maybe the government would forget to prove an essential fact? But we had to argue something affirmative, didn't we? What would it be?

As dangerous as it seemed, there was only one thing. We would have to tell the jury about the conditions in South Dakota that explained but might not excuse the incident. That was the motive for the trip in Brando's van—desperation in Indian Country—but it was too fresh. Wouldn't the jury feel threatened by Indians planning to use guns and explosives? Wouldn't they see it as a "give us back our guns and we'll show you our defense" defense?

For the first time, I realized that *Loud Hawk et al.*, my friends, were going to jail. Five, ten, twenty years in jail. They were no longer just names on the news or an interesting case as an antidote to the boredom of law school, but people I cared about. KaMook, especially, was a true human being—a *mensch* in Yiddish. I had talked with her, eaten with her, watched her speak about her heritage with pride and hold her children so lovingly. I had held those same children. Would she be able to see Tosh and TaTiopa only on weekends, through bars, until they were teenagers? Would Tsi-Am-Utza, who had once walked toward her daddy in court but was not allowed across the bar into his arms, have to wait until she had a baby of her own to have a real relationship with Russ?

I was scared for them, and angry, and sad. I forced my thoughts back to narrow legal issues: *Brady v. Maryland*, destruction of evidence.

On Monday morning, Hawk sat alone at the counsel table, to the left. Having arrived early, he had placed three empty seats between the defense end of the table and his side, a "neutral" zone with air space, away from Steenson.

As much as Hawk needed his distance, I felt awkward in mine. My fifteen feet from the lawyers made communication almost impossible. With each hearing I was growing more confident. I was eager to contribute. I ached, sitting away from the counsel table. But I could not get up, walk forward, whisper in an ear or pass a note, and walk back without being noticed. I had to weigh the importance of my novice, uncertain ideas against the disruption.

I watched from my seat just inside the bar as Hawk's first witness walked to the witness chair—William Fettig, the explosives expert. He was dressed in civilian clothes—a brown corduroy suit with a western shirt and a string tie. Hawk was nervous. His fingers flexed.

Hawk shepherded Fettig through his credentials, training, and experience, then, step by step, through the November events. He was ordered to Ontario. He arrived. Zeller was fingerprinting the vehicles. Zeller finished. Fettig removed the dynamite, took it to the pistol range, took two sticks from each case, and scraped them clean. He built a bomb with a time fuse, a nonelectrical blasting cap and one stick. He detonated it. He built another with a fuse, another nonelectrical cap, and three sticks. He detonated it. Then he burned the rest. The FBI took pictures. Fettig identified the FBI's photographs and one set of wrappers. They were entered into evidence.

Dennis Roberts, Dennis Banks's attorney (who had flown in from California on Sunday), objected whenever Hawk asked Fettig what he would have done if he had not been ordered by Lt. McCollum to destroy the evidence. Hawk's complexion became redder, and sweat congregated on his upper lip, as Judge Belloni's impatience became obvious. What difference, Mr. Hawk, did it make what Fettig would have done if he had had different orders?

Subdued, Hawk reclined in his chair and in a resigned tone, said, "Your witness."

Ron Schiffman leaned forward, staring at Fettig, thinking for a few seconds. He pushed his legal pad of prepared questions away.

"Mr. Fettig," Schiffman started, looking him in the eye, "are you aware of the manner in which dynamite is detonated?"

"Yes, sir, I am."

"Is that with blasting caps?"

"Yes, sir, electric and nonelectric."

"Have you had occasion to arrange for the transportation and storage of dynamite yourself?"

"No, sir, I have not."

Hawk sank lower in his chair. His head was on a level with the chair's back. Schiffman picked up speed.

"Would you agree or disagree with this statement?" he asked. "It would be unsafe to transport dynamite with blasting caps or detonator cord."

"It would be unsafe." Fettig's answer was authoritative.

"In looking at these photographs, officer," Schiffman said, matter-of-factly, "I noticed that you transported this dynamite in the trunk of a vehicle."

"Yes, sir."

"Was that a specially equipped vehicle of any kind?"

"No, sir."

"Did you place sawdust in the bed of this trunk."

"I placed emergency blankets on the bottom, sir."

Schiffman paused for a moment, inspecting the pictures. "I noticed," he continued, "there are other things in the trunk, such as a tire and long screws sticking out of the side of the cabin of the trunk. Is that the manner in which you transported it?"

"Just as you see it, yes, sir."

"I noticed that the trunk didn't completely close. Did you transport this with the trunk open?"

"About four or five inches open. It was tied down, sir."

Schiffman collected the FBI photographs from the counsel table and slowly walked to Fettig, his fingers shuffling through the prints, deliberately. "Looking at government's exhibit 1, would you describe the contents of the trunk, officer?" Schiffman handed the picture to Fettig.

"Yes, sir," the officer said. "It's the dynamite in question. It has my tool box, with my cap crimpers and unsparkable knife. All the tools in the box are unsparkable, sir."

"What is this yellow color right here?" Schiffman asked, pointing.

"That's a cord, sir."

"What kind of a cord is that?"

"An electrical cord, sir."

"And what is this red box right here?" Schiffman asked.

"The red box . . ." Fettig paused, and swallowed. "I'm not quite sure what that is, sir."

Schiffman examined the photograph again. He squinted, for effect. "I can barely make out the word," he said. "Does that say 'explosives,' officer?"

Fettig took the picture back. He pretended to inspect it. "Yes, sir, it does. That's a cap box, sir."

"That's a cap box?"

"Yes, sir?"

"A *blasting* cap box?"

"Yes, sir."

"And these little silver devices here with the leg wires on them, are those electrical blasting caps, officer?"

"Yes, they are."

"Sitting here in the trunk with all this dangerous dynamite?"

Fettig paused. He glanced at Hawk for help. Hawk's eyes were fixed on the clock high on the courtroom wall.

Everyone was silent, waiting.

In the quiet of the drama, I was distracted by a door opening at the back of the courtroom. It swung with a swoosh. The marshals let a chunky, middle-aged man in a business suit walk inside, ahead of all those waiting for a seat. I recognized him: Ron McCreary, our second, better explosives expert.

He stood for a moment, looked around the packed courtroom, then squeezed into a bench along the back wall.

I was alarmed. I watched the lawyers. Only Michael Bonds had noticed McCreary. Bonds had looked back into the spectator section and nodded "hello" to him.

Judge Belloni, at the defense's request, had ordered all witnesses excluded from the courtroom. But Bonds had acted as if nothing was wrong.

Schiffman was ready to pick Fettig apart. I thought of writing a note and handing it to one of the lawyers. But I was not sure. That might have destroyed Schiffman's moment. I decided against it.

"Officer Fettig, are those electrical blasting caps in the trunk with all this dangerous dynamite?" Schiffman asked, again, with an incredulous edge to his voice.

"That's right, sir," Fettig admitted, drawing a deep breath. He looked at Schiffman with a gaze of surrender.

"Officer," Schiffman continued, "you were asked by Mr. Hawk why dynamite of unknown origin should be destroyed, and in answering you said, 'Because it could become unstable and perhaps have a lower detonation.' Does that mean that it might *not* explode, officer?

"Yes, sir."

"Are you familiar with the effects of water on dynamite?"

"Yes, sir."

"What is that effect, officer?"

"The dynamite becomes unstable, and it may not function properly."

"So 'unstable' means that it may *not* function; is that correct, officer?"

"Yes, sir, it could."

"May *not* explode?"

"Right, sir."

"I have no further questions," Schiffman said. Fettig stood, ready to leave the witness stand. He seemed startled when Schiffman added, "Mr. Roberts wishes to examine."

Dennis Roberts's manner was elegant, smooth, classy, and familiar at the same time. He relaxed Fettig with a nod and a smile.

"Officer Fettig," he began, reverently, "I believe you testified that when you first saw the boxes, they were in the back of the station wagon?"

"No, sir. I said it was in plastic bags, sir."

"Plastic bags?"

"Yes, sir."

"What happened to those bags?"

"I believe they were also burned, sir." Roberts flashed Schiffman a quick wink.

"Now, if I understand you right," Roberts continued, "the dynamite was actually in cardboard boxes, and these boxes, in turn, were in the plastic bags."

"That's correct, sir."

"Now, those cardboard cases, did you burn those as well?"

"Yes, sir."

"I believe you testified that there was an FBI agent present throughout this time, did you not?"

"Yes, sir."

"And I believe you testified that there was a fingerprint man there. Did anyone print those cases before you burned them?"

"No, sir."

"Thank you very much. I have nothing further."

Roberts meant it. Fettig had destroyed Hawk's various explanations for the dynamite's destruction. Fettig had not decided to destroy the dynamite because it was volatile; he had been ordered to, by OSP Lt. McCollum. McCollum did not testify about who, if anyone, had given him his orders. And the debilitating effect of water on dynamite and Fettig's mode of transporting the material proved that this particular dynamite was less likely to explode than "normal" dynamite. It could and should have been stored.

There was also the destruction of the plastic bags and cardboard boxes. Zeller had fingerprinted every conceivable surface in and out of the vehicles: cornflakes boxes, bags of candy, cans of evaporated milk, scraps of discarded paper. But, somehow, no one thought to fingerprint the boxes and bags that the supposedly illegal explosives came in? And then they were burned? Certainly no one believed cardboard or plastic bags were hazardous to store.

Belloni ordered Hawk to call his next witness. Hawk glanced toward the back of the room. He seemed nervous, almost panicked. Then he smiled. David Nichols, the FBI lab man from Washington, D.C., had just arrived. He rushed to the stand.

Nichols had the results of chemical and microscopic tests on the dynamite wrappers. Hawk gasped when Nichols announced his results. His tests showed the presence of some fillers but no essential dynamite ingredients such as chalk or even a molecule of explosive. Either the dynamite was fake or a dud or Fettig had scraped the wrappers too well.

With no more witnesses to call, Hawk rested, the court record now devoid of any reason for the dynamite's destruction.

The defense called one last witness, McCreary. He came forward and sat down, filling the witness chair. He was sworn in. Hawk, so lethargic the moment before, actually jumped to his feet.

"Your Honor, before this witness testifies," he said, "I wonder if I might make one brief inquiry as to whether or not he was present in the courtroom during the testimony of any of the government witnesses?"

"Yes," McCreary said.

"You're excused," Judge Belloni said. "The defense has invoked the rule of excluding witnesses. That applies to both sides."

McCreary looked to the defense table, shrugged, and walked from the stand and out of the courtroom.

My high, which had only gotten higher during the hearing, became one of my lowest lows. I had *seen* McCreary. I could have prevented his exclusion. Instead, I had done nothing. Now, additional helpful evidence was going to go unheard.

I swore, at that moment, never again to assume that the lawyers always had everything under control. I'd be damned if my Indian friends ended up in jail because I was too reserved to say what I thought when I thought it.

I was dressed in a flannel shirt, blue jeans, and boots. I did not care. I walked to the counsel table, pulling my chair behind me. I sat next to Ed Jones.

Jones looked at me questioningly.

"I knew about McCreary," I said, "and I'm not going to be caught fifteen feet away again."

I was still angry at myself but became absorbed again in the proceedings. Counsel table was an entirely different world. Before, I had been in limbo, in legal purgatory, in front of the masses in a stuffed, fancy, oak-framed chair but an observer nonetheless. Now I was in the trenches.

As Judge Belloni signaled that the hearing was nearly over, Roberts stood. I knew what he was going to say from our prehearing meeting. I relished being able to watch his face while he spoke; before, I could only see the lawyers' backs.

In a pleasant voice, with a smile, Roberts said, "Your Honor, if I might request of the Court, it's my understanding, and perhaps this is erroneous, that the United States Attorney's Office has ordered the Ontario police and the Oregon State Police not to discuss any matter with the defense team. And I would respectfully request the Court instruct Mr. Hawk to rescind that order so that we might do some investigation here. We're absolutely handicapped in this case as a result of these instructions."

Three days before, Chelsea Brown, our investigator, had returned from Ontario. The trip had nearly depleted our investigation fund. He discovered that Hawk had ordered all the local cops to "shut up."

"Well, respond," Judge Belloni said, glaring at Hawk.

"Your Honor," Hawk said, "virtually all of the investigation reports of the Oregon State Police or all of the agencies involved in the apprehension here on the 14th were furnished to Mr. Schiffman and the other lawyers, long, long ago. That's normally how you get discovery in a criminal case. We supplied them with reports, reports of the officers and agents and whatnot, and they've been furnished with that information."

Belloni was clearly upset. "Well, the question here," he said, growling at the prosecutor, "is have you done anything to prevent law enforcement officers from speaking to defense counsel?"

"They called me," Hawk explained, "and said that there was an investigator who wanted to talk and asked what my position was. And I said, 'I would just as soon that if they want information, they come to me and I'll supply that information to them.'"

Roberts stood again, eager to pounce on Hawk's confession.

"Your Honor," he said, "I renew my objection and ask that Mr. Hawk be instructed to rescind that order so we can do some investigation and not have to rely on his bits and pieces of the reports that are mostly blacked out. These are serious charges! We have a duty to our clients, and we're handicapped by this kind of game playing by the United States Attorney's Office! I ask the Court to give us access to those witnesses and allow us to investigate this case fully, allow them to speak to us and allow them to speak truthfully. That's been absolutely sabotaged by Mr. Hawk's efforts."

Bonds was on his feet, adding to Roberts's indictment. "I might say," he said, looking first at Hawk and then directly at the judge, "that the very limited number of police officers who consented to speak with us gave us information 100 percent; 100 percent contradictory to the government; time of day, persons present, the scope of the investigation, the number of photographs taken, and everything else. So we have learned through personal discovery that we would be negligent in our responsibility to these clients if we blandly took the word that what's in the police reports is what happened."

The judge glared at the prosecutor, then turned toward Roberts and Bonds, purposefully away from Hawk. "I'm telling you," he said, "you can talk to anyone you want. I'll give you a court order if you need it!"

✙ ✙ ✙

THEY'LL STOP BULLETS

STEENSON, PARKINSON & LEA
ROOM 300, POSTAL BUILDING
510 S.W. THIRD
PORTLAND, OREGON 97204
(TELEPHONE 233–3490)
March 25, 1976

Tommy Hawk
Assistant U.S. Attorney
United States Courthouse
Portland, Oregon

Re: Loud Hawk et al. v. United States

Dear Mr. Hawk:

It has come to my attention that you might be interested in the following:
Flash! At approximately 9:55 A.M., this morning, I delivered my "blue" and only sports coat to a local laundry and dry cleaning establishment for refurbishing.

I received my information that you might be interested in this matter from confidential and reliable sources whose identities I will not disclose.

Sincerely,
TOM STEENSON
Attorney at Law

I pulled my cardboard box from its hiding place behind a pile of donated clothes in the defense house's office and slipped Steenson's letter into it. I envisioned Tommy Hawk with his copy—cursing at it, then crumpling and slam dunking it into his circular, government-issue metal wastebasket. He would be furious about Steenson's inversion of the parties in the case caption. Now it was the Indians accusing the government.

Along with Tom's letter, I put forty sheets of *Loud Hawk*

papers into my box. The three days after the court appearance had been constant work—in the library, at Steenson's office, at the defense house. The momentum from the hearing had to be ridden like a wave until all its energy dissipated. I found cases, drafted parts of the lawyers' motions, edited others, typed, strategized. After five drafts, a streamlined memorandum pounded point after point: there had been no legally justifiable reason for the government to destroy the dynamite and its containers.

Another memorandum complained of FBI monitoring and harassment of the defense camp. People were still followed—relatives of defense lawyers now, too. Ed Jones's cousins. Lynn Parkinson's wife. Telephones were haywire. And there were black bag jobs.

Sheila Lea had visited Peltier's lawyers in Vancouver, British Columbia. She worked with them late into the night, then returned to her downtown hotel. While she slept, her room was burglarized. She heard nothing. Her jewelry was not taken, but her pocketbook, right beside it on the dresser, was. Credit cards. Cash. Identification.

All were found on the hotel's roof in the morning. The only thing not returned was Lea's lawyer's diary. That was where she kept the names, addresses, and telephone numbers of *Loud Hawk* supporters across the country.

In late March, Judge Belloni ruled that the government had violated the *Loud Hawk* defendants' due process rights by destroying the dynamite. He prohibited the government from introducing any evidence of explosives at the trial on the remaining gun counts. He wrote,

> The destruction in this case occurred without notice to or presence of the defendants or their representatives or any neutral persons. All those present were law enforcement officers. The dynamite had been stored for nearly two full days before its destruction. There has been no evidence presented showing why it could not have been stored until defense counsel could have been appointed or retained.
>
> The boxes and plastic bags which contained the dynamite were also destroyed. The Oregon State Police, while attempting to take fingerprints from the outside of the station wagon, did not do the same with either the cardboard boxes or the plastic bags. The destruction of these

articles eliminated the possibility that the defendants could have pre-sented evidence rebutting this charge: i.e., they might have been able to show that their fingerprints were not on the dynamite containers.

Balancing the possible prejudice to the defendants against the gov-ernment's reasons for the destruction, I must find in favor of the defen-dants. Because of this destruction, it is impossible for the defendants to show that they have been prejudiced, but neither can the possibility of such prejudice be rebutted. In this situation, a presumption of such prejudice is created. This presumption, however, can be outweighed by valid reasons for the kind of destruction that took place here.

On several occasions, this Circuit has warned law enforcement offi-cers against the intentional and negligent destruction of evidence. Apparently, these warnings have gone unheeded.

Tommy Hawk was not a good loser. According to courthouse gossip, he approached the judge an hour after the dynamite order was filed.

"You can't suppress the dynamite, and you know it!" Hawk whined. "You'll be overturned on appeal!"

Judge Belloni turned away, closed the door to his chambers, and called Sidney Lezak, the U.S. attorney.

Lezak supposedly called Hawk into his office. Hawk reportedly stormed out, slamming the door. He was off the case.

April was beautiful. Camellias were in bloom. All the trees had budded. Flowers were everywhere, growing wild.

I was spending twenty hours a week at the defense house with Linda Coelho, Ramona, Russ (Kenny and KaMook were with Dennis Banks in California), and many others, including volun-teers like Connie Crooker. We were preparing for Dennis Banks's April 13 arrival for arraignment on the federal charges. Leaflets were printed. Documents, such as the affidavit quoting the South Dakota's attorney general's belief that AIM leaders should have bullets in their heads, were reproduced.

Judge Belloni's suppression order made everyone hopeful. A major part of the government's case—everything about bombs—was in disarray. Entropy could only help the defendants.[1] Yet

---

1. A trial on the gun charges, while not a great option, was at least better than a trial on both the gun and bomb counts. If the defendants were con-

strange things were still happening. One afternoon, Linda had been sitting at the kitchen table looking out the window and thought she saw a man with a handgun walking by, slowly, inspecting the house.

A week later, only two days before Dennis Banks was to arrive, I was in the middle room downstairs, just off the living room. A print shop had loaned us a huge stapler. It was almost five feet tall. It was green and had a large, worn, shiny metal foot pedal and a staple plate at chest level. I was lost in the rhythm of the machine, an extension of my arms and legs. Bang, slide the paper, bang again, pick up a folded, red, ten-page "The Longest War Comes to Portland" pamphlet, position it, staple it, slide the paper . . .

Russ and Linda were in the living room watching television.

"Hey!" Redner yelled. "Hey, there's a white guy on the porch with a rifle!"

In a second or two, I passed through emotions of shock and danger into clear thoughts: "He's probably FBI. . . . I'm a law student. . . . My role is to file an affidavit, describing the man—hair color, hair length, eye color, glasses, facial hair, color and style of clothes, type of gun. . . . Maybe I could pick him out of a lineup, proving he was working for the FBI."

I dashed to the front door and had my right hand on the knob when I heard a crash on the floor and felt my legs being pulled from under me.

"What are you, nuts?" Redner yelled from the floor, his arms clenching my legs.

"I've gotta see what he looks like, so I can testify," I explained.

"That man has a *gun*, for god sakes! Stay low and help me pull down the shades!"

Together we lowered the living room curtains. Redner ordered Linda upstairs. Then he crouched, heading for the kitchen, for the shades there.

---

victed, the jail time they would receive would be less, since they would be convicted of fewer charges. And if the government later managed to rescue the bomb counts by overturning Belloni's suppression order on appeal, the prosecutors would be hard-pressed to justify the expense of another trial on those charges. Also, if there were a later trial on the bomb counts, the defendants would have an easier time, already having had a free look at the government's witnesses.

At least twenty seconds had passed. My heart was pumping. I had not heard any steps on the porch. I peaked through a crack between the curtain and the front window. Seeing no one, I opened the door slightly, then walked to the edge of the buckled brown steps and leaned forward, peering into the overgrown bushes below, ready to run inside. I listened, cautious enough not to explore further. Hearing no one, I slipped inside and bolted the door.

"Did you get a good look at him?" I asked Redner.

"He was white, about six feet, dark hair—I think curly dark hair. I think in his thirties. Mostly, I noticed the gun. It was an M-16." Redner said he probably could not identify the man if he saw him again.

The door to the basement was through the back of the kitchen. A table had to be pushed forward to get to it. The stairs were narrow, green-painted pine planks that creaked in different keys. Some were only half planks. There was no light switch at the top. The button at the bottom did not work. Redner had to stretch to the left from the second to the last rung, trust the banister, locate the light bulb, and twist it tight. It would go on just as it sounded as if it would break.

The basement was all concrete, with regularly spaced, painted, partially eaten four-by-four beams bracing the floor above. A dozen old mattresses of various sizes, all of them stained, were scattered about. They had been donated and stored downstairs for the trial in May, when supporters from the Pine Ridge reservation would arrive by the carload and need a place to sleep.

Redner and I dragged the mattresses up the narrow stairs and positioned them against walls, behind the couches and chairs. When we had the last one in place, he called Linda downstairs.

"If you see anyone with a gun," he said, "get down on the floor, against one of the mattresses. And stay there. They'll stop bullets."

That night, I worked until 2:30 A.M. Then I woke Redner. It was his turn to keep guard.

CHAPTER 14

✝ ✝ ✝

JUSTICE, SOUTH DAKOTA STYLE

ONE hundred Indians and one hundred white supporters milled around the Portland airport, near the next to the last gate. Many held banners or placards or flags. Three young Indian men with long ponytails sat on blue plastic airport seats; another three crouched, bent forward on their knees. All six surrounded a bass drum, holding sticks, ready.

Television crews walked about, waiting. A cameraman focused on a pretty Indian girl with long, straight, black hair. A radio reporter, with a tape recorder slung over her shoulder on a thin black leather strap, wandered through the crowd. She picked two elderly Indians to interview. She put her microphone to their mouths and recorded their words, which were softly spoken over the hum of excited people.

The crowd reacted at every event. The plane landed. People pressed against the long, vertical plate-glass windows. The plane taxied to the gate. People pushed toward the doorway. As passengers appeared in the jetway, the crowd crushed inward, preserving only parts of a snaking two-foot-wide corridor. Television cameramen stood on chairs. Their lights, atop slender silvery tripods on either side of the gateway door, dazed the disembarking passengers.

When one hundred people had walked out, had been glanced at, and had been disregarded, Dennis Banks emerged. He was wearing a blue ribbon shirt and gray pants and was holding Tasina in his left arm. Beside him was KaMook, carrying Ta-Tiopa, laced into her cradle board. Ellen Moves Camp was to Banks's right. She looked uncomfortable, yet smiled for the cameras. Towering behind them was Dennis Roberts.

The television people formed a barrier in front of Dennis Banks, forcing the remaining passengers to cut a new path. The reporters shouted at him. "Mr. Banks, how will you plead to the charges?" "Mr. Banks, do you think Governor Straub will extradite you to South Dakota?" "Mr. Banks, the prosecutors have called you 'high risk.'"

"I'm pleased to be in Oregon for the very first time," Banks said in an even voice, into the camera lenses. "KaMook has told me wonderful things about the people here. That's all I can say. I'm due in court. I'm just happy to be here."

The reporters peppered Banks with questions, but he walked forward, flanked by a dozen Indian men in red ribbon shirts. Each wore an armband that read "AIM Security."

As the entourage moved toward the terminal, I zigzagged over to Roberts.

"Howdy, stranger," I said, tapping his shoulder. "How'd you like Belloni's ruling?"

"Far fuckin' out!" he said, putting his arm around me. "We've got 'em by the balls!"

Outside the airport, a caravan of forty cars formed. The lead vehicle was a late 1950s dark blue Ford pickup missing a rear gate and part of its left front fender. Two Indians, inside the truck bed, held a pole with a six-foot by eight-foot AIM flag. Dennis Banks's car was next—a beaten, white Chevrolet Impala fastback with a four-foot AIM flag sticking out of the right rear window.

Each of the cars following had smaller AIM flags, made of felt, slipped over antennas. The flags were six horizontal stripes of color. Blue, on top, represented the sky. Then red, white, black, and yellow, representing the four races. At the bottom was green, for the land.

To Lakota people, the four middle colors have additional meanings. Black is west; red, north; yellow, east; white, south. Black is night; red, earth and the blood of the people; yellow, the rising sun; white, snow and the sun at noon.[1]

The AIM flag tied the spirituality of the Indian movement to its politics of survival and sovereignty. In ceremonies, tobacco offerings were placed in small pieces of cloth in each of these colors, then strung together. Little flags of red, white, yellow, and black were also part of ceremonies.

---

1. See John Lame Deer and Richard Erdoes, *Lame Deer: Seeker of Visions* (New York: Washington Square Press, 1972), 104.

The six-colored flags, waving in the wind, strung forty cars together, creating a force on its way to meet the government at the courthouse.

William Youngman was a tall, stately man, in his thirties, with prematurely graying hair. Dressed in a finely tailored gray suit, he waited for the crowd to quiet. The judge had just taken the bench.

"Mr. Hawk will no longer represent the government," Youngman announced. "Mr. Hawk feels that since the government is going to appeal the Court's suppression ruling, the trial might be put over until late fall, in which case Mr. Hawk has other plans."

"Who will be representing the government?" Judge Belloni asked.

"Your Honor, I will, and Mr. Turner."

"All right. Good morning, Mr. Roberts," the judge said, looking to the right side of the counsel table.

Roberts stood slowly, respectfully, but not fast like a puppet. His client, Dennis Banks, sat to his right.

"Good morning, Your Honor," Roberts said. "I'd like the record to reflect my client's, my own, and codefendants' strenuous opposition to any continuance of this trial. We're ready to go to trial, we want to go to trial on May 12, we're prepared for trial, and we want to go."

"There has been no motion for continuance," Belloni responded, looking at Youngman, "and I also intend to try the case on May 12."

"How do you plead to Count No. 1, guilty or not guilty?" the judge asked Banks.

Banks stood at attention. "Not guilty!" he said.

"To Count No. 2?" the judge asked.

"Innocent!" Banks roared.

"The pleas of not guilty to all counts will be received," the judge said. "Trial will begin on May the 12th at 9:30 in the morning."

Banks, released without any additional bail beyond that posted in California, rushed out of the courthouse.

Cross-examination is a search for inconsistent detail. Words that best ferret out contradictions are "who," "what," "when," and "where."

The most damaging witnesses against the Indians would be the small-town officers who had stopped the vehicles and searched them. To cross-examine the officers sharply, the lawyers had to inspect the "scene of the crime." They needed to visualize their questions. Distance. Height. Orientation. Color. Sources of light. What could and could not be seen from where.

"Once a bell has been rung, it's hard to unring it," the legal adage goes. After Judge Belloni exploded, U.S. Attorney Sidney Lezak wrote to the eastern Oregon officers "rescinding" Hawk's order to be uncooperative with the defense and "encouraging" them to talk with us. The officers had to know that the first order was the intended one. But there was nothing to lose from another attempt to interview them.

Ron Schiffman, Michael Bonds, and I left Portland on April 15 in my brown Dodge Dart, going east on Interstate 80 North. Our first stop the following morning was the *Idaho Statesman,* Boise's main newspaper. A few weeks before, Schiffman had received a call from a reporter named Ken Matthews who said he had been at the scene on November 14.

"He claimed he had some 'key piece of evidence that would break the case,'" Schiffman said.

Matthews was a young man with an irrepressible smirk. He led us out of the newsroom to a corner at the end of a corridor. "I've checked with my editor and legal counsel," Matthews said. "I can tell you that I have some physical evidence, but nothing more. If you subpoena me, I'll assert a reporter's privilege."

"I know what you've got," Schiffman said. "One of the defendants remembers a reporter taking pictures."

"I'll tell you that it's not a photograph, but that's as far as I'll go," Matthews said.

"Expect a subpoena," Schiffman grunted. He turned his back to Matthews and motioned Bonds and me to follow him outside.

Matthews's assertion of a reporter's privilege was unconvincing, almost intentionally so. Perhaps he wanted to be paid for his "evidence"? In the parking lot, I asked Schiffman whether we should go back and find out what he really wanted.

"He doesn't have shit!" Schiffman said, while getting into the car. His tone left no room for debate. "Next are the TV stations," he said.

At KTVB, a pleasant young reporter named Randy McCarthy led us downstairs into a tiny screening room. He pushed papers off a table, positioned a projector, selected a can of film from a gray metal rack, snapped it onto the machine, and projected its raw, uncut footage onto a white wall.

Youngman had given us FBI still photos of the motor home. They resembled glossy advertisements from a Dodge dealership.

The television film showed something else. The windows of the motor home were blown full of holes. Some were the size of baseballs. The cameraman had walked up to the front windshield and shone a floodlight inside. The motor home was on the highway median—before any search. McCarthy ran the film over again and again in slow motion. The cups and plates and bags and jars and clothes from the cupboards were strewn all over the floor. But we could not see any bombs or bomb tools or wires or blasting caps or guns or gun cases or ammunition.

Were the guns planted or just well hidden? Even if they were just well hidden, I was excited by this photographic evidence. It proved the guns were not for use on the ride through Oregon in November 1975. It also meant anyone could have been inside the motor home without knowing about the "hardware." Since the government, inexplicably, had not charged the Indians with conspiracy to transport guns, it would have to prove that each one of the defendants, individually, knew the guns were there.

"How much would a copy cost?" I asked.

"About forty bucks," McCarthy said.

"We'll call you when we need it," Schiffman jumped in.

I whispered that we should order the film now. Randy might lose it, or the station might burn down.

"Can't," Schiffman said. "Chelsea's wasted trip shot our investigation fund." I suggested we use our own money. "Nah," Bonds said in a tone that ended all discussion.

We headed west. Our next stop was the Washington County, Idaho, sheriff's office. McCarthy had been at the scene on November 14, 1975, and remembered Sheriff Jim Johnston opening the back door of the station wagon. All the government reports said the Idaho officers stayed on their side of the river and that the OSP fingerprint man, Zeller, was the first officer inside the station wagon.

"Yeah, sure, I was there," the sheriff volunteered. "The whole thing was total confusion." Despite our prodding, he offered few details. He saw us as the enemy.

Next we drove to Fruitland, Idaho, a tiny community with a huge, bright pink bowling alley named the Gayway. Across the street was a cowboy diner, where we stopped for hamburgers. The service was intentionally slow. Five middle-aged men ate at a round table near the window. They stared at us. The word "hippie" was used during their meal.

"After lunch, let's get going to Ontario," Bonds said.

"Sure you don't want to spend more time around here?" I asked. "Sheriff Johnston said that everyone came to Ontario. Maybe we'd find someone who knows something useful. The prosecutors might not know about the Idaho guys."

"There's nothing more around here," Bonds said. Schiffman nodded.

Bonds pulled a map from his shirt pocket and unfolded it across the table. He pointed to back roads between Ontario and Portland, scenic routes we could take if we allowed enough time.

"What if we miss some key witness or piece of evidence that could win the case?" I asked.

Bonds laughed. "There's nothing here," he said. "This isn't like a law school examination, Ken. These guys got busted with all the shit. What can anyone possibly say?"

We drove past struggling clumps of sage that grew along the interstate between Fruitland and Ontario. Jackrabbits and prairie dogs scurried across the roadway. Beyond the chain-link fence at the edge of the road, there was nothing. Open desert. It would have been a great location to ambush the Indians, claim they tried to escape, and shoot them in the back.

We crossed the Snake River and within seconds were across the median from "the scene." It was, literally, a stone's throw from the water. We drove slowly, gauging the height of the fence that Peltier had allegedly scaled. Five feet, maybe a bit over.

We drove a half mile to a small, residential block. One building had an extended, painted, cinderblock storefront. A small sign read "Justice of the Peace."

The three of us walked in with our flowing hair and beards (mine was long and rabbinic, Schiffman's was cropped full and round, Bonds's was neatly trimmed), all wearing blue jeans, flannel shirts, and cowboy boots caked with desert. There were two wooden seats by the wall to the right of the front door. Sitting at a desk to the left was Judge Nita Bellows. She wore a beehive hairdo and clutched a telephone receiver with her chin.

She pretended not to notice us, even though the door chimed when we had walked in and she had looked up. We stood. She lit a cigarette, swiveled her chair away from us, leaned back, and said, into the receiver, "You know, I can't figure out what the hell those young legislators in Salem[2] are doing these days. You ask me, they're full of crap. As far as I'm concerned, the old laws are just fine, and those are the ones I'm going to follow, as long as . . ."

"Yes!" she finally said, as she hung up the telephone and spun her chair toward us. We introduced ourselves. She retrieved her burning cigarette from its glass ashtray, tapped the ash into the bowl with her forefinger, turned her back, picked up the telephone, dialed, and said into the receiver, "You won't believe the type of people they're letting into and out of our law schools these days."

We let ourselves out.

A few blocks away was Art's Garage, where the vehicles had been towed and searched. After the FBI finished with it in mid-November, Brando's motor home had been released to Mark Banks, Dennis's younger brother, who drove it to California. But the station wagon was still there.

A woman at the desk looked at the lawyers' bar cards, then showed us the white wagon. It had Zeller's black fingerprint powder all over and a fine layer of dust on top of that. Inside, strewn about, were pieces of clothes the FBI did not want. I picked up what seemed worth saving—blue jeans, shirts, a winter jacket, a pair of moccasins with red and black beadwork.

"Just leave the rest of that shit, and let's get out of here," Bonds said. It was already 3 o'clock, and he wanted to arrive at a hotel in the desert town of John Day, 130 miles away, by early evening.

The woman at the desk stopped us on our way out. "A reporter came here a couple of days after the FBI left," she said. "He said he

2. The state capital.

found evidence the FBI was doing something illegal. He went through our garbage cans and pulled out—what do ya call it—the negatives from a Polaroid. He said something in them didn't jibe with the FBI's story of when and where the dynamite was discovered. He told me he thought the FBI had planted the stuff."

"Was the reporter's name Ken Matthews, by any chance?" I asked.

"I'm not sure," she said, "it might have been."

We thanked her.

"That son of a bitch is getting a subpoena for sure now," Schiffman said, getting into the car.

"Let's make one last stop. It's on our way," Bonds said.

We drove past the town of Nyssa—site of a concentration camp for Japanese-Americans during World War II—into Vale, the Malheur County seat. The courthouse was a nondescript modern building, out of step with the "old west" architecture that lined the street. A large framed black and white photograph of the sheriff's posse was displayed on the lobby wall. The posse sat on horseback, a sagebrush-laden butte in the background. Although taken circa 1960, it looked like 1860.

There were things to do there. We had to talk to the jailers, the district attorney, his deputy, the clerks.

"It's late," Bonds said, "and the only thing we need here is a look at Peltier's court file. Sheila promised the Vancouver lawyers we'd look at it." Peltier's file listed witnesses to his alleged burglary of a farmhouse (from which a gun and vehicle had been stolen).

"Why don't we stay another day?" I said, noting that Peltier's files gave us additional names that would be worthwhile to investigate.

"Ken, there's nothing else here," the lawyers insisted. "Let's go see cowboy country."

We drove to Portland on a beautiful back road through small canyons and over buttes. Just east of Vale, a hawk hovered nearby, hunting a field mouse, careful that the shadow cast by the late afternoon sun was behind him. We passed through Prairie City. It had an old western brick hotel on its one street corner, across from the town's small, sloping "boot hill" cemetery. Its only public facility, the municipal rodeo, stood at the other end of the block, past real western storefronts and tie-ups for real horses.

I left Schiffman and Bonds at their Portland offices late the following afternoon, then drove to the defense house. I wanted to give Redner the clothes from the station wagon. I was excited. Having been in that vehicle somehow strengthened my bond to the case and the defendants.

"Hey," Redner said, grabbing a green plaid piece of clothing, "this is my favorite shirt."

He picked through the pile. All of a sudden, he became sullen. "The moccasins were Anna Mae's," he explained.

Bill Youngman and his associate, Assistant U.S. Attorney Charles Turner, filed a motion April 19, 1976, asking Judge Belloni to put off trial until after the appellate court reviewed his dynamite suppression order. Without waiting for the defendants' reply papers, Belloni denied the motion. Trial was still set for May 12.

"Betcha Ford was scared shitless, having a thousand Indians yell at him on the evening news, the week before the California primary," Dennis Banks said.

The Oregon presidential primary was the week the trial was scheduled to start. The first of the "thousand Indians" had already begun to arrive.

Trial was only one of Banks's legal problems. Even if the Oregon case ended in an acquittal or a dismissal, South Dakota still wanted him. Governor Robert Straub had to be persuaded that Banks's claim was just and that he would suffer more political damage from extraditing Banks than from offering sanctuary.

Banks had visible backers. There were the "lefties," like the Scotts and Bill Walton and Dick Gregory and Rev. Daniel Berrigan and William Kunstler. And then there were the entertainers, like Harry Belafonte and Tony Bennett, who offered to perform benefit concerts. Others, including Sammy Davis, Jr., were considering performing for him as well.

They would impress the governor, but Oregon voters would impress him more. Thousands of them—students, workers, craftspeople, teachers, lawyers, farmers—had signed petitions asking Straub to deny South Dakota's request. They were collected by Susan and Ron Williams of the defense committee, stacked, and delivered to the statehouse in thick bundles bound with twine.

No extradition fight would be taken seriously, however, without the support of the Oregon chapter of the American Civil Liberties Union (ACLU). It was *the* mainstream liberal legal organization. Its endorsement would reduce the political risk to Oregon's governor if he refused extradition.

On April 19, Stevie Remington, Oregon's ACLU director, led Dennis Roberts, Sheila Lea, Dennis Banks, and me into a large conference room in the ACLU office on SW Third Street. She had assembled the Lawyer's Committee, which voted recommendations on extradition matters.

Roberts opened his briefcase. "You've never seen anything so disturbing," he said, as he distributed thick packets of papers to the lawyers.

I watched these dozen attorneys, more traditional than my *Loud Hawk* attorney friends, as they inspected the papers with their technocratic lawyers' gazes. They turned the pages quickly, without emotion or comment. They were playing judge.

The papers had shocked me. The packet included the Rosebud Tribal Court disbarment judgment against South Dakota Attorney General William Janklow for allegedly raping a young Indian woman (Banks was the tribal attorney who had prosecuted Janklow's disbarment); Janklow's admission that Indians (like Banks) charged with the 1972 Custer Courthouse riot could not get a fair trial in Custer County (where Banks was tried and convicted); Janklow's statements advocating killing AIM leaders; Janklow's statements in support of a neo-Fascist organization called the Posse Comitatus; and Janklow's censure by the South Dakota Legislature for running through the capitol building with a submachine gun. There were also legal papers from other South Dakota Indian cases and other documents, affidavits, and letters.

A judge had dismissed a South Dakota case after nearly 250 potential jurors were examined and disqualified as being too prejudiced against Indian people.

Author Richard Erdoes, who had lived in South Dakota for more than twenty years, wrote,

Police brutality against Indians is widespread. I know of young Sioux girls, picked up by police on phony drunk and disorderly charges, who were taken to jail and there raped. I know of one Standing Rock Sioux who was shot in the back and paralyzed for life by a state trooper who objected to the Indian's 'loud muffler.' Every town in western South Dakota has its 'Indian Town.' It is generally poorly serviced without police protection, without running water, culverts, electricity. The fire department often will not go there. The houses are mostly tarpaper shacks with tumbling outdoor privies.

Court proceedings against Indians are travesties. Often they are rushed through in a few hours. I have yet to see an Indian among South Dakota jurors. I was in Rapid City, South Dakota, a few weeks ago. The county jail held 56 Indians and 6 blacks, but not a single white inmate, in spite of the fact that whites outnumber Indians eight to one.

National experts, such as attorney Roy Haber, wrote of the danger and racism in South Dakota jails. The U.S. Commission on Civil Rights reports documented the FBI's racist role on the reservation and its strange role in Anna Mae Aquash's death.

Then there were the papers documenting specific death threats against Dennis Banks. Cyril Griffin, a forty-two-year-old white living on the Rosebud reservation, said,

Dennis Banks is a marked man in South Dakota. Media coverage of his heavy activism for Native American human rights makes him a living target for every fear-ridden, violence-prone Caucasian in South Dakota. There must be over 1,000 white men in South Dakota who would consider themselves heroes if they shot Dennis Banks.

Father John Garvey swore, in an affidavit,

The threats upon the life of Dennis Banks are very real and very serious and are made by people with a physical and mental disposition to carry the threats out to completion. Affiant further states that because of his acquaintance with Dennis Banks and hospitality extended to Dennis Banks that affiant personally has been the victim of threats, to affiant and the building in which he resides.

Sally Rose Wagner, who had lived in South Dakota for almost twenty years and had written a book about the South Dakota history, swore,

On or about July 22, 1975, I went to the party at the home of Max Gors, who was then assistant attorney general of South Dakota. During the course of the party, the Indian problem and the trial of Dennis Banks, which was taking place at that time in Custer, S.D., were discussed.

In relation to the Indian problem, Mr. Gors said: "We don't have an Indian problem in South Dakota. The only problem we have is Dennis Banks and Russell Means, and if we get rid of them, we get rid of the Indian problem."

Mr. Gors' remarks reminded me of the kind of feelings which existed in 1876 at the time of the Battle of Little Bighorn, a subject which I had just been researching for the first chapter of my book, and I said to him: "That sounds like what the white nation was calling for in 1876—the extermination of the Indians."

Mr. Gors replied: "I'm not calling for the extermination of the Indians. I'm calling for the extermination of two of them."

Then there were the documents about Banks's trial and conviction on the Custer riot charges. The technical legal infirmities, while massive, were not as horrifying as the tale of a conviction engineered through official intimidation.

One of Banks's first witnesses was a law student. After he walked off the witness stand, the prosecution arrested him for perjury, right there. After Banks's trial, the charges against the law student were dropped. Favorable witnesses became too frightened to testify for the Indian leader.

Daniel Lee Jackson was Banks's court-appointed defense attorney. His affidavit was also in the packet the ACLU attorneys were glancing through. He swore,

> Janklow told affiant that the actions affiant had taken and was then in the process of taking in the preparation of a defense for Banks were improper and that if affiant continued to actively participate in Banks' defense that Janklow would make it a matter of public knowledge that affiant was a member of the Wounded Knee Legal Defense/Offense Committee. Affiant believed that such a characterization of him by the Attorney General Janklow would seriously impair affiant's stature as a reputable member of the bar and make it exceedingly difficult to obtain employment thereafter with firms from South Dakota.

Jackson quit the case.

Dennis Roberts augmented the documents with horror stories of life and death as an Indian in South Dakota that had recently been collected from the Indians who were arriving in town daily. There were also the other, better-known stories. Raymond Yellow Thunder, Wesley Bad Heart Bull, Pedro Bissonette, Buddy

Lamont, Byron DeSersa, Anna Mae Aquash—all had been murdered because they were Indians, and all were lesser targets than Dennis Banks. Roberts ended by giving the lawyers a feel for the man at his side.

"Dennis Banks was a youngster on a Minneapolis skid road who got drunk, committed a burglary, and ended up in jail," he said. He chronicled, in vignettes, how Banks, in jail, looked at his fellow Indians, talked with them, read, studied, and concluded that many of the problems of poor urban Indians were systemic, rather than individual. How Banks founded AIM, first as a monitoring group to follow the Minneapolis police and stop its routine brutalization of Indians. Then how Banks and AIM opened survival schools, where Indian kids who had dropped out of white schools excelled because they were taught to cherish their culture rather than punished for any reference to it. How AIM and Banks had been asked to come to Wounded Knee, where they helped lead a group of ragtag Indians in a desperate demonstration that the government turned into a siege. How Banks and AIM's actions at Wounded Knee helped many Indians gain a new self-respect and renewed hope—their first promise of a better life since Big Foot had brought the Ghost Dance to Wounded Knee in 1890 and was shot. And how, in 1975, hunted by the South Dakota government, Banks had gone underground.

The ACLU Lawyers Committee voted to authorize its director to write Governor Straub opposing extradition.

The *Oregon Journal* was Portland's evening newspaper. The afternoon of April 20, 1976, a banner front-page headline proclaimed, "TERRORISTS RAISE BOMB SCARE HERE."

According to the article, special police had been put at the federal courthouse, and other security measures and inspections were being implemented, because according to a government official, "Terrorist spokesmen have threatened to 'bomb hundreds of buildings' and 'blow your candles out.'" The article further noted,

> The steps were taken at this time to thwart any terrorism in connection with the trial of Dennis Banks, Chippewa Indian leader. Banks is scheduled for trial May 12 on federal firearms and explosives charges

arising from shooting between Indians and law enforcement officials near Ontario Nov. 14. The federal government plans to appeal, however, from a court decision ruling pictures of dynamite out of evidence in Banks' trial. Prosecutors forecast that the trial itself will not begin until fall.

By now the *Loud Hawk* lawyers and I knew that this was not a "normal" criminal case. Everyone had been followed and had had their telephones bugged. Tommy Hawk had even tried to short-circuit our investigation.

We knew. At Dennis Banks's Wounded Knee trial, AIM's chief of security, Doug Durham, had been invited to lawyer-client meetings to ensure their confidentiality. After the trial, he was disclosed as a paid FBI informant.

Perhaps, then, we should not have been as surprised as we were. The only possible reason for the *Journal* article, its front-page banner headline and wording, was a government attempt to poison the *Loud Hawk* jury. It smelled of FBI, associating Banks with terrorists and emphasizing the dynamite evidence, evidence that Belloni had ruled the jury could know nothing about. It provocatively referred to the eastern Oregon events as a "shooting between Indians and law officials" and associated increased security (all of which would be personally invasive—checking bags, putting people through metal detectors, possible frisks) with the Indian defendants. For one hundred years, everyone who entered an Oregon federal courthouse had simply walked in.

"Every time a juror walks in now and gets checked for bombs, they're going to think: dangerous, terrorist Indians!" Schiffman complained, as he and Bonds and I wrote a motion to dismiss because of this latest suspected instance of government misconduct.

CHAPTER 15

✝ ✝ ✝

ALL MY RELATIONS

BY Dennis Banks's second week in Portland, the defense house had become my home. Commuting between Salem, where I did not attend class, and Portland, where I worked on *Loud Hawk*, was a waste of time.

One late April evening, I was in the downstairs office studying cases about prosecutorial misconduct. Linda Coelho was upstairs, napping. No one else was home. The telephone rang.

"Hello," a male voice said, nervously, then tentatively, "is Dennis Banks there?"

"No," I answered.

"Do you know where he is?" he asked.

It could have been the FBI. I would not volunteer anything. But I did not know where Banks was.

"Sorry, I don't."

"Are any of Dennis's lawyers there?"

"No, they're not," I said, about to ask the caller who he was. He paused, then asked, "Who are you?"

"I'm a law student working on the case," I said.

"I'm Bruce Baker," he said, "chief of the Portland police." Banks had met Chief Baker the week before, to finalize a "rumor control" system. Banks had liked him. But I did not know if the voice was his.

"Chief Baker," I said, "I can get a message to Dennis to call you tomorrow morning."

"We've just received an intelligence report," he said. "A group of white vigilantes left South Dakota a few days ago. They're driving to Portland. They've come to assassinate Dennis. They may be here now. My suggestion is: find him, and get him out of town."

This might have been a hoax, an FBI setup, or real, but there was no reason to take chances. Anna Mae came to mind.

I thanked Chief Baker and called Banks's apartment on SE Oak Street.[1]

"H'llo," a gruff, sleepy voice said after seven rings.

"Hi," I said. "This is Ken, from the defense house. I need to speak to Dennis."

"He's not here."

"Know where he is?"

"No."

"Know when he's expected back?"

"No."

"Who is this?"

"Milt, AIM security."

"Milt, is there anyone there who might know where DJ is?" I asked, using Banks's nickname, so he would know I was a friend.

"Nope. I'm alone."

"When did Dennis leave?"

"'Bout an hour ago."

"Was anyone with him?"

"Why ya asking?"

"It's an emergency. Have any idea who he might be with?"

"Well, he left with Ellen Moves Camp and Russell Loud Hawk."[2]

"He had no speaking engagement that I know of. Are you sure you don't know where he is?"

It was hard to keep a calm, interviewer's voice. "AIM security" was an oxymoron. I visualized Banks lying on the ground, shot in the head.

After a lull, Milt said, "They might have gone to a movie."

"Great. You know where?"

"Nope."

"Do you know what film they were going to see?"

"Nope."

"Did they mention what time it started?" I was looking for any clue.

"Nope."

---

1. The defense house was too small for all the defendants. KaMook and Dennis had moved out.

2. Kenny's father, who had arrived from Oglala, South Dakota.

"Was it in a movie theater downtown, or Southeast Portland, or where?"

"Don't know. I think it might have been Southeast."

I thanked Milt, then called Ed Jones, Michael Bonds, and law student Connie Crooker. I told them what had happened and with an *Oregonian* movie page before me, assigned each of them theaters. I kept those in Southeast Portland and ran out of the house.

The attendant at the Mt. Tabor theater, where *Butch Cassidy and the Sundance Kid* was showing, had not "seen any Indians." I left my name and number in case Banks came to a later show.

Five minutes away, at the Baghdad theater on Belmont Street, where *One Flew Over the Cuckoo's Nest* was playing, a young, brown-haired ticket taker had seen Indians. "Go on in," she said, waving her arm. "They should still be inside."

"Thanks," I said, marveling that Portland was not like New York, where a theater employee would presume I was trying to get in free. I opened the swinging door and walked down the first aisle. None of the silhouettes in front looked familiar. I stopped and turned around, embarrassed that I was blocking peoples' views. My eyes acclimated slowly. I looked left to right, then right to left, up a row at a time, at faces lit in the dull light reflected from the movie screen.

Dennis and Ellen and Russell were ten rows from the back, toward the middle. I was two seats away when Banks noticed me.

"Dennis," I whispered into his ear, "someone who said he's Bruce Baker called. He said there's a group of vigilantes from South Dakota coming to town, looking to kill you."

Banks stood slowly. His face showed more disgust at the disruption than fright. He motioned to Ellen and Russell.

We started driving. Neither the defense house nor Banks's apartment were places to go.

Some things did not make sense. South Dakota was a long way from Portland. If there was some "intelligence," why didn't the FBI or the South Dakota police do something to stop the vigilantes? The FBI had issued APBs for Indians peaceably traveling in Marlon Brando's van but not for whites bent on killing an Indian?

Banks laughed when I mentioned the contradiction. "Janklow'd pin medals on their chests," he said.

We had no destination. We needed a place to stay for a day or two, maybe more, until it was safe to return to Portland. By default, I was the most seasoned Oregonian. But I could not think of any place to go.

Motels were out of the question. Banks's face was too well known from television. We needed a house to hide in. Nothing obvious, like a home of a defense committee member. Despite the government's sworn denials, there had to be informants. I ran through the possibilities.

"There's a law professor named Elliott Abramson," I said. "He's fairly progressive. He has a large house in West Salem, where no one would think to look for us. I'm not certain if he'd let us stay, but he wouldn't tell anyone he'd seen us."

There was also a law student named Jim, whose last name I did not remember. He lived in Mill City, a small lumber community thirty miles east of Salem, near the Cascades' foothills. Jim's wife taught elementary school there. "He's not political," I said, "but he's interested in the case. He's in law school on a mission to 'serve Jesus.' He's a good guy and would probably think of providing sanctuary as a good religious act. Neither the FBI nor vigilantes would know of him."

Hard as I tried, I could not think of anyone else. East was the desert, cowboy country, and west was the coast. In both places, three Indians and a Jew would stick out. North, Washington State, was no good either. The "Indian underground," born from fishing struggles, was there, but Banks needed Judge Belloni's approval to travel out of state. If he were captured in Washington, it would give the South Dakota authorities a third jurisdiction through which to seek his extradition.

I drove south, the only viable direction, where the two prospects lived. There was no moon. I memorized every headlight on the interstate. I slowed to forty miles an hour twice and sped to eighty four times. I was nearly certain we were not being followed. Banks had come to the same conclusion.

We were fifteen miles south of Portland when Dennis asked, "Where's Wilsonville?"

"Less than five miles from here," I answered. "I've never been there, but I've seen signs for it."

"Nancy Sanders is there. Let's go to her house," Banks said, adding that he thought he knew the way.

I was concerned. Nancy was a supporter, committed and energetic, although flighty. She had rented her father's old farmhouse and let the Indian people build a sweat lodge behind it. But she was well known to the FBI. If they wanted us, her house was an obvious place.

I argued mildly, then gave up. It was Banks's life. It also made sense to go where we knew we would be welcome.

Banks directed me through a few wrong turns, quickly corrected in the pitch-black night. He had been there only once before. At 10:00 P.M., an hour after leaving the movie theater, we pulled into the dirt driveway of a gray two-story frame house. Nancy—in her late twenties, with dirty blond hair—let us in and then, at Banks's request, lowered her shades. She showed me where to hide my car—behind her wood shed.

The kitchen had a wood stove, and Russell Loud Hawk already had it stoked. A pot of water was boiling on the gas range. Leaning against the kitchen door, to the side, was an old .30-.30 rifle. Nancy said her brother had used it in the fall. She found three shells in a stained bottom section of a cardboard box, on a small shelf above the back door.

Banks picked up the gun and inspected it. Because, as a youth, he had had a burglary conviction, he was an ex-felon. Ex-felons cannot possess firearms. That was one of the current Oregon federal charges against him. Whether or not he had committed a crime before, he was committing one now. Nobody would tell the authorities. But I wondered if he really trusted me. I was a newcomer. And I was distinctly aware that he and the others were now hiding only because of what I told them. Did any of them wonder if I was an agent, trying to lure Banks somewhere? Maybe that was why he had chosen the one place he knew of?

We sat at the kitchen table until 3:00 A.M. discussing the threat and security. The house was one hundred feet behind the county road. There was an old chestnut tree obscuring our view out front. And there were bushes—blackberries, a Concord grape arbor, roses—to each side. Agents in cars could sit fifty feet from the mailbox without being seen.

In back, the land continued half a mile, through fields and old orchards of apples and pears and Italian prunes, until it dropped off into the Willamette River. People could attack from there. I went outside, took two hundred feet of monofilament line from two Garcia spinning reels in my trunk (I had selected Willamette Law School in Salem, Oregon, for one reason—its proximity to good fishing), and tied them shin high between trees and shrubs all around the house.

Russell volunteered to stay up all night keeping guard, the rifle on his lap. In the black night, we reasoned, anyone sneaking around would trip. Russell would hear. He would wake Banks and me in the adjacent living room. Banks would run upstairs and get Ellen, Nancy, and her two-year-old son, Zack. I would run out the back door to my car. It was parked ready to loop around the shed, pick up everyone, and then either barrel out to the street or down an old dirt farm road toward the river.

I woke, startled, at 6:00 A.M. Two roosters were shrieking underneath my window. I thought that agents or vigilantes must have aroused them. Pulling the shade back an inch, peering out and seeing no one, I concluded that their commotion was probably a natural phenomenon.

I stayed in bed, unable to sleep. I lit my pipe. Banks still dozed across the room on his sofa.

Here I was, hiding out with a famous Indian leader. He had fled South Dakota's death threats, and now, within a safer state, he was still hiding from death threats. I was with him. I felt afraid and exhilarated.

We had stayed up into the early morning talking: politics, personalities, organizations, ethnic survival, both Indian and Jewish, the case.

"What's with this Sheila Lea?" he had asked me. I played dumb. I had heard that Banks had taken the lawyers into a sweat ceremony—Bonds had described it as an "intense sauna"—and that Sheila had tried to seduce Banks there. Bonds thought she was both crazy and disrespectful.

As we talked, I felt comfortable enough to criticize two things about AIM. "Lots of women do the best work," I said, "like Susana Gren and Lena Render, in the early days. But once the men came on the scene, the women were pushed into the kitchen or entirely out of the picture."

"You're right," he said. "But it takes time to work on prejudice."

"And it bothers me," I said, "that almost all the resources are spent on the big players—like you and Russell Means—almost to the exclusion of everyone else. Before you came, it was harder to get AIM as an organization working for Kenny and Russ. Seems to me that there has to be as much energy put into the foot soldiers' trials as the generals'."

I watched Banks's face across the dark room, lit in the glow of his pipe bowl as he inhaled. I thought he might be angry.

"I wish we had resources to help everyone who needs help," was all he said. Then he said good night and dozed off. Now, the roosters awakened him, too.

Russell Loud Hawk was still alert, sitting with the shotgun on his lap, in the kitchen. Soon everyone was awake. Ellen made coffee. Russell chopped firewood. Dennis played with Nancy's young son, Zack ("This little piggy went to Wounded Knee, this little piggy went to Oglala"). Nancy and I strolled to the mailbox in the morning sun, through the dewy grass. As we walked I glanced to the side, looking for anything out of place or any movement. I faked pulling an envelope from my pocket and pretended to put it in the box. Then I closed the tin door and raised the rusted red flag.

"Everything seems okay," Nancy reported, ten minutes later, when we walked into the kitchen. She took eight small brown eggs from her dress pocket. We had found them while looking for agents hiding under haystacks in the barn.

Breakfast was a feast. The sun shone through the country kitchen windows, and the crackling fire in the wood stove provided a sense of security.

"People in Portland must be freaking out," I said after my third banana pancake. "KaMook and the lawyers must be going nuts, wondering if we're okay. Maybe we should get word to them?"

"No way in hell!" Ellen screamed.

"I'm not proposing that we use Nancy's phone, Ellen," I explained, as she looked at me, angrier and angrier. "Either we make a quick call from a pay phone—'Hi, don't worry, we're okay, call you in a couple of days'— and hang up before they can trace it or maybe some of us drive into town, making sure we're not followed. If we are, we'd call back here and alert everyone."

"No!" Ellen screamed again. "That'll breach security."

"Ken," Dennis finally decided, "you drive into town and take Ellen with you. Drop Ellen at my place, and Ellen, drive back with KaMook, and tell KaMook to take my police scanner. And Ken, you can tell the lawyers and the people at the defense house that we're okay. I think they should know."

As we were leaving, I said, "I'll be back in a little over an hour."

"You don't have to," Dennis replied, looking surprised.

"I know," I said. "I want to." I wanted to help, and even more, I wanted Dennis to know I was committed and could be trusted.

No one followed us.

After reassuring Russ and Lena Redner and the lawyers, without telling them where we were hiding, I grabbed a clean set of clothes and headed back to Wilsonville circuitously, first going north. No one followed.

I passed the farmhouse, just to be sure. I made a U-turn a half mile down the road and then returned, parking behind the shed.

Dennis and Russell were behind the house, heating melon-sized rocks in a pit over blazing two-by-fours.

"We're going to have a sweat," Russell explained. "It'll take a couple of hours for them rocks to heat up nice and hot," he said. "They have to be white, you know."

I had never seen a sweat lodge before. I knew that sweats were traditional ceremonies of prayer. To Indians, a sweat lodge is like a church or synagogue, only the sweat lodge is more connected with the earth.

The lodge itself—twenty feet away from Russell's burning pit—was made from saplings bent into a semicircle ten feet wide. The branches intersected like a weaving and were tied together with rawhide, creating a dome. Over the saplings were canvas, rugs, and blankets to cut out light. In the center of the circle, on the floor, was a pit where the hot rocks would be placed.

Dennis asked me to go inside. "We have to check for light leaks," he explained.

He closed the flap, and I poked the areas where pinholes shown through. Dennis and I moved the covering materials until no point of light appeared. The lodge was satin darkness, despite the bright sunshine outside. Even without the rocks, it was stuffy and hot. I remembered Steve Suagee, an Indian who was one of the brightest workers on the defense committee. He had gone to a sweat here. It had become so hot he had panicked and run out. Indians laughed about it. Steve was embarrassed. He never came to the defense house again. It was as if he were emasculated. Having heard that story, I worried whether I could survive the heat.

Dennis opened the flap. I crawled out. We heard a car. Russell picked up the shotgun, lying against a pine stump next to his fire. Nancy and Zack were in the garden, fifty feet away.

We heard a car door slam, then another, then the front door of the house. Russell was cradling the gun as the back door opened. Ellen rushed out.

"They're massing down the road!" she yelled, in a panicked voice. She gasped for breath.

"There're twenty white men—in uniform—a mile back—getting ready to attack us!" she shrieked.

I had come down the same road not twenty minutes before and had seen no one. Why would a group of vigilantes, or FBI in their combat fatigues so familiar in South Dakota, be so brazen here? It did not make sense. But then again, Ellen could not be making it up. KaMook, who had driven back with her, had been holding TaTiopa and did not get a good look. Diane Ackerman, who was also in the car, had been paying attention to Tosh. But both thought they saw men dressed in military green.

Everyone rushed into the house.

Dennis plugged in the police scanner and extended its antenna. A series of twelve small red lights lit. He adjusted a dial so it stayed for only an instant on each band, except when someone was broadcasting. We listened for five minutes as Russell sat by the door with the gun. There was nothing unusual. Only two bands were active. A fire. An accident. Both miles away.

Russell and I got into my car, leaving the gun with Dennis. We would investigate. My brown nondescript Dodge Dart would draw little attention. Russell would look for familiar South Dakota FBI faces.

We were quiet, frightened, as we drove up and down the hilly two-lane road to the point where it forked. Ellen said that the men were in front of a house, a hundred feet to the right.

"I'll drive by at regular speed," I told Russell. "Then, if we need to take another look, I'll turn around and come back."

As I turned a corner, I saw the house Ellen described. I saw a dozen men in green uniforms. They were gray-haired World War I veterans, standing in front of an American Legion hall. Not one was under seventy.

The rocks were ready. KaMook and Russell kept watch, while Dennis, Ellen, Diane, Nancy, and I entered the sweat lodge. Russell took the large stones, white hot, and carefully carried them one at a time, balanced in an old rusted shovel, and then guided them into the pit in the middle of the sweat lodge only inches from our knees. They rolled off the shovel blade, clanging, then settled on the other rocks. Sparks flew.

When the rocks were in a heap, Russell closed the flap. Inside, we heard blankets drop over the opening. The last light disappeared.

We sat in a circle. In the dark, the rocks glowed. No one spoke. Dennis started the ceremony, speaking Lakota.

In the darkness, after prayers, the flap was opened for a brief moment, as a can of water was passed in, the tin ladle clattering against an old metal bucket. Dennis sprinkled water on the rocks. A blast of steam hissed, with no place to escape. We passed the pail and offered prayers for better lives and peace.

After each person spoke, or passed the water, we said "Mitakuye oyasin," meaning "all my relations" in Lakota. The words were a connection with nature and all the people before. I thought of the Passover Seder when Jews consider the Exodus from slavery in Egypt as if we had gone forth through the Red Sea into Sinai ourselves. Both cultures teach the need to understand our ancestors' battles, to visualize ourselves in their places, to learn the past as something present.

The ceremony lasted an hour. Tobacco was offered and cedar put on the stones. At times, the heat was so intense I was only a few seconds from bursting outside. Maybe running out would not be as bad for me as it had been for Suagee? I was not Indian. I oriented myself, knowing which way I would have to lunge to escape.

Finally, the flap opened. I caught a slice of cooler air. The water was passed to the others and finally to me. Instead of only ladling it over my head, I doused my beard as well. Moments before, sweating profusely in the darkness, I had remembered my high school physics: warm air rises.

When the flap closed, protected by total darkness, I bent over and put my face close to the ground. I folded my beard over my mouth and nose. The filtered air became breathable.

The flap was opened for the last time. The sacred peace pipe was passed in a circle, to be smoked. Then the ceremony ended.

When Dennis walked out of the lodge he said, "Look up!"

An eagle hovered slowly in graceful circles, directly over the sweat lodge. It had a huge wingspan. For ten minutes it circled above us. We stood, in our towels, and watched.

Indians regard an eagle as a powerful omen. I, a nonbeliever, was impressed with its size and beauty. Maybe the heat from the rocks, rising directly from the lodge, attracted the bird? Or perhaps eagles just knew who their friends were? To Ellen, especially, the eagle was a message from the spirits.

"They tell us everything is going to be fine," she said.

Hiding out in this war made life surprisingly more enjoyable, more real. My adrenaline had gushed since the call from Chief Baker. The sweat lodge was the perfect antidote. It extracted every molecule of worry and stress. At that moment, emerging from the ceremony and watching the eagle, I knew I would never be more relaxed and at peace.

The sky was translucent blue that day. Dennis and Tosh and I walked through Nancy's woods. He peeled red bark from a tree. "This is the tobacco used in the peace pipe," he told me.

Tosh had huge dark brown eyes. She did not talk much. But she giggled, looking back at me over her father's shoulder, as we played peekaboo while we walked to the old, forgotten apple orchards.

In her continuous smile was the promise of hope and joy. She did not remember a desert highway on a frigid night, holding hands with her mother and Anna Mae. She would know if her mom and dad spent her childhood in jail. I hoped my legal and defense committee work would help spare her that pain.

We raced to the courthouse. Judge Belloni had called Ron Schiffman's office at 10:30 A.M., Monday, April 26, 1976. He was convening an emergency hearing on *Loud Hawk* at 11:00 A.M.

"I had a letter from the government this morning," the judge said, in open court. "It reads: 'Dear Judge Belloni: The Court is aware that the government has filed a notice of appeal from the Court's March 30th, 1976, suppression order.

"'. . . In view of the notice of appeal, the government will not be prepared to proceed to trial on May 12, 1976. Although the Court has denied our motion for a continuance, it is hoped that it will not be necessary to summon a jury and that the time previously set aside by the Court for the trial can be utilized for other purposes.'"

He put the letter down and looked to the three prosecutors—Youngman, Turner, and their boss, Lezak.

"I want the letter and the position clarified," the judge demanded. "I still don't understand the government's position. As far as I'm concerned, there's going to be a trial on May 12th."

U.S. Attorney Lezak, in court for the first time on *Loud Hawk*, stood. His trademark bowtie quivered as he spoke.

"Maybe I can clarify it," he said. "We have filed a notice of appeal from Your Honor's decision denying the stay of the trial date. That appeal should be in the court of appeals today; and we expect to have a hearing on that by a panel of the court of the Ninth Circuit prior to May the 12th.

"Now, we, of course, hope that they will overrule this Court and grant us the stay. But, at least at this point, even if the Ninth Circuit refuses to grant the stay, we want to go to trial with the evidence that has been suppressed and we will take our chances on getting this Court reversed by the Ninth Circuit with respect to that evidence and we will suffer a dismissal at this time . . . rather than go to trial on the imperfect case that we would have to present if we were forced to trial now."

"So," Judge Belloni said, "on May 12th, if the trial date still stands because the court of appeals has refused to change it, then on that morning when the case is called for trial, there will be no jury needed because there will be a motion by the government to dismiss?"

"No, Your Honor," Assistant U.S. Attorney Turner said. "I don't think so. . . . I believe our present position is that if we move to dismiss, that would moot [kill] the appeal before the Ninth Circuit. I think that there would have to be a motion by the Court on its own or by counsel for the defendants to dismiss for want of prosecution."

Everyone on the defense team had trouble maintaining a look of disappointment. A dismissal was not as good as an acquittal but was much better than a trial—especially a trial where most of the defendants were likely to be found guilty, all of them if the government could prove that Dennis had been there.

"Has to be the Ford thing," Banks said, leaning over to me, while Turner spoke. "They have to be afraid of the attention we'll get while the national press is here for the primary. Otherwise, why wouldn't they just go for it on the gun counts?"

Bonds stood. "Your Honor," he said. "We expect and want to go to trial on the 12th of May. A reply to the government's motion for continuance in the Ninth Circuit will be filed this afternoon. We expect to go to trial on May 12th, and we will not waive our right to a speedy trial. Now, I'm afraid we're obliged to file another motion, and I think that this particular motion should be heard prior to the 12th."

Bonds paused for effect, then lifted a manila envelope from the counsel table. "We have been informed all along by the United States Attorney's Office, and I believe in good faith, that they would provide us with discovery in this case as it came into them. By that I mean FBI reports.

"Now, as recently as Thursday of last week, I was assured by one of the assistant United States attorneys that we had all the discovery. However, at the trial of Mr. Robideau et al. in Rapid City, South Dakota, involving the death of some FBI agents [the June, 1976, incident on the Pine Ridge reservation], discovery has been given there which is highly relevant and highly favorable to this case, and we have never received it.

"For example, there is a report of the 26th of February, 1976, saying that a latent print of a Marjorie Ellen Stephens was found on a radio transceiver's book inside the mobile home. There's an FBI report of January 27th saying that a latent print on a road atlas of Robert Robideau, a defendant in the case in South Dakota, was also found in the mobile home.[3] There is an FBI report

3. Other people's fingerprints in Brando's motor home would be very favorable evidence for the defense at trial. Additional prints would prove that people

dated March 12th with the results of the handwriting exemplars of KaMook Banks. There's a handwriting report dated March 15th on the handwriting report of Russell Redner and Kenny Loud Hawk.[4] And there are ten other FBI fingerprint reports dated as early as January and going through March of 1976 which we have never received, which are of an extremely exculpatory nature, particularly because the dynamite containers were burned along with the dynamite."

"What court proceeding was that, with such things as handwriting exemplars for Loud Hawk and Redner?" the judge asked.

"It's in the United States District Court for the District of South Dakota," Bonds said. "The case is going to trial this summer."

Belloni's face was crimson. For months, the prosecutors had pressed him to jail Loud Hawk and Redner for contempt for their alleged failure to give handwriting samples.

"I can't help but reflect on all the grief that was caused by the motion for handwriting exemplars of Loud Hawk and Redner in this case which, if they already existed, could have been avoided. It makes me slightly ill!"

"Well," Bonds said, "somewhere along the line, somebody is definitely dealing in bad faith."

---

other than the defendants might have hidden the guns and that Dennis Banks was not the only person who could have driven away from the scene.

4. The prosecution wanted the defendants' handwriting samples to compare with handwritten notes found in the motor home.

CHAPTER 16

✝ ✝ ✝

100 PERCENT PROOF

SOUTH Dakota was not giving up. Janklow's friends called Portland attorneys. On April 27, 1976, the ACLU Lawyers Committee reconvened and voted, 5–3, to rescind its support for Dennis Banks. "On reflection," the committee was not convinced that Banks was in "grave danger" in South Dakota. It referred the issue to the ACLU Executive Board, scheduled to meet May 8.

One early May morning, when the first roses were fully open, Dennis Roberts and Dennis Banks came to Salem to meet with Governor Straub. I waited for them on the steps of the capitol, having spent the night before in Salem studying for law school finals. They were five minutes late for their meeting.

Finally, a blue Ford with two AIM security people dropped them off at the curb. The three of us rushed into the capitol building, through the massive front doors, through the echoing chamber under the rotunda, up the marble steps to Straub's office. The governor's executive assistant shook our hands.

"Sorry we were delayed," Roberts said.

"Don't worry about it," the assistant said, as he immediately opened an oak door leading from the posh, carpeted waiting area into the inner sanctum.

I waited outside, inspecting the art along the halls, while Roberts and Banks and the governor met. Exactly fifteen minutes later, Banks and Roberts emerged. Neither said anything. They hurried outside. Banks walked across the street to the Ford. He got into the driver's seat, closed the door, and drove off, squealing the tires.

"Kenny, if I buy you lunch, will you give me a ride to Portland?" Roberts asked.

I was more curious about the scheduled thirty-minute meeting that ended in fifteen, without a word between Banks and his lawyer, than the finer points of contract law, my next exam. We drove to Boone's Treasury, an old brick building on the northeast side of Salem. It was dark, had high ceilings, served imported beer, and the sandwiches, although labeled with "crunchy granola" names, were not entirely smothered by sprouts.

"The *putz* doesn't realize that the governor can't be expected to run on Indian time," Roberts said. "I understand that in Indian culture, the shortest unit of time is a day, but still!"

He drew a deep breath.

"As soon as we got in, it started," Roberts continued, as we sat down at a small oak table and ordered two Dos Equis.

"The guy can't get out of his fuckin' ex-con mentality," Roberts lamented. "After ten minutes of friendly talk about sports and the weather, Straub picked up a file from his desk. The guy was real nice. He started with the easy stuff."

"'Mr. Banks,' he asked, 'How old are you?'

"Shithead fucking lied!

"Straub looked at his notes and asked, 'Weren't you born on such and such a date?'

"Banks said 'No' and gave another date."

Roberts gulped his beer and ordered another.

"Next, Straub asked where he was born. Dennis fucking made up a place! Straub asked, 'Wasn't it such and such?' Shit-for-brains said 'No.'

"The same thing happened when the governor asked how many kids he had. Straub, steaming, closed his file, got up, and said, 'Thank you, Mr. Banks,' turned his back, and walked out.

"Idiot Banks saw someone in authority and couldn't fucking give a straight answer! Every little, goddamn meaningless, inconsequential detail about himself, things that didn't matter a damn, he just couldn't tell the truth about. The big stuff—Indian relations, Pine Ridge, Indian rights, he'd talk straight about forever. We never got there. He just couldn't get out of his ex-con self-preservation shit! What a *putz*!"

Jury work was another part of the *Loud Hawk* case that was three-dimensional where law school was one. Law students learned that a defendant had a right to a jury trial if he or she faced a jail sentence. To select a jury of twelve from a larger panel, each side removed anyone who was biased ("for cause") and a limited number because, well, just because ("preemptories").

Law school did not teach how difficult excluding a juror "for cause" was. A juror could be prejudiced, but if he or she answered "Yes" when asked, "Can you put your prejudices aside and be fair in this case?" a for cause challenge would not succeed. To get a fair jury, preemptory challenges had to be used wisely.

These activist Indians would be tried by an all-white jury. It was statistically improbable that any member of an Oregon jury even knew an Indian. It was likely that that lack of contact would be a void filled with prejudice.

Studies proved that out of one hundred potential jurors, more than fifty started a case with a strong pro-prosecution bias. Most believed in a presumption of guilt—that because the prosecution charged someone, he or she was likely to be guilty. Less than 5 percent started with a counterbalancing, pro-defendant sentiment. The remaining 45 percent were willing to apply the law—the "presumption of innocence"—and make the prosecution prove its case.

"If you see a cop dashing down the street, chasing someone," a noted Oregon criminal defense lawyer explained, "you presume the person did something. If you're a juror, you're duty-bound to presume that the guy running from the cop did nothing unless and until the government proves its case, with evidence."

Jurors, like everyone else, harbored prejudices—racial and political. Like everyone else, they were either too embarrassed to admit to them or did not know they had them.

In some jurisdictions, lawyers tried to probe jurors' preconceptions through open-ended questions. "Do you know any Indian people?" "Do you think there is racism against Indians?" "Why do you think there is racism against Indians?" "Have you ever seen an Indian on skid road?" "Why do you think they were there?" "What do you think an Indian would feel if his child was taught that Columbus 'discovered' America?" "Would you like to be 'discovered'?" "What do you think about sports teams with Indian mascots and Indian names? Do you think Indian people have a right to be upset about that?" "Do you think the government might act improperly or illegally to convict people it doesn't like?"

In federal court, where the *Loud Hawk* defendants were to be tried, the judge, not the attorneys, asked the questions. Judges' questions were routine and brief, rarely prodding. "Can you be fair?"

In the early 1970s, a group of legal workers, the National Jury Project, applied social science techniques to jury selection. They hypothesized that if the defense used its preemptories wisely but without outside help, the jurors seated would be nearly half pro-government. If better techniques were used, with an error rate of 5 percent in determining which potential juror harbored which prejudices, only one quarter of the selected jurors would be pro-government and three quarters would be presumption of innocence jurors. Those numbers gave an unpopular defendant a fighting chance.

Former U.S. Attorney General John Mitchell offered the National Jury Project a small fortune to work on his post-Watergate trial. They refused. They wanted to help progressive people, like the *Loud Hawk* defendants. But their services were labor intensive and even at a discount, cost $10,000. The Indians did not have money, and the court would not authorize the expense.

Tom Steenson organized volunteers, including me and Sandra Phelan, a bright and dedicated worker whom Lew Gurwitz[1] had asked to come from Boston, to do some of what the National Jury Project would have done.

Portland's federal juries were selected at random from voter lists in Oregon counties within one hundred miles of the federal courthouse. Steenson's volunteers went to the county courthouses. They xeroxed voter registration lists. Steenson's statistician designed a computer program to select random names.

"There's less than one chance in a hundred that anyone we select would also be on the real *Loud Hawk* panel," Steenson said.

The hundreds of names culled from the thousands in the voter lists were divided among the volunteers. It took each volunteer a month to call those on his or her list—more if telephone taps were overly disruptive.

---

1. Gurwitz was a WKLDOC attorney, also from Boston, who had just arrived to help represent Russ Redner.

Some people refused to be interviewed. Others agreed. Some answered some questions, not others. How old are you? Have you ever been a victim of a crime? How much education have you had? Where do you get your news? How much television do you watch? Are you related to anyone working in law enforcement? How much money do you make? Have you ever been on a jury? Do you remember the Indians who were arrested in eastern Oregon last November? What do you remember about them? Do you think they're guilty?

Over 80 percent remembered the case. Nearly three quarters of those thought the Indians were guilty.

Steenson's volunteers marked answers on sheets. The sheets were tallied, and the statistician fed the computer. "A profile emerges," Steenson said. "What type of juror would be the least favorable, what the most favorable. We'll be able to tell based on observations and answers to the innocuous questions the judge asks. Say our data shows that a white middle-income male juror, twenty years old, with a high school education, who gets his news from television, who lives in Clackamas County and has never been on a jury before, is 90 percent certain to think the Indians are guilty, whereas a fifty-year-old grandmother, with two years of college, who has never been a victim of a crime, is 80 percent certain to be a presumption of innocence juror."

The information had another use. Over the government's objection, Judge Belloni released the names and addresses of the actual panel, from which the *Loud Hawk* jury would be chosen.

Without contacting the jurors, Steenson's most trusted volunteers drove by their homes to see the demographics. How old were they (were there toys in the yard)? How much money did they make (how expensive was the house, the car)? How did they get their news (was there a plastic *Oregonian* box on their fence post)?

Some houses gave extra clues. One small blue suburban cottage, neatly fenced from its neighbors with a high chain-link fence, had a forty-foot shiny aluminum flagpole planted in a square bed of concrete in the middle of the front yard.

"We don't know if the government is going to try the case on the 12th or not," Steenson explained to the statistician, as he ran the final numbers. "If the court of appeals denies their request to postpone the trial, they may go with the gun counts rather than have the whole case dismissed. If we're not prepared to select a jury on the 12th, we're in trouble."

I finished my last exam the afternoon of Friday, May 7. I packed my apartment throughout the night and stored boxes in a friend's basement at dawn. By 9:00 A.M., drooping with fatigue, I drove to Portland in time for a demonstration and march.

There had been three earlier marches for the *Loud Hawk* defendants. The first, in December, organized by Lena Redner and Susana Gren, drew 75 people on a trek to Redner and Loud Hawk at the Vancouver jail. A month later, 200 chanted and marched from downtown Portland to the BIA office in Northeast Portland, where they picketed the bureau's corruption and mismanagement. In February, 500 cheering Portlanders paraded from a park in Northwest Portland to the downtown courthouse. Traffic had been roped off. Motorcycle police had escorted the demonstrators, leapfrogging to block intersection after intersection.

This fourth demonstration assembled at the North Park Blocks. It was warm and sunny on May 8, in the high seventies. People wore T-shirts and shorts. Almost one thousand demonstrators assembled to walk downtown to the courthouse.

"This is the biggest march Portland's seen since Vietnam days, when Portland State was taken over, and we thought the revolution was coming!" Don Chambers, a rotund local attorney told me.

Banks and the first marchers left. They were five blocks ahead when my section finally moved. I walked with Lynn Parkinson, Kitsy, and their baby daughter, Megan. There were still a hundred people behind us. The chants of "Free the AIM defendants!" and "The people united shall never be defeated!" reverberated between downtown buildings, the sounds overlapping, sometimes in unison, sometimes not. The march was too long for a single, cohesive chant.

The procession, full of colorful banners and placards—"Free Loud Hawk, Redner, Banks and Banks!" "Sanctuary for Dennis!" "Stop the Genocide!" "Sovereignty for Indian People!" "U.S. out of U.S.!"—was more celebration than protest.

Four prostitutes from Ginger's Sexy Sauna, suggestively wrapped in pink bath towels, cheered from the sidewalk outside their work place as we walked by. "Right on!" they said, holding their towels with one hand and waving with the other. People ran out of restaurants to watch. "Join us!" marchers yelled. Some did.

As much as I enjoyed the revelry, I was there to work.

During the winter march to the BIA office, a young male with dark, scraggly hair and a dirty red flannel shirt and blue jeans, someone that no one had seen before, or since, had started chants. "Death to the pigs!" he yelled. "Burn the BIA!" he yelled.

At first, a few people chanted with him. Then his incitements to riot were ignored. The lawyers and the defense committee thought the man was either a nut or an FBI plant trying to discredit us. Luckily, the television stations did not film him. Instead they had focused on Lena and Tsi-Am-Utza Redner.

We knew that FBI agents watched us whenever we assembled. We saw their telephoto lenses behind windows on second and third floors of office buildings and from low roofs along the parade route. My job was to spot agents and provocateurs.

An FBI agent, in a tie, a short haircut, and trademark shiny shoes, walked sideways, ten feet to my right, five feet in front. His lens was pointed at me. He clicked his shutter while he shuffled. Click. Advance. Click. Advance. His focus never strayed. He took half a roll of film.

I was certain that the FBI had had plenty of opportunities to take my picture. No photographer could be so inept that he would have to shoot half a roll to get one good shot. This was intimidation. I smiled for the first ten shots. For the second ten, I extended my middle finger in front of my face. Then he left.

Three blocks later, Dennis Roberts found me.

"The FBI arrested two Indians," he said. "We gotta get to court."

The two had outstanding warrants for minor federal offenses. Their arrest violated a "rumor control" agreement: if any AIM member were to be arrested on outstanding charges, the authorities would let Dennis Banks bring him in.

Roberts, Bonds, Gurwitz, and I went into the courthouse. Even though this was a Saturday, Gus Solomon, a senior federal judge appointed by President Harry Truman, was working. He called an emergency session. U.S. Attorney Lezak—without a suit but still with his bowtie and short-sleeved shirt—represented the government.

As the judge was approaching the bench, Roberts leaned toward Lezak and whispered, "You've got egg on your face." Lezak, speechless, stared at Roberts in obvious anger.

"No, seriously," Roberts said. "You've got egg on your face, see." Roberts touched Lezak's chin, peeled dry egg yolk, and held it on his finger. Lezak turned away and addressed the judge.

"Your Honor," he said, "it will be an embarrassment if you release these defendants just because of community pressure and then they fail to appear."

"Your Honor," Roberts replied, "Mr. Lezak wants you to believe there will be egg on our faces if you release these defendants, who are being held on the most minor of charges. Well, we've all eaten our lunches," he continued, glancing at Lezak. "There will be a thousand hungry people outside your courtroom, Your Honor, if these gentlemen are not released. They made 900 sandwiches for the rally just now starting on the courthouse steps. The food is rotting in their truck."

Solomon freed them, and they arrived back at the rally with their sandwiches, to cheers, as Banks spoke from a plywood platform resting on a truck bed, parked across the street from the courthouse. He spoke about the rotten conditions Indians lived under. He repeated the phrase, again and again—"rotten conditions of unemployment, rotten conditions of hunger, rotten conditions of BIA corruption, rotten conditions of teenage suicide, rotten conditions of alcoholism, the rotten conditions under which my wife, KaMook, gave birth to our youngest daughter, TaTiopa, Iron Door Woman."

KaMook's grandmother, a skinny gray-haired woman in an old print dress, moved forward from the side of the platform. She spoke softly into the microphone. Dennis helped her move closer so she could be heard.

"We Indian people, we have faith in our Great Spirit," she said. "He is one who put us on this continent. We were here first. This is where we belong. When the white men came across, the Indian didn't fight them. They ate with them, showed them how to plant corn. They shared what they had. Now, in the end the white men hate us, want to get rid of us, move us so they can come in and get rich on the land. They're greedy for money and land. But they'll never be happy. But we are praying every day with our Sacred Pipe that we want justice. We're not praying for violence or anything else. Justice. We want justice.

"Our traditional men went to D.C. They want justice. They want the Treaty back. But Ford don't pay any attention to them. He didn't want to, I guess. I wish they understood Indians. We pray every day. We're happy. We shouldn't be happy.

"I'm not scared of no FBIs anymore since my son got killed. He volunteered, went in the service, volunteered to go across, fight for his country. Came back and he couldn't get no job and he couldn't go on to school. But I worked hard with my own money, and he went on to school, came back, tried to get a job, couldn't do it. And then in the end the government killed my son. He should have got killed overseas, I said. Then I'd feel much better if he's killed in war, fighting for his country, but he came back alive. He's my only son. Every day I go to church early in the morning and pray to the Great Spirit if he can spare my son to come back to me some day and he did. He came back to me without a scratch. Then he went into this Wounded Knee. That was his belief. And here comes Uncle Sam and killed him. He should have got killed overseas. It would look better and sound better, but instead he got killed right there on his own land, and what did they do about it? Nothing. I don't care how many thousands FBIs; they don't do nothing. They don't come and question me. Nothing. And I found out who killed my son. The government killed my son. And I have a good notion—sometimes I think that, well, he earned that flag alright, but in the end, his country, his government, killed him, so why should I keep this flag? I always think I'm going to send it to the Justice Department or War Department. What's the use?"

Roberts and I listened, as we each swallowed a rescued white bread, mayonnaise, and American cheese sandwich.

"C'mon," Roberts said, throwing away part of his sandwich with a squeamish look on his face, "it's time to deal with those mealymouthed, holier than thou bastards."

ACLU attorney William Snouffer, tall, with blond hair, and dressed in a gray suit, was already speaking when we walked into the conference room.

We knew Snouffer was against us. He had written a paper arguing against ACLU support for Dennis Banks. He had downplayed South Dakota's anti-Indian racism. He had painted Banks's riot conviction as untinged by any impropriety. He had defended Janklow, pointing out that the U.S. Senate had investigated the rape allegation and found it to be "without substance." That statement, true as it was, failed to give any credence to the contrary tribal court ruling.

What about Janklow's statement about bullets in AIM leaders' heads? That was not serious, according to Snouffer. It was just Janklow's penchant for using "exaggerated statements for their rhetorical effect."

Janklow was someone to be praised, Snouffer argued, as we walked in. He was "the only lawyer in the state willing to represent Indians for many years before he went into public office."

I whispered to Roberts. "That contradicts his written argument that racism against Indians in South Dakota isn't so bad. Even in Alabama in the '50s, there was more than one attorney willing to represent blacks."

Roberts made a note.

Snouffer quoted ACLU policy. "The ACLU does not object to extradition in the usual case in which it may be assumed that due process will prevail," he read from a booklet. "But an asylum state may not constitutionally grant extradition if evidence establishes the probability or reasonable certainty that the prisoner, if extradited, would be lynched or murdered in jail or tried in a mob-dominated court."

Despite the death threats, the countless murders of AIM people, the conditions of South Dakota jails, and the other horror stories, "Banks has presented no believable or persuasive evidence that 'establishes the probability or reasonable certainty' that he would be 'murdered in jail,'" Snouffer argued.

ACLU members Leslie Lazar, Eldon Rosenthal, and Nely Johnson had taken an opposite position. They wrote that "against the background of racism, widespread violence, and specific threats to Dennis Banks, coupled with the apparent inability or unwillingness of South Dakota officialdom to intervene effectively on behalf of American Indians, Dennis Banks's life is in danger *everywhere* in South Dakota."

Rosenthal and Johnson were to speak after Snouffer. Just as Snouffer finished speaking, Roberts erupted.

"What the hell kind of crap is this?" he yelled. "Am I hearing you guys right? You're saying we haven't established that Banks's execution would be a *certainty*?

"What the hell do you want? Do you want me to bring you the bullet from the jailer, the cop, the person from the attorney general's office, or the vigilante who wants to be a hero and say 'this is the bullet that is going into Banks' skull'? Is that what you want before you'll act!

"If this were a case asking you to support some Nazi asshole, you wouldn't ask for such proof. You'd jump in with both feet, to prove how liberal you were.

"But when an Indian's life is at stake, you ask for proof you know damn well no one can ever provide. You know the climate in South Dakota, the racism, the scores of murders of AIM members, the assassination attempts, the vigilantes who came here, to Oregon, to Oregon! looking for him, the 'open season' statements of the highest law enforcement officials, the farce of Banks's trial and conviction. What the hell more do you want?

"I'm sick of this intellectual charade. The man's life is in danger! People who have the power to kill him—including the top law enforcement officers of the state—have advocated killing him, have threatened to kill him. Can you live with that? How can you ask for certain proof, 100 percent proof, that he will be killed?

"If that's how you truly see this case, then I don't want your fucking support. Go screw yourselves! But if Banks is sent back and dies in a South Dakota prison, I hope none of you ever have another night's sleep!"

Roberts got up, pushed his papers together into a bundle, threw them into his briefcase, snapped the locks shut, and stormed out of the room, mumbling the word "assholes" under his breath. I followed.

A week later, the ACLU wrote Governor Straub:

The ACLU of Oregon urges you to deny South Dakota's request to extradite Dennis Banks because we believe his life would be in danger if he were returned. We are appalled that the Attorney General of South

Dakota has been widely quoted in the press as stating that AIM leaders should be shot and that Assistant Attorney General Max Gors had been quoted as calling for the "extermination" of Banks.

As May 12, 1976, approached, the government, in private, would not rule out going to trial. Yet, it bombarded Judge Belloni with additional requests for a continuance, such as the "Governments' Supplemental Memorandum in Support of Its Renewed Motion for a Continuance of the May 12, 1976, Trial Date." Those requests for delay were immediately denied, both by Belloni and the appellate court.

The government pleadings suggested that it was willing to suffer a dismissal, even a dismissal "with prejudice," if no continuance were granted. That was significant. Roberts explained it to me.

"Federal judges can dismiss a case in two ways," he said, "dismissals 'with prejudice' and dismissals 'without prejudice.' A with prejudice dismissal means there can be no further prosecution for the alleged illegal activity, unless a higher court overturns the dismissal order. A dismissal without prejudice means that the particular indictment would be terminated, but if the government later gets a new grand jury to issue a new indictment based on the same allegations, the case would start all over again, at the government's pleasure."

"So," I said, "let me see if I get this right. If Belloni dismisses without prejudice, that's really no better than a continuance. Once they finish litigating the appeal, even if they lost, they can just get a new grand jury to indict, right?"

"Right," Roberts said. "So, hopefully, Belloni will dismiss with prejudice." He added with a smile, "I've been checking the case law. I don't think any dismissal has ever been overturned where the government violates orders from two courts to go to trial. I think they really screwed themselves."

CHAPTER 17

+ + +

THE DISMISSAL

MY bedroom on the second floor of the defense house was actually a large closet on the way to the bathroom. A stained pink mattress was the only furniture. There was no room for anything else.

Linda Coelho woke me, unintentionally, as she stepped over the corner of my bed on her way to the toilet. The sun was up by then. A blue blanket, held by three nails over the room's single window, radiated a cobalt color. The blanket vibrated different blues as it shuddered in the faint breeze. I stayed awake, listening to the birds and the freeway traffic and smelling the crisp spring air.

There are days in life to look forward to. Days marking change: Bar Mitzvahs, births, weddings, graduations. May 12, 1976, was such a day.

Lena Redner was already awake. She was downstairs, stirring a fresh pot of Indian coffee. She looked especially radiant. Only weeks before, she had whispered her secret to me. She was pregnant. Lena cooked, and everyone ate while getting dressed.

"How does this look?" Linda asked, pirouetting in a print summer dress.

"Is this okay?" Russ mumbled, turning around, a half-eaten sugar doughnut in his mouth. He modeled his red ribbon shirt.

My usual court attire had been blue jeans and a flannel shirt. That would not do today. Neither would my only suit—double breasted, purple, worn through on the elbows, and too small in every direction. I had first worn it at my Bar Mitzvah, ten years before.

"Try this," Russ said. It was a black ribbon shirt with red and yellow ribbons across the front. I felt honored.

By 9:00 A.M., there was a crowd nearly ringing the courthouse.

Marshals were everywhere—on the street, in the lobby, on the elevators, in the hallways. Fifteen red-clad AIM security people also walked the halls.

As he had on earlier occasions, Dennis Banks unfolded a gray protective cloth, cradled the peace pipe inside, and carefully laid it on a small blanket at the front of the oak counsel table. If there was ever to be a trial, Indian witnesses would be sworn on that pipe rather than a Bible.

The counsel table was full. There were the three Dennises,[1] KaMook Banks, Russ Redner, Kenny Loud Hawk, Michael Bonds, Lew Gurwitz, Sheila Lea, Tom Steenson, Lynn Parkinson, Karen Spelke,[2] Ed Jones, Ron Schiffman, and me for the defendants. On the other side were Sid Lezak, Charles Turner, and Bill Youngman for the government. The table seemed unbalanced, in our favor.

The courtroom had dozens of reporters, court personnel, and nearly two hundred supporters. The seats in the jury box were taken by artists, sketch pads on their laps.

The Amnesty International couple sat by the clerk's desk. They were newly concerned. We had filed a motion regarding the hidden favorable fingerprint and handwriting evidence. Turner and Youngman had filed a reply. We had no complaint, the government lawyers said, since we had received the material from defense lawyers in the Robideau case, who, in turn, had received the material from the U.S. attorney in South Dakota, who, like Youngman and Turner, worked for the U.S. govern-ment. The inference was that the Oregon U.S. Attorney's Office was aware of the favorable evidence but did not want us to have it.

The tension in the room was tangible. Spectators talked. The doors in the back pressed open and were shut in unison by a marshal pushing on one side and an AIM security person pulling on the other. There was no more room. One hundred fifty people stood in the corridor; more were in the lobby five floors below.

Bonds walked over to Lezak, then returned and whispered to

---

1. A few weeks earlier, Judge Belloni had appointed Portland attorney Dennis Stenzel as local counsel for Dennis Banks. Stenzel was not integrally involved in the defense.

2. Dennis Roberts's legal assistant.

the rest of us. The government's supplemental, renewed motion for a continuance had been denied, and despite its inconsistent signals, the prosecution was ready to suffer a dismissal. There would be no last-minute change.

At exactly 9:30 A.M., Wednesday, May 12, 1976, Judge Belloni walked through his chambers door onto the bench. He waited for the crowd to quiet.

"This is the time set for the trial of United States of America versus Kenneth Moses Loud Hawk, Russ James Redner, Dennis James Banks, and KaMook Banks," he announced.

"Are you ready for the government?" he asked.

Lezak stood. "No, Your Honor," he said. "For the reasons stated in the memorandum filed with this court yesterday, we are not."

Judge Belloni nodded and turned to the defense.

"Is the defendant Kenneth Moses Loud Hawk ready for trial?" he asked.

Ron Schiffman stood, pulling Kenny up by the elbow. "Ready, Your Honor," Schiffman said.

"Ready," Kenny added.

"Is the defendant Russ James Redner ready for trial?"

Lew Gurwitz, Sheila Lea, Tom Steenson, Lynn Parkinson, and Russ Redner rose. "Ready, Your Honor," Lew said.

"We're ready, Your Honor," Russ added, firmly.

"Is the defendant Dennis James Banks ready for trial?"

Dennis Roberts, Karen Spelke, Dennis Stenzel, and Dennis Banks stood. "Yes, Your Honor, ready," Dennis Banks said.

"Ready," Roberts said.

"Ready," Banks said again. "Get it on!"

"Right on!" Redner added in a loud voice, ratcheting the courtroom's intensity level higher.

"Is the defendant KaMook Banks ready for trial?" Judge Belloni asked, ignoring Redner's enthusiastic outburst.

Bonds, KaMook, and I stood.

"Ready, Your Honor," KaMook said.

"Ready, Your Honor," Bonds added.

Judge Belloni looked at Dennis Roberts. "Well," he said, "do you have a motion to make?"

"Yes, Your Honor," Roberts replied. "We move that this case

be dismissed with prejudice. The government has been seeking one continuance and one delay after another. We stand ready for trial, as we have stood ready for trial these several months. Our defendants' rights to a speedy trial are being flagrantly violated by the dilatory tactics of the government in this case.

"We are ready for trial. We demand our trial. We demand our day in court now. We want our total and full exoneration by a jury. This is the day set by this Court many months ago for trial. We are ready, and we need our trial today!"

"All right," Belloni said. "I think everyone here realizes that this case will be dismissed against these defendants. Both this Court and the court of appeals have denied any postponement.

"I am ready to try the case commencing today. Both parties have had ample time to prepare. The defendants are ready to go to trial. For some reason, which I do not understand, the government is not, even though two of the counts are not even concerned with the subject of previously suppressed evidence. I don't want to dismiss this case without a trial. The factual and legal dispute should be heard and decided, but there is no way the Court can force the government to call its witnesses. My only recourse is to dismiss the case against these four defendants.

"Clearly, there has been unnecessary delay in bringing these four defendants to trial. Clearly, it's the fault of the government.

"The case is dismissed. All court-imposed restrictions on the activities of Mr. Loud Hawk, Mr. Redner, KaMook and Dennis Banks are now removed."

Turner looked pained and was standing, propped up by his left hand on the counsel table.

"Did you want to say something, Mr. Turner?" Judge Belloni asked.

"Well, I want to . . . ," Turner trailed off.

Lezak stood. "Your Honor," he said, "we would really like to be heard on whether or not the conditions of release can be set aside by the Court."

"Well, how can there be bail when the indictment is dismissed?" the judge asked.

"Your Honor, because the statute provides for that," Turner said. "We would respectfully request that the Court impose conditions of release."

"There should be no further proceedings based upon the alleged occurrence stated in this indictment," Judge Belloni said. "The dismissal of the indictment is *with prejudice*."

Waiting for that phrase—"with prejudice"—had been pleasingly painful. Those four syllables meant the difference between winning the case and merely prolonging it. All the lawyers and the defendants smiled. Bonds and I slapped hands below the counsel table, where Belloni could not see.

Turner was not smiling. He stood again and asked the judge to keep the government's witnesses under subpoena, even though the case was dismissed, and there was no new trial date.

"Your Honor," Roberts said, "this case has been dismissed with prejudice. The United States government has at its command the ability to serve subpoenas on anyone at any time, and for it to try by every back door tactic to keep a shred or a breath of life in this case strikes us again as a continuation of the government's tactics throughout."

Judge Belloni refused the government's requests for continuation of bail or subpoenas. The prosecutors handed a piece of paper to the clerk. It was a notice of appeal from the with prejudice dismissal, already typed and signed. Belloni received it, stood up, said "We're adjourned," and walked off the bench. As he did, the defendants, their lawyers, and their supporters hugged. Someone in the courtroom pounded a drum. Belloni stopped, his chambers door already opened, and whirled around, ready to say something. His lips pursed as he decided against it, and having already unsnapped the top three buttons of his black robe, he retreated into his chambers and shut the door.

Afterward, there were at least two hundred people on the courthouse steps. I pushed my way through, looking for Dennis Roberts, the tallest of the attorneys. He stood at the bottom of the steps, as his client spoke to reporters.

"What a fucking victory!" Roberts said, slapping my hand. "Indians haven't won one this big in a hundred years."

"You may be right," I replied. "Take a look up."

The prosecutors, sullen, were gazing down from their third-floor office.

Dennis Banks spoke to the crowd. "These prosecutors didn't want to go to trial because they knew they'd lose," he said into a bullhorn, as his supporters cheered. "They just wanted to keep us tied up on these charges, wanted bail, even though Judge Belloni threw them out of court. They're nothing but ambulance chasers!"

Roberts and I watched as Turner grimaced and walked away from the window.

The press interviewed the defendants and the attorneys. Television. Radio. Newspapers. Magazines. Wire services. Local press. Statewide press. National press. Foreign press.

An *Oregonian* photographer asked the defendants to pose together. They reassembled near the top steps of the courthouse's main entrance. The lawyers and I stood behind them, in the background.

Dennis Banks raised his fist in a sign of victory and defiance. We held our clenched fists high, too. That pose, in color, took up most of the front page of that evening's *Oregon Journal* and, in black and white, the next day's *Oregonian*. The dismissal was banner headline, front-page news, upstaging national events, even the arrival of presidential candidates on the eve of the Oregon primary.

It took just four days for euphoria to diminish into anticlimax. The defense committee had to be deactivated, bills paid, the house closed down.

The first afternoon, instead of accepting Redner's invitation to a lawyer-defendant-Bill Walton basketball game in Wallace Park, I spent hours on the telephone answering calls from all over the country, including those of William Kunstler, Daniel Berrigan, and Harry Belafonte. Telling them of the victory let me savor it longer.

On the second and third days, the lawyers and I drafted post-dismissal memorandums, reveling in the contradictory positions of the prosecution and analyzing its misconduct in refusing to proceed to trial. By the fourth day, every last ounce of rejoicing had been squeezed from the victory. Dennis and KaMook Banks had gone to California, Kenny Loud Hawk to South Dakota, Lena Redner to her home in Port Angeles, and Russ Redner to Vancouver, British Columbia, to run Leonard Peltier's defense committee. The Loud Hawk-Redner-Banks-and-Banks defense house was eerily quiet.

Lew Gurwitz and his friend Sandra Phelan were staying with Jack and Micki Scott. Gurwitz was scheduled to testify at Peltier's extradition hearing. The U.S. government wanted Peltier sent back from Canada to face charges of killing the two FBI agents.[3]

On the morning of May 17, Lew, Sandy, and I drove north to Vancouver, British Columbia, 300 miles and five hours away on the interstate.

For the first fifty miles, two FBI cars tracked us. One was blue and one was green; both were late model large passenger cars stripped of chrome. One would go ahead, then slow down, letting us go by. Then the other would go ahead.

"I'm not surprised they didn't stop tailing us after the dismissal," Gurwitz said. "They're more interested in Leonard anyway."

An hour out of town, at Castle Rock, Washington, both cars passed us and got off the highway. Fifteen miles later, we were relatively certain that no other cars had replaced them.

Just as we started to relax, Gurwitz pointed out the window, yelling. To the left, directly over the shoulder on the other side of the interstate, was an eagle. It was at least one hundred feet above the road, flying north. It was a fixture.

"It's a good sign," Gurwitz said, "flying along with us."

For five minutes, the bird moved at the same speed as I drove, never changing altitude. Then, just like that, it was gone.

The Vancouver Indian Centre was a large, gray, solid-looking building. Once a school, it had large rooms and polished hardwood floors. Despite its size, it was overtaxed. Children ran around unattended. Sleeping bags were on the floor, in the corridors, some folded up, some rolled up, some flat and partly kicked out of the way or stepped on by people walking past. Shopping bags with personal belongings were nearby. Shirts. Pants. Underwear. Hairbrushes sticking out on top, or toothpaste, to be easily

3. The extradition request also included two attempted murder charges against Peltier—one in Milwaukee (of which he was ultimately acquitted) and one in Oregon (for shooting at Griffiths; this indictment was later dismissed at the government's request).

retrieved. Some bags had food, bread, potato chips, and cheese doodles.

I had come to the Centre to see Russ Redner—leaving Gurwitz with Peltier's lawyers—but I did not see him. I meandered through the halls, smiling at the children, feeling out of place—one white face in a sea of Indians, none of whom I knew. I wore my "Free Loud Hawk and Redner" T-shirt to try to fit in.

I was feeling bored and ill—I had been fighting a cold the last days before the dismissal—when I saw Redner run through the lobby. "Got your car?" was his greeting.

I ran outside after him and followed his directions toward the U.S. border. "We just got a call," he explained. "Some whites are beating some Indians at a bar in Cloverdale."

It took twenty minutes to get there. We found the bar, but the crisis had ended. An Indian who had been involved was sitting on the curb up the street.

Redner went to him, sat on the curb, and talked. I watched as he put his arm around the man. After listening to his story, Redner pressed money into his palm. The man objected. Redner insisted.

On our way back to Vancouver, Redner stretched out in the front seat. He seemed exhausted.

"How's Lena?" I asked.

"We've split up," he said. "She told me that she had an affair when I was in jail. She denies it, but that other guy's the one who knocked her up. She likes to party too much."

"God, Russ," I said, shocked, "Lena didn't tell me about the affair—just the pregnancy—but the way she acted, how happy she was, and the timing, I mean, the kid *must* be yours."

"Well," he said, "maybe it is and maybe it ain't, but I'll tell you one thing; the case may be over, but it sure screwed up my life."

Redner was quiet for a while, then turned toward me. "Want to know what the mission in Brando's rig was all about?" he asked.

I did. But I felt a lawyerly responsibility. I did not want Redner trusting anyone.

"Thanks," I said, "but don't you dare tell me or anyone else. It's unlikely, but possible, that Belloni's rulings could be overturned. The last thing you need would be someone on the witness stand testifying, 'Russ Redner told me such and such.' I don't need to know, Russ. Believe me, if I ever do, I'll ask."

"Okay," he said, then fell asleep, his head against the passenger window.

Leonard Peltier's extradition hearing was in an old marble Vancouver courthouse. The interior steps divided to each side and curved their way past ornate windows to a mezzanine. The railing at the top of the stairs was unusually low. A person could fall over.

Spectators, even those with legal credentials, had to pass through a security checkpoint before entering the courtroom. I had visited prisoners in Oregon, going through an airport-style metal detector cranked up so high that the nails in my cowboy boot heels and the tin in my gum wrappers set it off. Here, that was only the first step. I passed through the machine, having dressed without metal.

"Take off your shoes!" a guard demanded.

I unlaced my sneakers.

"Hand them to me!" he yelled.

I bent over, picked them up, gave them to him, and watched as the guard looked inside, then stuck his hand in and moved it around.

"What're you looking for?" I asked politely.

"Hidden weapons," he said.

He handed the shoes back. Before I could lace them, he said, "Stand still, and lift your hands."

I did. He ran his hands up my legs, narrowly missing my crotch, then on my backside, then up my chest and arms. I was uncomfortable, sweating, invaded.

He took a Bic pen from my pants pocket. "You can't take this in," he said, accusingly, as if it were a knife.

"I'm a law student working on a related case in the United States," I said, trying to sound official. "I have to take notes."

"You can't take the pen in," he insisted. "A pen can be used as a weapon."

I left my pen and walked into the courtroom, winking to the frightened young Indian woman standing behind me, the next to be subjected to the routine. She forced a smile.

The courtroom had seven long oak pews for spectators, divided by an aisle. The bar in front was substantial, thicker and higher than those in American courts. Even though there was an opening for barristers and witnesses to pass through, the division between spectators and actors was more heavily drawn.

Like the British, the Canadians had a dock—an oak, fenced area of the courtroom. Peltier sat in it alone. He wore Redner's black ribbon shirt.

I recognized other people. I had met Peltier's lawyers—Don Rosenbloom, Tom Rafael, and law student Stuart Rush—over a seafood dinner the night before. They were sitting at a table, to the side, away from Peltier.

Gurwitz walked to the witness stand. Rosenbloom led him through the stories. Gurwitz's cases, over many years, defending Indians all over the country. The FBI manufacturing evidence. The FBI hiding favorable evidence. The FBI putting spies in lawyer's meetings. The FBI threatening him for representing his clients. The FBI intimidating supporters and supporting vigilantes. Some of his more recent stories came from Portland. Linda Coelho and the "How do you want to be buried?" episode. The hidden fingerprint evidence.

As Gurwitz spoke, I noticed a middle-aged man across the aisle and a row in front of me. He wrote in a notebook. I moved to the bench directly behind him. He was not a reporter taking short-hand notes. He was FBI, taking notes on Gurwitz. I could make out bits and pieces. "Criticizes FBI role," he wrote. "D. Durham," he wrote, referring to the FBI informant put into lawyer's meetings during Banks's Wounded Knee trial.

It took the agent five minutes to realize that I was reading over his shoulder. He moved to a different seat. I followed, sat behind his other shoulder, and smiled when he turned around. Two minutes later he tried again, finding a spot in a row behind him that was nearly full. I followed and squeezed beside him. He smiled and put his notebook away.

The movement in the courtroom caught Gurwitz's attention. He looked to the presiding judge and said, "Your Honor may not be aware, but these proceedings are being monitored by the FBI right now. Over there," he said, pointing to my immediate left, "is an FBI agent. I know this for a fact because, two years ago, he introduced himself to me during a court appearance in Minnesota. His name is Sidney Rubin."

The judge seemed shocked that there was an FBI agent in the audience without his knowledge. Rubin left.

Gurwitz was ending his testimony. "Your Honor," he said, "respectfully, I have some advice for you. Look at all the evidence against Peltier. Label that which comes from the FBI. Put it aside. See if what is left is enough to convince you that he should be extradited. If not, and you find yourself making a decision based on what the FBI swears is the truth, stop. Look at the evidence harder than you have ever looked at any evidence in your career. I know what I'm telling you may sound absurd. But I've seen too many judges learn this lesson the hard way. More likely than not, if you end up with one 'key' piece of evidence, and that evidence comes from the FBI, it's a lie."

Lew and Sandy and I left the courtroom and rushed to a downtown office building where a press conference was under way. We walked into the large, oak-paneled conference room that the Peltier defense committee had rented from a law firm. There were chairs, filled with people, all along the art-covered walls.

The television lights were focused on a young woman with blond ponytails and the trace of a southern accent. She was Candy Hamilton, a legal worker for the Wounded Knee Legal Defense/Offense Committee.

"Anna Mae was a good friend of mine," she said. "She told me that FBI agent David Price threatened to see her dead in a year if she didn't cooperate."

I knew the details. I listened as Candy described the body, found in a ditch. The severing of the hands. The autopsy claiming death from "exposure." The independent second autopsy. The obvious evidence of execution.

"I was with attorney Bruce Ellison," she said, fighting tears, "when he asked FBI agent Wood about Anna Mae's hands. Wood said, 'Wait a minute.' He walked to his car and came back holding a cardboard container. Wood was smiling.

"'Here,' he said, 'catch.' He tossed the box, as though it were a ball or a set of house keys or something. Bruce caught it. I could hear the hands rattling inside."

CHAPTER 18

WOUNDED KNEE

"I can't comment on that," Dennis Roberts squawked into a pay phone. An *Oregonian* reporter questioned the coincidence. Dennis Banks had extradition proceedings pending in two states. His California bail was secured by the deed to a supporter's house. The homeowner needed his property unencumbered the day before Banks had to appear in Oregon. While new security was being found, Banks was in a California jail, unable to travel.

As Roberts spoke to the reporter from the jail lobby, Banks sat on the edge of his metal cot. He smiled. Two officers were in his cell. They handed him a piece of paper.

Just as Banks signed, Roberts walked in.

"Let me see that!" he ordered, grabbing the sheet from his client's hand.

"Shithead!" he yelled, after he ordered the officers out. "You think these guys were sneaking in here, illegally, behind my back, to do you a favor?"

Banks started to explain something. Roberts held his hand up, not wanting to be disturbed. The lawyer walked around the small cell, reading. He stopped, then waved the paper at his client.

"You think this release agreement is such a deal, don't you!" he screamed. "It gets you out of jail right away, right?

"Idiot!" he roared, without giving Banks a chance to answer. "It's to get you out of jail, so you have no choice but to be in Portland tomorrow where, after your performance in the governor's office, you're sure to be extradited. You almost signed your own goddamn death warrant, you *putz!*"

The trial of AIM members Bob Robideau and Dino Butler began in early summer 1976.[1] Robideau and Butler had been indicted along with Peltier for killing two FBI agents the summer before. Peltier was not on trial yet, because he was in Canada, fighting extradition.

I had wanted to help. Gurwitz had invited me. He and Kunstler, whom I was eager to work with, were Robideau's and Butler's defense lawyers. But my father was ill. And I had invested three years in an infatuation with red-haired Mary Nathan. Her graduation from my alma mater, Bard College, was four days after I left Vancouver. I drove alone to Annandale-on-Hudson, New York, in three and a half days, fantasizing all the way about how wonderful it would be to see her, how pleased she would be that I had come three thousand miles, how her excited voice on the telephone, saying, 'It will be just *great* to see you, you can stay at *my* place' was really, finally, an invitation to her bed.

I spent her graduation night at her house. On her couch. "Oh, did I forget to tell you about Peter?" she asked.

Then there was my father. He was only sixty but was dying from a degenerative heart disorder. I watched as he shuffled rather than walked, how easy tasks were now too hard, how scared he was but could not discuss it, being a heart surgeon, knowing exactly what was happening to him. It was the last summer we fished together. I was scared but could not talk about it either.

And then, that summer, there had been "the decision." My law school grades had arrived in a white envelope, postage due. I had passed the December exams, cramming outlines the night before. But *Loud Hawk* had demanded too much. I had not crammed enough in the spring. By a few hundredths of a point—ten minutes of memorization for short-term regurgitation—I was on academic probation.

---

1. The trial was in Cedar Rapids, Iowa. Judge McManus had ordered a change of venue because it was impossible to find a South Dakota jury unbiased against Indians.

That jolted. Hadn't I always been a good student? Maybe law wasn't for me? Law school was torturous. The people were shallow. They made me angry. Was law school something I could endure? Would I have to go to classes to pass? I couldn't stand it! Did I really want to be a lawyer? I wasn't sure anymore. If I didn't want to be a lawyer, why should I spend two more years at law school?

To please my father, I took a year's leave of absence rather than quit. But I swore, from then on, to do only political work, organizing, like I had for the defense committee. Legal work I would leave to others, like Tom and Lynn and Michael and Ed.

Yet that summer I read about the trial in Iowa. What fun it would have been to be there, living what the papers reported. I wondered what was really happening. What were their chances?

The first *New York Times* articles told how Butler and Robideau had killed the agents in cold blood, execution style, without mercy, in a barrage of high-powered bullets from semiautomatic weapons, exploding their heads, exposing their brains. The agents had driven into the compound peaceably, to serve a warrant on a young man for stealing cowboy boots, the FBI said.

Then, slowly, over the next weeks, in small paragraphs, the defense story was reported. Witnesses claimed that the agents had come into the compound shooting.

I could picture Gurwitz with his gruff Boston accent, asking rhetorically, "Why does the FBI serve warrants for theft, which isn't under its jurisdiction, when it doesn't investigate murders of Indians, which is?"

The articles became more sympathetic. They described the extreme violence on the reservation. "The Indians say they thought they were under siege from the FBI and returned fire," one article reported.

A major legal battle erupted. An FBI bulletin sent to all major U.S. law enforcement agencies claimed that AIM was training 2,000 "dog soldiers" to disrupt the 1976 Bicentennial of the American Revolution. One of the alleged plans was to "fake car trouble and then kill unsuspecting police officers who came to help."

The memorandum heightened the tension around the trial and discredited AIM. The defense subpoenaed Clarence Kelly, director of the FBI. Under oath, Kelly admitted there was no evidence to support the "dog soldier" memorandum. U.S. Senator Frank Church testified. He was chairman of the Senate committee that had investigated the FBI political disruption scheme COINTELPRO. The FBI had spread lies about "left-wing" political groups to discredit and destroy them. Although the FBI said it "terminated" COINTELPRO before 1975, Church said the "dog soldier" memorandum was "reminiscent" of it.

The Iowa jury was entirely white. It believed that Robideau and Butler had shot the agents. But it found them not guilty. The jurors called the killing of the agents "an act of self-defense." The FBI was "stunned" by the verdict. I was depressed that I could not be there to live through the tension, then relish the victory.

A few weeks after the verdict, I said good-bye to my parents and left New York for Oregon. As I drove across Pennsylvania, into the flat expanses of Ohio and Indiana, Illinois and Michigan, I was eager to see the reservation where the events on trial in Iowa had taken place the summer before.

I drove through the Badlands onto the reservation, past the town of Wounded Knee, into the village of Pine Ridge, South Dakota. My rear bumper had a "Free Loud Hawk and Redner" sticker. Pine Ridge was a stronghold for Dick Wilson's Goons. But I needed gas. I decided it would be unprincipled to scrape the sticker off.

I pulled up to the red pumps at a Husky station. I hoped the gas would be better than the condition of the station suggested. Paint flaked from the silvery undercoating of the pumps. A rusted oil barrel, used as a garbage can, overflowed. A swarm of flies buzzed around it.

I waited. No one came. I got out to pump gas myself. Both pumps had slots in front for dollar bills. They spit out measured gas, a dollar at a time.

The owner saw me staring at the slots. "It's okay," he said, unlocking the door to his office. "I'll turn it on for you. Fill 'er up?" He did not notice my bumper sticker.

As I left, after paying with a traveler's check, Indians in an old metallic blue Chevy Bel Air pulled in. The car rocked when it stopped. The white station owner watched from his office as an

Indian man got out and stuck his hands in his faded blue jean pockets, fishing for dollar bills.

Oglala, fifteen minutes away, was small. Shacks were made of tarpaper and old road signs. Junked cars were dressed with torn curtains. Large groups of children played outside huts. I wondered how they slept, inside, in homes smaller than a garage.

Despite the poverty, there was harmony with the land. Each ramshackle house, each tarpaper hut, each car body looked curiously at peace with the earth around it.

I stared at the land. I fused a mental image, then deleted the structures. Nothing else changed. Not the feeling. Not the landscape. White people control nature around their homes; they plant gardens, cultivate lawns, cut down or add trees. The Indians just borrowed the land as it was. They left no traces.

My AIM bumper sticker, potentially troublesome in Pine Ridge, helped in Oglala. Traditional people were suspicious of white men as possible FBI agents.

There were no addresses. All the houses in the new "Oglala housing" were identical, bilevel, cheaply constructed boxes, in cul-de-sacs.

"Loud Hawk's the house right across from the one with all them junked cars," a friendly young girl with long black hair said, her eyes wide and smiling. Her mother grabbed the girl's small hand and pulled her away from my car.

I explored a dozen loops until I found a lawn with ten junked cars on it. I walked to the door of the house across the street. The neighbor's dogs barked.

Sam Loud Hawk, Kenny's older brother, lived there. His wife gave me coffee, despite the 100-degree heat. Neighbors came. I was escorted down the street to meet other neighbors, among them Gladys Bissonette, a middle-aged woman, a heroine of Wounded Knee. She described how young Pedro Bissonette, an outspoken AIM supporter, "my son," had been murdered by the Goons.

"Nothing's changed here," Sam said. Gladys and everyone else in the room nodded. "The Goons and the FBI keep after us. People are still getting shot every day."

The next morning, after sleeping on an old blue box spring without a mattress, with my underwear and socks folded into my shirt for a pillow, I was told to follow Sam's car to a house across the county road. Russell Loud Hawk lived there with his wife, Stella, and Kenny and Kenny's sister, Arlette.

"You drove through Pine Ridge with *that*!" Sam said when he saw my bumper sticker. "You're lucky you didn't get your ass kicked in Pine Ridge! Last year some attorneys got stomped on by Dick Wilson's boys, and they didn't even have bumper stickers. Some ended up in the hospital."

Russell Loud Hawk's house was on a dirt road that looked like two footpaths going in a similar direction. The building was made of discarded road signs, a billboard, and scraps of wood with different color paint. Inside, the rooms were small and sparsely furnished. The doorways were five feet tall.

Fifty feet away, larger than the house, was a shelter made of two rows of pine trunks stuck into the earth and connected with pine trunks above, lashed together. Branches had been tossed on top for shade. Another Indian-Jewish connection. It looked like a *succah*, the temporary structure Jews build on the holiday Succoth to commemorate the bringing of the harvest to the ancient Temple in Jerusalem.

Kenny stood to the side of the Indian structure, pumping a long iron rod into the muzzle of a gun. He pounded it in, pulled it out, pointed the gun, fired, smiled, reloaded, and fired again, either at nothing or at something only he could see. He walked away with the gun, into a field of rocks and brown weeds.

Russell went inside to help Stella, leaving me under the shaded structure with an old gentleman with graying hair, a cane, and a pockmarked face. Joe[2] was one of the Indians who had passed through the Portland defense house.

"Kenny," he said, "I know Peltier didn't do it, didn't kill them agents. I know this for a fact."

I was not sure what to say. I nodded.

A big smile spread across his face. He reached over and poked me in the arm. "You know who did it?" he asked.

His smile was from knowledge and pride. I knew he was going to tell me some relative—maybe a son—killed Coler and Williams. That was a secret I did not want to know.

---

2. Not his real name.

"How do you know I'm not an FBI agent?" I asked, pretending I was angry.

Joe's smile dismissed my question.

"I don't need to know," I said. "I really don't want to know, and if you don't want yourself thrown in jail for refusing to testify when some fed finds out you do know, I'd advise you to keep your mouth shut!"

I hoped my sternness had impressed him. But did he really know? Could his testimony free Peltier?

He would never testify. This was a war. He was an old warrior. In war, soldiers are not exchanged for prisoners; the enemy would keep both.

I smiled and shook the old man's hand. I did not mention my distress. His pride bothered me. He had spoken of the FBI agents like American soldiers in World War II talked about Nazis, about Gestapo, about killing them proudly. Agents Coler and Williams were not human beings to him, just dead enemy troops, faceless, nameless "FBIs." Their death generated pride and maybe, in a way, even hope. Joe had known scores of Indians during his long life who were murdered by whites with impunity. Maybe he thought the killing of two whites by Indians would stop the whites, make them think attacking Indians might be dangerous? Maybe they would not do it anymore?

Russell came out, with tea.

I had asked him the night before whether he would take me to Wounded Knee and show me what had happened. He had said "Yes" in a manner I thought might mean "No." (Indians are too polite to say "No" to a guest's request.) But why would he refuse?

I asked again. He gave another "no yes." A half hour later, I mentioned Wounded Knee again. I yearned to go there. Russell nodded and slowly walked to my car.

A mile out of Oglala, on the road back to Pine Ridge, he asked, "Do you want to see where Joe Stuntz and them agents died?"

He pointed to a dirt road no broader than the one to his house. It was not constructed; use had created it. It rose with the rises and dipped with the gullies. It turned radically, disappeared into a field of tall grass, then reemerged.

"The Jumping Bull place is up ahead," Russell advised. "The

little log cabin here," he said, pointing to the left, "was built for Dennis and KaMook."

It was charred above the windows. No one lived there now.

The Jumping Bull house was around the next corner. Three men had died there a summer before—the Indian, Joe Stuntz, by a shed, the agents in the field below.

We walked to the house. It was old, wood, and green.

"Looks pretty much like it did then," Russell said.

From the outside, thirty feet away, large-caliber holes were visible. From the inside, through the holes, I saw sunlit hills and a ridge in the distance with a single row of pines. Some of the holes were cannonball size. Lines of smaller holes, from automatic fire, extended back and forth, penetrating the thin walls cleanly, crisply, almost orderly. Hundreds of them.

Broken glass was still on the ground. In a corner there were fragments of a blue plastic picture frame that had been shattered by bullets. I did not find the picture it once held.

"Over there," Russell said when we walked outside, "was where the agents died, right up against their cars."

He was pointing to a gully one hundred yards away. It was a ravine in the middle of a field of tall grass.

"Is there another road down there?" I asked.

"Nope," Russell said, "only this road," pointing to my car.

No wonder the Indians thought they were under attack, with the agents sneaking up through a gully hidden from the house.

Soon we were on the main road again, heading to Wounded Knee. We passed a ridge by the highway, to the left, where there were small colorful flags blowing in the hot breeze.

"That's where Joe Stuntz and Annie Mae Aquash are buried," Russell said. Then he drew quiet.

"Sure you want to go to Wounded Knee, it's getting late?" he asked, as we neared Pine Ridge.

"I'd really like to see it," I requested. He nodded and was quiet again.

As we entered Pine Ridge Village, there was a telephone booth on the right near a school. It had been the only one I had seen on the reservation.

"Mind if I make a quick phone call to let my parents know I'm okay?" I asked.

Russell did not answer. His face was ashen, and a bead of sweat trailed from his forehead down his cheek. "If the Goons see me here," he said, "they'll shoot."

I drove through town, quickly, as Russell slumped in his seat. As we left Pine Ridge I remembered this brave man, calmly sitting with a gun by the door at Nancy Sanders' house in Wilsonville, Oregon, waiting for vigilantes to attack. In Pine Ridge, he was petrified just riding in a car.

My images of Wounded Knee had come from books and television. Guns. Army tanks. A church.

"The church was burned down," Russell said, as we parked on a gravel road near where the church had been. "The Goons did it," he said, "to destroy the evidence. There was lots of powerful ammunition—artillery, too—fired into the church by them Goons, the marshals, and the FBIs."

Only the foundation remained. An ironwork gate was behind the church. An entrance, it curved at the top. Behind, rimmed by concrete, was a mass grave. Big Foot and his followers' frozen bodies had been buried here. I walked around the grave, then stood silently in respect. The gate reminded me of photographs taken only fifty years later of the entrance to Auschwitz. Where, I wondered, at this Indian extermination spot, had the bodies lain before they were flung into the pit? Was I standing where some defenseless Indian had died, bleeding?

Where had Agnes Lamont's mother, KaMook's great-grandmother, spent that cold December night, as a child, a witness to such horror? Had she stayed here, hiding, or had she been old enough to escape right away?

I remembered Lame Deer's description of his grandfather, Good Fox, who saw a "dead mother with a baby nursing at her cold breast, drinking the cold milk." Was that baby Agnes's mom? One of Kenny's relatives? Some of them had been shot here, too.

"There was a meeting at Calico Hall," Russell told me, referring to the more recent Wounded Knee, "back down the road. Many people came. We decided to move to a bigger room in Porcupine. Wounded Knee was along the way. We stopped here.

"Wesley Bad Heart Bull had been killed," Russell said. "And that Dicky Wilson. He was corrupt, you know—sold our land, Indian land. People who opposed him lost their jobs. We were attacked by his Goon squad. We tried to impeach him. But he took over his own impeachment hearings. Even Nixon couldn't do that.

"We had demonstrated, you know. We even walked to the BIA office. The FBI and marshals come on the reservation, before Wounded Knee, with guns, to support Wilson and oppose us.

"There's not even supposed to be a tribal chairman, you know," he continued. "We have our traditional chiefs. The Treaty respects that."

As Russell talked, I looked around, standing near the church foundation. "From a military point of view," I said, "you guys couldn't have picked a worse place."

Russell nodded.

The church—the center of the takeover—was on a rise in a large bowl. Ringing the horizon, a mile or so away, was a ridge that went totally around. From its bunkers and armored personnel carriers, the FBI had shot down at the Indians, at the center of the bowl, in a raised platform. How could only two Indians have been killed?

"They tried to starve us out, you know," Russell said. "Some people snuck in backpacks, through the hills over there," he said, pointing to the side of the church. "The FBIs shot flares up all night long. The youngsters would run, fall to the ground when a flare went up, run some more, before the next flare. They got pretty good at it. KaMook and Kenny and Anna Mae did that, you know."

KaMook had been only sixteen then, and Kenny had not been much older. I imagined the intensity of those seventy-one days, at this spot, finally taking a stand, doing something, but at war, not being sure you would survive. KaMook's love for Dennis had blossomed here. Anna Mae Pictou had married Nogeeshik Aquash here. The siege here, the government's disdain for Indian lives here, and the mismatch of the firepower here—army tanks against .22s—had forged a commitment to survival here. The trip through Ontario, Oregon, two and a half years later had begun here.

CHAPTER 19

A BURNING BUSH

ALL of a sudden, the terrain changed. It was green all around, incredibly lush, and very familiar. There were two lanes of new white concrete in either direction, divided by grass and pine trees and maple trees and huge pieces of exposed granite, each a perfect natural sculpture.

It was a sunny afternoon. There were no other cars on the road. My windows were down. The air rushed in. It looked like the interstate between White River Junction and Barre, Vermont. How could that be?

As I drove farther, the landmarks were familiar. Little towns with white church spires in valleys engulfed by green hills. Fields of hay, neatly mowed, in sharply angled patterns. Red silos and old wooden barns with rusted weather vanes and crooked lightning rods. Fields of corn. Cows in black and white. Vermont.

There was a pickup truck in my rearview mirror, going 85 or 90 to my 65. As the road turned, the truck disappeared. It emerged in my mirror, closer, at the next straightaway. Soon it was right behind me.

It crept past. It was blue. It had a canopy on the back. It looked like a truck I had seen the year before, on my way to law school in Oregon. For twenty miles in Utah, on a sunny day, I had driven behind a blue truck with a canopy. It had had AIM stickers on the back—the first I had ever seen. "Support AIM." "I'm Indian and PROUD of it!" "Indians—America's POW's." "America—Love It or Give It Back."

An Indian girl, seventeen or so, absolutely beautiful with chiseled features and long, flowing black hair, had smiled at me through the canopy's rear window. I had waved in return.

This truck was not that one. It pulled into the right lane ahead of me. It was larger, recently washed, and had no bumper stickers.

Five seconds later, it decelerated abruptly. I was going to crash into it! I didn't have time to move to the left. My only chance was to slam my brakes and veer toward the right shoulder.

The truck's back gate popped down and flapped, an inch above the roadway. The canopy had a double door—glass surrounded by chrome molding. Both sides snapped open, smashing against the canopy in unison, as if they had been spring loaded.

Inside, two white men in white shirts and dark glasses were kneeling side by side. Each was holding a shotgun, pointed directly at me. They were FBI agents from Portland.

I saw the triggers on the guns pulled, as if in slow motion. I couldn't believe it. An instant later, there was a flash in the barrel of one gun, then the other. The dark-haired agent on the left smiled.

The air was sucked out of my lungs. I didn't feel pain. But I must have been hit. My side was warm and sticky. Gooey. I touched it. My hand was dripping blood. How could it be that it didn't hurt?

My right fender smacked the aluminum guardrail. The car jumped up in a violent heave. I couldn't breathe. The car was free-falling off a hillside. There were trees and jagged rocks below. I knew exactly where I'd crash. I was surprisingly at ease, at peace, resigned. I woke up, in a sweat, in a motel room in Hot Springs, South Dakota, just outside the Pine Ridge Indian Reservation.

The Portland Trail Blazers lost the first two games of the 1976–77 NBA championship series to the Philadelphia 76ers. Portland won the next two, and the fifth game. Game six, of the best-of-seven series, was at home.

That was June 1977. Micki Scott and I sat together, in her housemate Bill Walton's seats, five rows back. Jack Scott, with a press pass, was at courtside, cheering on the Blazers' star center.

It was the fourth quarter. Walton's Trail Blazers were comfortably ahead, 108–100, with only minutes left. Philadelphia cut the lead to 108–105. The Blazers called time out. Power forward Maurice Lucas hit one free throw. 109–105. Anticipation changed to fear when 76er George McGinnis launched a twenty-foot jumper. Swish! Blazers, 109–107.

Eighteen seconds were left. The Sixers had the ball. They could tie! Julius Erving fired. He missed. Philadelphia got the rebound! The clock ticked. Lloyd Free shot. It looked good. It missed. Philadelphia got the rebound! George McGinnis shot again. He missed! Walton tapped the rebound. Blazers guard Johnny Davis grabbed the ball. The clock stopped. The buzzer sounded. Micki and I hugged.

Ten minutes later, outside Memorial Coliseum, a thousand car horns honked. "Rip City!" a young man shouted. He was standing on the back seat of a black convertible, his hand extended, his index finger pointed to the sky. "We're number one!" "We're number one!" "We're number one!"

"This caps a wonderful turnaround!" Micki said, as we raced to her home to prepare the postgame party. She was not referring to the game alone. The year before the government had been threatening her and Jack with jail for harboring SLA captive-turned-soldier Patty Hearst.

After Jimmy Carter replaced Gerald Ford as president, the Justice Department dropped the case. Now, the pressure of grand jury subpoenas and indictments was gone, Micki was pregnant, and Bill, after two years of freakish injuries, had led the Trail Blazers to the NBA championship.

Things were settling for me, too. I was finishing a job working for the homeless in Portland's skid row and planning to return to law school the next fall.

My resolution of the previous summer—to stay away from law—had not lasted long. First there had been my new friends, the Scotts. They were warm, caring people, so different from the image the FBI had painted in the press. I *had* to help them.

And then, one fall night, Nancy Sanders called.

"A woman named Nancy Coupez, from Seattle, just received a subpoena," she said. "Her daughter is a member of the George Jackson Brigade.[1] Lezak subpoenaed her to a Portland grand jury—tomorrow—to testify against her own daughter!" Nancy organized thirty people to sit outside the grand jury room in support.

The next morning, Lynn Parkinson (who was now in partner-

---

1. An underground political group.

ship with Ed Jones)[2] was standing in a courthouse corner talking with a distinguished, fiftyish, tall, thin, well-dressed, gray haired woman. They looked concerned, confused about what she should do.

Parkinson saw me. He pulled me into the corner. He tested his ideas. I offered mine. I was hooked. I loved the emotional and intellectual rush. With good legal strategy and community pressure, the government eventually backed down.

And then there was Gerry Elbridge.[3] He was my age, a pleasant young man with a free-flowing beard. Elbridge's dream was to be a teacher.

He had grown up in Spokane, then moved to the Bay Area in 1975, where he had worked in a radical bookstore. He was recruited by a loony ultra-Left group, the Emiliano Zapata Unit of the New World Liberation Front. Before Elbridge figured out what he had walked into (the group was not only crazy but was run by an FBI informant), he helped steal and transport plastic explosives from logging camps in northern Idaho. The explosives detonated Safeway stores in California. The prosecutors had charts and maps, with tags in reds, blues, and yellows, showing where Elbridge had used credit cards on his trip through the Northwest while transporting the goods.

I volunteered 360 hours, writing motions, planning strategy, interviewing witnesses, preparing for trial. Then, on the Saturday before the Monday trial was to begin, the prosecution offered a plea bargain. Elbridge accepted. Six months at Lompoc, a "jail farm" in California, followed by probation.

The law in these cases was exhilarating. I would play with it, pull it apart, put it back together with integrity and professionalism, sculpt it, with a newly born internal logic, culled from the case law. That intellectual exercise actually helped people. In court, the issue would not be whether Elbridge's actions were justifiable; it would be whether he had been indicted according

2. After the *Loud Hawk* dismissal, Tom Steenson moved to The Dalles, in the Oregon desert, to work for Legal Aid. Sheila Lea went to Hawaii, where she lived with and represented marijuana farmers. Ron Schiffman moved into Michael Bonds's office, where he worked in partnership with civil lawyer Pat Watson.

3. Not his real name.

to internally inconsistent requirements of the U.S. Code. It would not be whether Nancy Coupez knew where her fugitive daughter was hiding; it would be whether the government could compel a mother to testify against her daughter. I had fifty cases analyzed for each argument, proving every point of every weakness in the prosecutors' cases.

This was an intellectual war, black and white. I enjoyed pushing the prosecutors two steps back for every three steps they thought they had gained. Soon, they were bound to tire and choose less-contested paths, with other defendants.

"It's an incredible case!" I said, staring across the light oak table at Jeanne Gross, thin, incredibly attractive, athletic, with long tan legs, straight golden hair, and emerald green eyes, wearing a partially transparent Guatemalan shirt and no bra. She was staring back.

We had escaped from an August 1977 legal conference to a quiet Japanese restaurant by the Seattle waterfront. Jeanne, a friend of the Scotts who had just moved to Portland, worked as a paralegal for the Willamette Valley Immigration Project.

"Was it exciting?" she asked, wetting her lips with her tongue as she finished the last syllable of her question.

"Not only were the defendants great people," I said, "but the case itself was *unbelievable*! The cops gave us a great issue when they blew up the evidence. We played it like a chess game. Their whole case unraveled."

"What happened on appeal?" she asked, her eyes wide.

"Nothing," I replied. "After it was argued in the fall of 1976, it just sat. First, I expected a decision any day. Then I forgot about it. Finally, the court ruled. Last week. Two to one, the court of appeals panel upheld Judge Belloni on *everything*, the suppression, the dismissal, everything!"

"You mean, your ideas actually got into an appellate court opinion?" she asked, impressed, leaning forward and smiling, resting her breasts on the table. My heart pumped.

Jeanne and I were inseparable for the rest of the convention. People at meetings, at meals, at parties, everywhere, congratulated Ed Jones, Lynn Parkinson, Ron Schiffman, and me for one of the biggest "wins" in years. Jeanne watched, impressed. And she was impressed that I was a friend of Lew Gurwitz's, whose plight was a topic at the convention. He had advised a group of Indians in Idaho to fish as was their right, recognized by treaties signed with the United States. They had been arrested, Gurwitz with them. The prosecutors said they might go after his law license.

Life, love, and friends were wonderful. I felt like I belonged. Then, as if to make me complete, for pure joy, the *Loud Hawk* case returned. The government had filed a Petition for Rehearing with Suggestion for Rehearing *En Banc*. The prosecutors wanted the entire Ninth Circuit Court of Appeals to reconsider the panel's ruling.

I raced through the petition, excited, afraid there might be ideas I could not counter. There was no argument I could not rip to shreds. I smiled, but I also cursed. "Fuckers!" I mumbled, as I read. The prosecutors' idea of "truth" meant nothing more than tactical convenience.

Before Judge Belloni, they had argued that the dynamite was so dangerous that they *had* to destroy it. When we proved that it was not so dangerous, they argued that the destruction was incomplete: some of the dynamite had been retained in scrapings from the wrappers the FBI saved. Their last-minute chemical analysis of the scrapings foiled that theory. Essential ingredients of dynamite were missing.

Before the appellate panel, the government had argued its third position: that the destruction had been in "good faith" and, therefore, should be excused. Judges Shirley Hufstedler and Walter Ely were not persuaded. Appellate courts had warned prosecutors that their cases would be dismissed if valuable evidence was destroyed.

The Petition for Rehearing had the government's fourth position: "We didn't do it. It was all the state cops' doing." What the federal government had taken credit for repeatedly, for years, as a reasonable act, it now swore it had nothing to do with. The idea was preposterous, both factually and legally.

FBI agents had swarmed onto the desert days before the explosives were destroyed. They had escorted Fettig to the gravel pit, taken pictures, accepted wrappers as evidence. Who would believe that the destruction was some wild lark by the state police, with forty FBI agents nearby?

The law said, even if that was how it happened, it did not matter. If a defendant's constitutional rights were violated by police, it made no difference where their paychecks came from.

The prosecutor's position was desperate, pathetic, and embarrassing. It also violated a basic rule of law: arguments not presented in the lower court cannot be made, for the first time, on appeal.

I read the petition again. My adrenaline rushed. More than anything else in the world, I wanted, right then, to stand before the appellate court, demonstrating in fiery oratory why the government had its collective head up its collective ass.

A few weeks later, Jeanne handed me the telephone at my end of her clawfoot bathtub. Bubble bath came off my hand, onto the receiver.

"You're not going to believe this, Ken," Michael Bonds said. "The Ninth Circuit has just withdrawn the panel's decision and voted to hear reargument."

"What!" I said, standing up, extinguishing two of Jeanne's rainbow candles with soapy water.

"What about the rules, Mike?" I asked, feeling betrayed. "I checked them myself. The court doesn't accept responses to petitions for rehearing. But they promise to ask for replies if they are seriously considering a petition. The court violated its own rules, Mike. They didn't give us a chance!"

"Apparently, the rules don't apply to this case," he said.

I spent the next two days at Bonds's office. The immediate problem was that none of the lawyers had spoken to any of the defendants in over a year. It was now October 1977. Kenny Loud Hawk was in Pine Ridge, without a telephone, drinking, the last we heard. Russ Redner, rumor had it, was in Nevada, newly remarried. And Dennis and KaMook Banks were living in California, where South Dakota's extradition request was still unresolved. Governor Jerry Brown had refused to send Banks back.[4] South Dakota was suing to overturn his decision.

---

4. Brown refused extradition because Banks's life was in danger. But he was certainly influenced by the reams of signatures that had been collected on petitions, many circulated by Jim Jones's parishioners.

Rumor also had it that Brown's decision was, in part, a payback to attorney William Kunstler—whose threats supposedly stopped a newspaper from print-

I called Dennis Banks. "Don't panic yet," I said. "There's no telling how long it will take to hear the case. They might decide in our favor. Even if they don't, we can ask the Supreme Court to review it. I don't think they would, but that will take time, too. No need to worry yet."

"Right-o," he said. "Ken, let me tell you about the Sun Dance we had here this year. It was the first one . . ."

He was more relaxed than I.

I pounded my typewriter, in polemical frenzy, writing a motion to reconsider. The panel's ruling was logical, correct, exact; the government's petition was spurious, erroneous, possibly unethical.

The government had complained that it had not been "forewarned" that refusal to go to trial on May 12, 1976, would lead to a dismissal with prejudice. "Forewarning" was required by *United States v. Simmons,* a case decided after Belloni's dismissal. How could Belloni have been expected to follow new guidelines before they were even announced? Besides, the government knew the case was being dismissed with prejudice. It had had its notice of appeal ready to file. Now it was telling the court of appeals that it had no idea. Liars!

"Watch out for the salsa," the waiter said. "It's a zinger." The Stepping Stone Café was a converted ground floor of a corner house in Northwest Portland. It fused '60s Bay Area hippie chic with '50s New York formica, chrome, and red plastic. Most of the waiters wore earrings. Most of the waitresses did not.

The café served fresh juices, home-baked breads, omelets, homefries (with or without green onions), pancakes, waffles, herbal tea, down-to-earth coffee, and a constant supply of salsa. No FBI agent could hide there. Even the *Loud Hawk* legal team looked out of place, in suits and ties, despite our beards and long hair. Roberts, Bonds, Jones, Parkinson, Schiffman, and I sat at a circular booth near the front window.

It was May 18, 1978. In October 1977, the court of appeals had denied our motion asking for reconsideration of its decision to rehear *Loud Hawk*. It heard argument and then, for almost five

---

ing a story alleging that Brown was gay, right before the 1976 California presidential primary.

months, was silent. In March, it ordered Judge Belloni to hold an evidentiary hearing and make findings on two questions: "1) Did any agent of the federal government participate in the destruction of the evidence?; 2) What prejudice, if any, was suffered by the defendants as a result of the destruction of the evidence?"

That hearing was now an hour and a half away. We had eaten. I was nervous. The lawyers spoke only of "war stories," recounting cleverness in past victories, like sparring tap dancers engrossed in a challenge.

"What's the plan for today?" I finally interrupted.

Silence.

"I've asked Ron McCreary—the witness who didn't testify in 1976—to meet us at the courthouse," Jones said.

"I sent Chelsea out to Ontario last week to investigate," Bonds added. "But his report doesn't help."

No one had prepared.

"I got a plan," Bonds said, after a long, awkward silence. He stood and grabbed the check. "Let's go in there and kick some ass!"

"Right on!" Roberts added. "Let's wipe their asses in it!"

I expected disaster.

None of the defendants were in the packed courtroom.

"Man, can you take care of that without me?" Redner had asked Parkinson, when he had heard the news through the Indian grapevine and called.

Motions were filed, orders signed, defendants excused.

The lawyers sat at the counsel table. Judge Belloni walked in and motioned Turner and Roberts to his bench.

"We're going into chambers," Roberts whispered, back at the counsel table. "Fettig has a brain tumor, and he's afraid he'll pass out or seize or something. I agreed to take his testimony in private."

Fettig looked horrible. He had aged twenty years. After the 1976 dismissal, he had had a brain tumor excised. Now it had returned. Surgery was postponed so that he could testify again.

In chambers, Fettig carefully lowered himself into a green wingback leather chair.

"Mr. Fettig," Roberts inquired gently, "who asked you to retain the dynamite wrappers?"

"Nobody specifically asked me," Fettig said, slumping further. "I took seven for our office and gave seven to FBI agent Dave Milam."

"If Mr. Milam had told you, 'Mr. Fettig, I want you to take those cases and transport them to a storage facility,' would you have done that?

"Yes, sir."

"If any of the other FBI agents there said, 'Look, we need some of these sticks of dynamite for evidence in this case,' would you have retained them?"

"Yes, sir, I would have."

Agent Milam, in fact, had ordered Fettig to hold onto other evidence from the motor home. Fettig's official report said the FBI "assisted in the destruction of the dynamite."

Satisfied that he had proved an FBI role in the destruction, Roberts stopped. Fettig was pale, out of breath.

Bomber Bill Fettig shuffled next to Roberts, on the way out of chambers. "Thank you, sir, for allowing me to testify privately," he said.

Roberts put his hand on the weakened, pasty-looking man's shoulder. "Sure," he said. "You get better, now." Fettig smiled.

Roberts and I walked into the courtroom together, as Fettig detoured down a side corridor. "That's the last we'll see of that guy!" Roberts whispered, then laughed.

I smiled back but thought of my father, who had died the November before from his own slow illness. I felt guilty. If *Loud Hawk* ever went to trial, the Indians would certainly be better off with Fettig dead. No one else could explain the destruction of the alleged dynamite step by step. But did that mean that I should want him dead so our clients could have a tactical advantage? Roberts apparently thought so. If I did not, did that mean I had less zeal, less commitment to my clients? Would I be an inferior lawyer, not willing to go to any length the law allowed to get my client off?

I forced myself to focus on the witness stand. Lt. McCollum, Fettig's boss, was testifying. It was official policy to destroy dynamite, he said.

"Where was it written?" he was asked.

"Nowhere," he admitted.

Ken Griffiths, the trooper who stopped Brando's motor home in Ontario, was next. In 1976, he had "resigned" from the Oregon State Police. He now drove trucks in Montana. His answers and those of the next witness, Corp. Clayton Kramer, painted the desert with FBI agents.

"The dynamite was on a conveyor belt to destruction," Judge Belloni concluded after Kramer left the stand. "One word by a member of the FBI would have stopped that conveyor belt!"

Surely the court of appeals could not ignore all the testimony and all that which followed, from Agents Milam, Hancock, and O'Rourke.

My anger at the lawyers, and fear of disaster from their lack of preparation, was replaced with pride. Maybe it was their good seat-of-the-pants skills? Or maybe there really was something magical about this case? It only got better.

Our dynamite expert, McCreary, was bulky. He dropped like a weight onto the witness chair. He had stubby fingers, like sausages. His left ring finger really was a stub. Somehow, he had either cut or blown it off just below the middle knuckle. He wore a college ring there, with a large, purple, inset stone. The setting looked the size of a napkin ring.

McCreary had been a civil engineer, specializing in heavy construction, drilling and blasting rock. He had detonated bridges. He had built tunnels, among them the tunnel that linked downtown Portland to its western suburbs.

"How difficult would it have been for Fettig or Milam or any of the other agents to check the stability of the dynamite?" Roberts asked McCreary.

"All they'd have had to do was look at it, taste it, touch it, and smell it," McCreary said. "And if it wasn't stable, that just means it might not have been as explosive as it once was."

Roberts was honing in on the second issue the Court of Appeals had asked about—prejudice to the defense from the destruction of the dynamite. He approached McCreary, carrying pictures the FBI had taken of the dynamite's destruction.

"Please look at the picture marked Government's 14," Roberts asked, handing McCreary the exhibit.

McCreary held it in his four-fingered hand.

"Now," Roberts continued, "does that look like three sticks of dynamite to you?

"Yes," McCreary agreed, "it does."

"Do you see the area on which those three sticks sit?"

"Yes, I do."

"Now," Roberts said, "if you were told that the dynamite had been detonated on that area of ground, would you expect to see rocks and gravel flying through the air?"

"A great deal," McCreary concurred.

"All right, sir. Now, let me show you a series of pictures on Government's 15, calling your attention to the top left and top right photographs."

McCreary put the single picture down on the oak railing to the right of his chair and picked up the light blue 8 x 11 sheet with four pictures stapled onto it.

"Do the pictures appear to be the detonation of dynamite?"

"No, sir," he answered matter of factly, "they do not."

The prosecutors and the judge sat forward.

"Would you tell me why, sir?" Roberts asked softly.

"The abundance of smoke, the lack of any flying debris, brush, rocks, sand, and silt."

"Thank you, sir. Now, looking at the picture labeled 'Government 14,' I see that there's something light colored wrapped around the three sticks. Can you tell me what that appears to be?"

"It appears to be primer cord, instantaneous detonating fuse."

"Now, looking at that picture, if someone were to have taken those three sticks and used a delay time fuse and a blasting cap the way they're wrapped together, set off the fuse, and the dynamite itself did not detonate, but the blasting cap went off and the primer cord went off, would the result be consistent with the photographs that you see on Government's 15 showing the smoke rising?"

"Yes, it is consistent."

Roberts had just established prejudice. If the dynamite was unable to explode, it was not illegal. He sat down.

"If the dynamite didn't detonate," U.S. Attorney Turner asked, "there wouldn't have been any sound, would there?" Turner knew the FBI agents had heard an explosion.

"Primer cord sounds like a battery of rifles going off. It scares the daylights out of anyone within half a mile."

"If the dynamite didn't detonate, wouldn't there be some residue left?" Turner knew the agents had not seen any.

"No, the primer cord would destroy the sticks and would burn the paper and simply scatter the insides—which are like peanut butter—all over the county."

Turner approached, inspecting a picture, his demeanor now changed from the meekness of his two prior questions.

"Mr. McCreary," he attacked, "what's this spot in this picture, right here." He pointed to a spot of light, a flame, and pounded on it three times with his index finger.

McCreary did not answer at once. He took the photo, put it on the witness box railing, reached into his interior suit pocket, extracted a magnifying glass the size of a small pancake, and picked up the picture again. He moved the glass toward the photograph. Then he moved it closer to his face. He reoriented the picture, twisting it, trying to maximize the light on his selected field. He squinted.

"The area seems to have a lot of sagebrush," he finally said. "The spot looks like something combusting. It is not dynamite, however."

"Well, then," Turner asked, snidely, "what is it?"

McCreary looked up. "It looks to me like a burning bush, Mr. Turner," he said.

Judge Belloni interrupted the gallery's laughter as Turner sat down, and McCreary slipped the magnifying glass back into his suit pocket. "Mr. McCreary," the judge asked, "as I understand it, dynamite is an explosive substance, such as nitroglycerin, mixed up with peanut butter and put in a tube?"

"Yes."

"And if the explosive has leaked out and is no longer there, you've just got a tube of peanut butter, it wouldn't be dynamite at all; is that what you're saying?"

"It's not quite that complete. When the nitroglycerin is gone, you have lost the punch that makes it destroy things. And so you have something that would probably not have enough oomph to detonate."

"I can't tell you what's going on with *Loud Hawk*," David, a twenty-five-year-old, clean-shaven lawyer told me over dinner at a Hunan restaurant in San Francisco. "Let's just say that every clerk who's been at the Ninth Circuit Court of Appeals during the last two years has worked on it."

David was also a clerk at the court and the housemate of my girlfriend Jeanne Gross's friend, Sharon. We were visiting them. David's information was not hopeful. It suggested that the case had been consumed in a power struggle between "liberal" and "conservative" wings of the appellate court.

It was the latest bad news that month—February 1979.

Two years before, Peltier had been extradited to the United States from Canada, had stood trial for killing the two FBI agents, and had been convicted. It was later discovered that affidavits the FBI used as part of its effort to extradite him were perjured.

His trial had been a sham. Judge McManus had been taken off the case. No one knew why. The new judge, Benson, refused to allow the jury to hear the "self-defense" evidence that led to Butler and Robideau's acquittal on the same charges.

Leonard Peltier was sentenced to two consecutive life sentences. His appeal was denied. Peltier petitioned the U.S. Supreme Court to review his conviction.

John Trudell, one of AIM's most articulate spokesmen, led a protest for Peltier on the steps of the Supreme Court Building. As a symbol, he burned an American flag. Hours later, his wife, Tina, Tina's mother, and their three young children were incinerated when their house burned, on Nevada's Duck Valley reservation. The FBI, according to Trudell, would not investigate.

CHAPTER 20

A NEW ROLE

I was nervous. For three and a half years as a law student, I had worked on Lynn Parkinson's and Michael Bonds's criminal cases. Black Panthers, antinuclear protestors, community organizers, drunk drivers, murderers, prostitutes, conspirators, con artists. I rationalized representing the ordinary criminals as practice for the extraordinary ones.

My first solo appearances—in three misdemeanor proceedings under a rule that allowed students to try cases—had gone well. I had not slept the night before each case, and my palms sweated in court. But I was prepared. Finally I was the one who stood and argued. All three cases were dismissed before trial, on my legal motions.

My first civil case was also my first full trial, with witnesses, evidence, and opening and closing statements. A household of political activists faced eviction. Gerry Elbridge, Steve Queener, Sherry Lainoff, Sheila Rubin, Glenna Hayes, and four others lived in an old gray Victorian building on a corner lot on SE Taylor Street. They complained because they had no heat. The landlord refused to fix the furnace. They complained again. The landlord threatened to evict them. They joined the Portland Tenant Union. The landlord started eviction proceedings. I represented the tenants and filed countercharges against the landlord.

As the trial began, supporters chanted outside the courthouse and marched in the park across the street, repeating slogans and holding placards. A dozen television and newspaper reporters attended the demonstration and the legal proceedings. After two days of acrimonious trial, the tenants won some of their claims, lost others, and were awarded money damages. After the verdict, the judge, Donald Londer, invited me into his chambers.

"Kenny," he said, "I liked your clients, but I just couldn't give you everything you wanted."

I nodded. The law was not as balanced as it could have been, and Londer had been exceedingly fair, even though he had given the landlord her house back.

"This wasn't like the landmark case I tried in 1976, you know," he said, needing to atone further. "The L&M case—you've heard of it—the one that established tenant rights in Oregon?"

I nodded. Londer was sympathetic to tenants. According to courthouse gossip, his seventy-five-year-old mother had once been evicted.

"You wouldn't believe the condition of that L&M house," he continued, leaning back in his chair, pointing up, his robe unbuttoned.

"There was a hole straight through the bathroom floor. It was right above the kitchen! And there were dozens of rotting old mattresses in the basement."

"Judge," I interrupted, "that house wasn't on SW Hood Street, by any chance?"

"As I recall," he said, looking surprised, "it was."

"I lived in that house," I said, "just months before the L&M case must have began. Have any idea why there were so many mattresses?"

"No," he answered. "That never came out in trial. As I recall, no one knew."

"Judge," I said, smiling, "mattresses stop bullets. Let me tell you a story."

That was the second time in three days the old defense house had come up. Micki Scott and her friend, Eva Kutas, had been sitting at the large round dining room table in the Scotts' new home on NW 24th Avenue.

"Take a look at these," Kutas said, her hands on a stack of papers. A Hungarian-born political activist, Kutas had been convicted in 1974 of harboring an escapee from the Oregon State Penitentiary. Her appeals had taken years and been denied. She had gone to jail and then, with the recommendation of her sentencing judge, was freed and accepted to law school.

The papers, her FBI files, had been released under the Freedom of Information Act. Her supporters had been spied on. I skimmed through the documents. Three inches in, I found one with a title in the upper left-hand corner: "Subject—Frank Giese,[1] Extremist."

The name of the source was blotted out, but it had come from an FBI informant, who had attended political meetings in early 1976, including one about Dr. Giese, whose case was then on appeal. Kutas had been at some of the same meetings, according to the informant.

On the third page, the document abruptly shifted from Giese's case to *Loud Hawk et al.* It detailed defense committee meetings, defense plans, who had attended (including lawyers), who had not attended, what was discussed. In part, the FBI document read,

> On 1/27/76, a visit was made to 3435 SW Hood; however, no individual, previously described as heavyset and wearing a red and black, large checkered flannel shirt, was observed. LENA REDNER was present and was being interviewed by reporters for the Portland Scribe [a community newspaper]. JOANNA LOHNES is known by sight, and she was present at VERNON BELLECOURT's presentation at 3435 SW Hood on Saturday, 1/24/76. She was also present at the benefit dinner given by the SCOTTs for LOUD HAWK and REDNER. JOHN BONN stopped at 3435 SW Hood and picked up numerous pamphlets explaining American Indian struggles.
>
> The occupants of 3435 SW Hood do not allow people above the ground floor; furthermore, there is limited access to the residence as the front door is kept locked.

The document even contained a detailed diagram of the defense house, showing how the downstairs, including the bedroom, was configured.

"The fuckers!" I yelled. "Look at this, Micki."

"You're not surprised, are you?" she asked, seeing her name listed as well.

"No," I said, "but this is *dynamite*. The prosecutors *swore* there were no informants in the defense camp. This report *comes* from one. If the court of appeals returns the case, this paper will blow it apart!"

---

1. Frank Giese was a professor at Portland State University. He had been convicted of conspiracy to bomb a Portland ROTC station during the Vietnam War.

I graduated from law school in May 1979 and passed the July bar exam. Then I flew to New York. My mother had cancer of the fallopian tubes. Her doctor hoped he had cut it all out. I was scared.

Michael Bonds, who had met my mother at graduation, called every few days to see how she was.

"I've got some bad news," Michael said this time. "The court of appeals just reversed."

The decision came in the mail. I sat on my mother's Brooklyn screen porch while she napped upstairs and read it again and again. I was enraged.

Judge Ozell Trask of the Ninth Circuit Court of Appeals said the federal authorities were not responsible for the destruction of the evidence since Bomber Bill Fettig—a state employee—had lit the match. But that part of the opinion did not "count." A majority had not agreed with him.

The opinion was broken into section and subsection. Different judges signed each part. Some parts, commanding a majority, had the force of law. Others, like Trask's, were merely "dictum," words.

Judge Anthony Kennedy (who would later be appointed justice of the U.S. Supreme Court) wrote the largest part. His counted. Yes, the government should not have destroyed the evidence. Yes, they had been forewarned not to do it. Yes, they should have notified court and counsel. Yes, there was no excuse for the destruction. And, yes, there was prejudice to the defendants' right to a fair trial. Almost enough prejudice to dismiss. Not quite enough. Just almost.

Judges Ely, Hug, and Hufstedler dissented. They accused their colleagues of bad faith.

Are the district court's specific findings of prejudice from the destruction of evidence clearly erroneous?[2] The simple answer is "no." In

2. Appellate courts generally cannot "find facts" because, unlike trial judges, they cannot hear and see witnesses and thus measure credibility by demeanor. Appellate courts are supposed to accept the trial court's findings of fact, unless they are "clearly erroneous."

seeking to avoid this result, the majority has devised a hypothetical scale on which it weighs non-competing interests against one another, discovers that prejudice is not prejudice, and thereby announces a result in favor of the government. . . . Three counts of the indictment were based on possession of a "destructive device." The material destroyed included the very substance that the government charged was the "destructive device." . . . The district court found that the destruction of the substance was prejudicial to the defendants. . . . All appellate inquiry should end with "affirmed." That result is unsatisfactory to the majority, and therefore, it is required to explain why the fact of prejudice is nevertheless not prejudice justifying suppression. . . . The majority . . . has inexplicably required the defendants to come up with proof that the government itself has destroyed.

The suppression order was only half the battle. After reinstating the dynamite counts, the majority looked to the gun charges, the ones the government had refused to bring to trial in May 1976, despite two court orders.

The court found no excuse for the government's actions. All the judges agreed that the prosecutors had created "unnecessary delay" and that Judge Belloni had been correct to dismiss. Nevertheless, a majority overturned the "prejudice" sanction, citing *United States v. Simmons*, the case decided after Belloni's dismissal, which held that prosecutors should be told what sanctions the court planned to impose for the government's prospective illegal behavior.

Belloni's only option had been to dismiss with prejudice. The prosecutors did not need warning; they already knew. Lezak had even walked into court on May 12, 1976, with a notice of appeal from a with prejudice dismissal in his hand, already signed.

But, the majority wrote, "It is the trial court that is required to warn the prosecutor, not vice versa."

The dissenters blasted the majority for distorting the law to rule for the government. In Judge Ely's words, the appellate arguments had been a "futile exercise."

On March 3, 1980, the U.S. Supreme Court announced that it would not accept our petition to review the court of appeals decision in *United States v. Loud Hawk*. No one was surprised. The high court takes only a few cases each year—and is more

likely to take cases it wants to overturn. I was scared for Banks.
Vic Atiyeh, a Republican, was Oregon's new governor. If Dennis
Banks had to appear for trial, Atiyeh would extradite him to
South Dakota.

Then things got worse. Judge Belloni either felt he could no
longer be fair to the prosecutors or was tired of the government
accusing him of favoring Indians. He took himself off the case.

For two weeks, Parkinson, Bonds, Schiffman, and I worried.
What if Judge James Burns, the presiding judge and a conservative whose greatest pleasure was sentencing people, took the
case? Everyone would end up in jail.

Meanwhile, we had problems finding all the defendants. It
took ten days phoning into Indian Country to locate Russ Redner. He had just left his second wife, Cindy, and their baby,
Tsoets-Up-Luht.

"We can waive your appearances at the first few hearings," I
told him, "but you'll have to come here by summer. If we don't
get it dismissed, trial should be in early fall."

"Shit," he said. His voice was despondent.

"This case keeps fucking up my life!" he yelled. "I thought it
might be coming back, when I read in the newspaper about the
Supreme Court not taking it. So I quit my job and went to see my
brother, on my way to Portland, to see you guys.

"I just got out of the hospital. My brother came home drunk
one night. He was so shitfaced, he didn't even know who I was!
He broke a beer bottle and flashed it at me. He gouged my eye
out. They just put in some goddamn glass eyeball. It just floats
around. I'm afraid to let anyone see me. Can you believe it? They
didn't even have a brown one. I got this one goddamned blue
eyeball!"

Dennis Banks asked me to be his Portland lawyer, even though I
was just out of law school. I would have been scared if I were
alone. But I was part of a team and proud that Banks and the
others wanted me. I had ghost-written all the papers in the last
year, including the Supreme Court petitions. I felt confident.
The love I had for the case and the defendants left no room for
insecurity, especially since Dennis Roberts would come for trial if
the case was not settled or dismissed.

I took a week from my new law practice and read every word of the 2,500-page *Loud Hawk* record, making notes in twenty legal pads spread over my office floor. I tracked every motion, tied every unresolved question to every appropriate page in the court file.

I carried boxes of paper home. I spent nights on the couch at the office. I was single-minded, a zealot studying a religion. I did not need the notes. I could picture every key sentence, every potential opening, every ill-conceived government admission.

I was crafting a role for myself on the *Loud Hawk* team. Everyone else had theirs. Ed Jones was the easygoing strategist, the games player, devising intricate plans and playing them with an innocent smile, beguiling the prosecutors.

Ron Schiffman was the impassioned realist. He expressed real hurt at every one of the prosecutors' misdeeds. And in 1976, when Redner had seen the case as a war rather than a legal proceeding, Schiffman had screamed at him, "Face up to it; you're going to be convicted and spend at least ten years in jail!" Sobered, Redner abandoned his plan to disrupt a pretrial hearing.

Lynn Parkinson was the hard-core political zealot. On good days, he was exceedingly clever and on bad days, paranoid. He was a good match for his client, Russ Redner.

Michael Bonds was the pure lawyer, "the natural." He could convince jurors of anything, even when hung over during his cyclic bouts with alcohol.

Lew Gurwitz and Dennis Roberts, as out-of-town counsel, also had roles. Gurwitz was the "crazy," the one with graying, flowing hair, who had played a part in many of the post–Wounded Knee Indian legal battles and could infuse that history into our Oregon court, not caring if he angered prosecutors in the process.

Dennis Roberts was "the heavy," the feared, consummate, smooth-as-silk trial lawyer, who commanded respect.

We needed someone in control of the details and dazzling on the law. I became the "keeper of the record" and "the scholar."

As soon as I digested every paper filed and every word spoken since November 14, 1975, I went to the law library. I needed new ideas. I started with the most recent cases, "slip sheets," decisions of the court of appeals too recent to be included in law reporters.

Within five minutes, I was standing in front of the copying machine, astonished, rejoicing at what I had found.

"Is everything okay?" Jackie Jurkins, the law librarian, asked as I was nearly dancing at the copier.

"You bet!" I said. "Jackie, I've got *Loud Hawk* won!"

Bonds, Parkinson, Schiffman, Jones, and I sat on large flat rocks by the Willamette River, across the street from my Milwaukie, Oregon, office, just south of the Portland city line. Barges and fishing boats passed by in the distance.

"James Griffin was an Arizona Roofer's Union financial secretary who was suspected of embezzling union funds," I explained. "The Department of Labor's investigation led to an indictment. But it also produced evidence of a crime not charged—that Griffin had defrauded the Veterans' Administration as well. Handwritten notes that were essential for defending the union embezzlement charge were destroyed by the government. When he learned of this, Griffin's lawyer filed motions to dismiss. Then the government got a new indictment, which also charged the fraud on the Veterans' Administration.

"Griffin alleged vindictive prosecution—that the increased charges were in retaliation for his motion. The trial judge threw out the union embezzlement charges because the notes were destroyed but refused to dismiss the Veterans' Administration fraud charges. Griffin appealed.

"*United States v. Griffin*, decided two weeks ago, resolved two issues. First, it permitted Griffin to raise his claim of vindictive prosecution before trial.[3] Second, the court ruled that once a defendant is charged and thereafter asserts any right, there is a presumption that the prosecution acted vindictively if new or increased charges are brought. In the court's words, an 'appearance of vindictiveness' is created. The burden, then, shifts to the prosecution to explain its actions, with reasons that 'dispel the

---

3. Most issues can be appealed to a higher court by a defendant only after conviction. That way, if a defendant is acquitted, an unnecessary appeal is avoided and time is saved. The only clear exceptions to this rule, before the *Griffin* case, were pretrial appeals about bail, double jeopardy, and congressional immunity issues, which are allowed before trial.

appearance of vindictiveness.'

"In *Griffin*, the fraud investigation wasn't completed until after the motion was filed. The appearance of vindictiveness was answered. Griffin had to stand trial."

"What does that have to do with us?" Bonds asked.

"Our gun charges are no longer dismissed with prejudice, thanks to the Ninth Circuit. But they are still dismissed. The government is going to have to reindict. If they make any change, even a word, and we can show that it increases the charges, we've won. The burden of proof is on the government. Either we get a dismissal or we appeal. Either way, we avoid trial, and Dennis doesn't have to come here. And given the time it takes the Court of Appeals to do anything, maybe the government will give up?"

"Good plan," Bonds said.

After I gave the other lawyers copies of the *Griffin* case and explained it further, Schiffman, Parkinson, and Jones left. Bonds and I stayed by the water and talked.

"I want to hold this and Eva's FBI report about the informant at the defense house back for a while," I said, tossing a rock into the river. "Let's see if we can get the case dismissed some other way and only use these gems if we have to."

"I agree," Bonds said. "Let's get a feel for Redden first."

"What's he like anyway?" I asked.

James A. Redden, a newly appointed judge, had just been assigned to replace Judge Belloni on *Loud Hawk*.

"Well," Bonds said, "he's a liberal Democrat, a Carter appointee, a former Oregon attorney general. But he hasn't been inside a courtroom in years. We ought to be able to run him around a bit. But he's a good guy. Years ago, at a bar convention, I got really drunk. I was outside throwing up over the balcony. I heard a noise and looked over. Redden was ten feet away, getting some air. We went out drinking the next night."

"Maybe he'd be receptive to a polished, straight legal motion seeking dismissal, something scholarly?" I suggested. "I have Ed and Lynn working on the motions that were unresolved in '76, and Ron is seeing if the law's changed on anything that was decided. I'm looking for new things, and I've got an idea that I didn't want to mention to the others yet."

Bonds looked up.

"What was the legal basis of the stop of Brando's motor home and the station wagon?" I asked. "As I turn it over and over again, there wasn't any. Trooper Griffiths had no knowledge of any potential crime. All he knew, and forgot, was that the FBI wanted intelligence if the vehicles were spotted. The All Points Bulletin specifically told him *not* to stop the vehicles. The Fourth Amendment requires there be some legal ground before a police officer can stop a citizen. Where was Griffith's 'founded suspicion' that anyone inside the motor home was doing anything illegal?"

"Good question," Bonds said.

CHAPTER 21

✛ ✛ ✛

VINDICTIVE PROSECUTION

THE clerk pounded the gavel. Judge James A. Redden appeared on the bench, like a jack-in-the-box. He closed the chambers door behind him and sat in Judge Belloni's chair in Judge Belloni's courtroom, four years to the hour after Belloni's May 12, 1976, dismissal.

Judge Redden was of average height, slightly broad, slightly bald, and surprisingly friendly. He actually smiled. He had not been on the bench long enough to acquire the appropriate judicial scowl.

"Your Honor," we argued, "Judge Belloni dismissed the gun counts when the government refused to go to trial, and the Ninth Circuit Court of Appeals left these counts dismissed for a reason. The Ninth Circuit certainly had the power to reinstate the charges if it had wanted to. But it only overturned the with prejudice aspect of the dismissal for technical reasons. If the government wants to proceed on those charges, it has to return to the grand jury and get a new indictment."

"I agree," Judge Redden said.

Turner was visibly angered. His words were choppy and his face red. He argued that the judge should simply reinstate the gun counts.

"I really can't see any purpose to be served by resubmitting the matter to the grand jury," Turner whined. "I don't know why we should have to go back to the grand jury!"

I was glad Turner was angry. Returning to the grand jury meant more work for him—finding witnesses, presenting his case. Maybe that was why, a month later, in June 1980, the new indictment he filed was so different from the one we had worked with for five years.

My worst fear had been that Turner would reindict from the

old indictment word for word. Instead, there were now *four* dynamite charges, not three (two alleging illegal bombs made with electrical blasting caps, two alleging illegal bombs made with nonelectrical blasting caps). That meant a potential of ten more years jail time for everyone, including Leonard Peltier, who was still listed as a defendant. And the gun charges had changed from an allegation of "interstate transportation of firearms" to "receipt of firearms that had once traveled in interstate commerce," which was easier to prove.

Turner also added another ten-year charge against KaMook Banks. KaMook's September 1975 Kansas gun charges had been pending on November 14, 1975.[1] It was, technically, a felony to possess firearms while under federal indictment.

"This *is* vindictive," I told Michael Bonds, as I read him Turner's new indictment over the telephone, ecstatic. "I don't even have to construct a complex argument proving increased charges; they *are* increased."

"The fuckers!" Bonds said. "After five years of unblemished behavior, the government tries to give them more jail time. The assholes! When was the last time anyone was ever indicted for possessing firearms while under indictment? Never!"

"The beauty is," I responded, "that even though the government will deny retaliating, it doesn't matter. *Griffin* creates a presumption of vindictiveness. It's Turner's burden to explain the new charges. I can't wait to draft the motion, then see him try!"

"Call your first witness," Judge Redden ordered Charles Turner at an evidentiary hearing in June 1980.

"The government calls Sidney Rubin," Turner replied.

A middle-aged man of medium height, with curly hair and wearing a light sports jacket, entered the courtroom at a deliberate pace. He sat in the witness chair comfortably, as if he had done so many times before. Rubin was the government's key witness for our Motion to Dismiss for Lack of Founded Suspicion. We argued that Griffiths had had no legally sufficient reason to stop the motor home.

---

1. She later pleaded guilty and received probation, which she had completed successfully by 1980.

As Rubin sat down, Lew Gurwitz and I flashed glances of recognition. Rubin had been the man I had hounded at Peltier's extradition hearing in Vancouver, British Columbia, four summers before. He was, indeed, an FBI agent from Seattle. He knew informants "A" and "B," whose identity the government would not disclose.

We listened, intrigued, as a new part of the story unfolded. "A" had told Rubin in late October 1975 that Dennis Banks was "in the Seattle metropolitan area and surrounding community." In early November 1975, "A" had told Rubin that Banks was staying at "the John Chiquiti residence at the Port Madison Indian Reservation, Kitsap County, Washington State."

"A" had said that Banks was using "a light-colored motor home and was planning to depart in a very short period of time to travel around the United States." "A" had given the FBI information on at least one hundred other occasions, and, according to Rubin, the data "proved reliable."

"B" had told Rubin in early November 1975 that Leonard Peltier was at Chiquiti's residence, planning to travel in a "large recreational home with New Mexico license plates." "B" had given information twenty times and each time had proven reliable.

How did Rubin confirm any of this? "I flew over the Chiquiti property on November 6, 1975, and took pictures," he said. "Below was a recreational vehicle and a light-colored station wagon, hidden in a thickly wooded part of the property. I flew over again on November 8, 1975. The vehicles were still there."

Turner showed him exhibits marked 3, 4, and 5.

"Yes," Rubin said, "those are the pictures I took. That same day agents went on the property, sneaking through the woods. They got the license plate of the motor home. New Mexico A8969.

"We flew over again on November 11, 1975. The vehicles were still there. They were still there on November 12th. On the 13th, however, they were gone. Here are the pictures."

Schiffman was seething throughout Rubin's testimony. "Your Honor!" he interrupted. "I sat in the office of the United States Attorney almost five years ago and was handed a pile of photographs, and I was told that this was all the photographs in the case. And today, nearly five years later, here are photographs that I have never been shown!

"Your Honor," Schiffman continued, "the flyover, Mr. Rubin's testimony, even Mr. Rubin's name, they're all news. I hope the Court can understand that we've lost faith that we will be treated fairly by the U.S. Attorney's Office. There's been a long history."

Redden, angered, criticized the government. But being new to the case, he did not impose sanctions.

At recess, Schiffman, Jones, Bonds, Gurwitz, Parkinson, and I huddled in an empty anteroom.

"Rubin raises a lot of questions," I said. "The FBI watched this little entourage for weeks before Griffith stopped it 500 miles away. If the FBI thought Banks and Peltier were at this Chiquiti place, why didn't it arrest them there?"

"Don't know," Jones said. "And if there were overflights, did that mean that 'A' and 'B' weren't part of the group, or did it mean they were part of the group, and the FBI was keeping an eye on their own people?"

"Why weren't the vehicles stopped along the way?" I asked. "Had the FBI lost them? Or were they waiting to stop them someplace else?"

"Shit," Parkinson said. "I always thought they planned to ambush them in the Idaho desert. The feds could have 'shot them escaping,' and there'd be no witnesses."

"I don't know," I said. "Rubin said something about them planning to travel around the United States. Maybe the ambush was planned for South Dakota? The press there would have been better—'Indians caught with guns and bombs.'"

"Can't wait to go after Rubin, that motherfucker," Bonds said, slapping his hands together.

Gurwitz nodded. He was almost salivating.

"I know the temptation, guys," Jones said. "But I think we ought to leave well enough alone. It's close. Given the way the record is, Redden may actually dismiss."

"He's right," I argued. "Look, it's the government's burden.[2] When founded suspicion is based on informants, two things have

---

2. If the informant information was reliable and sufficient to give a "founded suspicion" that people inside the motor home were committing a crime, Griffiths could stop the vehicle, even though he, personally, did not know that information. Legally, it was sufficient that other law enforcement officers did.

to be shown. Was the information sufficient to create a 'founded suspicion of crime'? And, was the informant reliable?

"Rubin testified that 'A' told him that Banks was at Chiquiti's in a motor home. That's a conclusion. Where are the facts? How did 'A' know? Would he be able to pick Dennis Banks out of a crowd? Did he see him there? Did someone else tell him that Banks was there? Was it just a rumor?

"Rubin wasn't any better on the informants' reliability. To say that the information was 'verified' is meaningless. How was it verified? How many of the 120 cases ended in arrests? What facts proved correct?

"All that Rubin showed was that the overflights and FBI ground surveillance corroborated the informants' stories that a motor home was at Chiquiti's. Nothing more. The feds didn't see Banks or Peltier there. There wasn't any testimony that the informants did either."

"Ken's right," Jones said. "It's a close call, but we'd better be cautious. Otherwise, 'founded suspicion' may come out of Rubin's mouth in answer to our questions."

"Emergency call from Charles Turner on line 2," read the note my secretary, Annette Murphy, slipped me a few days after the hearing ended.

"What's up, Charlie," I said, having cut my other call short.

"Ken," he said, "you won't believe it. I just got off the phone with the FBI in Sacramento. Some woman apparently stole Dennis Banks's briefcase from his office and turned it over to them."

"What?" I asked.

"She's apparently somebody the FBI knows," Turner said. "She's one of those, whatchamecallits, FBI groupies, unbalanced."

"Where's the briefcase now?" I asked.

"The FBI has it."

"There may be stuff about the case in it, Charlie. Tell them that it's privileged material, not to be opened."

"Sorry, Ken," Turner said. "When they got it, they inspected it because they thought it might have a bomb. And I told them to inventory it, without reading anything, so that there will be no confusion."

"Charlie!" I said, incredulously. "You mean to tell me that the

FBI, which knows there's an ongoing prosecution, gets a briefcase from someone it knows, who says 'Here's Dennis Banks's briefcase,' and they look through it, for bombs? Come on, now, Charlie! They probably put her up to it and knew damn well there was nothing in it except Dennis's private papers. And how the hell do you expect them to inventory documents without reading them? If Dennis had anything in there that's related to this case, his attorney-client privilege has been violated, and I'll move for dismissal."

"I expected as much," Turner said. "And you might win," he added in a resigned tone.

I called Banks immediately.

"Hi. How's it going?" I asked nonchalantly, now seeing the theft, a fait accompli, as another opportunity to win the case.

"Great," he said. "Just finished our third annual 500-mile marathon for the kids. Had 110 runners this year. And we're working on the Sun Dance for next month. So, how are you? How're things going in Portland?"

"Fine," I said. "The hearings went well. And I filed a new motion that I think will solve our problems for a while. I'll tell you more when I see you. Which may be sooner than you think. Dennis, let me ask you. Where's your briefcase?"

"Ah, it's right here, behind my, ah . . . Wait a minute. It's, ah . . . Maybe I . . ."

"It's in the Sacramento FBI office," I said. "I just got a call from Charlie Turner. Apparently, some woman who, according to Charlie, had a 'long history of contacts with the FBI' and some sort of psychological problem, stole your briefcase from your office and then turned it over to the FBI. Turner ordered the FBI to open it and make an inventory and give a sealed list to the judge and to us. That all happened before he called me. He agreed to return everything to Dennis Roberts. I called Dennis and he knows."

"Wow. Do you know who the woman was? I had some important stuff in that briefcase."

"Charlie didn't know the name of the woman, but he promised to call me back with that information."

By that afternoon—July 14, 1980—Banks had reported the burglary and theft to Lt. Hal Wolf of the Yolo County Sheriff's

Office. The next day, the press reported the story. It was front-page news in the Bay Area.

The woman's name was Diane O'Brien. The FBI knew her well. It kept a file on her. When she handed Banks's briefcase to the Sacramento FBI office and told them what it was, the agents went through it carefully, including the personal papers and books because, they said, it was Banks's briefcase, not because O'Brien had given it to them.

"This is just another in a series of FBI burglaries," Banks told a press conference. "They're worried about the Oregon case. It's like years ago, when they put an informant in my meetings with my lawyers and when they sent a spy snooping around the defense house in Portland."

I canceled court appearances on other cases and flew to Oakland for a meeting with Dennis Banks and Dennis Roberts. We met at a deli on Grand Avenue.

"So," I asked over a Reuben sandwich, "what was in the briefcase?"

I had not inquired over the telephone. As soon as the *Loud Hawk* case had been revived, the lawyers' telephones had developed squeaks and squawks and interference again.

"Well," Banks said, "I had some books, some articles, some notes from my classes and from The Longest Walk.[3] And some tapes."

"What were on the tapes?" I asked.

"Well, let's see," he said. "Some were videos of the last pow-wow. And about last summer's Sun Dance. And of the last

---

3. Dennis and KaMook Banks were living in Davis, California. Dennis, who had taken classes at Deganawidah-Quetzalcoatl University ("D.Q.") soon after Judge Belloni's 1976 dismissal, had graduated. Then he was elected the school's chancellor. He also taught Federal Indian Law at D.Q. and Indian Studies at Stanford University, where he was a visiting professor.

"The Longest Walk" was a cross-country trek Dennis had organized to protest anti-Indian legislation. He could travel only to the California-Nevada border (California courts had upheld Gov. Brown's refusal to extradite Dennis to South Dakota, but he could be arrested on an extradition warrant anywhere else in the United States). Nevertheless, the protest grew. Hundreds of Indians of all ages arrived weeks later in Washington, D.C., demanding respect for the treaties and defeat of bills designed to strip Indians of any remaining control over their land and resources.

Marathon—over 100 kids ran in that one. And there were some cassettes."

"What were on those?"

"Well, one was the cassette on my answering machine."

"You mean the one that people leave messages on?"

"Um hum."

"How long have you been using it?"

"For at least a year now."

"Great," I said, writing notes. "The FBI has the technology to listen to tapes that have been recorded over. So let's assume they have every message left on your machine for the last year. What else?"

"Well, there was also the one I was making for you. Dennis here suggested I make you a tape of all the things I've done since Wounded Knee up to my arrest in 1976. And I also put some questions about jury selection on it."

"You mean, if the FBI listened to it, it would know where you were on November 14, 1975, and the days immediately before and after?"

"Right-o."

"And our strategy for jury selection?"

"Um hum."

This was serious.

"I want to see your office," I told Banks. "But before we go, I have some good news."

I handed each Dennis a copy of *United States v. Griffin* and my motion to dismiss for vindictive prosecution.

I watched Roberts. He chuckled when he was a page into the motion.

"Far fuckin' out!" he kept saying as he skimmed further, then through the *Griffin* case.

"Banks," he said, "Kenny here just saved your fuckin' ass. This motion is worth its weight in gold."

"What Dennis means," I said to our client, "is that the case gets dismissed again or we appeal. Either way, you don't have to come to Oregon and face another extradition fight."

I explained the law of "vindictive prosecution" to my client as we drove to D.Q. University. Banks's office there had a pine door with a brass-colored spring lock. There were fresh scratches on the door frame. I felt splinters as I ran my hand along the edge. The FBI had said there was no forced entry.

Weeks later, after negotiation, the briefcase was returned. The key audiotape was missing.

"Those guys are getting pretty clever in their old age," I said at the next lawyers' meeting. "If they gave us the tape back, we'd know they copied it. But by not returning it, they could say they never got it—and then allege that either we made the whole thing up or that O'Brien took it before she gave them the briefcase."

Four days after I filed my latest motion to dismiss for government misconduct (the briefcase incident), the government filed its memorandum answering my vindictive prosecution claim. I savored it.

The government admitted that its new indictment increased charges and created the appearance of vindictiveness. It acknowledged its burden to refute that appearance. The government built its defense on two lean prongs.

First, it relied on a case from outside the appellate circuit (persuasive law but not binding),[4] saying that "different approaches by subsequent prosecutors" permit an increase of charges. That was no problem. The Ninth Circuit's cases were directly opposite. And these were no "subsequent" prosecutors. Turner and Youngman had been on the case for over four years. They both, supposedly, had prepared the case for trial in 1976. Youngman had been the first prosecutor—the one who arraigned Kenny Loud Hawk and Russ Redner in November 1975. And what about Lezak, who was a constant throughout?

Second, Turner swore in an affidavit that he "took no part

---

4. Federal courts are organized on three levels, like a pyramid. The U.S. Supreme Court sits on top, the district courts on the bottom. In between are the courts of appeals, which hear cases appealed from the district courts. Each court of appeals has jurisdiction over many districts. Each geographic area assigned to one of the appellate courts is called a "circuit."

Supreme Court decisions are binding on all courts below, but court of appeal decisions are binding on only that particular "circuit" and the district courts under its jurisdiction. The District Court for the District of Oregon was under the jurisdiction of the Ninth Circuit Court of Appeals.

whatever" in the initial indictments or complaint and that he never looked at the factual or legal background for the charges until he had to present the case to the new grand jury. Not until 1980 did he realize that electrical and nonelectrical blasting caps had been found in 1975 and that two different types of explosive devices could be made from them, hence the additional dynamite count. He also swore he had no animus for the defendants or their lawyers. "I have made a conscientious effort to remain uninformed about the American Indian Movement," he swore. "I have no knowledge of AIM, its origins, history, goals, and objectives, nor am I aware of whether any of the defendants are members thereof."

If Turner and Youngman, both of whom had argued the case in court, knew nothing about the case, that was an admission of incompetence, not an excuse for increased charges. Even I, as a first-year law student, had known that there were two different detonation systems found—electrical and nonelectrical caps, time bombs (to be made with the watches) and bombs detonated by fuse. McCreary and Key had mentioned that in their testimony, as did Fettig, twice. In fact, the two bombs that Fettig made in Ontario were constructed from fuse, caps, and dynamite, whereas the original indictment charged the Indians with possessing devices made with pocket watches and other equipment for electrical circuits. How could Turner not know? And Turner swore that he did not know that Dennis Banks was a member of the American Indian Movement!

I read the entire record again, over seven days, and filled ten legal pads with notes. Each pad contained dozens of categories, each designed to disprove something Turner had sworn to. Turner knew that dynamite could be detonated with either electrical or nonelectrical blasting caps. Turner knew of AIM's goals. Turner knew Banks was a member of AIM.

Then I read everything written about vindictive prosecution. By our August 5, 1980, court appearance, I could recite, explain, and expound the law of vindictive prosecution effortlessly, like Lenin could explain Marx or the pope, Catholicism.

In five minutes, I took Redden step by step through the case law. I attacked the government's legal analysis and showed why its reasons for the increased charges did not rebut the appearance of vindictiveness. Defendants had the right to defend themselves without fear of revenge for their assertion of rights. Retaliation came from the government, which had the power of indictment, not from an individual prosecutor, who did not.

"The law of vindictive prosecution could be circumvented by changing prosecutors," I argued.

I held up Turner's affidavit. For forty-five minutes, I listed every fact in the more than 2,500-page record that contradicted what Turner said he did or did not know. I stopped when the court reporter's fingers were numb.

Turner and Youngman called a recess to discuss what to do. On his way out of the courtroom, Youngman put his arm on my shoulder. "You must have spent two weeks putting that together," he said. "I'd never have the patience to comb through a record that way." It was a gracious compliment. I knew I had impressed Redden, too.

After the recess, Turner took the stand to prove that he had no animosity toward the defendants. I pestered him with facts from the record and asked whether he was familiar with them. Time after time, Turner did not remember. He probably had not read this or that. Yes, he had argued the case before the Ninth Circuit without reviewing key transcripts. Yes, he had signed court pleadings—including sworn ones—without knowing what they referred to.

Turner was a zealot. He could be worn down. He did not like any of us. He believed our clients were evil. And Schiffman and Gurwitz and Roberts and I were all Jewish. Although it was difficult to prove (one Jewish lawyer on his staff told me that he had never been discriminated against by Turner), each of us felt that Turner might be an anti-Semite. He had that edge, beyond his propensity to quote Hebrew Bible passages to us at the most peculiar times. It was in his eyes. Our feelings were supported by a Bay Area lawyer who had grown up near Turner. "His family were awful anti-Semites," she said.

I knew he could not disguise his hate if I pushed hard enough. Turner swore that he tried to remain totally ignorant about AIM and that he had succeeded, but even if he had not, it would not have mattered, because AIM's goals and objectives were irrelevant to him.

"You say that the defendants' AIM membership is totally irrelevant," I asked. "Why, then, would it matter if you knew anything about it?"

"I said it was irrelevant!" he snarled.

"If it is irrelevant, why would you make an effort to remain uninformed? How does it hurt you to know about it?"

"Because, Mr. Stern, I don't want to be caught up in a game of AIM and its objectives. I'm not interested in that. The fact that you are or your client, that's all right, but the government should not be interested in the goals and objectives of defendants in any organization they belong to."

"You still are not answering my question," I persisted. "Listen to me carefully. If knowing something is irrelevant to your action as a government prosecutor, why would you make an effort to remain uninformed?"

"Because, Mr. Stern, I have heard you and other folks in this case say from time to time that the government is engaged in a policy of genocide against the American Indians and possible attacks against the American Indian Movement. And the less I know about that, the better off I am and the better off our office is."

"The less you know about it?"

"The less we know about the American Indian Movement, the less involvement we have in that type of a game, the better off we are. As far as I am concerned, you folks simply use the media and the press in an attempt to galvanize yourself into a better position than you should have!"

Turner leaned forward. "In my opinion," he continued, his voice booming, "if you had been a gang of bank robbers, you would have been in jail a long time ago!"

Turner had forgotten that he had taken the stand to prove his lack of animosity.

The next day I was in the courthouse on an unrelated case when I heard voices from behind a closed door in a corridor. As I walked past, a loud voice said, "But they *knew* KaMook Banks had been under indictment back in 1975. If they wanted to bring those charges, they should have done it *then*." A second voice said, "Right!"

I was tempted to listen further but walked on, smiling. These must be Judge Redden's clerks, writing a draft of his ruling on the vindictive prosecution motion. They were on our side.

On August 7, Redden denied our motion seeking dismissal based on the contention that there had been no legal basis to stop the vehicles. But on August 8, he ruled that the new indictment had created an appearance of vindictiveness. That appearance had been explained and eliminated toward the male defendants: the increased dynamite charges were the result of the "independent judgment of subsequent prosecutors." But the vindictive appearance created by the added gun charge against Ka-Mook was not dispelled. All charges against her were dismissed, with prejudice.

I was disappointed that the charges had not been dismissed against everyone but thrilled nonetheless. From the defense side, criminal cases thrive on disorder; this was maximum entropy, one defendant dismissed, the others not. Dennis Banks could relax in California.

CHAPTER 22

✛ ✛ ✛

AWAY FROM SOUTH DAKOTA

WHEN I was a law student, I went to court every few weeks to learn from Michael Bonds. He was the best trial attorney in Portland. One rainy winter morning, Bonds defended a married woman in her forties who was charged with prostitution. She ignored his warnings not to testify. The jury returned before we finished our first cup of coffee in the eighth-floor coffee shop.

"Let's get out of here," Bonds said after the jurors were excused, having found the woman guilty. "Stupid clients are one of the worst parts of law," he complained, as he strode through downtown and I did my best to keep up with him. "Let me show you something good about law," he added.

We walked into an old, gray stone courthouse, through its polished brass post office lobby, then up worn stairs. A single courtroom occupied most of the second floor.

The U.S. Court of Appeals for the Ninth Circuit, based in San Francisco, heard appeals from U.S. district courts all over the West Coast. It sent a panel here—to the Pioneer Courthouse—for three days every other month, on the theory that it was cheaper to send three judges north than to fly a score of lawyers south to argue a dozen or more cases. The courtroom was empty now.

The bench, where the judges sat, was polished oak, raised, majestic. The counsel table, the seats for the audience, the chairs for the lawyers, the podium and the coatrack in the rear were the finest antiques, as were the roll-top desks and other fixtures that filled the courtroom and the hall outside.

"Some East Coast courthouses were dismantled years ago, and an Oregon judge claimed the finer pieces," Bonds explained, as he pointed to a pair of fancy antique lanterns with pale smoked glass globes.

The courtroom itself was like Wedgwood. The walls were pastel green, with designs in white relief. Although it was a gray day, light beamed through the red, white, and blue stained-glass windows. A fireplace was carved into the rear wall, behind the spectator section. Logs sat in it. Unkindled, it added warmth to the courtroom on this rainy winter day. It evoked history. Lincoln, I thought, must have argued in a courtroom with a fireplace.

"I hope once in my career," I said as we closed the door and walked down the stairs, "I have a chance to argue in this room."

I had not expected it to happen so soon. It was now January 7, 1981. The vindictive prosecution briefs had been filed in the fall. Since Christmas, I had worked only on *Loud Hawk*, rereading the case law and practicing the argument.

On January 6, with a six-month growth of hair and beard, dressed in blue jeans and a faded, frayed flannel shirt, I walked into the courtroom, quietly. Judges Anthony Kennedy, Warren Ferguson, and Stephen Reinhardt, all men in their forties or fifties, were listening to a lawyer plead his client's case. They looked up as I—the lone spectator—closed the door, hung my old wet raincoat on the oak and brass coatrack, and sat in the last row, where I stayed silently all morning. I gauged their styles as they asked lawyers questions.

Kennedy stared at me, then smiled in recognition the next morning as I sat in front of the packed courtroom, neatly trimmed, dressed in a new, light gray, three-piece Pierre Cardin suit.

I walked to the counsel table, put my papers down, and stepped to the podium. "May it please the court," I began, "the government admits that its new indictment creates an appearance of vindictiveness because new charges were brought after we asserted rights—especially our right to a grand jury indictment. Mr. Turner, however, claims that he is a 'subsequent prosecutor,' and therefore, his alleged 'different approach' justifies the increased charges my clients face.

"Mr. Turner is not a subsequent prosecutor. He's been on this case since March 1976. But even if he were new to this case, under this circuit's law, it would not matter.

"Mr. Turner relies on cases from outside this jurisdiction. Those cases hold that mistake, oversight, prosecutorial inexperience, a different approach by subsequent prosecutors, or a failure of communication within the United States Attorney's Office may be sufficient reasons to rebut an inference that the prosecution was vindictive *in fact*. That's a different standard.

"In this circuit, the law requires the prosecution show 'independent reasons or intervening circumstances that dispel the *appearance* of vindictiveness.' That's a harder task than disproving vindictiveness *in fact*. And dispelling the *appearance* of vindictiveness is essential, for otherwise, defendants, fearing retaliation, will be deterred from exercising constitutionally protected rights, whatever the government's real motives may be for increasing charges after a case is begun.

"What reasons dispel the appearance of vindictiveness? The cases binding in this circuit are explicit. There is only one reason: the prosecution must prove it was impossible to bring the increased charges at the outset.

"For example, in the case of *Blackledge v. Perry*, the new charges, upped from attempted murder to murder, were allowed because the victim died after the defendant was charged with attempted murder. . . ."

First Kennedy interrupted, then Ferguson, then Reinhardt. "Shouldn't prosecutors be able to reindict whatever charges the grand jury is willing to bring?" "Does this circuit specifically reject the case law the government relies on?" "Did you 'set up' the government by opposing their request that the gun counts be reinstated?"

I answered each question, working my way back to the case law, the facts, always focused on my argument—that the government's reasons for upping the ante were factually and legally insupportable.

I encouraged the judges to ask more. I understood why each judge asked what he did, and I answered while pushing my argument ahead. It was easy, fun. Their questions were not interruptions to fear but opportunities to exploit. In less than a second, I could spit out cases, facts, and analogies. The judges and I connected. A half hour later, my time was up. But the court kept probing. Fifteen minutes more elapsed before Judge Kennedy noticed the clock.

"Your time's up, counsellor," he said, smiling.

Jack Wong, a handsome veteran U.S. attorney, walked to the

podium. "May it please the court," he began, "since Mr. Turner's motivations are at issue in this appeal, I am going to argue for our office."

He had not completed a sentence when Judge Kennedy interrupted. "Isn't it true, Mr. Wong, that the search of the vehicles—three days into this case—produced two types of blasting caps and that Trooper Fettig, as early as March 1976, testified that two distinct types of bombs could be constructed from them?"

"I'm not certain, Your Honor," Wong responded. "But the point is that Mr. Turner wasn't aware . . ."

I felt for Wong. The *Loud Hawk* record was now over 5,000 pages, and it was not his case. While Wong equivocated, I hungered to answer. "Yes, it's true, judge," I tried to say, with telepathy. I was nodding unconsciously.

"A prosecutor should be able to bring charges at any time, as long as they are brought in good faith," Wong continued.

"But, sir," Kennedy interrupted, "Mr. Stern would say that your standard is one that gauges actual vindictiveness; doesn't the law in this Circuit limit reindictment after a defendants' assertion of rights to reasons that dispel the *appearance* of vindictiveness?"

Wong hesitated. I wanted to answer, "Yes, judge, and here are five cases, three examples, and two logical progressions, weaving the facts of *Loud Hawk* into all."

It was painful to wait my turn to speak again. I nodded assent, now aware that the judges and the court clerk were watching me.

"What about the *Demarco* case that Mr. Stern cited?"

Wong apologized for not knowing it well enough to discuss. The judges peppered him with questions. But the bench now looked to me, not to him, while he answered.

Judge Kennedy, the judge who had contorted the law to give the government back its case when it appealed Judge Belloni's 1976 dismissal, was frustrated, his tone harsh. "Mr. Wong," he accused rather than asked, "the government has flirted with *disaster* since the inception of this case!"

Wong ignored the outburst and went on as best he could. Finally, winded, he sat down. Kennedy looked to me. Even though I had used fifteen minutes beyond my allotted time, he allowed me twenty minutes more to dissect the major flaws in the government's positions. The judges and I agreed. There was no doubt. We had won, even though, as it always does, the Court took the case "under advisement." Its decision would be announced in a formal written opinion.

Walking down the antique steps, surrounded by Indians and defense lawyers who gushed congratulations, pleased with my performance and gratified that two senior attorneys told me that I had presented "the best appellate argument" they had ever heard, I watched a somber Wong, Lezak, Youngman, and Turner, half a flight ahead. Wong looked especially downhearted. He muttered to his colleagues, "This is the worst day I've ever had as a lawyer, ever!"

He was undoubtedly right. We had just spent an hour and a half in court, talking about how the government had violated the law. No one had asked about Indians with firearms, 350 pounds of explosives, and what they planned to do with them. Our case was best that way.

At first I expected a decision any day. Then my expectations slowed. By summer, I had almost forgotten. Other things kept me busy. Jeanne and I had split up (she had fallen in love with someone else), but now I was in love again, with Margaret Butler, a senior at Lewis & Clark College with lovely long brown hair, a wonderful nature, and a beautifully twisted smile. Since *Loud Hawk* was on hold, I had more time for her.

My law practice was fulfilling. I was winning most of my trials, feeling more confident, and taking on high-profile cases. Dennis Roberts and I sued heiress Patty Hearst for our friends, Jack and Micki Scott. In her book, *Every Secret Thing*, Hearst claimed that she had never been able to leave the Symbionese Liberation Army, even when harbored by the Scotts. That was a lie. Jack and Micki, and Jack's parents, had offered to take her to her parents, and she, in response, had yelled, "Take me the fuck where you're supposed to, or you'll be dead!" The Scotts won a settlement.

In another case, I challenged a Portland city ordinance that made it a crime "to camp." The law was designed to drive the homeless out of town. I proved that middle-class teenagers waiting overnight for concert tickets and middle-aged women who bought linen from downtown department stores, then put their shopping bags on the ground while waiting for the bus, also violated the law. I enjoyed using the suit to argue to Portlanders that the homeless needed help, not prosecution.

As much fun as these cases were, the others—the vast majority—were increasingly wearing. Drunk drivers I never liked, and after my first twenty trials, their cases were no longer challenging (if my client had refused a breath test and appeared at trial sober, I could usually win an acquittal). As I began representing more serious offenders, I found less and less to like about my clients as human beings. Some of them belonged in jail. On the streets, they would rob or attack innocent people again. The rationalizations that they deserved a fair trial, that the state had to be put to the test so that innocent people would not be convicted, while unquestionably true, were harder for me to internalize. I felt stress fill the places where zeal had departed.

Where were clients like Dennis Banks? There was little ambiguity in his case. The government was trying to jail him for longer than any of the truly dangerous people I represented. Keeping him free would make the world a better place. His work guided Indian children away from lives of despair, from crime, from drugs, from alcohol. My role in his freedom contributed to their hope for a better future.

Give me another Banks case! It had everything: a client I honestly loved and respected and counted as a friend; a case the press paid attention to, focusing on the problems of Indian people, allowing me to attack racism.

On the legal side, it was perfection. Fascinating, novel issues: destruction of evidence, vindictive prosecution, government misconduct, FBI spying, wiretaps, stolen briefcases. It was depressing to think this case was unique.

My mother's cancer returned in the summer of 1982, in the scar tissue. This time, she needed more surgery, then radiation treatment, then chemotherapy. I flew to New York once a month. Every return trip to Portland was a visit—to catch up and then prepare to go east again.

One June morning, sitting on my mother's Brooklyn porch as she napped upstairs, I read a small article in the back pages of the *New York Times*. The Supreme Court had ruled in a case called

United States v. Goodwin. From the single paragraph, it was impossible to tell exactly what the high court had decided. But the claim was vindictive prosecution. The court had ruled against it.

Three days later I read the full opinion. The Ninth Circuit's law rested on the analytical foundation of a presumption of vindictiveness. If charges were increased after a defendant exercised a right, there was a presumption that the new charges were retaliatory. In *Goodwin*, the Supreme Court outlawed this presumption and suggested that there was no problem with prosecutors acting vindictively anyway.

The delay in *Loud Hawk*—eighteen months since argument—finally made sense. Judges Kennedy, Reinhardt, and Ferguson must have known the *Goodwin* case was pending. There would be a *Loud Hawk* opinion soon, and it would be against us.

I read *Goodwin* carefully, charting its facts and the Court's ruling and reasoning. Torn to its underlying assumptions and then reconstructed, the *Goodwin* case could be stood on its head when blended with *Loud Hawk*'s unique circumstances.

Two weeks later, the Supreme Court decided a second vindictive prosecution case, *United States v. Hollywood Motor Car*. The Court, overruling *Griffin*, held that vindictive prosecution claims could be appealed only after trial and conviction.

On July 29, 1982, Judge Reinhardt wrote for a unanimous panel in *United States v. Loud Hawk et al.* Hinting that we would have won if the Supreme Court had not changed the law, he nonetheless dismissed Loud Hawk's, Redner's, and Dennis Banks's appeals, finding that they no longer had a right to a pretrial appeal, according to *Hollywood Motor Car*. He also reversed the dismissal of KaMook Banks, citing *Goodwin*.

Two weeks later, I filed a petition for rehearing. It took the court of appeals until October 1982 to reject it. The only option left was the Supreme Court. I knew it was unlikely to take the case. It had, after all, just ruled on two vindictive prosecution claims. But I had no choice.

California Governor Jerry Brown's term was ending. Republican George Deukmejian had just been elected. He vowed to extradite Banks to South Dakota. Banks had to leave California by Deukmejian's inauguration day in early January 1983.

The timing of the return of the Oregon case was critical. If

Banks had to come to Oregon for trial, Oregon's Republican governor, Vic Atiyeh, would send him to South Dakota.

Banks was no longer safe in either California or Oregon. I had to find a way to delay, just enough, a few weeks, until he could get settled someplace else.

The only legal option was a petition for Supreme Court review. It was difficult to draft. It barely passed the "straight face" test.[1] But my client's life was more important than my reputation for skillful arguments. And the petition was not frivolous—only unlikely to persuade an increasingly conservative court. I hoped I had written it so authoritatively that the court could not deny it in a matter of days.

Dennis Banks gave a huge "Farewell to California" party on December 17, 1982. Then he disappeared.

George Deukmejian was sworn in on January 3, 1983. Banks was now subject to arrest. Influential leaders, including many Republicans, asked Deukmejian to change his mind. They cited the serious threats to Banks's life in South Dakota and his "exemplary" contributions to California, including his teaching at D.Q. University and at Stanford. Deukmejian did not care.

On January 14, 1983, the *San Francisco Chronicle* quoted an FBI source saying the agency had "good reason to believe" Banks was hiding on the Onondaga reservation near Syracuse, New York.

---

1. Using antitrust law from complex litigation, I argued that it would be chaotic to sever KaMook's case from the others and that since she had a good claim on the merits, the others should be able to "attach" their dismissed appeals to her live one. (The government was appealing Judge Redden's dismissal of the charges against KaMook for vindictive prosecution, while the male defendants were appealing Redden's refusal to dismiss the charges against them for vindictive prosecution. The *Hollywood Motor Car* case took away the defendant's right to a pretrial appeal; it had no effect on the government's right to appeal a dismissal.)

The argument made sense because if KaMook won her vindictive prosecution appeal, there would be a good chance that the other defendants would also win. But first they would have to go through the time and expense of a trial before having the appellate court consider their claim separately. Conversely, if KaMook lost on appeal while the others were sent back for trial, it would mean that the government would have to try her alone later, again wasting time and money.

I was surprised to learn that two members of the U.S. Attorney's Office thought my petition was "masterful."

The chiefs of the Onondaga Nation confirmed the FBI reports. Banks was there, seeking sanctuary. His timing, as usual, was excellent. The Supreme Court had refused to take our case just four days before.

For the first month of Banks's refuge on Onondaga territory, no one knew what would happen. His chief New York attorney, William Kunstler, planned to ask New York Governor Mario Cuomo to grant Banks sanctuary. Cuomo's staff said consideration of asylum was "premature." Upstate New York newspapers were filled with debate, Dennis Banks as fleeing felon versus Dennis Banks as Indian hero. The Onondaga chiefs held meetings, over days, into nights, then granted Banks sanctuary, conditioned on his abstinence from political activity.

The South Dakota attorney general kept pushing for Banks's arrest and extradition. Two weeks after the Onondagas' announcement, a federal official, who requested anonymity, said, "We're going in to get him." "I hope they're not stupid enough to try," Kunstler responded in the press. For the next three weeks, there were daily threats of invasion.

As I sat in Oregon, rereading the now more than 7,000-page record in preparation for the first *Loud Hawk* appearance before Judge Redden in nearly three years, I hoped that somewhere in Washington, some wise person was weighing the government's desire to "get" Banks against the cost of so doing. Banks's choice of the Onondagas had been well considered. They were fiercely independent, unique among the Indian nations. They were part of the historic Iroquois Confederacy, Indian nations bound together for centuries. Despite living the last few hundred years under the domination of white people and white governments, their culture, traditions, sports (lacrosse is their game), and governmental systems survived intact. Their government flowed from a constitution older than ours which was a model for both Benjamin Franklin and Karl Marx. It begins, "We the People."

Banks had a long relationship with that nation's chiefs. Oren Lyons and Herb Powless had led a delegation of Onondagas to Wounded Knee in 1973 and helped Banks and the Sioux hold off the FBI and army when it looked like a government attack was imminent.

The Onondagas' small land base was more sovereign than

other Indian nations'. Onondagas traveled on Iroquois passports. Unlike the Sioux or the Navaho, they had never been conquered by, had no relationship with, and thus had no dependency on the federal government. Their bond was with New York State, with which, in the late 1700s, they treatied as equal partners.

The city of Syracuse was built on Onondaga land, leased to New York for two hundred years. That lease was nearly up. This was no time to anger Indians, impugning their claim of sovereignty with an invasion.

Onondaga sanctuary was a pledge to protect Banks—with guns. The *Loud Hawk* case was actually a defusing force. It offered another way for the government to "get" Banks, if it was patient. He would either have to come to Oregon for trial and would be extradited to South Dakota from there or, if he did not appear for trial, there would be less criticism of a federal invasion. The U.S. marshals would not be serving a South Dakota warrant pushed by racist officials but a warrant signed by Judge Redden, a liberal Democrat from Oregon, for violating a release agreement.

When six weeks passed without the promised raid, I knew that the authorities had chosen the "Oregon" option. Sanctuary was now the status quo.

Bruce Ellison, a South Dakota attorney for AIM member Leonard Peltier, won a bitter Freedom of Information Act suit against the government in 1982. One of the documents he won— a report of an FBI scientific examination of a bullet casing— proved that the gun the prosecutors said Peltier used to kill the two FBI agents could not have fired the relevant bullets. The document, known by the prosecutors at the time of trial, had allegedly been hidden from the defense and thus not known by the jury. Ellison filed papers asking for a new, fair, trial.[2]

Another document won in the suit did not help Peltier, but Ellison knew I would be interested in it. Two gas station atten-

---

2. The court of appeals denied Leonard Peltier a new trial, even though it found that if the jury had had this evidence, it might have acquitted him. In late 1987, the Supreme Court refused to overturn that decision. Peltier, however, was dismissed from the *Loud Hawk* case at the government's request. It apparently thought two consecutive life sentences were sufficient.

dants in eastern Oregon, Richard Schricker and Eugene Strain, had seen the motor home, the station wagon, and their occupants on November 14, 1975. Each had identified Peltier. That was why the government had given the documents to Ellison. Those same attendants, however, had not identified Dennis Banks; Strain identified another fugitive who was not among those arrested in Ontario.

These hidden reports would be potent at trial. "Ladies and Gentlemen of the jury," I fantasized arguing, "the government wants you to believe that the only person who could have driven the motor home from the scene was Dennis Banks. But it hid interviews with *eyewitnesses*. None of them identified Banks. One of them identified *Frank Black Horse*. Frank Black Horse was an AIM member, a known associate of Leonard Peltier, who was arrested with Peltier in Canada, in possession of a gun stolen from an Ontario area farmhouse on November 15, 1975."

These reports created reasonable doubt. I did not want to use them yet. I would keep them to myself and, when appropriate, challenge Turner in open court. "Mr. Turner," I would say, "do you swear again that you've given us every favorable piece of evidence, as the Constitution and the cases of the United States Supreme Court require?"

He would swear to it. I would draw the FBI reports from the middle of a yellow legal pad, walk to the bench, and hand them to Judge Redden. But, for now, the reports gave me another idea. Unless something else was being hidden, the prosecution must have no witness saying, "I saw Dennis Banks in the motor home." Without any eyewitness to identify him before a jury, there was no compelling reason for him to be at the trial. He had a right to be present, but shouldn't he be able to give up that right?

I filed a Motion for Trial in Absentia. If Dennis had to appear in Oregon, he lost. He could be acquitted but would be sent to South Dakota, where he might be killed.

"The case law says a defendant waives his right to be present when he absconds during trial," I argued. "The trial continues in his absence. Shouldn't a defendant, whose life is endangered if he had to appear, be permitted to waive his same right legally, by motion?"

I analyzed the federal rules. They referred to a defendant's "presence." They didn't say "physical presence." I argued, "Of the five senses, only those of sight and sound are important to a defendant's right to be present at trial. Mr. Banks can be electronically present. We can have a closed-circuit hookup between this court and the Onondaga Nation."

The beauty of this motion was that the Supreme Court, in *Hollywood Motor Car*, announced rules to determine when a defendant had a right to a pretrial appeal. The question had to be something separate from the central issue in the case. It had to be something fully decided, yes or no, before trial. It had to concern a right that could not be protected by appeal after trial.

The "trial in absentia" issue fit. If Redden ruled against us, we could appeal before trial. If he ruled for us, Banks would be tried from afar. Either way, he would not have to come to Oregon, a stop on what would certainly be a trip to a South Dakota jail.

CHAPTER 23

CAMPS

AFTER three years on the trial bench, Judge Redden had become confident and relaxed. "Come in, gentlemen," he said, like a madam, as he opened his oak chambers door and waved the lawyers in.

"Hi, Judge," we each replied in turn, as we passed by and staked a position around his long, polished conference table.

Redden sat at the head. I sat to his left. Michael Bonds, Lynn Parkinson, Ed Jones, Tom Steenson,[1] Mike Rose,[2] Ron Schiffman,[3] Charles Turner,[4] and Ken Bauman[5] sat around the table.

"Everyone agrees this meeting is off the record, right?" Redden asked as his secretary, Julia Plummer, closed the door. Everyone agreed.

The judge sat in a dark leather high-backed chair. Behind him, between leather law books in a built-in bookshelf, was a

---

1. Tom Steenson, who left Portland after the 1976 dismissal to work for Legal Aid in The Dalles, had returned in 1981 and joined Parkinson and Jones's partnership.

2. Mike Rose was my law partner, in our firm Rose & Stern.

3. A month before this meeting, in March, 1983, Schiffman had asked Judge Redden to be relieved. "Kenny Loud Hawk deserves someone in active practice," he had explained. "I'm retired. I'm running a seafood restaurant in Cannon Beach."

"Your request will be granted, if you find someone adequate to replace you," Redden had said.

No one of Schiffman's caliber could be found.

4. Charles Turner was now *the* U.S. Attorney. Lezak had resigned after Ronald Reagan was elected president in 1980. Reagan appointed Turner.

5. Since Redden's 1980 vindictive prosecution ruling, Bill Youngman had also gone into private practice. His *Loud Hawk* replacement, Ken Bauman, dark-haired, in his thirties, had once been an FBI agent. Turner had enlisted him to read and organize his two five-drawer *Loud Hawk* file cabinets.

brass scales of justice. The scales were ever so slightly off balance, the right side lower than the left. I thought the unevenness unintentional but was unsure.

"See that can?" Redden asked, pointing behind his right shoulder with his left index finger. "We won't need that, because we're all going to talk straight here, right?"

A can of Anti-Bullshit Spray was one shelf above the scales. He looked around the room, staring at each lawyer, waiting for each to nod assent.

"Okay," the judge continued, "you all received my letter. I know this case has an acrimonious history."

He picked up a stack of papers with two hands, held it aloft for effect and then put it down. These were the *Loud Hawk* pleadings, including our old, unresolved motions (such as the "briefcase incident"), and new motions, including one to dismiss for lack of a speedy trial.[6]

"We're gearing up for trial again," Redden said, his hand on the papers, "and, like I said, before the engines get lit, and there's too much fire in the belly, I wanted to see if this case can settle. Mr. Turner, what do you have to say about that?"

"Thanks, Judge," Turner said, turning to Bonds. "We considered your letter, Judge. We're prepared to offer each of the defendants a plea of guilty to one count of our choosing. The remaining charges would then be dismissed."

"What about a sentencing recommendation, Charlie?" Bonds asked, as if on cue.

Turner paused, looked to the judge, then back to Bonds.

"Judge Redden knows this case. We don't need to make one," he said.

"That sounds reasonable to me," Bonds said, excitedly. He looked at Judge Redden and asked, "After seven years of de facto probation and two dismissals, I suspect my client, KaMook Banks, is a good candidate for probation?"

Redden nodded.

---

6. Even though the case was now seven years old, there was no violation of the statute of limitations. The statute of limitations defines by what date a prosecution must begin; the "speedy trial" right limits how long a prosecution, once begun, can take.

"Judge," I interrupted, "before we go too far, I think everyone knows I'm the problem here. My client is trapped on the Onondaga reservation. If he leaves, he'll be arrested and sent to South Dakota. We may have something to talk about if he can plead guilty over the phone from the reservation and if he were sentenced to unsupervised probation. It wouldn't work if he had to report to the probation office in Syracuse, and I suspect the Probation Service isn't fond of house calls."

"I suspect not," the judge agreed. No one spoke while he thought.

"Why don't you ask your clients?" Redden continued. "I'd want a presentence report, and if it's favorable, I might be willing to sentence Mr. Banks over the phone and not jeopardize his sanctuary. I understand the threats. You know," he said, looking at me, "I actually met South Dakota's governor once when he and I were both attorneys general. What's his name again?"

"Janklow," I said.

"Yeah," Redden said, "I thought he was a horse's ass."

Clouds had come over late in the day, and although no snow had fallen, the skies were ominous. At night there were no stars. Everything was black. That was good. If the FBI wanted us to lead them to Banks's Onondaga hideout, they would have a hard time driving to avoid detection—without headlights—on the curvy roads Joe Heath, Banks's Syracuse lawyer, was racing through.

At first Heath's headlights lit only trees and frozen land, then a few tiny ramshackle houses, dark, with smoke coiling out of some chimneys and heaving out of others. It was still winter in New York in late March.

I had called Banks from the pay phone outside Redden's chambers the week before. Even so, his underground phone-of-the-week might have been tapped. We did not discuss where he was staying.

"That's an amazing deal!" he had said.

"Damn right," I had replied, still not used to the idea that the case could go away so easily. "I'm coming to explain the details to you."

Now, driving with Heath, I wondered why Banks was no longer as enthusiastic.

"He's been weird the last few days," Heath said. "Sort of sullen, resigned. I don't understand it. He should be elated!"

As we passed each small cottage or dark trailer, I wondered if this was the place. I had hoped Banks would be living in a centrally located house. The reservation was small, and if he was staying near the borders, the feds could sneak across and grab him before anyone knew. The more people they had to pass, the better.

"We're here," Heath said, all of a sudden, and pulled off the road into the short dirt driveway in front of a run-down wooden shack that looked like a stereotypical trading post.

The house was dark and clammy like a cave. There were thick curtains over the windows. I did not know if they were for insulation or security.

The Onondaga man who let us in left us alone in the living room. A black and white television was on. The volume was low.

After a minute, KaMook appeared from behind a curtain. She looked exactly the same. We hugged. Three little girls were holding onto her legs. Tosh was not the cuddly, sweet infant I remembered. She still had sparks in her dusky brown eyes, but she was now a pudgy nine-year-old. TaTiopa, seven, although cute, had harder features, more like Dennis. She had been in a cradle board when I last saw her. Chubbs, whom I had never met, was a toddler.

"Tell me how the people in Portland are," KaMook asked, offering us coffee.

"Everyone's doing fine," I said. "Michael and Ann Bonds just bought a co-op; Ed Jones got married, and he and his wife, Jenny Cook, are expecting a baby; and Ron Schiffman keeps trying to retire and run his restaurant, but this case won't let him."

"How's that Sheila Lea?" she asked.

"Haven't seen Sheila in years," I said. "The last I heard she was living in Hawaii in a commune that grows marijuana."

"That Sheila Lea," she said again, laughing. "I remember when we went to her house. She had this big metal tray full of marijuana, right in the middle of her living room! 'You guys want any?' she asked. Gee, I never saw anything like that. I couldn't believe her."

"So," I finally asked, "what do you think about the plea deal?"

"It's great!" she said. "I told Michael Bonds a long time ago that I wasn't going back to jail. Hey, can I plead over the phone, too, or will I have to go to Portland? It's always raining there."

Before I could explain that she would probably have to come, Dennis walked in. We greeted and talked and ate dinner and reminisced. But Heath was right. Something was weighing on him. Dennis was quiet when he was troubled. He was less talkative than I ever remembered.

"There's a good probation officer named George Minor, preparing a report for the judge," I explained between bites of fry bread. "Turner's a loose cannon, and I don't trust him, but the way it's worked out, we don't need to."

Dennis grunted. "It's a good deal," he finally said, as though he were convincing himself.

"You get to serve your sentence here," I said, "in the custody of the Onondaga chiefs, where you are anyway. You avoid South Dakota, and Indian people can point to the plea procedure as a federal recognition of Indian sovereignty."

Dennis motioned for the papers I had brought and signed them. "We'll work out the final details later," he said, swooping up Chubbs in his arms. "Got to go to a meeting."

"Dennis," I asked as he walked to the door, "are you really safe here? The feds could mount an operation and only be minutes away."

"That's not your worry," he said sternly. "If they try, fifty armed Onondagas will fight them off."

Lynn Parkinson had always been a bit strange. His hairstyle was early beatnik—thin, greased, whisked-back hair and a wispy beard. His mannerisms were those of an early rock and roll bass player, long, low, and slow. His politics were paranoic. His intentions were honorable, but he saw conspiracies wherever he looked. Under stress, his voice cracked.

"There's nothing more I can do!" Parkinson proclaimed the week after I had returned from Banks's hideout.

Dennis and KaMook and Kenny Loud Hawk had agreed to the deal. His client, Russ Redner, the only defendant who had come to Portland to prepare for trial, had not.

"I tried to explain if we go to trial, all those guns will be dropped on the counsel table, and he's going to jail," Lynn said.

"He doesn't care. Russ just said, 'This case has ruined too much of my life. I'm a warrior, and warriors don't surrender, and that's all there is to it.'

"So," Parkinson continued, "I figured I had to get him focused on something else. I told him I could use connections to send him to Nicaragua to fight the Contras. That's a war. He said no. So, shit, I guess I'm going to trial!"

"Did you tell him that this might screw up Dennis's deal and that Dennis might have to go to South Dakota if the thing falls through?" I asked.

"Yeah," Parkinson said. "Russ said Dennis is a sellout, and KaMook would do whatever Dennis wanted. He said he'd talk Kenny into trial."

I tried to call Parkinson later that day, but he did not return my calls. I did not see him until a week later, at a meeting in Redden's chambers.

"My client won't let me participate without a court reporter," he announced as he walked in, late. He had not mentioned that to anyone before. Redden looked angry.

"Judge," I interceded, "if we all agree that no one will ever order the record of these proceedings and that they will never be transcribed without your order, then we can continue our gentle-man's understanding with a court reporter present, and Mr. Parkinson's client will be satisfied."

Everyone agreed, although Parkinson looked unhappy, as if some well-thought-out plan had been ruined. "Your Honor," he said after the stenographer arrived, "my client has instructed me to tell the court that he rejects the plea bargain and insists on his right to trial."

"All right," Redden said. "Mr. Turner, we can't force anyone to plead. Even though this was proposed as a package deal, I presume as long as Mr. Banks is willing to enter his plea, you're willing to take it and try Mr. Redner afterward."

"That's my inclination, judge," Turner said.

After the meeting, Parkinson, Bonds, and I walked to the South Park Blocks, a street with a canopy of old elm trees shading the well-kept lawns, benches, and statues below.

"This is a sad day," I said, as we walked. "The best thing about this case has been its unity. Now we have to figure out how everyone can do what they need to, without hurting anyone else."

"Um hum," Bonds agreed. "And tell Russ that Ken and I will come to court and do anything we can for him after the pleas go down."

Parkinson did not say anything right away, but his pace slowed. Then he stopped. Bonds and I turned back to him. "Look," he said, "we've been through a lot. I owe it to you guys to let you know. I've figured out Russ's defense."

"Sure," I said. "We'd be more than willing to brainstorm."

"Listen, Ken," Parkinson yelled. "My defense is that *your client* did everything. I'm pinning everything on *him*. And I'm filing a *subpoena*, to have the marshals serve in New York, to have him brought back as a defense witness."

My mouth fell open.

"You heard me!" Parkinson yelled.

"You crazy?" Bonds asked, his voice squealing.

"Lynn!" I said. "This is Janklow's dream come true. And you know Dennis has nothing to say that could help Russ."

"I know," Parkinson said, "but Dennis should be here. He should be a warrior, too! And, anyway, the marshals probably won't go in and get him because it's too hot, and then Turner will have to dismiss, since the government won't get me a witness I need."

"You're nuts!" I said. "This is just the ticket the feds need to go onto the reservation—Banks subpoenaed by another Indian!"

"Well, like Russ says, if Dennis is still a warrior, he should be here!" Parkinson retorted.

"Lynn!" I said, "you know damn well why he can't be here. You tell Russ that this is a stupid move. It will either say that Indian people have nothing to fear in South Dakota despite all the murders, overt bigotry, and abject terror or that Russ is no better than a snitch, endangering Dennis's life. And you haven't seen Onondaga. They're committed to protecting him. It's a sovereignty issue, for god's sake! There are *kids* on that reservation, Lynn. Ask Russ if he's prepared to have some of them die in the crossfire!"

"Ken," Parkinson responded, "Dennis is an anachronism. Russ is the warrior. There's a war on. Sometimes people die. That's part of war. I'm sending you guys and Ron a letter. If you want to speak to my client from now on, it has to be with my permission and in my presence." He turned his back and walked away.

I met Redner and Parkinson once, the next week, in the recreation room of Lynn's apartment complex. I tried to convince them not to file their subpoena. I talked past Parkinson, who looked filmy gray and exhausted, directly to Redner. He was angry, focused, confused, passionate.

"How can you still respect the guy?" Redner hollered. "He's hiding out!"

"Russ," I said, "you know he's in danger if he goes back to South Dakota."

"Well," Redner said, "warriors face danger. Anyway, I don't like how he's always the center of attention. I was pissed when I saw that poster in your office. Where were Kenny and me? Nowhere! Just Dennis Banks this and Dennis Banks that!"

"Russ," I said, "the poster was from California, from the campaign to have Governor Deukmejian give him sanctuary. It had nothing to do with the case."

"Still," Redner said, "if he were a man, he'd be here!"

He stood, grabbed his coat, and walked out of the meeting. Parkinson followed, then turned around, stopped, and smiled a psychotic smile, as if his client had followed his lawyer's suggested script perfectly.

The evening of April 12, 1983, was warm and dry in Portland. The camellias were in full bloom. Michael Bonds and I were in my Northwest Portland apartment, with the windows open.

"I can't believe this case," I said. "After all these years, it's going down the fucking toilet! Like any other multidefendant criminal case, when trial comes close, it's 'fuck the politics—every man for himself.' And the politics are the best defense!"

Ron Schiffman had called me an hour earlier, fighting sobs. Redner had finally coerced Loud Hawk into trial. "There's nothing I can do!" Schiffman said. "Kenny wants to plead guilty, and he knows if he goes to trial, he's going to jail. But Russ demanded. Russ was adopted into his family after the first dismissal. Kenny said, 'Russ is my brother, and I have to do this.'"

After hanging up with Schiffman, I called Banks and told him about Parkinson and Redner's subpoena. For over a week I had hesitated, rationalizing that the telephones were probably tapped and that I did not want the feds to know Parkinson's plans. In truth, I hoped reason would prevail. It did not. The plea deal, which was secret, had been leaked by Parkinson in and out of the Indian community. People called me about it from all over the country. Banks was furious when I told him. He said he would talk to Redner. He called back a half hour later.

"Those guys—Parkinson especially—are trying to blackmail me! You tell Parkinson that he if subpoenas me, I'm coming out, and when I step off the plane, I'll tell everyone that Lynn Parkinson is the reason! And you tell Redner that when I'm there for trial, I want a severance! There's no way I'm going to trial with him!"

Bonds, hearing parts of this conversation, poured himself a second bourbon. This case was not fun any more. A week later, with nothing resolved, Bonds was in my apartment again, sipping Jack Daniels.

"Listen to this," I said. "Dennis called me this afternoon. The Onondaga chiefs met. They considered four options for Dennis. First, the hard line—Dennis has sanctuary; no one can do anything to him. If anyone comes in to get him, its war. Damn the Oregon charges! Second, Dennis could plead guilty over the phone. Third, Dennis could be tried in absentia. Fourth, Dennis could leave Onondaga, fly to Portland, and be tried in person. Get this. They chose number three!"

"Did you explain to them that the plea deal is cut and that Redden probably wouldn't allow a trial in absentia?" Bonds asked.

"Yes," I said. "I reminded him that if Redden denies the in absentia motion and we appeal, it wouldn't take forever; and that if Redden allowed a trial in absentia, with Dennis in Onondaga, and he were convicted, that would pose additional problems. He could be sentenced to a federal jail. The plea is the only certain way to avoid South Dakota. I told Dennis I thought I could get Redden to sentence him to probation to the chiefs. That could be interpreted as recognition of their sovereignty by a federal judge. They could use it in other cases. I bet Redden would do it if he realized that that's what it took to get the case to go away."

"So, what did Dennis say?"

"He said he'd talk to them but that they already decided, and he thinks that's that."

"That's bullshit!"

"No shit," I said, as Bonds guzzled another drink.

I walked out of the judge's chambers on April 27 feeling guilty and confused, unsure of how to balance friendship to a lawyer and duty to a client. I had said nothing when the judge called an emergency meeting. He had had the marshals explain the new security arrangements. The lawyers would be taken up a back elevator, kept from the crowd. There were numbers to call for protection, night and day.

I had said nothing when Schiffman, nearly white with fright, talked again about getting off the case, explaining how he lived with his wife and his infant son eighty miles away on the coast, in a small community with no real police protection.

I had said nothing when Parkinson rambled on aimlessly about the tensions between "camps" of Indians—those who would plead and those who would go to trial.

Only when everyone was finished did I explain that I, personally, was not worried, that AIM was not a violent organization, even when people had different opinions.

"So you're saying it wasn't necessarily Indians who beat up Michael Bonds?" the judge asked.

"Judge," I said, "all Michael Bonds was able to describe was a large fist."

Bonds had just been released from the hospital. The evening Banks said the chiefs insisted on a trial in absentia, he had left my apartment, saying he was going home. He was tipsy. I would not have let him drive. But he lived three blocks away and appeared able to get home. I had not insisted when my offer to walk him there was refused. I should have.

"When I got to my front door," Bonds told the police, "two guys jumped me. I really didn't see them. They beat the shit out of me. I managed to crawl up my steps, but I passed out at the top. My wife, Ann, found me when she got home."

The way Ann and I figured it, Bonds had stopped off at a bar for another drink or two or was more intoxicated than I thought when he left my apartment. He either fell down his steps or was easy prey for the street people who camped in the neighborhood. When Ann found him, two hours after he had left my apartment, he was unconscious on the porch, bruised but also thoroughly drunk.

There was no way I could let anyone know that Bonds's claim of unpremeditated attack, which all the other lawyers presumed had to do with a war between Indians, was baseless. It would embarrass him, no one would believe it, and I would harm a friend and lose an ally. And my client and I needed an ally. Chiefs Lyons and Powless were coming to Oregon to meet with Judge Redden.

"They're coming to explain to the judge why Dennis can't plead guilty and why the Onondagas will only allow a trial in absentia," Joe Heath lamented over the telephone.

Bonds recovered enough to meet them, with me, the night before they were to see the judge. Over dinner at the "Chinese Tastee Freeze," a new Hunan restaurant in an old Northwest Portland Tastee Freeze building, we explained how the trial in absentia was not as good as the deal.

"We're not convinced," Chief Lyons said. "But we won't make any demands of the judge. We're going in on a fact-finding mission."

The meeting—without any lawyers, on Friday, May 13, 1983—lasted over an hour. It had apparently gone well.

"He's a good man," Chief Lyons said afterward.

The chiefs and the judge were about the same age, and each had a sense of humor.

"We told him we wanted the trial in absentia," Chief Lyons reported. "He said he hadn't made up his mind. And he also said that he wouldn't until he ruled on the motion to dismiss for lack of a speedy trial. He said he might dismiss on that motion, and he didn't think it would be fair to dismiss Kenny and Russ while taking a plea for Dennis and KaMook."

Two days later, Redden heard argument on that motion in a packed courtroom. He seemed unusually interested in the legal give-and-take. The government had refused to go to trial in 1976. Judge Belloni and the Ninth Circuit Court of Appeals had both said there was no good reason for that delay. The first appeal took over four years; the second, over two. The delay was now seven and a half years. Defense witnesses had died.

To buttress our claim, I used information from the reports[7] Ellison had given me about the two gas station attendants who had not seen Dennis Banks but had seen others. My investigator, Don Grant, had telephoned them. They no longer remembered anything. They would have remembered seven years before.

The question was whether Redden had the guts to blame the delay on the appellate courts, which had had jurisdiction of the case for six and a half of the case's seven-and-a-half-year life. Pretrial appeals were rare and thus, pretrial appellate delay even rarer. There was little law telling how to count it. But whatever Redden decided, I would be relieved. At least I was not going to trial. That would be disaster.

Redner was determined to make war. Parkinson was crazy. In fact, he had turned his attention from me and Dennis Banks to Ron Schiffman and Kenny Loud Hawk. He now planned an additional defense pointing to the number of fingerprints Loud Hawk had on items in the motor home, contrasting that with the number of Redner's.

Schiffman was not holding up well either. "I'm absolutely convinced that Redden is going to dismiss based on this technical defect I found in the indictment!" he said, calling me late one night. His argument, although interesting, was weak, even desperate.

And my friend and ally, Michael Bonds, was getting worse every day. In court, he had argued eloquently on the speedy trial motion. He spoke about the effect of delay on KaMook's life, how she had given birth in jail, how her seven-year-old daughter had never lived a day without fear that her mother might go to prison. But, with unfailing confidence, Bonds had misstated facts: when KaMook had given birth, where she had given birth, to which daughter she had given birth. He knew KaMook's children. He had lived through the events. Was his drinking affecting his memory?

"What are you doing up?" Margaret asked, her hands rubbing my back.

---

7. I did not let the prosecutors know I had the reports themselves.

It was 3 o'clock in the morning, and I was sitting at my oak dining room table staring out the bay window, watching the peach tree in my neighbor's backyard sway in the wind.

"This case is fucked, that's all," I said.

"What's wrong?" she asked.

"Well, first, I'm worried about Michael. Friends in his office tell me he's coming to work with alcohol on his breath, even in the morning. So, on top of everything else, some of us met with a psychologist, who told us we had to plan a confrontation. That's no fun. And then there's Banks," I added.

"You told me that Lynn's trying to force him into trial," she said, sitting down.

"Lynn went to South Dakota two weeks ago," I said, "and told everyone that Dennis has committed his honor to going to Oregon to fight the charges. Maybe that got back to him? Anyway, right before the chiefs came out, Dennis asked me to tell the judge that the deal was off. I told him there was no reason to do that yet. There was no percentage in cutting off options unnecessarily. And I told him that if we had to, we could do it later. They couldn't force him to plead guilty. He ordered me to tell the judge anyway. I refused.

"When the chiefs returned to New York, everything was copacetic. Then Banks called me again today. 'I won't plead to count one,' he said, 'it has to be to count two.'

"'What difference does it make?' I yelled. 'They all carry the same penalty.'

"'I won't plead to that one,' he said. 'That's the one Judge Belloni first dismissed. I don't want to do it; I'm not gonna do it. Either get Turner to get the count changed, or the deal is off!'

"So, I called Joe Heath and asked him what's going on. Hell if he knows. He says Dennis is worried that they might try to stick some of the 1975 bombings around the reservation on him. Joe explained that if they had evidence to do that, they would have done it a long time ago, and anyway, the statute of limitations is long past.

"Joe thinks something else is going on. He's not sure why the problems keep coming up. He said it may not be a tolerable situation for Dennis there, with the gag order imposed by the chiefs keeping him from political activity and the travel limitations. He tried talking to Dennis again. Intellectually, Dennis knows that anything but the plea is suicide. But, as Joe said, Dennis just doesn't want to plead. He's said it in enough different ways, at enough different times. So, what am I supposed to do, while my client fucks himself?"

Margaret shrugged.

"And I'll tell you what else is bothering me," I said. "I'm getting more and more burned out with my regular clientele. And this is the case that's supposed to make up for all that!"

The plea was less than a week away. I express mailed more papers to Heath in case he could get Banks to change his mind. Banks was furious that I had not told Redden that the deal was off.

"I'm not saying anything until the judge rules on the speedy trial motion," I said. "If I tell him it's off, he'll be pissed at you. I don't want him pissed at you while he's making up his mind. Anyway, if he thinks that some folks want to plead and the others are going to trial, he is more likely to want to put everyone in the same boat by dismissing the case. It's neater that way."

"Tell him!" Banks instructed.

"I'm not going to," I said, with equal firmness.

I had not offered to resign, and Banks had not fired me. That might be the next telephone call.

At 4 o'clock in the afternoon, May 19, 1983, Julia Plummer called. "The judge's opinion will be ready to be picked up at 1:30 tomorrow afternoon," she said. Her voice was upbeat.

Opinion? He could have written an opinion denying the speedy trial motion. It was a meaty issue, deserving a well-considered written ruling. But if he were going to deny it, a one-page order would have done the job. I hoped.

At 1:25 P.M. on May 20, Annette Murphy and I were in the courthouse elevator on the way to Redden's sixth-floor chambers. As the door opened, Steenson was running down the hall toward us, a document in hand. He was skipping. With each hop, he shook the document high above his head.

We hugged. Redden had accepted all our arguments! He ruled that the delay had denied the defendants a right to a speedy trial *and* that the prejudice from the death of witnesses and the failure of memories over seven years had denied us "due process of law," fundamental fairness.

I called Dennis Banks.

The press was waiting outside the courthouse. "Dennis is relieved," I said as reporters wrote and the cameras clicked, "and commends the judge for his courageous ruling."

"What if the government appeals?" a reporter asked.

"After seven years and three dismissals, it would be gross harassment and a waste of taxpayer money," I said.

An hour later, Kunstler called me. "It's on the wires," he said. "It's an *amazing* result! I was *crazy* with this guy going to go out there."

"I know. Could you believe that? He was being *meshugie*."

"His wife was gonna kill him."

"For good reason."

"You had the right judge."

"Absolutely. Not only is he a good guy but he saved what's left of AIM from self-destruction without knowing it."

CHAPTER 24

THE SUPREME COURT

I awoke at 7:00 A.M. on May 21, 1983, and rushed to the corner newspaper box, just as I had in 1976 after the first dismissal and in 1977 when the Trail Blazers won the NBA championship. A banner headline spread across all five *Oregonian* columns: "JUDGE DISMISSES FIREARMS CASE AGAINST INDIANS."

Redden's dismissal was reported around the country, in the *New York Times*, in Syracuse, in the papers of the Dakotas. The Sioux Falls, South Dakota, *Argus Leader* quoted Mark Meierhenry, the state's new attorney general, lamenting the end of this possible path of Banks's return. Meierhenry said the Oregon prosecutors "blew it" and called *Loud Hawk* "some of the saddest work the taxpayers have ever gotten."

The only person who seemed to be more upset than the prosecutors (who filed an appeal) was Lynn Parkinson. He had been out of town when Redden dismissed. The following week he charged into my office. "I'm furious," he said, pounding my desk for effect. "I wanted a trial, not a dismissal! I may file a motion disassociating my client from the speedy trial motion!"

Was he out of his mind? Possibly so. Two minutes later he said, "The case got dismissed because I prayed for it when I burned sage with Indians in South Dakota."

On January 4, 1984, I argued the speedy trial appeal to a three-judge panel in the Pioneer Courthouse on behalf of all four defendants. Judge Clifford Wallace, a conservative Republican who coveted the next Supreme Court vacancy, was hostile.

But Judge William C. Canby, Jr., a liberal Democrat (and Democratic presidential candidate Walter Mondale's brother-in-law) was friendly. The deciding vote would be that of Senior

District Court Judge Walter Craig.[1] He had sat silently, not asking either side any questions.

Craig had been a trial judge for decades. Appellate judges routinely castigate trial judges for delay. I could not imagine a Senior District Court judge passing up the opportunity for revenge.

I was right. In August 1984, the court of appeals upheld Redden's dismissal, two to one. Predictably, Turner filed a petition for rehearing in September.

At 9:00 A.M., October 8, 1984, Dennis Banks was brought in chains for sentencing on the 1973 Custer riot charges. Tired of his confinement in Onondaga, he had surrendered to South Dakota authorities weeks before. He had not forewarned any of his lawyers.

The sentencing took all day in a packed courtroom. Kunstler led Banks's witnesses through their testimony. California community workers told of his help to Indian and poor people. Elderly Indians from the Pine Ridge reservation told of whites killing Indians, over and over again—Gordon, Custer, Pine Ridge. The government did not care. Then Banks came and tried to stop the murders. He had a "big heart for his Indian people," they said.

Kay Cole, an elderly white woman from California, a daughter of a Daughter of the American Revolution and granddaughter of a civil war soldier, told how she had met Dennis and KaMook in 1980. Within weeks, she was helping to coordinate a cross-country walk to educate people about Indian demands for cultural, religious, and economic freedom. She helped Banks organize a tribunal of indigenous peoples from every continent to explore their common conditions and experiences. She helped him arrange a rescue mission of food, clothing, wood stoves, and quilts that was to be brought by airplanes, helicopters (piloted by Vietnam veterans), cars, vans, and trucks to poor Indians who were freezing and starving in Arizona and in the Black Hills of South Dakota. She spoke about Banks's commitment to his family and to all children and about how he had welcomed her into his family and encouraged her to reconnect with estranged members of her own.

1. To reduce appellate backlogs, district court judges routinely sit on court of appeals cases.

Others testified too, including those who worked with Banks in his fight against child abuse and alcohol and drug use. Each had stories about how Banks had directed habitual alcoholics to sweat lodges and Sun Dances and turned their lives around. Now they did not drink, and many now helped others.

Jim Bear Big King, a member of the U.S. Armed Forces, was denied leave to attend the Sun Dance. The navy did not recognize Indian religion. He told Banks that he was going AWOL. Passionately, Bear Big King told Judge Marshall Young that Banks had dissuaded him from that decision and had guided him through the grievance process so that he and all others Indians could have their rights respected. Partly because of Dennis Banks's work, he said, President Carter signed a law in 1978 recognizing Indian religious rights.

People testified about Banks's part in the beginning Indian struggles during the Johnson administration. Indian children who were taken to boarding schools (frequently against their will), usually more than a thousand miles from their homes, were beaten if they spoke their native tongue or refused to participate in Christian ceremonies. Dennis helped found "survival schools," where Indian children learned to take pride in their history and culture. In the late 1960s, when Banks was working at Honeywell Corporation in Minneapolis, he found young Indian people in the slums and directed them to jobs, into alcohol programs, and out of trouble.

Priests from South Dakota, Presbyterian lay workers from Syracuse, and teachers from Onondaga (carrying hundreds of letters from students) spoke about Banks's substantial contributions to the betterment of Indian people: the running coach, helping a young Indian athlete recognize his potential as a world-class competitor; the compassionate leader, excusing himself from a meeting with a congressman to comfort a youngster crying in the next room. Geraldine Armendariz spoke. She had faced great obstacles as a woman and as an Indian when she was trying to become an attorney. Each time, Banks was there, encouraging her to go on, to strive, to learn. "He said I should be a role model for other Indian young women," she explained. She had persevered because of Dennis Banks.

Finally, Banks stood, ready for his sentence. "Your Honor," he said, "there were a lot of circumstances involved in my decision to come back. Certainly, the long outstanding warrant was one of them. But since I left, I had a very productive life and a very moving life.

"Onondaga wasn't small. It was a giant nation. It was a place where the heritage and the music and language is still spoken; where the clan system still exists as the governing mover of a nation. I've often asked other chiefs, other council members across this country, to come to Onondaga and to see real jurisdiction and real sovereignty.

"In nineteen months, I never heard or witnessed or even heard gossip about any murder on that nation, never heard of robbery or rape.

"Prison time has never been an issue with me. I am an ex-convict. I have committed crimes against this society, and I went to jail for them.

"When I got to prison and, for the first time in many years, away from alcohol, I finally began to understand the word 'discrimination.' For the first time I wanted to challenge it. For the first time I wanted to understand what it was, racism and discrimination, and I came out of prison in 1968 determined to build a new road for my life. Out of all of this came the American Indian Movement.

"Throughout my life I've felt the snide war whoops and the yelling war whoops by people as I go down the street. That used to hurt me. I'd feel very angry about that, growing up and reading the textbooks filled with racist remarks and derogatory statements and pictures about Indians. A feeling of being ashamed, being ashamed to be Indian, began to creep into me, and it was inside me all that time.

"I ran into Eddie Benton, who I've known all my life. I ran into Clyde Bellecourt, Mary Jane Wilson, Peggy Bellecourt. We began to return to our own Indian ways. I began to feel a sense of pride, and I realized that this is what I was looking for. I believed I had found a trace of that pride in our people, and I set out on a journey to bring it out in full force.

"In the meantime, Indian people were still being hurt all over this country. In Arizona, Philip Solayo was shot in the back by a deputy sheriff. Manslaughter charges against him were dismissed.

In California, Richard Oaks was shot to death by a white man; no charges. And then in 1972, Raymond Yellow Thunder was brutally beaten to death. The Yellow Thunder family asked the FBI to investigate. They refused.

"As a last resort, the family called the American Indian Movement. We went to Gordon. We had heard that this man had died brutally, from cigarette and cigar burns and castration. We exhumed the body. There were cigarette burns all over his body. He was not castrated. We asked for the Hare brothers to be charged. The authorities weren't even going to charge them, but they were eventually charged. They were found guilty of manslaughter. We went to Alliance, Nebraska, Gordon, and Chadron, setting up Human Rights Commissions and race relations committees, almost always after an Indian had been beaten up or murdered. And that's all we asked, that race relations committees be established.

"In January of 1973, I received a call from Sarah Bad Heart Bull. Her son was murdered in Custer. I called the district attorney. We had a meeting, he and I and Ramon Robideau, our attorney. Hobie Gates said he didn't have any evidence connecting Darold Schmidt to the murder. He said to Ramon, 'You go out and you find the evidence and bring it back to me. I'll issue a warrant.'

"Two days later Ramon had five affidavits. Then ten more, and they all incriminated Schmidt. Hobie wouldn't make an arrest. I called Ramon, and I didn't know what to do. We called the press. But there was never anything said about it, and so Sarah kept pushing, asking for something to be done about her murdered son.

"I called Hobie Gates. I called the mayor. We got hold of a minister, and the purpose of the February 6 meeting was to come here and establish a Human Rights Commission and see if Hobart Gates would arrest Darold Schmidt.

"What happened when we got here was racism. I pleaded not guilty. I tried to argue my case. My counsel was scared off. I never could present my case here, why and what happened on February 6.

"I'm prepared to do whatever time you give me. I'm prepared also to help build South Dakota.

"Ten years ago, when I was held prisoner here, there were eight prisoners in my cell block, and all eight of us were Indians.

"Yesterday, thirty of us went out to play basketball. Twenty-five of us were Indians. Racism still exists.

"Why did I come back to South Dakota? I came back because progress is too slow. Progress in trying to bring together Indian people and white people is too slow.

"I'm fearful for my life in prison. Maybe not the prison guards, but somebody might try to make a name. Kill the American Indian Movement leader. Put a bullet in his head.

"I'm forty-seven years old. In the ten years KaMook and I have been together, we started buying a house. Then we had to move. Then we started building a house. Then we had to move. It was always hanging over me. I could never raise my children the way I wanted to.

"I've been running a long time. I've been running from discrimination. Now, and in 1968, I wanted to turn around and meet it head on.

"I will never try and flee from prison or jails. I will never consider suicide, ever, so there should never be a story of me found hanging myself or being shot escaping prison."

Judge Young sentenced Dennis Banks to three years in the South Dakota state prison, the longest term given to any of the Indians convicted in the 1973 Custer Courthouse riot.

The U.S. Supreme Court building is solid and ornate. History lives there in portraits and busts: Holmes, Brandeis, Frankfurter, Black, Cardozo, Douglas.

I wore a new blue suit, a new red silk tie, and black shoes with laces instead of my brown cowboy boots. I called it my "Ed Meese outfit," after the style of the former attorney general.

The Ninth Circuit Court of Appeals had rejected Turner's petition for rehearing. But the Supreme Court had taken the case, wanting to further define the right to a speedy trial.

"The Department of Justice thinks it's a slam dunk," my informants in the Oregon courthouse told me. I didn't care. I was going to argue before the United States Supreme Court!

Regardless of their eventual ruling, I knew that ten years of delay before trial—most of it waiting for appellate courts to issue opinions—deprived my clients of a speedy trial. I had refused new cases to work five hundred hours on the briefs and another three hundred hours on the argument, even though the court paid just $2,000.

I was relaxed, confident. I knew all the rules and subtleties. I had read all the books, articles, cases, and law reviews. I had traveled to Washington the week before to watch the court. I had concentrated on every detail: how the justices spoke, what type of questions they asked, the distance between the counsel table and the podium, how high the podium was, where the water glass was. I even looked at the ornate ceiling, to see where the light came from. I wondered, so high up, who changed the light bulbs, and how did he or she do it?

Every lawyer must begin with the same sentence: "Mr. Chief Justice, and may it please the court." That is the tradition, the rule. I practiced, "Mr. Cheap Justice, and may it please the court." My sister, Alice, who came from Boston to watch, yelled "Stop that!" She worried that I would slip.

At 10:00 A.M. exactly, November 12, 1985, the justices emerged from behind a dark curtain and took the bench—the Chief Justice in the middle, the others arranged by seniority. Chief Justice Warren Burger and Justice William Brennan were five feet from me. I exchanged nods with both.

Bruce Kuhlick, the deputy solicitor general, went first. His argument was technically correct but serviceable, bland. To practice mine, I had practiced his and done it better. He was representing the government. I was representing friends—and the hopes of many Indian people.

I stood and paused a few seconds for dramatic effect. I was surprised that I was not nervous. I looked to my colleagues, Tom Steenson and Michael Bonds, sitting to my left, and Kuhlick, my opponent, sitting to my right. Then I began. "Mr. Chief Justice, and may it please the Court. Nine years and 363 days ago . . ."

Chief Justice Burger interrupted, furious about the age of the case. He blamed it on the defendants rather than the slowness of the appellate courts. I answered and diffused him. Everyone, except Justice Thurgood Marshall, asked questions. None of the questions were as difficult as the ones I had asked myself in preparation.

Justice William Rhenquist's eyes lit when I mentioned that the Ninth Circuit was understaffed by thirteen judges during most of the appellate delay. Justice Sandra Day O'Connor seemed sympathetic—such a long delay; subject to restriction at any time; no special procedures used to speed up pretrial cases; no excuse for the courts to take four years on the first appeal and two and a half years on the second.

"The government believes that no defendant *ever* wants a speedy trial," I said, "and that if he asks for one, he's lying. Well, I don't believe that a speedy trial should only be provided to those who the government believes are sincere. If a defendant demands a speedy trial, and the government has the ability to provide one, and the district court orders the government to proceed to trial, and the court of appeals orders that trial proceed, the government should provide that speedy trial or suffer the consequences."

I played the court like a jury. The emotion worked. Justices Brennan and Marshall, the two "moderates" left from the Warren Court, now termed "liberal" in relation to their increasingly conservative brethren, were my only "solid" votes. I had arguments designed for the rest, especially Justices John Paul Stevens and Harry Blackmun, who had dissented from another recent case—*United States v. Dr. Jeffrey MacDonald*—in which the rejected speedy trial claim was weaker than ours.

I needed to win all four of them and one more. But no other justice was likely to vote for me. My only hope was that Chief Justice Burger would be upset with the magnitude of the appellate delay and have enough political savvy to use the case to ask Congress for more appellate judges to reduce backlogs. When my half hour was up I was satisfied, racing intellectually, yet unfulfilled. I had put so much effort into such a short performance that I wanted to be invited back to do it again and again.

"Great argument!" an older member of the Supreme Court bar said as I walked out. John Privitera, Leonard Peltier's Washington attorney, winked at me from a rear bench and flashed a "thumbs up." Charles Fried, President Reagan's new solicitor general, walked through a crowd to me, shook my hand, and said my advocacy had been "masterful." Television, radio, and newsprint reporters waited to interview me on the Supreme Court steps. Court watchers called that afternoon and said that my argument was "the only one that had the justices leaning forward in their chairs all day."

We had won the argument. Three hundred hours of practice, driven by the fear of screwing up, had made me polished. But the politics of the case remained. If the Court wanted to rule for us, there was no reason for it to have taken the case in the first place; it would have let the court of appeals opinion stand.

While cloistered, preparing for argument, I had decided. I no longer enjoyed my practice. I wanted out—from criminal law, private practice, and Oregon.

After ten years, I needed the ethnic diversity of New York again. I hungered for the flavor—people of different color speaking different languages, eating real food, like fresh bagels and pastrami sandwiches offered without a choice of wheat bread, sprouts, or mayonnaise. I missed the large Jewish community, where anti-Semitism was less visible, where "Stern" was always spelled correctly (without an "i" or an extra "e"), and where I was more likely to find a Jewish woman with whom to fall in love.

I had had an idea in October, when the Palestine Liberation Organization (PLO) hijacked the *Achille Lauro* passenger ship, killed wheelchair-bound American Leon Klinghoffer, and dumped his body overboard. There were organizations advocating for victims of domestic crime, but no one stood up for the victims of international terrorism. I researched the PLO. It owned property in the United States. It had multimillion-dollar bank accounts here. Unlike with indigent criminal defendants, there was someone to sue for a victim's injuries. The American Section of the International Association of Jewish Lawyers and Jurists, of which I was a board member, approved the project—a national organization advocating for victims of terrorism. I was elected director.

I returned to Oregon the week after the Supreme Court performance, eager to close my remaining cases, pleased that I was ending my private practice with a Supreme Court argument, and conflicted about leaving friends and the beauty and ease of the Northwest. But my immediate concern was Michael Bonds.

Bonds had shown up late at the Supreme Court the week before, only minutes before argument, looking horrible, pasty, fidgety. At a postargument lunch, he made a trip to the bathroom every fifteen minutes. He sniffed constantly. He was jerky, staccato. His hands shook with classic DT's.

When he returned to Portland, his newest lover,[2] a talented young attorney named Jonna Schuder, had found him frozen, one side of his body paralyzed. I heard about his condition when I returned to Portland. I called him. He sounded bewildered, although by then he had been released from the hospital and his feeling had returned.

The next day, when I called again, he was drunk again. "Fuck that!" he yelled, revolted, when I suggested an inpatient alcohol program. "Yeah, Kenny," he said, calm all of a sudden, with a singsong cadence, "I know I have a problem, but believe me, it's nothing I can't handle."

I had witnessed Bonds's spiraling alcoholic bouts twice before. Each time, he plunged lower. The last time, his friends had planned a confrontation. Before it could be arranged, he was arrested for drunk driving. He was fine for a while. Jail had jolted him. He went to counseling. Then he started drinking again. This time, I worried there was no longer any room for him to sink.

A day later, Ann called, frightened. "Mike just phoned me," she said, "He asked where his guns were." We hid them.

I was back in New York in January 1986, running the antiterrorism project from my mother's attic until grant money came in. It was fun, new law. Both former U.S. Supreme Court Justice Arthur Goldberg and Vice President George Bush wrote letters of support. Key senators were interested, as were international law scholars and Jewish organizations, including the American Israel Public Affairs Committee (AIPAC) and the American Jewish Committee (AJC). I had already been to Washington twice to gather support for victims of terrorism and to discuss specific legislation.

One January afternoon I expected a call from a reporter who was considering a feature story. A newsman called and asked about "the decision."

"What decision?" I questioned.

"The Supreme Court's decision in *Loud Hawk*."

"What was it?"

2. He had left Ann.

"Don't you know?"

"No."

"The dismissal was reversed, five to four."

I was sad but not surprised. Two days later, I was actually relieved when I read the text. Justice Lewis Powell's majority opinion had a dozen serious factual and intellectual errors. Things that he said had happened (for instance, defense motions being denied) had not happened (the same motions were granted). The whopper was his statement, "The government introduced evidence at trial showing that Dennis Banks was the driver of one of the vehicles."

What trial? That had been the point of the entire case! If the Court had assumed there was a trial, then it must have assumed that the defendants were *convicted*, because if they were acquitted, there could have been no appeal. The government cannot appeal acquittals. That was significant. The standards of review were different for an untried person (presumed innocent) and a convicted felon.

I would ask the Court to reconsider, especially as the two new "rules" it created in *Loud Hawk* were contradictory. Justice Powell said that if people are not "incarcerated or subjected to other substantial restriction on their liberty [during a pretrial appeal, such as the *Loud Hawk* defendants, who were either on personal recognizance or on no restriction at all], a court should not weigh that time toward a claim under the Speedy Trial Clause." Four pages later he said, in "assessing the purposes and reasonableness of . . . [a pretrial government] appeal, courts may consider . . . the seriousness of the crime, [which] must be sufficiently serious to justify restraints . . . on the defendant pending the outcome of the appeal." In other words, the delay would "count" against the government in reverse proportion to the seriousness of the charges against the defendant, on the theory that the government had more reason to appeal adverse pretrial decisions on serious cases.

Together, these two standards were irreconcilable. If a defendant were released without restriction, the speedy trial clock would not tick. And if the charges were serious enough to keep the defendant in "restraints" pending the appeal, the speedy trial clock would not tick. Either way the defendant lost, the prosecution won, and the constitutional right to a speedy trial meant nothing.

I wrote a hard-hitting Petition for Reconsideration and filed it on my next Washington trip to meet senatorial staffers about the terrorism project. A few weeks later, the Court denied the petition. The order came in an envelope with a misprinted return address: the "Supreme Court of the Uniteb States."

Within hours, Charles Turner called. "Ken," he asked, "do you think Dennis would still be interested in a plea?" Turner never knew that Banks had rejected the deal in 1983. I thought he would be less interested now, since he was in jail in South Dakota and no longer had any fear of appearing in Oregon.

I equivocated, wanting to keep Turner hopeful about a plea so that he did not spend time preparing his case. "But before we discuss any deal," I said, "we have to finish litigating Redden's 1983 dismissal."

"What?" he asked, perplexed.

"Charlie," I explained, "Redden dismissed because he found a violation of the right to a speedy trial *and* because he found a violation of the Fifth Amendment right to due process of law because of the unavailability of the dead witnesses and the loss of memories of live ones. You may have a good argument about the due process question, but it's never been ruled on. Technically, Redden dismissed on that basis, too, and no higher court has touched it. Since that part of the order has never been overturned, the case remains dismissed."

He was unsure. He talked to an expert in the Justice Department named Kathleen Felton and called me the next day. "Felton agrees with you," he said.

Turner filed a motion and a brief asking the Ninth Circuit to overturn the due process dismissal. I filed papers in opposition, quoting settled "blackletter" law—that the government had had to ask for that relief when it appealed Redden's order nearly three years before and could not raise it for the first time now.

We waited again. In March 1986, the court of appeals issued two rulings three days apart. The first said, "The order of the district court dismissing the indictment is vacated, and the case is remanded for further consideration in light of [the Supreme Court opinion]." The second said, "The motion by the government for an order reversing dismissal of the indictment is denied."

Judge Redden gathered the lawyers[3] on the telephone the afternoon of April 17, 1986. "Two orders came down," he said. "As I understand it, the first one had the effect of saying my due process opinion was incorrect and to proceed from there, and the second one is the opposite of that."

Turner suggested that everyone ask the court of appeals for clarification. It was in the *Loud Hawk* defendants' interest to argue that the orders made perfect sense.

"When the first order was issued," I said, "the court of appeals hadn't realized that dismissal order had anything more to it than the speedy trial ruling. That was all the government ever mentioned in its briefs and all the Supreme Court had considered. When, three days later, the panel realized there was a second, independent, dismissal ground that the government had never appealed, its order was clear: the case was still dead." Redden was intrigued.

On the tenth anniversary of Judge Belloni's first dismissal, I filed a twenty-three-page memorandum tracking all the opinions (filed as a 215-page Appendix) and proving that the court of appeals had been unaware of the due process claim because the government had abandoned that issue on appeal. The case law was clear. Failure to raise an issue on appeal, in the briefs, waived (i.e., abandoned) it.

On June 23, 1986, Judge Redden filed an opinion. He had dismissed the case in 1983 because the delay had prejudiced our due process rights to a fair trial—witnesses had died, others had lost their memories. This holding was independent of, and in addition to, the speedy trial dismissal. The due process ruling had never been appealed. The case, therefore, "remained dismissed."

Despite resounding criticism, Turner filed his fourth appeal.[4] Briefs were filed in fall 1986. Argument was heard in San Francisco in March 1987. I flew in, argued, and returned to New York, pessimistic. The Court of Appeals panel had been composed of

---

3. Except for Michael Bonds, who had left his law practice to travel around Europe for a year.

4. The *Oregonian* editorialized: "Surely Charles H. Turner can find more productive things to do with his time than to continue the government's 10-year-old case against Dennis Banks."

two Reagan and one Eisenhower appointees, none of whom seemed favorable. The only highlight was that Tosh, now twelve, was attending school in San Francisco for one year and had watched the argument.

"What do you want to be when you grow up?" I asked her later, over lunch.

"A lawyer," she said.

"God forbid!" I said. "Okay, why?"

"To help people like my daddy," she replied.

"Good reason," I said. "That's why I do it."

On May 7, 1987, five days before the eleventh anniversary of Judge Belloni's first dismissal, the court of appeals reversed Judge Redden and sent the case back for trial. In early fall, the court of appeals declined my petition for rehearing. *Loud Hawk et al.* was finally heading for a jury.

CHAPTER 25

HEADING FOR A JURY

"OKAY kids, we need to have a meeting here," Dennis Banks ordered, as he lifted Chinopa from his lap and landed him like a parachutist on the kitchen floor. His four children—Tosh, now thirteen; TaTiopa, eleven; Chubbs, seven; and Chinopa, three— didn't debate. They each grabbed a bagel, fresh from Brooklyn, and went downstairs.

I arranged my legal papers on the wood kitchen table where the bagels had been. "We have to decide," I began, "whether we want to go to trial or take the deal, which, by the way, has improved since 1983. If Dennis and KaMook plead to one count, Turner will dismiss Russ and Kenny."

"What are the chances we'll go to jail?" Loud Hawk asked.

"Well," I said, "if we take the deal, none. And if we go to trial, I don't think Dennis would be convicted. But I think you and Russ and KaMook would be, because you were caught there."

"That's right," Bonds said, sitting across from me, below the bulletin board where KaMook kept the kids' school lunch menus cut from the Rapid City, South Dakota, newspaper.

"And," I continued, "there are no guarantees. But I don't think Redden would send anyone to jail, although you never know. If all that hardware sits on the table for two weeks, and there's bad press, he might. But I can say, for sure, after so many years, no one is looking at anything substantial, although, of course, insubstantial jail time is no fun either."

"I may be interested in a deal," Dennis said, "but only if they dismiss KaMook too. Then I'd have to think about it."

Dennis had looked down when he said that. And his voice lacked conviction.

"Nobody's taking any deal if KaMook has to plead!" Redner

yelled. His manhood seemed threatened by the prospect. "What are our defenses?" he asked, his voice now calmer.

"First," I said, "there are technical things. We have a hook for every count. For instance, for the first four counts—the bombs counts—they have to prove the dynamite was explosive. The only physical evidence they have are pictures. Our expert says they don't show dynamite exploding, only Fettig's blasting cap and primer cord."

"When we first got the stuff," Banks said, "I tried shooting at it—put a couple of sticks on a log and fired maybe a dozen rounds. Nothing happened. I think the stuff was too wet."

"Well," I said, "you guys must have thought some of it was good, or you wouldn't have bothered lugging it. Anyway, it's the government's burden of proof. They'll have a hard time with a jury since they destroyed it.

"There are also issues on the firearms counts," I continued, "and the idiots have never figured out that Dennis wasn't technically 'convicted' of the Custer riot charges until he was sentenced in 1984, not in 1975, as they allege in the indictment. Convictions aren't legally 'entered' until after a person is sentenced.[1] But all that is defensive; we need an affirmative message for the jury."

Dennis nodded as KaMook left the table and warmed fry bread in a microwave oven.

"In 1975," I said, "all we had was a 'give us back the guns and we'll show you our defense' defense." Redner smiled. "Now, in the fall of 1987, after a collective fifty years of good behavior, self-defense won't be threatening to a jury. It's historical. They won't worry about you guys picking up guns as you walk out of the courtroom."

"I think we should do what we did in St. Paul," Dennis said.[2] "We had testimony about the wretched conditions on the reservation that led to that demonstration and the violence of the government. All the jurors we talked with favored acquittal."

---

1. In order for Banks to be found guilty of being an ex-convict in possession of firearms, as charged in the indictment, proof of a prior conviction would have to be presented to the jury.

2. Banks's 1974 trial for the Wounded Knee takeover, held in St. Paul, ended in a dismissal for government misconduct.

"I agree," I said, "but we also give up something. If we say 'here's why we had the stuff,' a jury is more likely to think the dynamite *could* explode; and it's hard to jibe a defense of 'prove I was there' or 'prove defendant in vehicle number one knew about the scary guns hidden in vehicle number two' with what is, essentially, a justification defense."

"I understand," Dennis said.

At a break in our two days of meetings, Bonds and I left the Banks's house and walked to a ridge nearby. We could see the white and red lights of Rapid City below and the outline of the Black Hills in the distance as nightfall approached with a touch of dusky gray in the October skies.

"Did you catch what Kenny said to Dennis as we were leaving?" I asked.

Bonds shook his head, "No."

"He said, 'Man, you're really into green. It's not like the old days.'"

"Shit," Bonds said.

"Well, it's understandable," I said. "Dennis's middle-class home looks palatial to Kenny. And did you notice the tension between Kenny and Russ?"

"Yeah, what's the story?" Bonds replied.

"Well," I said, "First, Russ married a woman whose family were Goons. She's very nice, but she's not full blood. Her first husband was white. Her kids have blond hair. The Loud Hawks look at that as my great-grandmother would have looked at me marrying an ex-nun.

"And then there's Loneman School in Oglala. Apparently there was a fight over control. Russ was teaching there, trying to push the kids forward, increase their expectations and confidence. He told me he even had the football team calling audibles. But there's an old guard that controls the board and liked the status quo. It fired Russ. Kenny's relatives dominate that faction. Ka-Mook says that's why they're here in Rapid City now, instead of on the res. Rather than choose sides, she picked up the kids and left."

"Shit," Bonds said. "How are we going to get these guys through a four-week trial together?"

"Don't know," I said, "but it seems only fair. Last time it was the lawyers going crazy."

We slept only a few hours that weekend, meeting all the time, the distance between the defendants controlled by each but hidden by none. Some things seemed to bind them together—not the nostalgia or the mission of twelve years before but the current racism. They all nodded when Bonds and I commented on the bigoted caricatures of Indians in public places, including murals depicting "savages." There was subtle racism, too. On one coffee run, Redner put a five-dollar bill on a convenience store counter. The clerk picked it up, made change, and left it on the counter for Redner to retrieve. "Watch what she does with the next customer," Redner whispered. He was a white man. She handed him his change directly, into his palm, hand touching hand.

When Bonds and the other defendants had left and KaMook and the kids were at the Rapid City mall, Dennis and I were alone for the first time since the spring of 1976, when we had been hiding from vigilantes in Nancy Sanders's farmhouse, talking into the early morning.

I had never asked him, point blank, what had happened back in November 1975. To represent him, I had not needed to know. For the first time, we were close to trial. I told Dennis, in roundabout ways, that I might need to know soon. He sat in his kitchen chair, quietly puffing his pipe. The room smelled of Red Cherry tobacco. Cans and pouches of that brand had been found all over the motor home. The prosecutors had never made the connection.

"When you come to Portland," I reminded him, "leave that blend behind."

He smiled and said, "Right-o."

I was bending over, packing legal pads into my suitcase, when Dennis added, "You know, I was in that motor home."

"Um hum," I answered matter-of-factly.

Dennis puffed on his pipe for a minute, then tamped it on a glass ashtray. Smoke coiled from an unextinguished ember.

"After that trooper pulled us over and KaMook, Annie Mae, Tosh, and Leonard got out," he said, "I stayed inside." He paused for an instant, drawing a dirty pipe cleaner through the discolored pipe stem. "I put it in gear," he continued. "I was going straight down the highway, doing 45 maybe, driving like this."

He demonstrated in front of the refrigerator. Standing, his left hand was outstretched to the imaginary steering wheel while his right hand, also extended as far as it could, held the imaginary mobile home door open. His legs were spread-eagled.

"I was balancing like this. When the rig slowed a little, to say 35, I let go the wheel, then jumped onto the highway. I hit the concrete and rolled over and over, then watched it keep going, then veer to the left, onto the V-shaped median, where it slalomed up and down until it stopped."

As I waited silently, Dennis picked up his pipe, reconnected the stem to the bowl, packed another pinch of cherry tobacco, and lit it with a wooden kitchen match. "I ran to the highway fence," he continued, "scaled it, and cut the hell out of my hands and legs on the barbed wire. I ran as fast as I could, due south, where it was dark, until I was out of breath. Then I walked, kept walking 'til I found some bushes and hid. Even from there I could see the lights from the highway and hear the shots."

"You must have been scared shitless they got KaMook and Tosh," I said.

Dennis swallowed and rested his pipe against the box of kitchen matches. "I didn't know what the hell was going on. I stayed there until after the lights went out and the shooting stopped. Then I went south. It was a gravel road. I found a beaver hutch. I crawled into it. It was cold and wet. Luckily, I had a double layer of socks on and fleece-lined rubber boots. I took one set of socks off and put them on my hands, which were cut and bloody."

Dennis looked at his hands, obviously remembering the fright of his escape. "I didn't sleep all night," he continued. "Just as the sun was rising, I heard dogs barking. Then some shots. They were close by. I was *petrified*, not of the cops, though. I remembered as a kid, I used to shoot into beaver hutches. I thought it was a kid. I stayed as still as I could. The dogs and the shots were close. I heard them pass by. I stayed there, awake, for three days. On the fourth, I watched as the owner of the land approached. I thought I might have to run, but my legs were so cold and cramped I didn't think I could. I watched as the man took a bucket of water, poured half of it out for some purpose, and put it on a stump. He walked away."

"You are one of the luckiest sons of bitches I ever met," I said.

"Well, listen," Dennis continued, looking me straight in the eye. "I hadn't had anything to drink in three days. I crawled out, guzzled the remaining water, and crawled back into my hiding spot. Five minutes later he came back, looking for the pail, as if he had forgotten where he had put it.

"That night I had to sleep. I snuck into the barn, which was close by. I made a bed of two stacks of hay, placed side to side. The next morning I was cold, hungry, and thirsty. I woke when I heard the owner again. He was packing his truck. I decided to take a chance. I walked to the truck and edged up to him.

"'Hi,' I said, 'I've been out all night. My car broke down, two or three miles back, and I've been walking all over, looking for a telephone. Mind if I use yours?'

"The guy looked skeptical. He studied me. He stared at my cuts and my clothes, which were really dirty.

"He just stared at me for a minute and then asked, 'You're Dennis Banks, aren't you?' He didn't wait for me to respond. He said, 'They're looking for you, you know? Wait here. I've got to go inside.'

"He walked through his porch door. I still remember hearing it slam shut," Dennis said, as he paused and looked out the window.

"I was panicked," he began again. "I thought I should run, that this white guy, from cowboy country, for sure was calling the sheriff or the FBI. But I was too tired. I just couldn't run any more. So I waited. It seemed like fifteen minutes. I'm sure it was less. Finally, he came out. With his wife. She was holding a platter of turkey sandwiches."

"Amazing!" I said, laughing.

"That's only part of it," Dennis said, fending off my interruption of a story he had been waiting nearly thirteen years to tell. "While I was eating my first food in four days, the man was telling me they were moving to Nevada the next day, with their truck and trailer. I had $80. I offered him half for gas, to take me wherever he was going, and to let me off by a freeway.

"'We talked about it already,' he said. 'We'll take you, no need to pay.'

"They didn't want me in the cab with them, so they moved some boxes and stuck me in the trailer. They left a slot for me to peek through. We left the next morning, on this really bumpy gravel road. I felt every jolt. There were still roadblocks up. At a gas station, I saw police look into the back of the truck, but they didn't bother with the fully packed trailer.

"We reached Nevada that night. The couple checked into a motel. They bought bread and cold cuts, which they shared with me. I called John Trudell, who lived on the Duck Valley reservation, about three hours away. 'John,' I said, 'this is Dennis. I need your help.'

"'Where the fuck are you, man!' he asked. I told him. John picked me up.

"I never did learn that couples' name," he said, "because I wanted to protect them. But before John came, I asked them why they helped me.

"Months before, they had been traveling through Nebraska and detoured to hear Marlon Brando and me speak in Lincoln. We spoke in this big hall, about all the terror on the reservation, all the murders and trials, you know.

"Marlon gave an impassioned plea, asking for help. We passed a collection plate. The couple had only $2.50. They said they cried when they couldn't contribute.

"When they left, the wife said to the husband, 'I hope someday, we have a chance to help these people.'"

I returned to New York on the red eye. I waded through the record again. The Supreme Court litigation had swelled the file to over 20,000 pages. I made notes and prepared novel defenses.

Dynamite, otherwise legal, had to be registered if the owner had a "nefarious" intent. If Banks and company planned to use it for self-defense, was that a nefarious intent? And if they planned to use it in South Dakota, as the government would certainly allege, did they have to register it in Oregon, a state they were only passing through? Wouldn't their intent in Oregon be only conditional? What if they never reached South Dakota, or changed plans along the way?

And what about the government certificates—pretty papers with blue ribbons—that "proved" the dynamite had not been registered according to federal law? The papers said that none of the defendants had destructive devices listed in their names on the date the records were checked—at the U.S. Attorney's request—in 1980. There was nothing retrospective to prove that no bombs had been registered in their names in November 1975.

And there was also the question of venue. The government

had to prove that the crime took place in Oregon. The indictment alleged that the guns were "received" in Oregon. But the
proof was that the guns were received in California, where they
were bought, or Washington, where they were supposedly hidden
in the motor home, minus their serial numbers.

I also pondered facts that would not be mentioned at trial.
Banks had told me that the motor home had traveled for weeks
before being stopped. It had even gone back to South Dakota. "It
was scary being on the fringes," he said.

This was the mid-1970s, when the ultra-Left became the freaky
Left, when the Weather Underground and the Symbionese Liberation Army and even part of AIM thought social change came
through bombs. Banks, like others I knew, caught up in the
emotion and the government attacks, had crossed a line.

Since then, we had both changed. If he had crossed that line
now, maybe I wouldn't defend him? In 1975, I was zealous, thinking that the rightness of the cause justified nearly everything—
good ends excusing almost any means. The Banks I knew now
would not hesitate to help the people who needed help any more
than he had then. But would he do it with guns? If they needed
them. But his definition of "need" would now be less romantic.

Regardless, the real culprit now was the government. Banks
had changed, mellowed perhaps, but Turner had not. There was
no justification for him to continue this prosecution.

By early November I had reread the record, packed it, shipped
it to Oregon, flown to Portland for Banks's arraignment, returned
to New York, arranged a leave of absence from my new job,[3]
returned to Portland, rented a computer, and set up a desk at
Tom Steenson's office. The case was on a sure track for trial. Trial
was worrisome. The defendants were not getting along. And no
one, except Redner, was eager to visit Portland and do all the
work a political case required—create an effective defense committee and seek constant interviews in the press. Even the lawyers were not that interested anymore.

---

3. I had worked for seven months on the terrorism project, waiting for
funding to materialize. It did not. Since I couldn't work without a salary, I
found a job. I was environmental enforcement counsel for the New York City
Department of Sanitation when I returned to Portland for *Loud Hawk*.

Time had passed this case by. In 1975–76, the marches and protests and letters and press had had an important effect beyond educating the community to the problems in Indian country: they kept the prosecutors off-balance. I still remembered an older U.S. marshal pulling Bonds and Roberts and me into a corridor in 1976 and, with an approving smile, asking, "What the hell are you guys doing to make the prosecutors so *crazy?*"

What the case needed was to be stirred up again. Turner was combustible. Pressure could detonate him. My new role in the case—now that I had no other Oregon client who might suffer in retaliation—was to drive Turner literally nuts. That was our best defense. I would prod him, he would explode, and then he would decide that the case was no fun and give up. If not, he would get carried away at trial and either alienate the jury or say something so outrageous that the case would end in a mistrial or dismissal. I felt guilty that I enjoyed the idea of Turner experiencing the same stress he inflicted on my clients.

My first step was to paper him to death. With my rented word processor, I spit out nearly five hundred pages of motions in slightly more than three weeks. None of it was polished. But it was weighty. It would discourage Turner.[4]

After I filed most of the pleadings, Judge Redden's secretary called. "The judge wants an emergency hearing," she announced. "He has an agenda." One of the items on the agenda would certainly be my paper mountain.

One of the motions I planned to file the following week was a new dismissal request, based on the papers from Bruce Ellison that I had held onto for five years about the two gas station attendants who did not identify Dennis Banks in the motor home but instead identified Frank Black Horse, another AIM member who had been arrested in Canada with Leonard Peltier.

The motion challenged the suppression of this favorable evidence from the grand jury. According to transcripts, one of the grand jurors had asked the prosecutors if there was any eyewit-

---

4. Even though the motions were well founded, I knew Judge Redden was unlikely to grant many. Having dismissed the case three times, only to have the higher courts reverse, he wanted the case concluded.

ness evidence concerning Banks. The prosecutors did not tell the grand juror of these essential witnesses.

Now was the time to play these reports. They would allow me to take control of the "emergency hearing" and diffuse Redden's inevitable displeasure at my massive pleadings.

To set the stage, before the hearing, I gave Redden a copy of a letter I had received from Senior District Court Judge Fred Nichol, who had presided over Dennis Banks's Wounded Knee trial. The letter detailed the government misconduct in his case.[5] The

5. The letter read:
Dear Mr. Stern:
   You have asked me to write you regarding my experiences in the BANKS/MEANS case.
   I began this case with the assumption that the government would treat Mr. Banks and his codefendant in the same manner as it would any other defendant. I ended this case with the firm conviction that the government would go to any end, including hiding exculpatory evidence, fabricating evidence, and lying to the Court, in order to convict Mr. Banks. As I said in my last opinion, the "waters of justice ha[d] been polluted."
   The common denominator in your case and the BANKS/MEANS case was the identity of the defendant Banks, and the American Indian Movement. The government's demonstrated disregard for fairness and legal ethics exhibited in the case before me deprived Mr. Banks of the rights any criminal defendant is entitled to.
   In my case there was misconduct both by the FBI and the prosecution. The FBI withheld documents from the prosecution, so that when the prosecutor said something didn't exist, in fact something did exist. Ultimately, I had to order that all potentially discoverable material within the FBI files be kept intact, and made available for both the prosecution and defense counsel to review. The search produced 131 discoverable or arguably discoverable documents which the FBI had not turned over. I had to recess trial for well over a week so that that search could be conducted. (Only the FBI knows if there were more documents that did not surface.) Documents which should have been provided for defense examination of government witnesses were in many instances not released until well after the witness had testified. In many instances, they were not released at all. And in some instances, the documents were intentionally altered (e.g., renumbering pages so that the defense would think that a document ended before it actually did).
   But the total disregard of truth and fairness in the government's attempt to "get" Dennis Banks "by hook or crook" did not stop at the doorstep of the FBI. The U.S. Attorney's office was an active participant. The prosecuting attorneys' actions were shocking. The Court was intentionally deceived. Some of these lies also related to issues of disclosure, some of them resulted in delay, and all of them evidenced a deep desire to convict Mr. Banks regardless of the truth.
   The fact that both the FBI and the U.S. Attorney's office were active participants in this pollution of justice convinced me that there was a systemic, in addition to an individual, desire to convict Mr. Banks by means well beyond those which were ethical and fair. After all, in other cases in my district I had both FBI agents and these attorneys before me regularly. But the willingness to lie and fabricate and withhold evidence was only exhibited against Mr. Banks and his AIM codefendant. And it was exhibited with a

implication was that Turner was continuing that misconduct by withholding favorable evidence. There is no evidence more favorable than a witness who says, "The man you've charged is not the one I saw; I saw this other person instead."

As the hearing began, I stood, walked to the bench, and gave the judge the eyewitness reports of Strain and Schricker, with another copy to Turner. Redden read them with an intensity I had not seen before. Turner looked shaken. Bauman, his assistant, was ashen. He had personally reviewed the files in 1983 and filed a sworn statement that no such "favorable" reports existed.

Redden called the papers "significant" and asked Turner to explain. Turner said he was "chagrined" that the documents were not turned over before. He promised to review the file, personally, to see if there were any more such papers. Bauman sank into his chair. It was decent damage control, and Turner knew he was damaged.

Just then, Redner[6] stood and asked the judge if he could "say something."

_____

vengeance. Whatever the reasons were for the Government to act in the manner it did, they were certainly deeply seated.

By the way, it was also discovered after the trial that the Government had a spy at meetings of the defendants and their lawyers. Of course, the Government had denied this allegation to me all through the trial.

If my experience has taught me anything, it is that the past is a good indication of the future. The broad and pervasive nature of the FBI and prosecutors' misconduct in 1973 and 1974 reflected patterns and beliefs that were deeply held. I doubt that they would be abandoned easily.

Sincerely,

Fred Nichol

6. At the defense table were Ed Jones, attorney for Kenny Loud Hawk, Michael Bonds, attorney for KaMook Banks, Tom Steenson, attorney for Russ Redner, Russ Redner, and me. (The other defendants' appearances had been waived until trial.)

Ron Schiffman was beyond inducing out of retirement, and since Ed Jones had left the Steenson et al. firm (which still represented Redner), he no longer had a conflict of interest when he took Loud Hawk as a client. (A lawyer has a potential conflict of interest when he or she represents two defendants in the same case, as each can claim that the other "did it.")

Parkinson was out of law altogether, no longer listed as a bar member. Rumor had it that he had agreed to resign rather than face disciplinary action. He now was much happier, selling books in a downtown used book store.

Veteran AIM counsel Lew Gurwitz planned to be at trial, helping to represent Redner.

"No, sir," Redden said, telling him he had a lawyer and that he should sit down.

I watched Redner's hands twitch. He was about to explode. Steenson, on one side, and I, on the other, exchanged glances, then put our hands on Redner's legs and held him down.

"We'll have plenty of opportunity to work this out later," I whispered to him. "Just give the judge the benefit of the doubt for today."

When Redner still stirred, I whispered, "Trust me!" He glared at me as if I had better be right, but he stayed seated.

Redden was now discussing trial dates. Turner was hoping for February because an earlier January date conflicted with "the holiday schedule."

Bonds bounded from his seat, interrupting. "I was the first person to jump up and say January 1st is okay with me!" he said, meaning February 1st. "Not being a follower of Jesus, I don't give a hoot about the holidays. As far as I'm concerned, frankly, no lawyer on earth will ever be ready to try this case! All we can do is the best we can do. If you want to try KaMook Banks on January 4th, I'll be glad to do that!"

His speech was slightly slurred. Everyone stared at him. I had smelled alcohol on Bonds during our walk to the courthouse a half hour before. I had dismissed it. He seemed sober. But he must have guzzled some right before we left. He was drunk now.

Redden judiciously ignored the outburst and went on about trial dates. Bonds stood again, and now in a castigating and angry voice and in a total non sequitur to Redden's comments, shouted, "Sir, may I say, I continue to observe the sanitation of our language, and I read where Anna Mae Aquash died. Eisenhower died; Kennedy was murdered; Anna Mae Aquash was murdered; and the United States Civil Rights Commission has certainly given the international community reason to believe her death is

---

And Dennis Roberts swore he would not come to Portland to help represent Dennis Banks again. After months of coaxing, I made him promise to appear the first day of trial, for a cameo appearance. I knew, and I think he knew, that once in the courtroom, he would stay for the duration.

somewhat more complex than the official explanation."

Redden, red-faced, said, "I am not going to sit here and listen to lectures from any of the attorneys!"

I was tugging harder and harder on the back of Bonds's suit jacket, trying to pull him into his chair. Redden ended the hearing, and Bonds sauntered out.

I approached Craig Meyer, the judge's clerk, and told him that I knew Bonds held the judge in the highest esteem and that he had been through days of difficult hearings on another case and probably had not had much sleep. Craig looked unconvinced. I intended my words to get back to the judge and dull his anger.

Five minutes later, I was in the basement coffee shop when Jerry Harris, the court reporter, said, "Seems Mr. Bonds had a couple too many at lunch." He was the third person to make such an unsolicited comment. This needed more serious damage control.

I took the elevator back to the sixth floor, walked into the judge's chambers, apologized for Bonds, and told the truth: Bonds had a drinking problem, and I was worried about him.

"Just last week," I said, "I called Michael. He was home at three in the afternoon. He said he was just tired, taking a nap. Judge, his words were slurred."

I reminded the judge of the 1983 incident in which Bonds was injured. "Remember that I seemed unusually unconcerned about that when everyone else assumed that the Redner-Parkinson faction was out to maim the Banks-Bonds-Stern faction?"

Redden nodded.

"Judge, Michael was drunk that night," I said. "He was his own victim."

"Think I should shock him by threatening to take him off the case?" Redden asked.

"No," I said, "not yet. Let me see what I can do."

"Okay," Redden said, "but if you want me to do something, let me know. And if he does this again, I *am* taking him off the case!"

I thanked him. But my thoughts were not only of Bonds and the horror and embarrassment he would feel if Redden removed him from the case. Worst-case scenario: Bonds would show up at trial drunk; KaMook would get a mistrial and maybe everyone else, too. Bonds's problem was, at least, another possible defense, although, as our best trial lawyer, our clients needed him sober.

I put everything else aside and spent the afternoon and evening with other counsel and with Russ Redner, discussing Bonds. Redner had the best idea.

"Let's get him together in a room with all the lawyers and have a ceremony, with an eagle feather," he said. "We'll tell him how much we all love him, how much more important he is than the case, and have him hold the feather. We'll ask him to pledge that he'll remain sober throughout the trial."

When I went home that night (I was camping in Bonds's extra bedroom), he was already asleep. The next morning, Jonna, his lover, was downstairs, reading the *Oregonian* in an overstuffed chair. Since I planned to spend two nights at the office straight through, writing more motions, and the ceremony-confrontation was planned for the day after, I wanted to let her know what had happened so that she could be supportive of Bonds.

"Jonna," I said, "there was a problem. Michael was drunk in court."

"Oh, shit!" she said. Then, after a pause, "He was doing *so* well."

I told her of Redner's and my plan and the concern of the other lawyers. "Sorry," she said, "He should be talked to right now! If you don't do it, I will." She walked upstairs.

Bonds was outside on the porch, smoking. I started softly. "Listen, Michael," I said, "we've got a problem that we've got to talk about, about what happened yesterday." He looked at me, more accusative than inquisitive. "What?" he demanded.

"Well," I said, "you were drinking before court."

"No I wasn't!" he yelled. "That's just bullshit!"

"Look," I said. "Three people came over to me and said, 'Did Michael have one too many before coming into court?' I smelled an odor of alcohol about you."

"I swear I didn't drink. I haven't had a drink in ages. This is bullshit!"

There was no going back.

"Michael, Russ Redner said when you and he drove to Eugene a few weeks ago to speak with potential expert witnesses, you also had a couple of drinks."

"Well," Bonds yelled, walking back into the house where Jonna was now downstairs, listening, "that's just bullshit, too. I had one beer!"

"Michael, you just told me that you have had 'nothing to drink in ages,'" I said. "Anyway, that's not what Redner tells me. He said he smelled something on your breath before you drove down to Eugene and that while you were down there you had two doubles."

"Well, that's all just bullshit!" he hollered, storming up the stairs.

Jonna followed him into their bedroom, opening the door he had already slammed shut. I took a shower, and when I finished, he was gone.

Jonna said they spoke and added, "I tend to believe him. He tells me when he's drinking."

"Listen, " I said, "you know me. I wouldn't accuse Michael unless I really believe it. And I believe it. I didn't see him drink, but I saw how he acted, and I smelled how he smelled."

"Well," Jonna offered, "lots of times Michael smells of alcohol. I've been around him when I know he hasn't been drinking, but he smells that way."

"Jonna, he acted like he was drunk, and he smelled like he was drunk. And it wasn't only me who noticed. I even had to apologize to the judge for him, it was so bad.

"This is awful," I continued. "We have four people's lives at stake, clients we love. Those eyewitness reports were saved for *years*, for exactly this opportunity. Redden should have come off the bench thinking, 'Oh my God, the fucking government, what the hell are they doing, these documents they're hiding, despite their sworn promises to me.' Instead he came off the bench thinking, 'What the fuck is wrong with Michael Bonds?'"

CHAPTER 26

✝ ✝ ✝

INVESTIGATING INDIAN COUNTRY

I spent three days without sleep writing motions, memorandums, pleadings, and affidavits on every aspect of the case. My writing was not only designed to win legal points and drive Turner crazy. Redden had to be primed on an issue that would determine the verdict—how much evidence of the times and circumstances he would allow the jury to hear. The case law gave him wide discretion. If he kept the legal issues narrow, we would lose.

I detailed all the government misconduct again in a memorandum of more than thirty pages. I argued that we needed wide latitude to make up for the government's dirty tricks. And, I concluded,

The only truly fair trial for these Indian political activists is one that allows them to have the jury understand them—as Indians, as activists working for the survival of a way of life under siege, and as victims of lawlessness by the FBI.

The jury will not be able to understand the defendants or their defense if they do not know that, between the end of Wounded Knee and the beginning of this case, the FBI was an occupation force on the reservation. And while they were there, scores of people were killed, mostly AIM members. And during that time, there was not a day going by when a person did not know someone who had been run off a road, or shot at, or beat up, or killed. It was a poor society under siege—but, to our embarrassment, the people responsible for that siege were those who were supposed to enforce the law. And this conflict, driven in part by the engine of racism, made the FBI act in shocking ways in its "investigations" of AIM cases.

The backdrop of this case is Wounded Knee and the death and violence in its wake. To present a defense which is honest and accurate, that backdrop must be firmly established. Otherwise, the equivalent would be like trying the Sacco and Vanzetti case without mentioning racism against Italians, like representing the Rosenbergs without mentioning McCarthyism, or like defending Dred Scott on a straight contract theory.

The papers filed and Michael Bonds having disappeared—so that the confrontation had to be scrapped—Redner and I headed north, to investigate the "Indian underground."[1] We drove the interstate in the opposite direction Marlon Brando's motor home had come over twelve years before. We were looking for information about informants "A" and "B"—who had told the government about the motor home—and about whether there might have been some more significant unmentioned "C."

"Russ," I asked, "remember when we were in Vancouver for Leonard's hearing in 1976? You wanted to tell me what happened, and I told you you shouldn't tell anyone unless they really needed to know?"

Redner nodded.

"I really need to know," I said.

"Well," he said, leaning back in the passenger seat, "after I got back from Vietnam—you know I was shot up—I was angry. I had to get back to who I was. I got a job with the Indian community in California.

"When Wounded Knee happened, I filled a car with 'skins and a few guns, and we headed east. After Knee, I went back to California, to my community work. That's about the time I met Leonard, who was an AIM organizer in the Seattle area. Leonard had a great sense of humor, but unlike a lot of people who were just flakes, Leonard was disciplined and dedicated. He was dynamic—a general.

"I said to myself, 'If Leonard's ever in a situation where he needs help, I'll be there.' I didn't see him for a long time. Then,

---

1. Redner had calmed down since the court appearance. I had filed a Motion to Transfer Case to International Jurisdiction on the theory that this was a legal conflict between the U.S. and foreign (Indian) nations. Even though it had no chance of being granted, I requested that Redner argue it. Redden could live with controlled participation of a defendant, and the motion would allow Redner to speak about Indian sovereignty, the heart of the ideology of American Indian resistance.

in 1975, I was living in the Seattle area, too.[2] I was working near Tacoma, counseling Indian kids. I got to know the people in Northwest AIM. The group included Leonard, his cousins Steve and Bob Robideau, Dino Butler, and lots of others. They were tied into the more established Indian network, people like Janet McCloud and Hank Adams and Sid Mills and Hazel Bridges, people who had started organizing for fishing rights in the late 1950s and early 1960s."

"I take it that the AIM group was a little more adventurous?" I asked.

"Sure," he said. "We were warriors. We went on missions. And before that a lot of those guys—Leonard, Dino, you know—were bodyguards for Dennis. That's partly why they were all at the Jumping Bull compound—to provide security for Dennis during his Custer trial.[3]

"Anyway, the month before the Oregon case started, I heard that some of those Northwest AIM guys had blown up the BIA building in Pine Ridge."

Redner named some of the Indians he thought were involved. That was troubling. I had met many of them. In my youth, I was embarrassed to remember, I would have thought bombing property was almost romantic, a sign of defiance, especially given the terrible FBI and Goon violence in Pine Ridge. Now, even though I still intellectually understood the act, I could no longer condone retaliatory violence. If it happened today, under similar circumstances, I would condemn it, but there was no need to tell Redner that.

"Anyway," he continued, "I heard that Leonard was hiding in the Northwest in late October 1975. I decided to help. It was a mission, to get these guys and their weapons safely to Pine Ridge. I didn't expect to get out alive, though. The security was too poor."

"Did Dennis ever leave the Chiquiti place?" I asked.[4]

2. The year before, Russ had married Lena, who had grown up in Port Angeles, Washington.

3. The Jumping Bull compound was where the two FBI agents and Joe Stuntz were killed on the Pine Ridge Indian Reservation in June 1975.

4. Dennis and KaMook Banks, Kenny Loud Hawk, Anna Mae Aquash, and Leonard Peltier, along with Marlon Brando's motor home and the station wagon, had been hiding at the home of John Chiquiti, on the Port Madison Indian Reservation.

"Yep," Redner sighed. "One night, he even had a speaking engagement in Seattle. So he drove in, spoke, and then came back."

"Shit!" I said, remembering Dennis Roberts's favorite word for my client—*putz*. I now feared a room full of witnesses from Seattle saying that Banks had spoken there days before the stop in Ontario.

"Leonard didn't lay low either," Redner added. "In fact, he and Anna Mae once went into town and came back freaked. They thought a man on the ferry across Puget Sound recognized him."

"These guys were hiding?" I asked. "This was the best-kept secret shared by every Indian north of the Oregon border!"

"It wasn't that bad," he assured me. "It was just the Indian underground who knew."

That was still too large a group to make any lawyer happy.

"So you joined up right before they left, for one mission?" I asked.

"Yep," he replied. "I was the newcomer. I never felt totally trusted, especially by Anna Mae. She treated me like a rookie, and I was the one with all the combat experience!" he said, with resentment still fresh after twelve years. "I knew they had some guns," he continued, "and I asked her if I could take one in the station wagon. She turned me down."

"You know," he said, after a moment's reflection, "if I had had one of those Valmets, rather than just the .44, I would have wasted that cop. But with just the .44, I knew there was no way, so we just pulled over hoping that that would create a diversion. Dennis had told us if the motor home was stopped, we should drive on. But we stopped instead."

In 1975, Redner really did see this as a mission in a war. Griffiths, a cop, was a uniformed enemy, fair game.

I did not say much for the next hour. I was haunted by how this case could have been so different. Instead of a fun old weapons case, it would have been a human tragedy, a murder case with Ken Griffiths dead by the side of the road, his wife a widow, his daughter fatherless; Tosh and KaMook and all the others shot dead in a chase; TaTiopa, Chubbs, and Chiopa never born—all if Anna Mae had liked Russ enough to have given him a semiautomatic rifle.

I wondered if the Ken Stern of 1975 would have rationalized

the officer's death and worked on the case anyway? Probably. Redner could still rationalize it. He had shot at many people, with more powerful guns and for less reason, in Vietnam.

Janet McCloud greeted me with a firm hug. She had forgotten how, twelve years before at Linda Coelho's house, she had lamented how she was "always having to sit next to white men."

Janet was still saber-tongued and bright-eyed. Sitting in her huge Yelm, Washington, kitchen with a large pot of coffee brewing, she kept Redner and me engrossed with stories of the fishing struggles of the Northwest, going back to the late 1950s. Out of those fights—Indians shot at or arrested for exercising their treaty rights—the Indian underground had developed, spiriting away people the state wanted, mostly taken by small boat north across Puget Sound to refuge in British Columbia. That network was still intact when AIM needed it in the mid-1970s.

Janet had not seen Dennis Banks or Leonard Peltier when they had been hiding at John Chiquiti's place. "But I heard they were around," she said. She named people who might have seen them or had ideas about who the snitches were. As we talked, Janet's nine-year-old grandson strode through the room, removed his jacket, said "Hello," snatched something to eat, and took his homework into a back room.

"You know what happened to him last year?" she asked.

Redner and I shrugged.

"For three months, the school board allowed a bus driver to keep all the Indian kids in the rear of the bus. You see," she explained, "the driver felt that Indian kids were just plain rowdier than white kids."

"What are you doing about it?" I asked, expecting to hear of ACLU and lawsuits and firings and pickets and a new, younger, Rosa Parks.

"Nothing," she said. "I've been through too many battles. I'm leaving this one to my daughters."[5]

---

5. I was astonished that no one in the Indian community in Seattle or Portland knew of this incident. Unlike the African-American, Jewish, and Asian-American communities, Indian people had no defense agencies that monitor, expose, and combat bigotry.

✢ ✢ ✢

The next morning we drove to the Port Madison reservation. I wanted to see the hiding spot so that I could cross-examine FBI agent Sidney Rubin with details I was sure he had long forgotten.

Redner's memory was stimulated as we approached. "The dynamite got there the day before we left," he said. "It was raining real hard. The boxes were soaked through. I helped put them into plastic bags, and then we loaded the station wagon. When we decided to leave, the motor home got stuck. We waited for hours until some friend of Chiquiti's—a white guy—came with a Cat and pulled it out if the mud.

"We stopped off someplace on the way to Oregon, and then, the next day, the 14th, we drove through Portland. We got about thirty miles into the Columbia Gorge when Leonard decided he wanted to see an old girlfriend in Portland. I couldn't believe it! They turned around, leaving Kenny and me waiting for hours in the station wagon, near the Bonneville Dam. I was pissed!"

"Do you think that this girlfriend might have been 'A' or 'B'?" I asked.

Redner shrugged.

"That would explain one thing that never made any sense to me," I said. "The All Points Bulletin Trooper Griffiths read referred to the station wagon as a 'lead car.' That's an unusual fact. You would expect the teletype to say that the vehicles were traveling 'together,' especially as you told me there was no set plan about who would go first. Maybe the girlfriend told the FBI that the station wagon was waiting ahead and that got translated into 'lead car?'"

"Could be," Redner said.

It was midmorning, sunny, but only in the 30s when we pulled into John Chiquiti's driveway. The house and the grounds were as Redner remembered, except that the trees had grown and a trailer that had jutted from the wooden house was no longer there. It had been that white trailer that had hidden Brando's motor home from view of the road the day or two before it departed but not from Agent Rubin in his airplane.

Redner walked to the front door and knocked. A young blond woman with a red-nosed toddler by her side answered the door. She picked up the boy, excused herself, then returned. Chiquiti was upstairs. He had told her to show us in.

My image of Chiquiti came from a famous Wounded Knee picture. His long hair braided, he sat erect on a horse with a rifle in his left hand and the reins held tight in his right. He was confident.

He was now older, in bed, totally groggy. His wooden room was dark. A single window looked out to thick tree branches. Moss clung to the window edges. A .30-.30 shotgun leaned against the wall by his bed. It was presumably loaded, pointed up, within easy reach. A huge elaborate bong rested on the floor near the gun. Chiquiti offered us marijuana. We declined.

The conversation was stilted, cautious, with Redner doing most of the talking while Chiquiti laughed, nervously, his language peppered with "hey, mans" and "shee-its" and "fucks." We showed him the FBI flyover photographs. He said that after Anna Mae had been killed, two agents "showed up with these same pictures." He said he told them, "These pictures aren't of my place."

I found it hard to believe that the FBI had visited him only once—and then so long after the stop. Anna Mae's body was discovered in February 1976. The FBI was desperate to find Banks and Peltier, and Chiquiti's should have been among the first places the feds would have looked after the Ontario fiasco.

I thought we might get more information if he and Redner were alone. I left to survey the property. First, I measured the distance from the county road to the driveway in front of the house. About one hundred feet. From the roadway, there was a clear view to where the trailer had been, obscured only by occasional trees, all of which were larger and fuller than they had been twelve years before.

Across the road was a hill. Although it was now clear-cut, it had been heavily forested in 1975. This hill was where Rubin's "protective screen" of FBI agents had been hiding while two agents had sneaked through the brush to read the plate number on the motor home. It was a good spot from which to watch, to launch an assault on the house, or to stop a vehicle on its way out.

Farther down, away from the county road, behind the house, was a little gravel lane that bent past Chiquiti's salmon smokehouse. The incline was steep.

A quarter mile farther, through a young tangled forest, I found the spot where I thought the motor home had been first hidden, before it was moved closer to the house and the trailer. I mapped the trees, finding patterns of triangles and rectangles of the larger ones Rubin had photographed from the air, matching them to the same patterns I found from the few thick trunks rising from the ground.

The spot, clear years ago, was encased in ten-foot-tall underbrush. But I could sense the distance to the house and to the older woods and gauge the shape and feel of the land.

As I made notes, I heard footsteps. It was Redner. Behind him was Chiquiti, who first continued to deny that the vehicles or their occupants were ever here and then, with a smile, commended me for finding the right spot. I explained how I figured it out from the trees.

"No problem," Chiquiti said, "you just tell me which ones, and I'll be right out here with an ax and chop the fuckers down."

I laughed. "John," I said, thinking of the thousands of sheets of paper filed in *Loud Hawk*, "too many trees have been sacrificed to the case already. Anyway, the major landmark is not these trees but your house, and I wouldn't ask you to get rid of that."

He offered again. "Okay, but just let me know if you change your mind, and I'll take out those trees, man, just let me know."

"Thanks," I said again, "but what would really help would be your memory of the time—who was around, who was suspicious."

He led us back to his house, into his living room, which had many windows but was somehow just as dark as his bedroom. There was a huge stone fireplace on the far wall, unkindled. Redner and I sat facing Chiquiti, who relaxed into a large chair. We kept our coats on. It was colder inside than out.

"Yeah," he said, "guys named Dog and Rocky and Nacho and Steve Fernandez, all of them had been in and out while Dennis and Leonard were here." They could have been snitches, he said, but he had no way of knowing.

"Who else?" I asked.

"Well, there was this guy who supplied the dynamite at the last minute. I think he was the son of the Yakima chief of police. He had stolen the stuff."

An interesting new fact.

"John," I finally said, "one thing I don't understand. If the FBI knew that Dennis and Leonard were here, why didn't they just come in and raid the place? With the hill behind, the thick woods, and no way out except the county road, it would have been easy."

John offered no hypothesis.

"Think there might have been an informant placed so close to the group that the FBI felt confident of catching them somewhere else?" I asked.

"Could be," he said.

"The impression I had was that these guys were not too careful," I added.

"Shit," John said, "most everyone knew they were here, right after they arrived in early October."

I glanced at Redner, signaling that Chiquiti had told us all he would. "Nothing I've heard today makes me change what I've been thinking," I said as we got up, "that 'A' and 'B' were local people who had heard about the AIM group, while there was some other more involved informant that the government's keeping secret."

We left Chiquiti's and drove to the right on the county road and then, reaching town, circled back to the left. There was no way, on this tiny winding two-lane road, that the FBI could have lost a huge motor home like Brando's. Peltier was wanted for killing two agents. Why wouldn't the FBI post at least one agent close by to watch? Or it could have put two people miles away, one to the right and one to the left, in any one of a hundred different spots by the road. There was absolutely no way vehicles could have been missed.

And once on the road, it was hard to believe that the vehicles could have been lost. It made more sense that the FBI felt confident that it knew the plans. So they were sitting back, when the plans changed—maybe when the motor home got stuck in the mud or when Peltier stopped off in Portland.

Near town, Redner saw a man named George[6] who had been a regular at Chiquiti's. He was sitting by the side of the road. In his

6. Not his real name.

late forties, he had an alcoholic's glow. As he spoke, strands of saliva joined his lips together.

"Yeah, I remember being around there," he said, looking at Redner.

"Hey, you know what?" George asked, in a whisper. "There's ten more cases of that shit buried in the woods. You guys couldn't take all of it, remember, and after the bust, we just buried the rest. What do you want us to do? We can dig it up, or move it, or burn it, or whatever you want."

I had never imagined that seven cases were all they could fit into the station wagon rather than all they had had. My first thought was that the dynamite might confirm a defense. I remembered the Panther 21 trial in New York in the late 1960s. Black Panthers were acquitted of conspiracy to bomb stores. One night New York cops switched fake dynamite for the real thing. I had already contacted participants in that case to prove that it was possible to have something that looked like dynamite, said "DYNAMITE" on the wrappers, but was not.

Maybe the same thing had happened here? Except the theory was better as a jury argument, a suggestion of what might have been. If I dug up the dynamite and had it tested, I had nothing to gain (because time could make this batch bad whereas the seven cases in the station wagon might have been potent) and everything to lose.

"Just leave it," I instructed.

As Redner and I got back into the car and headed to Port Angeles, I wondered aloud what Turner would think if an unaccounted-for wrapper showed up.

Redner smiled. "Maybe he'd think his snitch wasn't playing straight," he said.

"What do you make of all this?" I asked. "As far as I can tell, there were a lot of people who might have been snitches."[7]

---

7. In addition to the supplier of the dynamite, Rocky, Nacho, Steve Fernandez, and Dog—all seemingly unbalanced characters (Dog was now disabled; he had robbed a bank so successfully one morning that he tried it again, at the same branch, that afternoon and was shot in the head)—there were two more candidates. One was Glen McNeeley, a man who had bought one of the guns found in the motor home; the other was Nancy Chiquiti, John's former wife. Although everyone remembered her as a "righteous" woman, I wondered. She

"I don't think we'll ever know," he said. "Oh, on that score, you know what I heard?"

"What?" I said.

"That the FBI's investigation of Anna Mae's death is heating up again. And I heard a rumor that Denver AIM held a trial, found her guilty of being a snitch, shot her, then drove the body to Pine Ridge and dumped her there."

Lena, Tsi-Am-Utza, and Redner's son greeted us as we pulled into their driveway. Lena, like KaMook, had not changed much in more than ten years. She was still youthful, bubbly, and very attractive. Tsi-Am-Utza, however, now looked like her mother's sister. She was tall, prematurely formed, and very self-assured. She completely ruled her mother. I was not surprised. Sam (as she was now nicknamed) had been doing that when I last saw her—before she was two.

Lena and Ramona—Lena's mother, who lived across the street—asked about the legal people and support committee; I told them whatever I knew. Even five-year-old information was interesting to them. I asked about the Indian people I had not seen in so many years.

"What about Ida Stuntz?" I asked. I remembered Ida as a forlorn widow, her husband the overlooked Indian corpse at the June 26, 1975, Oglala shootout.

"Ida's living here, doing well," Lena said. "She never remarried. In fact, one of the kids who was here when you guys arrived was one of hers."

"Did either of her boys turn into an artist?" I asked, remembering the day I bought her older son a huge box of crayons. Ida and her children had visited the Portland defense house in 1976, and

---

had cracked up not long after the arrests and was now living on skid road. She had owned a new model Polaroid when those were expensive. A picture taken with such a camera, at Chiquiti's, was found among the items seized from the motor home—but not until Assistant U.S. Attorney Ken Bauman discovered it in the *Loud Hawk* evidence room in 1987. Dennis had a Che Guevara beard in the photo. KaMook remembered a Che Guevara Banks picture posted outside her Kansas hospital-jail room when she gave birth to TaTiopa in December 1975 just in case Dennis was stupid enough to visit.

I had felt sorry that the boy had had only defense committee pencils and pens to draw with.

"Yes!" Lena said, surprised that I asked. "The older one draws all the time. Everyone thinks his work is really amazing."

Sam seemed glad to see her father but not exactly sure what to do with him. She had wanted to spend the previous summer with him on Pine Ridge, but he backed out when the tension over Loneman School became too intense. Sam was too young to understand the politics—that on Pine Ridge, there was always the risk of violence. She had to feel newly rejected by the father she had not seen since she was a baby.

Sensing the tension, Lena asked Sam to show us her scrapbook. First she handed me a faded, crumbling proof sheet of black and white photographs.

"They're from the benefit at Jack and Micki Scott's!" I said.

"Yeah," Lena said. "That's all Sam has of those early days."

Sam flipped the pages. After the sheet of the early fund raiser in the Scott/Walton home, she had dozens of clippings about her junior high softball team. Sam was the star pitcher and hitter. She had inherited her father's athletic ability. She asked Redner if he would play a game of basketball with her the next day. His eyes lit.

After a turkey dinner, I left for Portland, leaving Redner behind. I heard that Sam went out with friends right after I left, and even though Redner stayed for four days, she did not return to see him.

It must have been so hard for her. The Oregon experience had been a catalyst in Dennis Banks's transformation from free spirit to dedicated family man. He even cut important trips short so that he could watch Tosh cheerlead. Redner's family was destroyed by the case, however. "Lena liked to party too much," he used to say, referring to the affair she had while he was behind bars. The son he had thought was not his looked exactly like him. It brought tears to my eyes when this boy, now eleven, who had gone through so much without a father—including open-heart surgery at age three—approached Redner with anxious timidity and whispered, "Dad, would you teach me how to smoke a peace pipe?"

CHAPTER 27

+ + +

INVESTIGATING COWBOY COUNTRY

WHEN I returned from Port Madison, a packet of FBI reports was waiting on my desk. Charles Turner had no way to know if we were hoarding other unreleased documents, the disclosure of which would embarrass him. He therefore released another half-dozen eyewitness reports, which he claimed his office had "overlooked."

All of these "new" eyewitnesses had been interviewed within days of the Ontario stop. Each had seen the vehicles and their occupants; one, at a garage in The Dalles, had spent half an hour with the Indians, trying to fix a faulty windshield wiper on their motor home. No one identified Dennis Banks.[1]

I spent a day speed reading through the record. I found one of the "new" eyewitnesses—Gloria Lightle, a waitress—on a 1978 government witness list. How could they have "overlooked" her? I phoned Mrs. Lightle. "I've been under government subpoena since 1975," she said. I filed another dismissal motion based on government misconduct.

Aside from proving prosecutorial misdeeds, the new reports were startling for another reason. One of the eyewitness reports Bruce Ellison had given me years before had mentioned a *third* vehicle, a powder blue Mercury Comet, traveling with the Indians. Everyone assumed that was a mistake—another car that pulled into a gas station at the same time, perhaps.

One of the new eyewitnesses also saw a powder blue Comet

---

1. One identified Bob Robideau, another member of the Northwest AIM group. Robideau's fingerprints were also in the motor home. However, he was in a Kansas jail on November 14, 1975.

with Indian occupants traveling with the motor home and the station wagon. The new eyewitness had seen the Comet in The Dalles, Oregon. The old eyewitness, later that same day, had seen it in Baker, two hundred miles away. Redner swore there had been no blue Comet with them. Maybe it was a tail?

I called every AIM activist I knew, asking if anyone remembered a car like that on any reservation. John Trudell, like the others, did not remember the car. But he was passionate about one thing.

"You know what I think you ought to do?" he asked.

"What?" I answered.

"Subpoena Marlon Brando."

"I already mentioned that to Dennis," I explained. "He doesn't seem eager to bother him. Apparently, Marlon's over three hundred pounds, and he's embarrassed to be seen. But I definitely want to talk with him before trial. Bill Kunstler suggested I should, too."

"He owned the mobile home," Trudell said, slowly, for emphasis. He repeated, "He *owned* the mobile home! The weapons that were found there were paid for with $100 bills. Those $100 bills came from Marlon Brando."

"Oh, really," I said, sensing Trudell was ready to spit information.

"That's right. Mark Banks[2] paid for them."

"That I knew," I said. "The government gave us a receipt, showing that Mark bought the guns under his own name."

"Shit, Mark bought $3,000 or $4,000 worth of weapons.[3] And they were paid for with $100 bills. The government knew this. The money could be traced back. Brando is a very, very key person in all of this. And if Dennis and the others are serious about saving themselves and if Brando is serious about being supportive of the Indian cause, he has got to come out."

"Um hum," I said, not wanting to interrupt.

"People talk about wanting to save their lives, stay out of jail and shit, yet they want to protect Brando. We're not talking about them turning over somebody's name who's unknown."

2. Dennis's younger brother.
3. The guns were legal, until they later had their serial numbers removed.

"That's true," I said. "Anyway, too much time has passed. Marlon couldn't be indicted."

"He couldn't be indicted now, and even if he could, think of the amount of attention it would create just by daring them to indict him. Brando could help pull these guys through. He's the key person. If you subpoena Marlon Brando and had him sitting there in the courtroom, the jury's going to see there's favoritism here.

"John, I don't know if the FBI ever questioned him. The government never alleged that there was a conspiracy, or that anyone beyond those found in the vehicles was involved.

"Well, sometimes I kick around the thought," Trudell interrupted. "I wonder if people were getting set up, if outsiders were playing abstract games with peoples' lives? Because you know as well as I do if that mobile home had gotten to South Dakota, they would have been killed."

"Absolutely," I said.

"John," I asked, "have any idea why the feds didn't go in and get them at Chiquiti's? It was a secluded place."

"They wanted to get them back to Pine Ridge with these weapons and so-called explosives and kill them there," Trudell said. "Here's what I think. I have questions about people. You see, someone stepped in and taught people how to make bombs. There had been some bombings in Pine Ridge. Someone planted bombs. I figure that the original person who planted the bombs was either going to continue or he taught someone else how to. And I know who this person is. And one of my feelings is that the feds never pursued this because the guy that made the bombs and taught us how to make bombs was working with them. This person surfaced in a couple of situations connected with bombings, and he's never, ever, been charged, or even dragged through the court system. But he was definitely linked a couple of times, and he was let go. And any time they even get a suspicion we're doing something, they don't let us go."

"That's true," I said.

"So I figure that they were going to let the mobile home get to South Dakota, and the ambush was there, because the order was not to stop them."

"That's what the APB said."

"That's right, Ken, the stop was an accident. I don't think they needed two informants. I think they were monitoring the activities all along. You see, before the firefight,[4] we didn't have access to these things. People weren't bringing us loads of dynamite, buying us guns and shit. Then the firefight takes place. Yes there were some semiautomatic weapons there, but basically it's a ragtag army collection of weapons, nothing there. The bombings weren't happening prior to that."

"John, when did the bombings happen?"

"The bombings started at the time of the firefight. The day after the firefight there was a bombing at Mt. Rushmore. And it was a frivolous bombing. Someone went and planted a bomb there and broke some windows. It wasn't a serious bombing. The person who planted the bomb knew enough about bombs to place it in such a way that it would do minimal damage. But public relations-wise, it turned the world against anyone who was an Indian at that time. And the person was picked up on that and released."

Figuring that must be public record, I asked, "Who was picked up?"

"Drew Hopkins."[5]

"Drew Hopkins, that's a new name to me."

"Picked up and released on that, although I don't know for a certainty that he was the one who planted the Rushmore bomb. But it was after the firefight that all of a sudden these guys—the people who were being hunted—all of a sudden had access to more shit. People started bringing it in to them. And when you go back to it, Butler, Robideau—when they were busted [on the September 1975 Kansas charges, the same charges as KaMook, when their vehicle exploded]—every one of these people were busted on weapons charges after the firefight. And that's all they were held in jail on. They hoped to get Peltier and Banks on that, and they didn't get them on that. Our people did not have the bomb-making capabilities; it was brought into us. When I think about things that went on with the Weathermen, the

---

4. The June 26, 1975, shootout at the Jumping Bull residence on the Pine Ridge reservation, where the two agents and Joe Stuntz died.

5. Not his real name.

various people who would come in and teach people how to make bombs, I remember that the people who learned how to make the bombs were always caught, and those who taught them always walked."

"One of the pieces of paper in the motor home with bomb-making instructions came from Patty Hearst's SLA," I said.

"Um hum! One of the guys you talked about before, one of the possible snitches, Dog, I remember he once talked about weapons and told me 'the state has to arm you before they can kill you. That's how they justify it.' You can toss that statement either way, but I always remembered it."

"Got anything else you think I should look into?" I asked.

"Brando's the name. He's the one person. He's in this one up to his neck."

It was a beautiful, crisp desert day, and the drive to the Idaho towns bordering the Snake River brought me back to an August twelve years before, driving the same route, eager for the new adventure of Oregon and law school. I also remembered a trip here the following spring, with Ron Schiffman and Michael Bonds, and Lynn Parkinson's theory that there had been an ambush planned somewhere in Idaho. This was a desolate stretch of highway—just flat land, no houses, no trees, no witnesses, and no place to hide.

"I can't tell you know glad I am to come back here," I said to Michael Long, my beer-bellied investigator.[6] "I've always felt we missed an opportunity in these towns."

Fruitland, Payette, and Weiser were clean, quiet, and small. Their buildings were either wooden with false fronts or western block or brick. In each town there was a local police department with a cop or two.

After five hours, I was discouraged. Almost every officer had been in elementary or junior high school in November 1975. Yet

---

6. We had already visited Boise and tried to find Ken Matthews, the *Idaho Statesman* reporter who had refused to talk with us in 1976, and his photographer. Neither were in town. We collected names to call for leads.

We also tried to find the old TV footage of the shot-up motor home that Ron Schiffman and Michael Bonds had decided not to buy. The station no longer had it.

every time I introduced myself and said we were there "about an old case involving American Indian activists," there was instant recognition. The night the leadership of the American Indian Movement was caught near the river and then escaped was now folklore, told at station houses on cold winter nights.

Sheriff Jim Johnston of Washington County, Idaho, had been on the job in 1975. In his fifties, somewhat graying, distinguished, he was a man whose love for his work showed on his face. He led us to the end of a quiet corridor and, leaning against a soda machine, spoke in a relaxed voice.

"I was on duty that night," he said. "We got the call of 'gun-fire.' When I got there, the highway was shut off, and the mobile home was just before the bridge. Idaho state troopers were at a roadblock on the Idaho side of the river. I was told to guard the station wagon. Don't remember who was with me. I remember two guys were taken from the station wagon. They were taken away, and later, I helped escort the station wagon to Art's Garage."

He did not remember talking to any FBI agents but said, "I remember the two big names that the state troopers said were involved, 'Banks and Peltier.' And I remember that the motor home had a very sophisticated scanner radio system. But mostly, I just remember being cold, standing guard near the station wagon."

He thought for a moment. "You know," he continued, "even though I don't remember who was with me, I remember him smoking. Because then I realized that there was dynamite under the blankets in the back, and then we didn't smoke anymore."

I was excited to find something different from the FBI reports. According to the FBI agents, the dynamite was discovered the next day when Zeller had been fingerprinting the motor home and the FBI "suggested" he stop that search and check the station wagon. Now we had proof that despite sworn statements, the dynamite had been discovered by the time the FBI arrived the day before. The government had hidden the truth from the courts about the events that had led to the destruction of evidence— events that were crucial to the first dismissal and appeal. Certainly, if the dynamite had been discovered earlier and under different circumstances, there would have been more telephone calls made and more people involved before it was destroyed.

We thanked the sheriff, who offered to testify for us. It was now well after 5 o'clock and we were driving south, retracing our route back to the interstate. We stopped at the Fruitland Police Department and found Chief Tom Smith working late.

Smith had been chief since 1978. In 1975, he had been working for Probation and Parole in Idaho Falls. But even though Idaho Falls was far away, he had heard about the AIM case.

"Back then," he said, leaning on his desk in his small, dark office, "the freeway wasn't finished. I remember a roadblock was being set up in Caldwell. The feds set it up, and let's see, there would also have been Canyon County Sheriff's Office and Caldwell P.D. involved in that. Yeah, I remember hearing about how Griffiths, that Oregon trooper, spoiled the party."

I was excited. If this information was confirmed by other witnesses, the prosecutors would have their cops, but we would have ours, too. Ours would show that theirs were hiding things, including a planned Caldwell, Idaho, roadblock, mentioned nowhere in any FBI document.

The next morning Long and I drove halfway back to Boise, looking for witnesses to the canceled Caldwell, Idaho, ambush, hoping that Smith was correct.

Caldwell was a larger small town, a county seat, richer than Weiser or Payette or Fruitland. The houses were grander and better kept. There were more stores. The newer sections looked less like cowboy country and more like suburbia, with large food stores surrounded by clean asphalt parking lots painted with bold yellow lines.

The police department was away from the prosperous part of downtown, literally on the other side of the tracks. It was on the ground floor of an old brick building, with a tiny front door and a small lobby. Inside, next to a stack of complaint forms and three-inch eraserless pencils, was a box of candy canes. Christmas was coming. A dispatcher was speaking into a microphone on the other side of the lobby counter. We waited, then said why we were there. "The sergeant might remember," she said.

An officer took us to the back office where Sgt. Irv Reich, in his fifties, greeted us with a wild-eyed smile and a pumping handshake, as if we were celebrities. He offered us two seats near his desk.

"I know why you're here," Reich said. "Sorry I can't help you guys. We had the roadblock set up, you know, but they never made it this far."

"That's okay," I said, trying to look unexcited. "We're just interested in any little detail you might remember."

"There were people on the roadblock both from the county and city police," he said, "and I think some 'staters.' The staters had asked us to help, and I presume, the FBI had asked the staters to coordinate the roadblock."

"How many people manned the roadblock?" I asked.

"There were a couple of dozen who went to the Middleton overpass, right outside of town," he said, "and waited in the cold."

"Was everyone armed?" I asked.

"Sure," he said. "Each guy had a rifle."

"Were there any FBI agents there?"

"Yeah," he said. "I remember there were agents there, but I don't know as I remember who. One might have been George Calley. He was the agent stationed in Boise."

Was it possible that, so many years later, Sgt. Reich might be confusing roadblocks? After all, if the Caldwell area was a good place to stop vehicles, it must have been used other times, too.

"Sergeant, do you remember anything particular about the vehicles you were supposed to stop?" I asked, fearing the answer would be "No," or worse, "a pink Caddy" or "a Borden milk truck."

"Sure do," he said. "We were looking for Indians in a motor home and a station wagon."

He had the right incident. But maybe he was confusing the right vehicles with the wrong roadblock. Maybe he had been one of the Idaho officers who went scrambling to the east side of the Snake river that night, thirty-two miles east of Caldwell, and sealed that side of the bridge.

"Did you ever go near Ontario that night?" I asked.

"Nope," he said. "We waited and waited. Then some cars, I think they must have been ISP (Idaho State Police), went speeding through, heading west. We got word that the stop had happened up the road instead, in Ontario, so we all just came back here and packed it in. Went out to eat, as I recall. That's all there was. Like I say, sorry I can't help you much, because everything happened up the road."

The sergeant gave us names of another half-dozen officers who might have been waiting for the Indians with him. We now had more than just a suspicion of an Idaho roadblock. We had an actual witness, a credible participant, a police officer, a sergeant in charge of operations.

We stopped at the Middleton exit and took two rolls of pictures as exhibits. It was the perfect spot. The road from Oregon inclined up as it came to the overpass. At the top, it made a slight turn to the right. A mile back was another rise. The police could see the headlights as they crested that hill, almost a minute before the motor home arrived at the roadblock. The Indians would not have been able to see the officers until they made the turn at the top of the second hill, only one hundred feet or less from pointed guns.

Photographing the scene was eerie. I kept thinking of Griffiths. If he had not misread the teletype and stopped the motor home thirty-three miles before, my friends might have died here. If any had survived, I would never have met them; they would have been tried in federal court in Boise.

I started thinking like a lawyer. The existence of a second roadblock[7] was not, in any way, a defense to the charge of possessing unregistered firearms and explosives. Yet Sgt. Reich's testimony would show that the FBI and the prosecutors were still hiding facts of the "true story." There must have been an integrally involved informant relating the latest plans; without one, how would the feds have known where and when to erect a roadblock?

The roadblock also supported the defense claim that there was an FBI war going on. Here, in the middle of nowhere, the FBI had backwater cops aiming firepower at Indians whom the FBI knew were unlikely to stop. Stopping for Griffiths, who might have been pulling them over for a broken taillight, was one thing; stopping when you think you are going to be blown apart the next instant is another. The FBI knew this, and I was certain I could find experts in police procedure to testify this roadblock

7. The first one we knew about was set up by the Idaho State Police by the Snake River *after* Griffiths stopped the vehicles as part of the search for the people who had escaped.

was designed to get rid of Banks and Peltier rather than to arrest them.

Driving back to Ontario, excited about the ability to prove what we had long suspected, I compared this investigation to the depressing sojourn of the month before into Indian country. We still did not have a cohesive trial defense, but cowboy country was giving us many bits of good interlocking offenses. It was a start.

We found Bill Fettig at his home in North Powder, Oregon, a tiny town between Baker and LaGrande. It was a crisp, clear, beautiful desert afternoon, but Fettig, now long retired, was work-ing in his windowless shop in the back of his large, self-made, aluminum-framed garage.

His enclosed space said much about the man. His tools were all around him, each in its proper place. His military memorabilia—plaques and certificates and tarnished, fading medals—were on this side. On that side was a fishing rod, suspended from a rafter, ready for a warm spring day. Sawdust was scattered on the wood floor from some recent project, but even though there were many little messes, there was no clutter. This was Fettig's cocoon, the one part of the world that was totally his. If he had been a lawyer or a doctor instead of a policeman and a bomb expert, this would have been his den.

The last time I had seen Fettig was right before his second brain tumor operation, in May 1978, when he testified at a hear-ing in Judge Belloni's chambers. Ten years later, he seemed youn-ger. Retired now, he was still strong-willed and free-spirited, with a hard, telling, silent smile. The sawdust on the floor was from stools he was making for North Powder's children as Christmas presents. The boxes in the corner were for the local food bank.

We brought him up to date on the case; it was his almost as much as ours. We told him about our investigation in Idaho, hoping those revelations would open him up. He just smiled.

"Between you and me," Fettig finally said, "I'm rooting for you guys. I think a lot of the people involved were horses' asses. And I don't see any reason for this case to continue. Yes, I understand that there were regulations about explosives broken, but all this time and money going into it! I don't like it."

"What about the FBI?" I asked. "Were they just there watching, or calling the shots?"

Fettig winked. "On the record, I'll wait until trial to talk, counsellor," he said. I did not push. He would be a friendly witness.[8]

On our way out, Fettig said, "Say hello to that nice lawyer for me, the one who wished me well when I finished testifying in the judge's chambers ten years ago. I appreciated it a lot."

"Sure," I said, neglecting to mention that Dennis Roberts had laughed, then whispered to me, "That'll be the last we see of that guy!" as Fettig hobbled down the courthouse hallway.

Former OSP Lt. Kleinsmith lived just north of Ontario, on a precipice above the Snake River. The Snake did not wind or weave there. It gracefully bent, opening up a wide streak of blue-green through the brown valley below. This was quiet. Simplicity. Power.

Retirement suited Kleinsmith well. He seemed to enjoy life as much as Fettig did but with a calmer core. He sported a new, neatly trimmed, short white beard.

I understood why all the troopers we had interviewed the last three days said good things about their old commander. He was smart, precise, orderly, and caring. Even though Ken Griffiths had given up police work shortly after the stop of the motor home and station wagon, he still kept in touch with his old boss. Kleinsmith had just received a Christmas card from him.

"Griffiths had a tough choice to make, and I backed him up," Kleinsmith said. Implicit in his statement was the FBI's displeasure at his subordinate.

"This incident, you know, ended Ken's career in law enforcement," he said, speaking more of Griffiths's jolt of being shot at

---

8. A month later, I interviewed another OSP trooper, Dennis Lien. According to Chelsea Brown's old investigator notes, he had been willing to talk with the defense in 1978 at the time of the hearing before Judge Belloni ordered by the court of appeals, but none of the lawyers had bothered to contact him.

"There was no question about it," he said. "I remember sitting there in the office when all the agents were around, on the phone. I don't know who they were talking to. But that was how the decision to destroy the stuff was made. It wasn't Fettig. It was the FBI."

and shooting back than pressures from on high. "This happened before there were psychologists to counsel officers involved in shootings," he explained. "He still doesn't think he hit Peltier."

"Actually," I said, "he did. Peltier was shot in the right shoulder." Kleinsmith did not look surprised.

"Were there many reports produced?" I asked.

"There were at least two feet of them," he said.

"I mean state reports," I clarified. Most of what I had were FBI reports; the state records were no more than an inch thick.

"Yep, state reports," he said.

"Were there many teletypes?" I asked, knowing that three unsensational teletypes Ellison had sent me from Peltier's files were the last reserve of unreleased documents I had.

"Gobs of 'em," Kleinsmith said. Turner or the FBI were *still* hiding papers from us!

He gave us more names of officers who might remember. Our list now contained well over fifty names. One of the officers, Ken Leathers, lived down the road from Kleinsmith. He was now, like Ken Griffiths, a trucker. We pulled into his driveway, where he and his son were repairing the underside of a tractor trailer. Leathers stood, rubbed his soiled hands on his pants, then decided they were still too greasy for a proper handshake. He apologized.

We talked about the case for a few minutes. He did not remember much—he might still have his notes, he said—as it was such a long time ago.

All of a sudden, his manner became intense. Angry, Leathers said, "You know, those fuckers almost *killed* one of our guys! I mean . . ." His face was red. His voice was inappropriately loud. I edged toward our car in case I needed to escape, and I was about to explain how we did not actually represent Leonard Peltier, who had allegedly shot at Griffiths, when I realized he was not talking about the Indians but the FBI.

". . . the fuckers knew where these guys were and let them go, playing some game, and the result was, one of our guys almost got killed. And then they had the balls to blame everything that went wrong . . ."

I could have signed Ken Leathers up for the defense committee.

As our interviews went on that day, and the next, our new

witnesses got even better.[9] One, Mike, a skinny man in his late forties, wearing a dirty oil company baseball cap, was a driver at Art's Garage.

"Yeah," he said. "The FBI asked me to go into the motor home after the tear gas wasn't so bad anymore."

"Why did you have to go inside?" I asked.

"Because the rig was in the center of the highway, in a ditch," he explained. "I couldn't get the tow truck down to it; I had to drive it to the lip of the shoulder first."

"Did anyone fingerprint the steering wheel before you touched it?" I asked.

"No, sir," he said. "Far as I know I was the first one in. There was no print powder, and I even had to kick a whole bunch of shit out of the way to get to the driver's seat. Seemed everything had spilled out of the cupboards."

"Did you see any guns or bomb-making equipment?" I asked, holding my breath.

"No, sir."

Here was a witness who would prove that someone could be in the motor home without knowing of the firearms and paraphernalia (even after almost everything had spilled out of the cupboards) and that the FBI allowed the fingerprints on the steering wheel—*the* key piece of evidence tending to show who drove the motor home away—to be obliterated.

Like everyone else associated with the garage, Mike remembered swarms of FBI agents in the days following November 14. He remembered three FBI cars there at a time. After talking with more than one hundred people over four days, we had found additional witnesses on all the important new facts—the Caldwell roadblock, the "gobs" of state reports, the earlier discovery of the dynamite.

We still had another hundred to question but had to get back to Portland. We made one last quick stop at the Idaho State Police headquarters in Boise.

---

9. Even Justice of the Peace Nita Bellows, who had treated the young *Loud Hawk* lawyers of 1976 so coldly, was now friendly. She regaled us with stories of her childhood and of the cultural programs she was bringing to Ontario. About the case she said, "I never felt good about the way the FBI handled it."

Richard Skinner and Charles Pugh were two names Idaho officers had mentioned frequently. We found Skinner near a glass-enclosed exhibit in the lobby. It held antique uniforms, old tin badges, even old radar devices, including one like Griffiths must have used in 1975.

"Yes, I was on the force then," Skinner said. "No, I wasn't directly involved."

We asked about Pugh.

"Pugh?" he said. "Good luck. That son of a bitch is harder to catch than a fart in a pan."

No sooner had he said that than Major Pugh walked by.

"Hey," Skinner said. "These guys are looking into that old Indian case."

"Sorry," Pugh said. "Can't help you much. Yep, after all the waiting, the damn thing got called off."

Another witness to the Caldwell roadblock. I asked about details to test his memory.

"Remember what time it was?"

"Yeah," he said, "daytime."

Everyone else had said it was night.

"How long did you wait at the roadblock before it was called off?"

"Didn't," Pugh said. "We stayed in the barracks."

Nothing meshed.

"We were told that there was a station wagon and a motor home full of Indians who were transporting cigarettes without tax stamps," he explained. "They were coming our way from Washington State. They'd been surveilled up there, and supposedly, they were being followed. I was told it was Dennis Banks and his wife we were waiting for.

"The block was to be between mileposts one and three [on the Idaho side of the Snake River]. We waited at the barracks in Ontario, playing cards, but apparently, we were told, they had a change of plans. Must have either left late or took a different route, because it got called off after a few hours."

As I questioned Pugh, it became clear why so many local officers had thought the stop of the motor home and station wagon had happened in the desolate area between mileposts one and three on the Idaho side—which also had an incline, like the Middleton overpass. That had been the original plan.

Driving back to Portland, I was newly optimistic. "The case won't be cops against Indians any more," I said to Long, "but FBI against homegrown folk."

All the local cops, without exception, hated the FBI for its arrogance and felt for the Indians. What one said stuck with me.

"You know," he said, "I don't like what those Indians did, but I understand it. They were fighting for their land, just like we fought for it. I know why they had to be charged twelve years ago. They have to realize they lost this war, and that's what comes with losing. Yet, I feel for them, and hell if I know why the government is still after them."

CHAPTER 28

✝ ✝ ✝

CAPTURING THE WAR

THREE Indian kids, about twelve years old, are sitting in a circle on an old yellow carpet, the television flickering in the background. Snow covers the ground outside. It is late December. They are discussing Christmas.

The first kid says, "I know what Christmas is. It's when you go out, and everyone gets dressed up weird and collects candy. Then you come back and count the candy, and the one who has the most wins."

The second kid, with knowing disdain, says, "Nah, that's not Christmas. Christmas is when everybody takes some eggs, colors them, and hides them. The one who finds the most wins."

The third kid, the oldest, instructs, "You guys are both way off. Here's what they do. What they do is they take this white guy, see, and they put him up on a cross and leave him there for four days. Then they take him down, and stick him in a cave for four more days. Then they put this big stone in front of the cave. Four days later, the white guy comes out and stands in front of the rock and looks down. If he sees his shadow, there's six more weeks of winter."

Dennis Banks had told this story at a Portland church fund raiser in 1976. When only the Indians and I laughed, Banks whispered, "You Jewish?"

It was now the day after Christmas 1987. Tom Steenson and I had flown to Rapid City, South Dakota, to prepare *Loud Hawk* for trial.

Dennis and KaMook had a plump Christmas tree in the corner of their living room. The following days, on the reservation, Steenson and I saw more trees. Almost everyone had one. They were scrawny things that had been hacked from the hills. They looked like skeletons, poor and emaciated. They fit a place where people struggled to survive.

"Seeing Christmas trees worries me," I said to Steenson. "Most Jews would never have a Christmas tree. It's an alien symbol that has deep meaning for Christians but is tied to our oppression, a threat to tradition and survival. It's no less so with Indians. Maybe it's because Indians have less experience than Jews preserving their faith while adapting to life under the domination of other religions, but it seems, as with alcohol and diseases, Indians, for sociological reasons, also lack a certain cultural immunity."

"Wouldn't Indian kids feel deprived without a tree?" Steenson asked.

"They should feel special about their own traditions," I answered.

"But Christmas is a secular holiday," he protested.

"You'll convince me of that when it's celebrated on the last Monday in December," I replied.

Our visit to South Dakota was not just to educate Steenson about the reservation and its contradictions. We had to find witnesses for the trial and meet with the defendants.

After a night's sleep at the Banks's, Steenson, our South Dakota investigator Candy Hamilton (whom I had first met in 1976, when she described for a Vancouver press conference how Anna Mae Aquash's hands had been returned by the FBI), a friend of Candy's named Sue,[1] and I drove to Oglala. It had snowed heavily the night before, but the roads were clear until the border of the reservation.

"There's no money for snow removal," Candy explained.

As we drove through the Badlands, which were serene covered in white, I dug the front tires of our rental car into the small paths blazed by the few pickup trucks and old cars that had come before. The underside of our Oldsmobile scraped snow. The car became muddy. I was glad. Only the FBI drove shiny cars on the reservation.

Sue and Candy, both in their thirties and both with blond hair, had been living on the reservation during the mid-1970s.

"Shit, everyone was armed back then," Sue said, as Candy nodded in agreement. "You'd be nuts not to. The Goons were getting people right and left. Even kids were getting shot. And the FBIs were just as bad. They didn't do shit to stop the Goons. Especially after the two got killed, they just went ape shit."

---

1. Not her real name.

"Maybe I should add you to our witness list?" I asked. Her message was good, and I could control her language.

"Shit," she said, "you know the bombings after June 26?"

"Uh-huh," I answered. "You mean the Rushmore bombing and the bombing of the BIA headquarters in Pine Ridge?"

"Yeah," she said, with a twang in her voice. "We had teams. The night of the BIA bombing, there were teams of us on the res. One bomb was for [Tribal Chairman and chief Goon] Dickie Wilson. We were going to blow him up in his house. But while we were getting ready to set the bomb, some woman or kid got up and was walking around. It was 3 o'clock in the morning. Wilson never knew how close he was to buying it," she said, chuckling.

I said, "Uh-huh," sat silent for a minute, then changed the subject, not wanting my discomfort to be obvious. As I drove, I thought again about what might have been. The only people the American Indian Movement had killed were the two FBI agents, in what was clearly a firefight. A jury in Iowa had ruled that self-defense. Where would the self-defense have been if Dick Wilson, for all his terror tactics and Goons, had been blown to pieces along with his family?

I knew what Sue would say. "Maybe Byron DeSersa and Anna Mae would be alive." Maybe. Or maybe Anna Mae had died from the same revolutionary rationalizations that had led a "team" to Dick Wilson's house with a bomb?

I felt relief after dropping Sue near the town of Porcupine. Rather than concentrate on how easily events of a decade earlier might have been different, Candy, Tom, and I searched for potential witnesses to what had actually occurred. We drove to isolated houses and knocked on doors. There were few telephones to call ahead to.

Charlene[2] was a woman in her forties, living in post-Wounded Knee prefab, decomposing housing. Nothing—inside or out— had been painted in a decade. The floor was once shoddy off-white linoleum squares. Now, most were either missing or broken, exposing the graying plywood below.

Charlene greeted us warily. We pounded the snow off our boots at the door, removed them inside, and walked up the half-

2. Not her real name.

dozen stairs to the living area. She sat at her cracked formica kitchen table, having collected the four usable, mismatched, metal or wooden chairs she owned. She served Indian coffee, thick as I remembered, in old, stained, blue plastic teacups. She smiled now and then but never looked directly at us. She talked with Candy, who was gently prodding her, interspersing questions about the old days with ones about friends and their children.

Candy had told us about Charlene. She was not AIM. She was simply an Indian who wanted to live in the tradition of the old ways as fully as the demands of the new ways allowed. She was quiet, religious, and respectful.

Two weeks earlier, Candy had talked with Charlene and asked if she would sign an affidavit. Charlene had said yes with a yes that meant yes. But when Candy returned with a typewritten draft, Charlene said yes with a yes that meant no. This had happened with ten other witnesses. People would talk privately, wanting to help. But to sign a piece of paper dredged up old fears.

"The FBIs will come," Charlene had said.

Candy had replied, "We can give you a piece of paper, like in the old days, telling them that you insist on your rights and that unless they have a warrant to search or to arrest, they have to leave."

Charlene had looked down and said, apologetically, "But that won't stop them from coming."

Steenson and I were here to listen and to urge her to come to Portland to testify. She would do well; she was straightforward, honest, simple, soft-spoken, sincere. After an hour, she started to open up. Then she stopped abruptly, looking at Candy.

"Are you sure these guys aren't FBIs?" she asked.

Candy laughed. "If they were, we'd have found out a long time ago. They're okay, Charlene."

"Well, you know what it was like," she started. "Them FBIs was everyplace, and they never come alone. Always three, four, five cars of 'em, all dressed like soldiers, carrying guns, running around like they owned the place.

"I got shoved around by them many times. Many times they come here, asking questions about people, pushing, threatening, pointing guns. Even at the kids. Four and five and six years old, had guns pointed at them.

"One time, I was in a sweat, and them FBIs come, ripped open the lodge in the middle of a ceremony! It was cold. All we had was towels. They pointed their big guns into the sweat lodge and ordered everybody out. I don't know if they were looking for someone or just wanted to be mean. But they had no respect for our ceremonies. They come in, pointed their guns, laughed. If they just wanted to freeze naked women in the snow, at least they should have waited until we finished praying."

This was not the only incident of religious harassment I would hear, nor was it the only story of the FBI's fondness for cold as a weapon. Oscar Bear Runner's son had been forced to take off his T-shirt and stand, rigid, in ten degree below zero weather until he was frostbitten.

We heard more horror stories as we traveled around the reservation the following days—about the Goons shooting at old people driving down the road, about the FBI invading Oglala as if it were a battlefront in Vietnam. Everyone had lived in constant fear of death. So many years later, the trauma was still fresh. Young adults pulled up their shirts and pant legs, showing us wounds they received as children—from bullets that scarred their arms, legs, and chests. People as exhibits for a Portland, Oregon, jury.

Richard Broken Nose's hut was behind his house. The structure was one room. It was empty, except for backless wood benches resting against two of the four walls and an old white enamel gas stove. The oven door was open, and all four burners were lit for heat.

Even though it was night, all the windows were sealed with blankets. Steenson sat next to Dennis, and I sat next to Steenson at the end of a green bench. TaTiopa and her sisters were on the floor next to us, nestled under a blanket. KaMook, also on the floor, held Chinopa in her lap. Russell Loud Hawk, Sam Loud Hawk, Kenny Loud Hawk, KaMook's mom, Cheyenne, and Ka-Mook's niece, Stephanie, were also in the room, along with twenty other people I did not know.

"That's Rudy Runs Above," Dennis whispered. An elder spiritual man from the Rosebud reservation, he knelt in the center of the room. Tobacco offerings in tiny colored ribbons had been strung together by Rudy's wife.

I watched as Rudy stuck small staffs with colored flags—black, red, yellow, and white—into old tin Maxwell House coffee cans full of gray sand and then put each can in its proper spot. Rudy carefully poured sand on the floor, in the center between the square made by the cans with the staffs. He spread and gently molded it with an eagle feather. This was the altar.

A young boy circled the room, giving each person a sprig of sagebrush. Steenson and I watched as the others placed them behind their ears. We did the same. Then the single light bulb was unscrewed. The stove was turned off. The ceremony began.

Lame Deer said of this ceremony,

Imagine darkness so intense and so complete that it is almost solid, flowing around you like ink, covering you like a velvet blanket. A blackness which cuts you off from the everyday world, which forces you to withdraw deep into yourself, which makes you see with your heart instead of your eyes. You can't see, but your eyes are opened. You are isolated, but you know that you are part of the Great Spirit, united with all living beings.

And out of this utter darkness comes the roaring of the drums, the sound of prayers, the high-pitched songs. And among all these sounds your ear catches the voices of the spirits—tiny voices, ghostlike, whispering to you from unseen lips. Lights are flitting through the room, almost touching you, little flashes of lightning coming at you from the darkness. Rattles are flying through the air, knocking against your head and shoulders. You feel the wings of birds brushing your face, feel the light touch of a feather on your skin. And always you hear the throbbing drums filling the darkness with their beating, filling the empty spaces inside yourself, making you forget the things that clutter up your mind.[3]

I did not feel birds' wings, and nothing knocked me, but I had never been in such a moving and totally dark environment. Opening and closing my eyes made no difference. It *was* jet black velvet.

The drumming, the singing in Lakota, the green sparks shooting from the rattled gourds were mesmerizing. With my eyes open but seeing only darkness and flashes that did not illuminate, I could not fight off a state very much like dreaming.

3. Lame Deer and Erdoes, *Lame Deer*, 172.

Conscious, I was debating myself, my 1975 self a real life entity, a spirit, coming inside me in the dark, challenging my 1988 self.

Yes, these people had a way of life under attack. Yes, they had to fight to survive. But, yes, crimes could have occurred. People could have been killed when AIM went off the deep end for a few months. It almost seems providential that Wilson, or Griffiths, or the Bankses, Kenny Loud Hawk, Russ Redner, or Leonard Peltier did not end up buried with the two agents and Joe Stuntz and Anna Mae.

But legal advocacy for my clients demands that I see only good on their side, discounting any evil. That is not truth. That is not life. Life is grayer. Sure, Wilson's Goons were murdering AIM people and the FBI did nothing except encourage that, but that did not mean I should ignore the fact that AIM people were capable of murdering others, too, and only chance stopped them. Of course, this is not a balanced equation—a few potential murders versus many real ones. But because one side is racist and rotten does not mean that the other side can do anything it wants.

I feel awkward. It still hurts that people I support, some of whom are my friends, could have planned to kill other human beings. Yes, of course, it was war. Death is a necessary part of war, but those planned deaths—Ken Griffiths and Dick Wilson—were proved unnecessary. Yet, but for freak fortune—a misread teletype, Anna Mae's dislike of Russ Redner, a 3:00 A.M. decision to raid a refrigerator—they would have happened.

I am haunted by Byron DeSersa's severed leg and Anna Mae Aquash's severed hands and all the kids shot and elders beaten and killed, mad as hell about all the racism and the destruction of a beautiful way of life, but I am still saddened by the death of the two agents, haunted by what those bullets fired just down the road did to the lives of the wives and children and parents and friends who knew nothing more than that Williams and Coler were cops who died when they did not have to. I wonder if they were really shot the way the FBI said—wounded, begging for their lives, one of them pleading, "I have a family!" on his knees, then having his head blown off. Somebody I have met or talked with in a friendly way—Butler, Robideau, Peltier— may have done that to another human being.

This is a feeling I can never admit to my clients. They would no longer trust me. I do not trust me any longer. Intellectually, I can discount what could have happened, and did not, and focus on what did happen, and why. People were getting shot. Many Indian families were torn apart—more widows, more orphans. Dennis came back, at risk to himself, to help. And the real crime is that the government knows that any antisocial behavior on his part was a matter of the times. Those times are long past. Yet the case continues. What a waste!

If I am ever going to try this case, I am going to have to push the sympathy for everyone who died or could have died well down, bury it, and paint a picture for the jury that is unequivocal—all good on our side, all evil on the other. That is my duty to my clients. I have a month to shape my mind, feel the zeal without the doubt.

The light came on. Sam Loud Hawk spoke, explaining in English what the spirits had told him, in Lakota.

"The Spirit Red Boy came," Sam said. "He looked into the hearts of the lawyers. He looked deep. They are both committed. The one on the left, however, is troubled, has doubts. But those doubts will be gone by the time of trial. The Spirit Red Boy will stand with you. He will be in that courtroom, standing by your side."

When Tom Steenson and I talked the next day, we each thought we had been "the lawyer on the left."

After the ceremony we slept one night on the Loud Hawks' linoleum floor and then, to balance feelings, the next night at Russ Redner's double-wide trailer. The feud was still strong. The Loud Hawks were upset at Redner for missing the ceremony, and Redner was mad at the world.

"Shit," Redner said, "for the first time things were going well, and now, it's all falling apart. We move into this trailer—Debbie's dream home—and then I lose my job, and we have no way to keep up the payments. That's why I didn't go to the ceremony. It was at Richard Broken Nose's. The Broken Noses and Loud Hawks are family."

Then, changing the subject, he said, "I spent last night thinking. When I get back to Portland, I'm taking that judge head on. I put Redden and Turner not only in the same ball park but on the same team!"

"Russ," I said, "Redden is a *judge*. You can't expect him to be any better than he has been. After all, he's dismissed the case three times."

"I don't care," he asserted. "If I go down, I don't want to go down without having fought, dug in, every step of the way."

The next morning I left Redner waiting in the car with Candy Hamilton, while Steenson and I knocked on the Loud Hawks' door to take Russell and Kenny Loud Hawk for a meeting with Dennis and KaMook.

"You decide without me," Kenny said, having just emerged from the shower, his long hair trailing down his bare back, a towel around his neck. His wife and two young daughters watched him silently.

"Kenny," I said, "important decisions have to be made, and they can determine whether you go to jail or not. You've *got* to be there."

"I don't give a shit anymore what these guys want," he yelled. "Whatever they do is okay with me. I don't have any patience for this shit! Just go without me!"

I looked at Russell with exasperation, then at Kenny, and said, "Kenny, just stop it, get dressed, and get in the fucking car."

Russell, embarrassed, his eyes down, walked over and whispered to his son. Kenny, disgusted, threw his towel on the floor and charged out of the room. Russell looked at me and nodded.

Five minutes later, Kenny was sitting in the back seat with his father and Candy. Redner, Steenson, and I were in front. Only my conversation with Russell penetrated the silent wall between front and back seats, each containing a defendant who ignored the other.

"That's Sheep Mountain," Russell said, as we drove near the town of Scenic. "That's Indian land," he continued, pointing out the window. "Two hundred thousand acres. World War II, the government asked to borrow it for a bombing range. Indians wanted to help. The government promised we'd get it back right after the war. That's more than forty years. We keep asking, but they don't give it back. It's Indian land, you know."

An hour later, we were sitting around the Banks's sun-drenched kitchen table.

"A lot has happened since October," I began. "We filed a motion to dismiss based on Turner's failure to tell the grand jury about favorable eyewitnesses. Redden denied it, saying it was a close question. But our timing couldn't be better. There's a new

case that gives us the right to appeal. It's another narrow exception to the rules that ordinarily prohibit a defendant's appeal
before trial. The theory is that the right to be free from an
improperly obtained grand jury indictment is lost if you have to
go to trial."

"What are our chances?" Dennis asked.

"For everyone except you, almost none. The eyewitnesses don't
have much importance for anyone arrested at the scene," I said.
"Ed Jones thinks you should appeal, and everyone else should go
to trial. He says that would throw Turner's case into chaos. But I
think everyone should appeal. The issue is not frivolous. It will
keep everybody together. And it will buy us more time to prepare
for trial."

"Okay," Dennis said, "if they want Dennis Banks, they'll have
to fight every step of the way. File the appeal."

"Fine," I said.

"And if we lose," he continued, "how's the trial shaping up?"

"Well," I said, "we've found a couple of witnesses, but we're
having a difficult time finding good ones about the time and
conditions. People who were good witnesses ten or fifteen years
ago don't come across well now or have died. And there are a lot
of people who are still afraid."

Dennis puffed on his pipe and nodded.

"Think it would help if we had some witnesses who used to be
Goons?" Redner asked sheepishly, looking away from Kenny.

"What do you mean?" I asked.

"Well, Debbie knows people who would be willing to say one
of two things. Some would say 'I was with Wilson back then, but
knowing what I do now, if I had to do it all over again, I'd be with
AIM. They were the ones really fighting for Indian people.'

"Then there'd be some who wouldn't go that far. But they'd
say 'I didn't like those AIM people, still don't, but back then,
everyone was armed. You'd have been crazy not to. I can't blame
those guys for having that stuff. Everyone did.'

"Dennis," he continued, "you've told me you had people like
that coming up to you. You're even doing adolescent alcohol and
drug counseling with the sheriff who arrested you on the Custer
charges, right? Think these people would help?"

Dennis nodded.

"I just *love* the reverse English on this!" I said. "I know Turner. It's finally dawned on him, after all these years, that Redden will let the jury hear some of the history. So I'm sure he's looking for people to say there were good Indians and bad Indians, and you guys certainly weren't the good ones. We'll pull in some of Wilson's old boys and confuse the hell out of him. Not only will their testimony help justify the weapons, it'll send a powerful message to the jury: the Indians have put this war behind them; the only party that can't is the government—the government that has had its case dismissed four times. It'll give a jury another reason to acquit. I *love* it!"

KaMook and Dennis liked it, too. Kenny looked at Russ and nodded. Marrying into what traditional Indians called the "apple" (red on the outside, white on the inside) Indians was one thing; using them to testify in court was another.

Bruce Ellison lived just outside Rapid City in a comfortable wooden cabin with huge picture windows, just feet from a stream that trickled through a canyon spotted with ponderosa pine. The hills ran almost straight up from the water, leaving just enough ground for the house and the narrow dirt road behind it. It was a fairyland, the snow and ice covering the tree-studded horizon as well as most of the brook.

Ellison had come to Indian country right after Wounded Knee and never left. Although Jewish, his dark hair had grown out long and straight, and he kept it in a ponytail, the fashion of a Lakota male. He represented AIM members in South Dakota, although when they wandered, so did he. He had represented Dino Butler (one of the two AIM members acquitted of killing the two FBI agents) on another murder case in Oregon.[4] He continued to represent Leonard Peltier, now serving two consecutive life sentences in Leavenworth, Kansas.

Steenson and I arrived in early afternoon. "I have a lot to show you," Ellison said. He handed each of us a beer, pointed to his living room couch, and turned on his VCR. One tape had feature stories about Peltier from Canadian television. Another had interviews after the June 26, 1975, firefight. But most impres-

---

4. Dino Butler was acquitted of killing a grave robber.

sive was one with raw NBC News film footage of the FBI occupation of Pine Ridge in the summer of 1975.

I *had* to get this before a jury. It *was* Vietnam, just as I remembered on television growing up, except that the combat soldiers
were FBI agents and the Vietnamese were Sioux. The footage
was not cut, not edited for television, not in any order, not all
focused. It captured rather than presented.

FBI Special Agent Joseph Trimbach, in combat gear, speaks to
the press, saying, "Two of our agents . . . ran into some gunfire. . . .
I don't know if they were alive when they were shot in the head."

"What's your total force number?" a reporter asks.

"We have between 125 and 150 agents," Trimbach answers.[5]

Cut to nighttime. A road. A dark green bus, huge, with ARMY
NATIONAL GUARD stenciled in small white letters near the
front door, license plate US ARMY 1M5153.

"Stack 'em up!" someone hollers. "Stack 'em up over there
somewhere."

Through the bus door, sliding onto the concrete, come gun
cases. One, two, three, four, five, six, seven, eight, nine, ten, on
and on, endless. The camera catches the sound of the Samsonite-
like cases, black with little metal balls underneath, dropped on
the ground and then a crackling, running sound as the agents
slide them along the roadway.

Out come boxes of ammo. More boxes. One agent in a blue
blazer with a khaki shirt underneath it instead of a dress shirt and
tie, carries more ordnance. More boxes. One large one is labeled
"MEAL COMBAT INDIVIDUAL C." Did they plan to stay a
while?

Two agents strain, each carrying a strap of a heavy duffel bag.
Another gingerly transfers a cardboard box to another vehicle.
This box had been taped shut. Large letters say "DO NOT
DROP." Another such box, handled with equal care, follows.
More ammo boxes. Another heavy duffel bag. And another.
Footsteps of agents marching on the roadway, two at a time,
crunch in rhythm.

---

5. The Canadian television program *The Fifth Estate* reported that the forces
(under FBI command) included "over 250 state troopers, U.S. marshals, and
FBI agents [who] poured into the area."

Cut. Agents, dressed for battle in flack jackets, carry rifles. It is almost dawn. They check their rifles, M-16s, hold them up, look at them, then walk to trucks and cars.

"Okay, are we ready?" one asks.

Cut. An agent peers over a hill, careful not to expose his head. Another joins him and squints through a rifle scope.

"Hi," the new arrival says, "what're we going to do, make a sweep?"

"Yeah," the other agent replies.

More green-clad figures run on the edges of a field, making a sweep, ready to attack. Birds chirp. Someone screams something unintelligible but frantic in the background. Diesel trucks drown out the birds. A helicopter overhead drowns out the diesel trucks. The militarized FBI is at war.

Cut. A sunny, windy day, in a shaded structure made of tree trunks. An Indian man reads the beginning of a proclamation: "We the undersigned members and supporters of the White Clay District, Pine Ridge Indian Reservation, do hereby request the removal of all alien law enforcement personnel . . ."

Cut. An older Indian woman, crying, picks up the corner of an orange tent as though it had been her only worldly possession.

"They ripped down the tents and *everything!*" she sobs.

Cut. A news conference. "I haven't heard of the petition," an FBI agent says. "We certainly don't plan on leaving the area until we have completed our assigned job here."

Cut. A young Indian man speaks to a reporter. "About fifty of 'em," he says. "They surrounded our house! They were all armed with M-16s, battle fatigues. There was nobody at the house except women and kids. They came down and were all flashing around and everybody got scared. What would have happened if I hadn't gone down there to talk to them? My grandfather, he was pretty scared. They came without a warrant. When they ask to search the house, there's not much you can say with fifty guns pointing at you."

Cut. An older Indian woman dressed in black stands in front of her house, with her family. An FBI agent stands to the side. The camera focuses on the woman, her face wrinkled, her anger fired with a rage that does not fit her age or her grandmotherly stature. She is under five feet tall. The camera looks down to her.

"He come in!" she yells. "He come to the door. He accused me of killing two FBI men . . ."

The agent interrupts. "As a matter of fact, Ma'am, no one said anything about that."

She tugs at her shirt as she spoke, in quick jerks, in rhythm with her words, as if in mourning.

"I've got plenty of witnesses!" she yells. "Your lying days are over! Don't push no more lies down my throat! My people! My people are being *slaughtered*—beaten and killed every day! Don't you have any conscience!"

The agent walks away, his back to the camera.

Watching the tape, I wondered. How do I get this in front of a jury? How many of these witnesses are now dead or no longer compelling, their attractiveness to a white jury ruined by the effects of poverty and time? "I don't know how to sort all this," I said to Steenson, who also seemed overwhelmed. "We'd better collect all we can and figure out what we can use later."

Ellison nodded, turned off the VCR, and popped an audio-cassette into his tape recorder.

"A reporter named Kevin McKiernan was actually there the day of the shootout and recorded it," Ellison said. He pushed the play button.

Feet marching. Metal clanging, in step. Foot. Foot. Foot. Foot. Foot. Foot. Pop. Pop. Pop pop pop. Pop. An exited, rapid voice, "Now you can hear the fire. The BIA agents are going behind their trucks."

Pop pop pop pop pop pop pop pop.

"High-caliber bullets."

Pop pop pop pop.

"There it is again!"

Pop. Pop. Pop pop pop.

"Ricochet. Automatic fire!"

Pop. Pop pop pop pop pop pop. Vrrrrrm! An automobile accel-erated, hard, as if in a drag race.

"There goes a car with an Indian family in the area, tempo-rarily leaving it. A very heavy volley of shots just before that."

Pop pop pop pop pop pop pop.

"There they go again! . . . Federal cars continue to race up and down the roads, over the ridges, rolling plains. Yet, from where I am, I can see little Indian children playing by these tarpaper shacks, and horses continue to play in the meadows all around. The FBI plane has moved out of gunshot range. There's some firing now!"

Pop. Pop pop pop pop. Pop.

"Some of the shots sound like firecrackers. There are a couple now! Those are more than firecrackers."

An unidentified white male voice: "It was up to me to make the final decision. I made the decision that we would assault."

An elderly Indian woman, speaking over the sound of a baby coughing in the background: "It looks like they're trying to kill *all* us Indians. Some girls were sitting there, and some marshals or FBIs turned around and said, 'We're going to kill some more Indians before we leave.'"

Pop pop pop pop pop.

A voice that I recognize as John Trudell's: "FBI agents that grew up watching John Wayne and cowboys and Indians come out there and want to play cowboys and Indians, then they gotta suffer the consequences, just as we do. They are the aggressors. We will make no apologies for the death of two pigs who did not belong there in the first place."

Pop pop pop.

"Those sound like high-caliber bullets. I'm down behind the back bumper of my truck. At this rate there's surely going to be some blood spilled here."

I listened to more interviews intercut with gunfire, then clicked off the tape recorder, having heard enough. I could cut out the interviews and use the gunshots for the jury. They captured the war—and the fear.

CHAPTER 29

JUSTIFICATION AND RICHARD NIXON

"HERE," the OSP lieutenant in charge of archives said, with a broad grin. He lifted a heavy cardboard box from the corner of a dusty basement in OSP headquarters and handed it to me.

After talking with Lt. Kleinsmith the month before, I had filed a subpoena for the "gobs" of Oregon State Police reports. Then Charles Turner "advised" the lieutenant not to honor my request. Then I threatened to go to the judge. Then Turner backed down.[1]

"I threw in a little present for you too," the lieutenant said, watching my face. When enough time had passed for dramatic effect he whispered, "We had a copy of the early FBI files."

"Thanks!" I said, amazed. Turner or the FBI must have really pissed this guy off. I put the box down and shook his hand again.

"If they say this isn't the real thing," he added, "you call me as a witness!"

Hundreds of papers fleshed out the FBI's activities. People in Portland had been followed in late November 1975 and after, the FBI hoping to catch Peltier and Banks. Informants had been more deeply involved. For example, on the 13th and 14th of November 1975, the FBI expected a *third* vehicle, a "white Jeep Wagoneer," to be traveling with the motor home and the station wagon. More facts. More leads to follow.

There was even a report with two more eyewitnesses—waitresses in a Baker, Oregon, restaurant. According to the agents,

---

1. Judge Redden was so concerned that the government was still hiding evidence that, weeks before, he had ordered Turner to turn over his entire file for judicial review.

these two women served food to Dennis Banks and an Indian woman on November 14, 1975. I called both witnesses. They had identified pictures but did not remember who was in the pictures.

"Did the FBI ask you to initial any photographs or write down anything about who you picked?"

"No," they both said.

Both were furious at the prosecutors for continuing the case for so long. "Don't they have any heart?" one asked.

It was disheartening to learn that the government, after all, had witnesses who might be able to identify Dennis Banks in eastern Oregon on November 14, 1975. Yet their testimony was now so weak that at worst, it would not hurt us, and at best, it would backfire on the government. (What juror would believe that these witnesses had identified Banks when FBI agents had not asked them to initial the photographs they had supposedly chosen?) Having information from these papers that the government thought we did not—details about their witnesses, small pieces of their investigatory puzzle—was also satisfying.

The papers also proved more government misconduct. The prosecutors had misled Judge Belloni, Judge Redden, and the Court of Appeals in the first two appeals about what they knew and when they knew it.[2]

And the FBI had, in fact, investigated Marlon Brando. Agents had talked to him at his motor home during the filming of

2. One document proved that the prosecutors knew about the dynamite *before* Fettig destroyed it and wanted it "rendered safe." They had told the courts that all the decisions about the explosives were made by the state authorities.

Another proved Turner misinformed Judge Redden in 1980, when he swore he had played "no part whatever" in the initial charging decisions. According to the FBI memo:

On November 16, 1975, SA XXXXXXXXXXXXX [blacked out in original] telephonically advised that as a result of discussion with Assistant U.S. Attorneys KENNETH BAUMAN, CHARLES H. TURNER and JACK G. COLLINS, it was determined that a complaint would be filed against LOUD HAWK and REDNER for aiding and abetting a federal fugitive, Title 18, U.S. Code, Section 3.

Assistant U.S. Attorney advised that in addition to the harboring complaint, an additional charge would be filed on the morning of November 17, 1975, charging both LOUD HAWK and REDNER with possession of an explosive device. Mr. TURNER advised that unless he phoned to the contrary, that the complaints for harboring and possession of explosive device, Title 26, Section 5861(d) would be filed with the U.S. District Court.

Missouri Breaks. That was in August 1975, when Banks had fled after having been found guilty of the Custer riot charges. It was Brando acting a high comedy. According to the agents, when they asked him a question, he "would simply smile and go on to another topic of conversation."

And Trudell was right. After the Ontario arrest, the FBI must have known that Brando had given Peltier money. According to a report, two agents investigated a North Hollywood Radio Shack. The employees pulled records for September 4, 1975. On that date, two Indians bought $1,000 worth of radio equipment with "crisp one-hundred-dollar bills." One employee picked Peltier's picture from a photo spread. "They said it was for a movie," the employee told the agents. "Columbia Pictures. They needed the stuff to communicate between vehicles—a van and a car."

Two FBI agents also spent an afternoon with Brando at his Beverly Hills home on December 1, 1975, two weeks after his motor home had been stopped in the Oregon desert. They filed a nine-page report. Brando, who was "very gracious and courteous," refused to talk about the Oregon case. But he told the agents about his interest in Indian affairs.

The situation of the American Indian today is terrible. A national shame. Cruel, driving poverty. Lack of hope. Malnutrition. And our government is part of the problem. Representatives of several tribes, Indian elders, asked for an audience with President Ford about the plight of the American Indian. The delegation was ignored. Meanwhile the people who are trying to do something about it are being hunted down.

I was with Dennis Banks when he was on trial for Wounded Knee. I was there when Joseph Trimbach, the Regional Director of the FBI, repeatedly lied under oath. Judge Nichol asked Trimbach if he had ever authorized a wiretap of Wounded Knee village. He swore he had not. Then the defense produced proof that he had, with his signature on it. It was dismal. And Trimbach has never been reprimanded.

I was also with Dennis Banks after his conviction for the Custer courthouse riot. Dennis was very remorseful, but afraid that he would not get a fair sentence. He had received word . . . that he was going to get ten years, and probably be "hit" after his incarceration. I know the man. He truly believed his life was in danger.

I advised him to go through the process, because the ideals he stands for were worth the two or three years he'd probably spend in prison. But after Durham, his closest advisor, was exposed as a police informant, Dennis suspected everyone. Including me.

Banks, as I'm sure you guys know, is a very intelligent individual. I honestly can't comprehend why he chose to make himself a fugitive. He's more intelligent than that. But, then again, he told me that during this time he had seen a hit list containing American Indian names who were targeted for assassination by either the CIA or undercover FBI agents. Given how many have died over the last few years, I could understand his concern. Especially after the two FBI agents were killed. I fear that that incident will work like poison in other agents' minds when they go after Indian fugitives like Dennis Banks.

You know, I tried to speak out more about this. I called Johnny Carson, and asked him for time. Carson told me I could have a spot, but that the Indian cause could only be a small segment. I told him, "Johnny, you can't discuss the situation of the American Indian sandwiched in twenty minutes of levity."

I wouldn't play Carson's "silly ass" games. I'll probably never appear on the Johnny Carson show again. I really couldn't give a shit!

Then I tried Henry Kissinger. I knew that as secretary of state he was a very busy man, and that his job didn't include internal problems. But he listened to me, and I hoped, because he was close to President Ford, that he'd explain the situation to the president. I doubt it, though. I don't think the president was ever told about that conversation.

I also tried to contact Don Rumsfeldt of the White House staff. But hard as I tried, that went no place.

It was February 2, 1988, Groundhog Day. I sat at a wooden table in a windowless room in Alexandria, Virginia. Every few hours I motioned with a stretch of tired arms. A librarian pressed a silent alarm that summoned another librarian, who pushed a paper-filled gray metal cart away from my table, through double glass doors. Five minutes later he or she brought the cart back and with it, another half-dozen gray cardboard boxes.

I read the documents on fast forward, a thousand pages an hour, deciding by a date, a name, a word. I clipped the ones I wanted reproduced and scribbled a description on a list, already fingering the next page. Weeks later the copies, all certified from the Presidential Papers of Richard Nixon, would be mailed to me in Portland.

With the trial date now tentatively set in mid-April 1988 (due to the delay from the appeal of the grand jury motion), there was enough time to prepare a full defense. I knew now I could make the jury see the terror of South Dakota circa 1973–1975 in historical perspective. The defendants, solid citizens, would no longer be threatening.

Yet I dreaded the day when all the weapons would land on a courtroom table. The guns had to be buried. But burying them behind the motor home's cornflakes boxes and bags of peanuts, as they literally had been, would not work. I decided to bury our guns with their guns through a defense known as "justification."

"Justification" was the usual trial tactic of nuclear protestors and of ex-felons found illegally possessing guns. It rarely worked. Nuclear protestors said they should be acquitted because the potential harm of nuclear power was greater than any damage caused by their technical trespass at a reactor gate. But in order for the defense to work, they had to prove the danger was imminent. Clear and present. Right now. They could not.

An ex-convict might have a gun for protection against a real, imminent danger. ("The man was coming back for his money, and threatened to kill me. I knew he'd do it, too. He carved up Joey real bad last week.") His justification defense failed because, in theory, he could have called the police for help.

The Indian justification defense—it was okay for them to possess weapons to defend Indian people under attack—had neither problem. First, there were scores of witnesses who would testify about the combined Goon-FBI reign of terror on post-Wounded Knee Pine Ridge. Weekly deaths were real, clear, present, and graphically bloody. We had pictures. Second, how could the traditional Indians and AIM have called the cops? The federal police were at war with them.

Of course, there were problems with a justification defense. The government would have an easier time arguing that all the defendants knew about each of the guns. And if Turner gave the case more thought than he had in the past, he would realize that even if Indians were justified in possessing weapons, they did not necessarily have to have guns and bombs without serial numbers, the lack of which rendered them illegal.

But justification let us get their guns into evidence to cover our guns. Their guns were larger, scarier, and there were many more of them. Ours would disappear.

This defense also dovetailed nicely with international law, the concept of sovereignty so important to Indian people. What if Luxembourg were occupied by Germany? Wouldn't its soldiers have the right to transport arms for collective self-defense through enemy territory? Why not Indians, too? They have some aspects of sovereignty left. Isn't collective self-defense the last, core, rock bottom concept of sovereignty?

My defense—"You have to prove it all," coupled with justification/self-defense, flavored with sovereignty—was unusual. Evidence codes were made for the expected. That meant that where the evidence most neatly fit the rules, I would have to offer as many government guns and as much justification as I could. That is why Brando's December 1975 interview was so intriguing. It led me to the Presidential Archives.

I already had reservation witnesses to prove the Indians could not call the local FBI for help. But could I also prove that the upper echelons of government were no source of help either? If Brando could not get a message through, how could the Loud Hawk gang? And if a message had gotten through, wouldn't it have been futile? Didn't the government already know about the conditions and the murders and the FBI's vendetta?

Proof of that futility would be in the presidential papers of Richard Nixon and Gerald Ford. Who else had tried to intervene? What was the official reaction to the radical Indians? Did the White House want them to go the way of all "bad" Indians?

I filed a subpoena for the White House tapes,[3] which would take weeks to process. Declassified papers, unlike the tapes, were immediately accessible. From January 1969, when Nixon took office, to August 1974, when he resigned, the documents—letters, internal memorandums, briefing papers, news digests—painted a

---

3. Judge Nichol had been the first judge to order the release of Nixon's White House Watergate tapes, during Dennis Banks's Wounded Knee trial. Supposedly, there were conversations about Wounded Knee in the Oval Office.

Nichol had backed down with pressure from White House Counsel, "but there may be something there," he told me. There was a good chance that Nixon said an "expletive deleted" about Dennis Banks.

I expected Nixon's lawyers to object to my subpoena, especially after the archivist told me that there was "a lot there." I instructed the archivist to tell the lawyers that if they objected, I would also subpoena Nixon himself.

fascinating picture of the White House's policies on Indian affairs. There were occasional voices of sympathy, or at least interest. But it was a dismal record that only looked passable by comparison to the neglect or outright animosity of other presidents.[4]

Familiar names permeated the papers I spent four days poring through: Watergate figures John Erlichman, H. R. Haldeman, John Dean, Bud Krogh, Charles Colson, Jeb Magruder, Dwight Chapin, Rosemary Woods. All had a hand in Indian affairs, especially Krogh. Other names, also involved, were one layer below: George Bush, Frank Carlucci, George Schultz, Pat Buchanan, Alexander Haig.

The files contained thousands of letters and telegrams from private citizens, congressmen and senators, state officials, school-children, Indian leaders, all complaining about the plight of Indians, demanding that something be done. Reorganize the Bureau of Indian Affairs. Stop unequal justice. Free funds impounded for Indian health care. Free funds impounded for Indian housing. Almost every paper was addressed to the president. Most were redirected by his staff to lower-level bureaucrats for "suitable responses," not action.

The president sent his personal greetings to the Miss Indian Arizona Pageant and was photographed with a newly elected Republican tribal chairman in the Oval Office. But he would not even see a telegram from Janet McCloud of Yelm, Washington, about Indian youths being gunned down there, or a telegram about Indians dying in a South Dakota natural disaster, or a letter about teachers torturing Indian children at federal boarding schools, or an old chief's plea for the return of Sheep Mountain.

The administration had the statistics and the reports. "The Indian is a refugee and an administered person; he has no control over his destiny. . . . The suicide rate is ten times that of the

---

4. Nixon signed a bill returning Blue Lake, a sacred piece of Taos Pueblo land, to that tribe. As commendable as that act was, it was for show.

"Blue Lake is *the* symbolic issue for the Indian community," Bobbie Kilberg of the White House staff had written. "The 'Indian problem' has achieved a level of national attention and sympathy from our white population. We are out in front on this issue but stand to get it snatched away by the Democrats if we don't move on Blue Lake."

nation. . . . Alcohol-related deaths are extremely high. . . . Crime [is] fantastic. . . . The BIA is the worst agency in Washington. . . . [They] have long been told that [they] are not legally a person. . . . Justice is a mockery. . . . Literally dozens of homicides against Indians [in one year near the Pine Ridge Reservation] go undetected—prosecutors have kept their hands off. . . . Police brutality against Indians is widespread. . . . Indians are kept at the bottom of the BIA. . . . Health services for Indians are inadequate."[5] Yet nothing was done.

The Nixon administration suffered three political crises with American Indians: the occupation of Alcatraz Island in 1969; the takeover of the BIA building in Washington, D.C., in November 1972; Wounded Knee in February 1973.

The Nixon papers proved that the federal war against the Indians at Wounded Knee, and the violent move to crush AIM in its aftermath, resulted in part from the White House's failures during its two prior Indian emergencies.

In mid-November 1969, a group of young Indians with a keen sense of publicity[6] appeared on the deserted federal prison island, Alcatraz, in San Francisco Bay. Petitions, letters, and telegrams arrived at the White House. Most were supportive of the Indians. Even Ruth Milhous, the president's aunt, wrote, "Dear Richard:

5. From Howard Glickstein's (U.S. Commission on Civil Rights) 31-page summary on Indians, sent April 1, 1970, to Daniel P. Moynihan, counsellor to the president.

6. Their proclamation said,

TO THE GREAT WHITE FATHER AND ALL HIS PEOPLE

We, the native Americans, reclaim the land known as Alcatraz Island in the name of all American Indians by right of discovery. . . . We feel that this so-called Alcatraz Island is more than suitable for an Indian reservation, as determined by the white man's own standard. By this we mean that this place resembles most Indian reservations in that:

1. It is isolated from modern facilities, and without adequate means of transportation.
2. It has no fresh running water.
3. It has inadequate sanitation facilities.
4. There are no oil or mineral rights.
5. There is no industry, and so unemployment is very great.
6. There are no health care facilities.
7. The soil is rocky and unproductive, and the land does not support game.
8. There are no educational facilities.
9. The population has always exceeded the land base.
10. The population has always been held as prisoners and kept dependent upon others.

We don't want this administration to go down in history as another that dishonored our treaties with our Indians. Why not let the Indians pay the bills of rebuilding that old rock and win their real gratitude?"

The administration feared ugly television images. "The Alcatraz episode is symbolic of the lack of attention to the unmet needs of Indians in America," an early White House memorandum noted. "Our response has to be one of *restraint*."

John Trudell, the Indians' spokesman, rejected the government's plan, which called for the creation of a park with "maximal Indian properties." "We will no longer be museum pieces, tourist attractions, and politicians' playthings," he announced to the press in March 1970. He gave the government a new deadline for a better proposal: May 31, 1970.

The Indians wanted a spiritual center, not monuments, a thriving university, not a stale museum. Most of all, they wanted control. As long as they stayed, they had power.

For the next year and a half, the government debated what to do. Plans were considered, then rejected. "Impound the small vessel now making daily supply trips. Install foghorns of such volume that sleep would be virtually impossible on the island. The army has an anti-intrusion device producing sound of such shrill intensity that it is impossible to remain in the area." Yet a November 1970 White House memorandum ended, "Having tolerated this problem for a full year, we might conclude that it is a condition rather than a problem that demands an immediate solution."

By June 1971, Erlichman, Krogh, and their cohorts changed their minds. They wanted the Indians off Alcatraz long before the November 1972 elections, fearing how "troublesome this 'symbol' can become." The Indians were escorted off the island in June, 1971 by a heavily armed Special Operations Group (SOG) of U.S. marshals without incident.

Both sides learned. Emulating Alcatraz, other young Indian activists occupied other facilities. Leonard Peltier was part of a group that took over Fort Lawton, surplus federal land, near Seattle. The federal authorities learned not to let occupations fester. That was easy for a while. The Indians who imitated Alcatraz focused on seizing land, not on articulating any basis for its restoration. These youngsters only represented themselves, not Indian nations. Without any philosophical basis for their acts except anger against racism and terrible conditions, the young Indians did not generate publicity in the papers, support among whites, or passion among other Indians.

By 1972, however, a new radical Indian ideology was forming. The young Indians began reconnecting with their heritage. They rediscovered treaties. The tribal governments, bogged down in day-to-day BIA regulations, did not care much about these hundred-year-old documents. But traditional elders did. The land claims, the broken promises, and the history and pride symbolized in these sacred agreements made between nations lashed the young activists to the older religious reservation Indians.

The youngsters began to learn Indian ways, Indian spirituality and Indian religion, as a glue and a channel for their anger and despair. The older reservation Indians accepted the youngsters and their talents for political confrontation within the white man's world.

Although Indian activists were also influenced by the civil rights movement, the Black Power movement, and the antiwar movement, the lessons learned were in style rather than content. "Civil rights," an attractive concept for black people denied equal treatment by mainstream society, was a frightening notion for Indians. Indian problems stemmed from a dominant society that wanted to take them off the reservations, blend them into white America, take away their heritage and culture and land. Traditional Indians, and now the young radicals, did not want equal rights; they wanted respect for their rights as Indians—"treaty rights."

The American Indian Movement, started by Dennis Banks in 1968 to monitor the daily harassment of Indians by police on the streets of Minneapolis, had become the preeminent Indian organization by 1972. It drew both urban and traditional reservation Indians as members. It challenged the regular killings of Indians by whites, spoke about treaty rights, and reconnected Indian people to their heritage and religion through survival schools and religious ceremonies. In the summer of 1972, many AIM members attended a Sun Dance on the Rosebud Sioux reservation.

"Maybe we should do something like the civil rights movement's 1963 March on Washington?" someone suggested.

By the fall, a Trail of Broken Treaties (TBT) was agreed upon. It would be a cross-country caravan starting at three separate points on the West Coast and picking up Indians as it went along, arriving in Washington, D.C., right before the 1972 presidential elections.

The Indians arrived on November 2, 1972 (two days late), in beat-up cars bearing bumper stickers: "Custer had it coming, and so do some others." "Remember Crazy Horse." "United States Is Indian Country." They came with a twenty-point plan for "securing an Indian future in America" that included land rights, water rights, fishing rights, prosecution of those who committed crimes against Indians, and abolition of the corrupt Bureau of Indian Affairs. But the preeminent issue was treaty rights. Congress should relate to Indians through treaties. The old ones should be observed. The ones signed by the Indians and never ratified by Congress should be adopted. New ones should be created. Sovereignty had become the core of Indian ideology.

The Indians' ideology was more organized than their logistics. Whoever had the responsibility for finding housing in local homes and food in local churches had not done his or her job. A few Indians were housed in a church, with the assistance of the Department of the Interior. The church had rats. The Indians left as hundreds of others arrived, with no place to go and nothing to eat.

The Indians met at the BIA's auditorium, awaiting word on housing. When no place could be decided on, the Department of Interior offered its auditorium. The Indians accepted.

On the way out of the BIA building, some young Indians were shoved out the door by a few of the guards. The youngsters (possibly including Anna Mae Aquash), already angry because the government would not let them hold a planned religious service,[7] believed they were being shoved outside into a waiting District of Columbia riot squad.

They stopped. They turned around. They seized the building.

---

7. Ira Hayes, the infantryman who had helped raise the American flag at Iwo Jima in a pose known to all Americans as a symbol of victory, was an Indian. He was buried at Arlington National Cemetery. The Department of Defense had refused the Indians' request for a peaceful religious service at his grave site.

They barricaded the doors, blocked the windows, upended desks, and piled metal chairs against doors in great heaps. American flags were worn or rehung upside down. A sign, printed on a cloth, hung from a window: "Native American Embassy." Sovereignty. Indian land.

Days of negotiation produced nothing. The administration was panicked. Its major concern was the election and, according to Krogh, "a real need to get *good* publicity."

At 2:30 P.M. on Monday, November 6, 1972, a judge ordered the forcible removal of the Indians by 6:00 P.M. that day. Hearing of that order, the young Indians, determined to make the BIA building the final line in a battle for Indian survival, lost control. The building was trashed.

"The atmosphere [inside the BIA building] is getting worse and worse," an informant told the White House. "The plan of the leaders is to wait until 5:45 P.M. If they had not heard anything positive, or seen any police movement, they'd set the building on fire and charge out of it as it burned."

Bobbie Kilberg, of the White House staff, raced to the BIA building, arriving at 5:30 P.M. She, along with staffer Sandy McNabb, forced their way in. Kilberg described what happened next in an internal White House memorandum.

[We were escorted] to the Commissioner's office on the second floor. The building was a shambles. At the second floor stairwell landing, smashed typewriters and furniture had been piled high. The entire corridor was lined with ripped files and strewn paper, broken equipment and furniture. The walls were a mess. The pile of stuff on the floor was two inches deep. The smell of gasoline was everywhere. Some canisters were visible. People were warning others not to smoke. The Commissioner's office was a complete wreck. Pictures were torn down. There were gashes in the panelled walls. His furniture was damaged. His rug was ruined.

The Steering Committee, about 25 to 30 people, was meeting in that office. All had clubs (mostly made from furniture legs) or makeshift spears. Their faces were painted. They were ready for war. The atmosphere was choking with determination, desperation, pride, and hostility, all mixed together. People were willing to die. Some seemed anxious for martyrdom.

The group just stared at us when we walked in. Finally, Russell

Means asked us what we wanted. Sandy McNabb said that the police had been pulled back, and would not come anywhere near the building that evening. Their reaction was one of intense disappointment. They were all psychologically geared up for their "last stand" confrontation. We had outmaneuvered them.

After a round of cursing, the group fell silent. Then Clyde Bellecourt [an AIM leader] ordered us to get an answer on whether the President would set up a Commission. Sid Mills [an Indian leader from the Pacific Northwest] gave us to midnight. If a Commission wasn't created by that time, they'd burn down the building that night. Dennis Banks then summarily dismissed us.

Eventually that night, White House counsel Leonard Garment, along with Office of Management and Budget (OMB) Director Frank Carlucci, Secretary of the Interior Rogers Morton, and Commissioner of Indian Affairs Louis Bruce, agreed to negotiate with the Indians. It was a decision dictated by politics. Highlighted in Krogh's handwritten notes were the following lines, written that night as the decision to negotiate was made: "If still there, remove Wed. A.M.—Get best press possible;—Look strong. Not tolerate illegality any longer;—Defer *violence* until Wed. A.M." Wednesday was the day after the presidential election.

By election morning, Garment, Carlucci, and Bruce met with the Indians. A federal task force was agreed on. It would examine wide issues in Indian country. Amnesty was promised. The Indians were given money for transportation home. They left before a 9:00 P.M., November 8, 1972, deadline.

Both the administration and AIM were heavily criticized over the Trail of Broken Treaties. Tribal officials from all over the country sent telegrams to the White House strongly disparaging of AIM and dissociating themselves from it. "THE OGLALA SIOUX . . . TRIBE DOES NOT APPROVE OR CONDONE ANY AND ALL ACTION TAKEN BY THE AMERICAN INDIAN MOVEMENT," wired Dick Wilson, tribal chairman of the Oglala Sioux. Many people, white and Indian, had been upset by the televised image of another Oglala Sioux, Russell Means, with a smug smile, wearing a bright red ribbon shirt, braids down each shoulder, holding a glass-enclosed, black-framed, three-foot by four-foot black and white photograph of President Nixon over his head, as he walked out of the BIA building.

Nor were people comfortable with the hundreds of thousands of dollars worth of damage in strewn paper, mangled machines, twisted chairs, and ripped walls left behind. Congressman Wayne Aspinall, Chairman of the House Committee on Interior and Insular Affairs, held hearings. How were the government's decisions about the occupation of the BIA building made? Was the president involved? Why did the Indians get money? Why did the government agree not to prosecute anyone? The administration was embarrassed and on the defensive.

Alcatraz had been tolerated, then ended in time to avoid conflict with the election. Then these same Indians invaded the capitol on election eve. The next time, there would be no toleration. In the White House's own word, these were twentieth-century "renegades."

As I started reading the Nixon papers about Wounded Knee, the event closest in time to the stop in Ontario and thus the most relevant legally, I searched for documents to prove two prongs of my justification defense. I already had documents proving that the administration knew about the problems in Indian country and did not care. It was more important to prove that these Indians had an honest fear of massacre by federal forces.

Some of that proof would come through reservation witnesses and experts.[8] But other evidence would be in the papers. There had to be documents—telegrams, letters—showing that others, even whites, feared another military genocide against Indians.

Wounded Knee started on February 27, 1973, when a traditional chief, Frank Fools Crow, called a meeting at Calico Hall, a community building on the road between the traditional hamlet of Oglala and the village of Pine Ridge, where the descendants of the "hangs around the fort" lived. The traditional reservation Indians had had enough. Mothers did not want to stand by, doing nothing, waiting for the next inevitable, racist death of one of their sons. Just weeks before, Wesley Bad Heart had been killed in Custer, South Dakota, by a white man, whom the authorities did not want to charge with murder.

---

8. Indian history is oral, not written. The stories of a hundred years before—like the massacre at Wounded Knee—were almost as real as stories of ten years before. Their fear of atrocities from the government was a constant.

Too many people showed up for the meeting. The leaders decided to move to a larger hall across the reservation. On the way, the Indians in the caravan passed the tiny hamlet of Wounded Knee, where the frozen, twisted bodies of Big Foot and his followers, including many women and children, had been spread on the snowy ground—shot to death by the U.S. Army—eighty-three winters before. The cars stopped. The town was taken over.[9] The Catholic church was occupied. Its white spire stood in front of the mass grave where scores of dead Indians had been dumped in a trench and buried.

News of Wounded Knee '73—images of Indians with warpaint and a few guns making a stand—filled the newspapers and made colorful footage for the evening news. The news was largely supportive.

Wounded Knee press coverage was featured in the News Summaries that Richard Nixon received every day.[10] This is what President Nixon saw. Presidential News Summary, major stories, Wednesday, March 1, 1973, stamped THE PRESIDENT HAS SEEN: "US officers sealed off entire Oglala Sioux reservation where about 300 militants of Amer. Indian Movement seized Wounded Knee, SD, and took 10 hostages and exchanged fire w/officers. Story led NBC and was subject of lengthy reports of ABC/CBS. . . . All nets noted trading post was stripped of food, clothes, guns and Indian relics as Indians who say they'll die for cause attempted to force attention on what they say is corruption and mismanagement w/in BIA."

Nixon, in broad handwriting, had circled the letters "BIA." The circle connected with a line drawn to the border of the page, where he wrote, for Erlichman, "E—*when* are we going to get action on this *mess?*"

Wounded Knee figured prominently in the president's press summaries for the next three months. In the first week, they reported the fast-changing events.

March 3: Apparent firebombing of an AIM leader's home

9. A white couple, the Gildersleeves, owned a trading post, a "see how they live" place where Indian artifacts were sold. They were held initially by the Indians, then released.

10. A White House staffer compiled the stories from all forms of media, prioritized them, and wrote a paragraph about each, showing which networks and papers had which stories as their "lead."

"stirred" up everyone; "CBS w/ ominous film of Indians fixing sights on weapons and Armored Personnel Carriers (APCs) in area. Meanwhile food supplies of Indians and villagers are dwindling."

March 5: "'Tension grows worse every day,' said a typically ominous report on NBC Sunday. . . . 'Another showdown is in the making at Wounded Knee,' said NBC Sat. where gov't's 'flexing of the muscles' w/the APCs was featured along w/Molotov cocktails and 'fortresses' being built by the hopelessly outmanned Indians faced by gov't demands for 'unconditional surrender.'"

Except for the news summaries, the White House documents about Wounded Knee for the first week of March 1973 were still classified, as were many of the papers covering the later weeks. (I left a subpoena.) Yet events were clear.

By March 7, 1973, there was a stalemate. The Indians, dug in, were surrounded and shot at by FBI agents and U.S. marshals and Dick Wilson's Goons. Erlichman discussed Wounded Knee with Nixon that day. "Indians" were two items higher on his hand-written list than "Watergate."

By the fourth day of my search at the presidential library, I was growing tired. I had read tens of thousands of pages about Wounded Knee and Indian affairs in the Nixon administration. All were fascinating. Only a few would be useful for trial.

"By the way, did anyone send telegrams about Wounded Knee?" I asked librarian Bonnie Baldwin. That afternoon she declassified a huge box with thousands of pink Western Union slips. These were my proof. It was not only the Indians who feared that the militarized FBI—the new Seventh Cavalry—was actually capable of wiping them out.

PRESIDENT RICHARD M. NIXON, THE WHITE HOUSE, DC, DON'T COMMIT GENOCIDE. HELP INDIANS AT WOUNDED KNEE, HEN-STRAND, HARLEYSVILLE, PA

NO MAI LAI AT WOUNDED KNEE PLEASE WITHDRAW TROOPS AND NEGOTIATE, CONSTANCE PINKERMAN, MD, LOS ANGELES, CA

IMMORAL TO KILL INDIANS AT WOUNDED KNEE. SLAUGHTER-ING INDIANS IS REVERTING TO WILD WEST TIMES, REV JAMES STARKEY, SUNFLOWER, KANS

DISPATCH KISSINGER. . . . TALK IS PREFERABLE TO FURTHER

BLOODSHED AND NATIONAL DISGRACE, ANNE MEDLIN, EXECU-
TIVE VICE PRESIDENT VATICAN II, LOS ANGELES, CALIF

DEEPLY DISTURBED AT REPORTS OF IMPENDING TEAR GASSING
VIOLENCE AND MILITARY ACTION AGAINST INDIANS AT WOUNDED
KNEE. . . . CONGRESSWOMAN BELLA S ABZUG

WE ARE FIFTH GRADE CLASS COMPTON. PLEASE TALK TO MR
DENNIS, WOUNDED KNEE. NO GUNS, FIFTH GRADE CLASS KALLY
SCHOOL COMPTON, CALIF

IF YOU KILL ONE SINGLE INDIAN AT WOUNDED KNEE I HOPE TO
SEE YOU IMPEACHED, HEATHER KIRK, SEATTLE, WA

AS DIRECTOR OF AIM IN HUMBOLT CO WE APPEAL TO YOUR
SENSE OF JUSTICE TO HALT ALL AGGRESSION AGAINST INDIAN
PEOPLE, RUSS J REDNER, ARCATA, CALIFORNIA

RE INDIANS POW WOW DONT POW POW, R A OLSEN, GRAND
RAPIDS, MICHIGAN

I URGE YOUR PROMPT ACTION TO PREVENT ARMED CONFRON-
TATION AND POSSIBLE BLOODSHED AT WOUNDED KNEE. . . .
HUBERT H HUMPHREY, US SENATOR

RECOMMEND LANCING WOUNDED KNEE BOIL WITHOUT ANES-
THETIC IMMEDIATELY, MR AND MRS BILL PARSON, HONOLULU,
HAWAII

Wounded Knee ended in May 1973 when AIM members put
down their guns and walked past the roadblocks. Despite the
hundreds of thousands of rounds fired by the government, only
two AIM members died. One law enforcement official was paralyzed. The White House saw Wounded Knee as "a great psychological and fund raising victory [for AIM]."

Wounded Knee also finalized a vendetta that had started with
Alcatraz and accelerated with the BIA takeover. The White
House staff "asked that OMB orchestrate a thorough audit" of
AIM in spring 1973. But as mad and embarrassed as the administration was by Indians who controlled the media better than it
could, the FBI was even more outraged and embarrassed. It ordered an investigation of every AIM member and supporter in
the entire United States.

CHAPTER 30

✛ ✛ ✛

TERROR TIMES

INDIANS were starving in Pine Ridge, South Dakota, in December 1970. According to White House documents, Congressman James Abourezk asked the U.S. Air Force to airlift "150,000 pounds of food, clothing, and books." Nothing happened.

South Dakota Senator George McGovern interceded, fearing that children would die from delay. The senator's staff "was informed that the Air Force was assisting in accordance with DOD[1] directive regarding domestic actions assistance, i.e., on a space available basis at no additional cost to be incurred by the government."

Finally, with more political pressure, the air force agreed to ship 20,000 pounds of food. It demanded, however, that the food should first be trucked to Scott Air Force Base in Illinois. The air force would fly it to Ellsworth Air Force Base in South Dakota. The military refused to take the supplies from there to the people on Pine Ridge.

Feeding starving Indians in the 1970s was one thing; shooting them was another. I was sitting at a wooden desk in the Minnesota Historical Society in St. Paul examining one hundred boxes containing materials about AIM, many donated by WKLDOC lawyer Ken Tilsen. Thick binders strained with lists of munitions the military had shipped to the FBI when the agents sealed Wounded Knee. What a reaction to a protest!

2/28—Army convoy arrives with APCs [Armored Personnel Carriers]. . . . 3/2—FBI getting slap flares and M-16s. . . . 3/3—15 additional and 1 replacement APCs for WK. . . . 2/7—DOD approved loan

---

1. Department of Defense.

of 20 sniper rifles (M1-D1). . . . 3/12—Col. Warner and Colburn author memo for military type seizure of Wounded Knee under APCs.

The supplies rolled in, page after page after page, from all over the country. To shoot 200 to 300 poor Indians, hiding in a reservation church:

Ft. Carson, CO 44,200 rounds, M-16 ammunition . . . 4 March; Ellsworth AFB, SD 50,000 rounds, M-16 ammunition . . . 3 March; SDNG, 5,800 rounds, M-16 ammunition . . . 3 March.

Page after page, listing after listing:

1,000 rounds, tracer, M-1 ammunition . . . 500 star parachute flares . . . 216 star parachute flares . . . 400 star parachute flares . . . 1,050 star parachute flares . . . 2,000 star parachute flares . . . 1,000 rounds, ball, match, M-1 ammunition . . . 2,000 rounds, tracer, M-16 ammunition . . . 950 star parachute flares . . . 8,000 rds M-1 ball ammo in clips . . . 10,000 rds M-1 ball ammo (clipped) . . . 11,760 rounds, M-16 tracer ammunition . . . 30,000 rounds, M-16 ammunition."

Equipment was even sent for field testing: "100 vests, experimental protective—29 March."

Some dedicated WKLDOC legal worker had indexed the hundreds of pages of military documents. The contents read like a war manual:

Aerial Photo Reconnaissance . . . Supplies and Equipment (weapons and arms) . . . APCs . . . Helicopters . . . Other Aircraft . . . Flares . . . Trip Flares . . . Gas . . . M-16, M-14, M-1 . . . Grenades . . . Military Personnel . . . Advisers . . . Troops . . . 82nd Airborne . . . 6th Army . . . 18th Airborne . . . Air Force and Navy . . . Military Intelligence . . . National Guard.

Here was proof for my jury. This *was* a war. The FBI's own documents proved it. Their orders had been to shoot to kill. At first, they used sidearms. Then M-16s. Then M-16s with sniper scopes.

Army Col. Volney Warner had ordered the APCs. He thought the FBI agents would be less vulnerable to stray bullets in APCs than in patrol cars. In safety, he reasoned, the agents would not feel obliged to respond to single shots with a hundred-round barrage. The documents showed that the FBI hated AIM so much that the military's presence was actually a calming factor.

FBI agents were used to living in towns, going to work, coming home at night, and kissing their children before tucking them into bed. Now their nights were spent at Wounded Knee, in the cold, at war. Some of the agents left as replacements came. But most of the FBI army at Wounded Knee were just that—an army, in the dead of winter, on foreign soil, far away from home. They were cold.[2] They were being shot at. If they shot back at these "renegades" and ended it all, they could go home sooner.

The military people were more patient. Wars took time. Soldiers did not go off duty at night. In memorandum after memorandum, Warner implored the FBI not to carry out its plan to end Wounded Knee with an assault. He feared the massive bloodshed the FBI did not care about. He repeatedly told his superior, Gen. Alexander Haig, "Time is on our side."

Harassment techniques, considered for countering the occupation at Alcatraz, were used here. The military flares were endless, lighting up the sky every night as though it were day, making it difficult to sleep. In the seventy-one days of Wounded Knee, the government used more flares than it had during the entire war in Vietnam.

The dusty boxes at the historical society not only contained military logs. There were pictures, many of Indians. Some were of those murdered before, during, and after Wounded Knee: Buddy Lamont, Frank Clearwater, Anna Mae Aquash, Byron DeSersa, Pedro Bissonette.[3]

Here was tangible evidence. Here were my exhibits: the aerial reconnaissance photographs, military maps, pictures of FBI men in combat gear, pictures of APCs, the group picture of AIM

---

2. From Fort Carson alone, the military delivered "100 mittens w/trigger finger—12 March; 130 mittens w/trigger finger—13 March; 130 arctic boots—13 March; 130 parkas (large)—13 March; 100 blankets—14 March; 30 mountain stoves—14 March."

3. Buddy Lamont and Frank Clearwater had been killed at Wounded Knee. Pedro, leader of the Oglala Sioux Civil Rights Organization, had been murdered by BIA police. Byron DeSersa was a legal worker who had been killed following the June 26 shootout.

members before they walked out that May 1973 day, proud, in disdain of the FBI they had faced down.

There were articles and interviews and congressional reports and legal pleadings and thousands of pages of transcripts from all the trials. Everything that had been sent to AIM lawyers between 1973 and 1976 had been collected. There were even articles and pleadings I had forwarded to AIM headquarters from the 1976 Loud Hawk-Redner defense committee. *Loud Hawk* was, literally, a museum piece.

Among the legal papers were hundreds of witness interviews, verbatim statements about Wounded Knee—the events before it and those that followed. Here were more good witnesses, with old details graphically recorded on paper.

Affidavit:

My name is Dorothy Brings Him Back. I was harassed and assaulted on February 19, 1973, by three men whom I believe to be members of Dick Wilson's Goon Squad. I was returning to Oglala from Rapid City. While we stopped near my house [one of the Goons] told [my brother-in-law's brother] Julius that he had a warrant for his arrest. After Julius got out of the car [another Goon] dragged me out. The men began to beat me. They slammed my face against the car. They sprayed mace in my face. Julius and I were taken to Pine Ridge jail. [A jailer] twisted my left arm until the shoulder joint popped. I was kept in jail until the next day without any charges. I was released to the hospital in Gordon, Nebraska. Dr. Wallace treated me there for two black eyes, a broken nose, a rash from the mace, head pains, and an injury to my left arm.

Statement of Mary Ann Little Bear, a young Sioux girl:

On August 24, 1973, I was in a black and white car. My father Dallas Little Bear was driving. We turned down the road. We heard shots coming from Randall's house and my daddy said to get down on the floor. I got down on the floor and then a shot hit me in the head. It is very hard for me to remember and think back what happened. I don't like to think about it now. I can no longer see out of my right eye.

Even lawyers were not immune from the terror. On February 26, 1975, three legal workers, Roger Finzel, Joanna LeDeaux, and Eda Gordon drove to the Pine Ridge airport. They parked their two cars, waiting to meet a small plane carrying a WKLDOC legal team. It was early afternoon. The plane was late. As they waited, cars traveling at high speed, with squealing tires, careened into the parking lot near the airport. "We were clearly observed," Gordon wrote in an affidavit.

The plane landed. Attorney William Rossmore was the pilot. His passengers were legal workers Madonna Gilbert and Katherine James and attorney Martha Copelman.

"Madonna immediately left with Joanna in her car," Gordon recalled. "The rest of us piled into Roger's car." It was a blue 1965 Pontiac Bonneville with a black convertible top.

The lawyers and their assistants had planned to interview defense witnesses on the reservation for one of the post-Wounded Knee trials. Their car was stopped by the tribal police. They were detained, then allowed to leave.

When they returned to the airport, they found their plane "riddled with shotgun blasts." It was unsafe to fly. The WKLDOC workers took all their personal possessions and legal files and crowded into the Pontiac. As they did, cars sped into the parking lot. Women and children were being driven out of the area.

"Something must be going on," one of the legal workers speculated.

The blue Pontiac reached the airport exit and turned onto Route 18. Tribal Chairman Dick Wilson's car immediately pulled alongside, on the left. He motioned with his hands for the other cars to follow.

"Instantly," Gordon wrote, "six cars blocked our way, at least three directly in front of us." There were two others on the left, including Wilson's, and one other on the right. This inner circle was enclosed by another circle of ten cars. The highway was blocked.

A fat Indian man jumped out of a light-colored pickup truck on the left and held a shotgun "with both hands, as if ready to pump it," Gordon recalled. "He held it with the barrel up, toward us, his finger on the trigger. We instantly locked the doors of the car. Twenty-five to thirty men suddenly converged on all sides of our car, trying the doors to open them." One man, about six feet tall, began screaming at them, ordering them out of the car.

"No!" Finzel said.

"Get out!" the man screamed, again and again, as others surrounded the car. They began rocking it.

"What do you want?" Finzel asked.

"We want to talk to you," the first man yelled, as the others continued to chant, "Get out! . . . Get out!"

"You can talk to me through the window," the lawyer answered.

"Get out!" the first man screamed, as two men jumped onto the hood and began stomping their cowboy boot heels into the windshield glass. Two others pounded the back window with their boots.

One of the men thrust his knife down through the fabric, the long blade ripping the convertible roof directly over Finzel's head, barely missing it. He yanked the blade through the black top. Then with the opening wide enough, he grabbed each end and tore a larger hole. He snatched Finzel's hair and tugged it. He reached in and punched Finzel in the face.

"You're crazy!" Finzel, stunned, managed to say.

Wilson walked up.

"What do you want us to do with them, Dick?" the man with the knife asked.

Wilson shouted, "I want you to *stomp 'em.*"

The rest of the top was ripped off, leaving only the convertible's frame. Both windshields were kicked through.

"Let's get out! It's better to get out!" Gordon yelled. She wrote,

William Rossmore opened the door and walked off carrying his briefcase. I heard Martha Copelman scream, 'They have Will!' I didn't see him accosted. I was trying to pull Roger away from the driver's side. I had my arms around his head, trying to stop the punches.

Roger got out of the car. He was kicked and knocked to the ground. Ten men stomped and kicked his chest and back and head. I tried to cover him as much as I could with my body. The beating went on for several minutes. One man grabbed Roger's hair, pulled his head back. I didn't know what he intended, to slash his face or slit his throat. I pulled Roger's head down with my arms and hands to shield him and saw the knife cutting at Roger's hair, which the man still held in his left hand."

After the legal team had been thoroughly beaten—muscles separated from bone and cartilage broken—they were allowed back into what remained of the car. The dashboard was cracked in two places. But it drove. They were allowed to leave.

"Don't come back," one man yelled. "If you do, we'll kill you!"

These were terror times in Pine Ridge. In the first six months of 1975, at least seventeen people had been killed there. Countless others, like the legal workers, had been assaulted and thought they were about to die.

The FBI did little or nothing. Complaints were lodged. Copies were in the historical society files.

Senator Abourezk asked to meet President Ford, to urge him to take "direct action" to end the "anarchy" on the reservation. "The people must be able to stop living in fear," he said. Ford's staffers apologized. The president "was unable to clear . . . his schedule" to meet with the senator.

The traditional chiefs and headmen sent a petition to President Ford, in both Lakota and English. Nothing happened.

WKLDOC lawyers wrote to federal judges, to congressmen, to senators, to the attorney general of the United States. Nothing happened.

No one pushed the FBI to investigate assaults and murders of the Indians it disliked. The agency was otherwise occupied.

According to affidavits in the historical society, only five weeks before Trooper Griffiths stopped Brando's motor home in the Oregon desert, John Abelone Walsh, a journalist, had been sleeping at WKLDOC headquarters. Three white men, FBI agents, walked in and came over to him. One yelled, "Get up!" Another shouted, "Don't move!" A third came forward, took a handgun from beneath his blue windbreaker, pointed it toward the young man, and shouted, "Freeze!"

Lawyers and legal workers were at the headquarters. Four FBI agents were in the front yard, four in the back. They tore through the headquarters and threatened the staff. They did not have a warrant. "We don't need one," one of the agents said. "We're looking for someone. He could be in the tent, in the car, or up your ass, so quit while you're ahead."

CHAPTER 31

✝ ✝ ✝

PLEADING ELOQUENTLY

IT was now mid-February, and I was back in Portland. I had a defense. I could prove the terror of the times. And I had Turner worried. He still thought of *Loud Hawk* as a simple case, two vehicles with four Indian defendants and eight illegal weapons and seven cases of dynamite that he, technically, no longer had.

No one else thought this "oldest pretrial criminal case in United States history," as the newspapers referred to it, was that simple. Nixon's lawyers pondered our subpoena. Foreign newspapers wrote about *Loud Hawk* as an example of the worst in American justice. National media, including the *New York Times*, planned to cover the trial. Amnesty International was sending an observer. Senior U.S. District Judge Nichol offered to testify as a defense witness. And I had flown to San Jose at the invitation of Congressman Don Edwards. He was "deeply concerned," he said, with this long vendetta.

In Portland, the Turner stories were flying. "Turner's really going nuts," a person on his staff told me. One state prosecutor said, "I've never seen Charlie this stressed out. What the hell you guys doing to him?" Another attorney said, "I heard that Charlie had his blood pressure checked at the gym the other day. He *never* does that. He said his insides were getting eaten up from this case."

My strategy had worked. He couldn't even say my name correctly any more. In person, in court, I was Ken Sterns. On paper, Dennis Banks and I had merged into one evil entity—"Kenneth Banks."

"Charlie is absolutely despondent," another lawyer on his staff volunteered. It was the latest appeal that had finally gotten to him. "Charlie was happy as a clam after the court of appeals granted summary affirmance,"[1] I was told. "But your motion for reconsideration has him totally depressed."

It was now the third week of February. Charlie had asked the court of appeals to return the case immediately. His request had been denied. "Charlie thinks the case may be stuck in the appellate courts for another year or two," I was told. Apparently, Charlie thought more of my appeal than I did.

I called South Dakota. "Dennis," I said, "I think Charlie's on the edge of losing his sanity. It might be a good time to try to press him on a plea bargain. Like we talked about before. Everyone else would be cut. You'd plead to one count."

The old Dennis Banks would have hemmed and hawed. "If you can get everyone else dismissed and get the judge to promise no more than one-year bench probation," he said, "I'll take the rap. Go for it!"

I was not convinced. "Okay," I said. "But you have to tell me now that you'd do it, you'd get up there and say, 'Yes, I was there and it was my stuff.' I remember the last time, in '83. You weren't eager, you keep looking for every subtle way out. 'It can't be this count, it has to be that count. . . . It can't be a guilty plea, it has to be a no contest plea.' We can't do that this time. If you want me to try to get a deal, you have to tell me now, that you'd get up in the courtroom and damn well plead guilty. Otherwise, if I get something together, and then you back out, you'll be in terrible shape."

He paused. I heard him exhale. "Yep," he said, "go for it."

There was still hesitation in his voice. He did not like giving in. But a plea would end the stress of uncertainty. I could tell. His love for KaMook—who did not want to come to Portland or to take the kids out of school for the trial—was stronger than his animosity toward the government for hounding him for so long. And he knew, like I did, that Loud Hawk was drinking again, and Redner—who was quoting the freakier statements of black prison revolutionary George Jackson of late—might combust at trial.

I called Bonds, the only defense lawyer with whom Turner was

---

1. In early January, the court of appeals denied our latest appeal—in which we complained about the failure of the prosecutor to tell the grand jury about the favorable eyewitnesses.

still talking.[2] "Michael," I asked, "since Charlie seems so stressed out, think this might be a good time for you to push him to drop KaMook?"

"He's getting very discouraged," Bonds agreed. "But the problem is that he sees this as a real test of wills. I'll call him in the morning when he's fresh, but I'm afraid his reaction is going to be knee jerk on this two for two thing."

"Let's get him a bit more discouraged then," I suggested. "I've been saving more of his lies to use against him. Now may be the time. The FBI files I was given by the state police show that the *Loud Hawk* investigation began with an informant tip from Rapid City,[3] not from the overflights of the reservation in Washington, as Charlie told Redden. And it also shows that Charlie was integrally involved in the U.S. Attorney's initial charging decision, even though he swore in open court in 1980 during the vindictive prosecution hearing, that he had taken 'no part' in that 'whatever,' that he was a 'subsequent prosecutor,' remember?"

"Um-hum," Bonds said.

"Well, the papers show that he even told the FBI what the initial charges were going to be."

"No shit?"

"No shit. So wait a day while I soften him up a bit more. I'll send the reports to Redden, with copies to Charlie."

Bonds agreed.

The following morning, by coincidence, the *Oregonian* printed its annual lawyers' ratings of judges. Redden was near the top. His rating would have been higher, the paper reported, except that it was weighted down by those who identified themselves as federal prosecutors. One member of the U.S. Attorney's Office had even written that Redden was "prejudiced and would do just about anything to act on those prejudices." It was a cheap shot.

An older courthouse employee called to ask me if I had seen the newspaper. "It might as well have been signed!" she said, angrily. "I hope you *do* drive him crazy!"

---

2. No other defense lawyer had dissociated himself from my continuing accusations of government misconduct.

3. The exact information had been blacked out.

"Believe me," I answered, "these days, all it takes is for me to be in the same room with him. I don't actually have to *do* anything; I think he sees me as a demonic presence."

Another source called me that afternoon. "Believe it or not," he said, "the story around the courthouse is that Charlie called Redden to tell him that it was not his questionnaire. As far as I can tell, no one in the building believes him."

I called another friend in the courthouse, who was on close terms with some of the judges. "I've set up a conspiracy," I said. "Bonds is going to be talking to Turner at 10:00 A.M. tomorrow morning, trying to convince him to cut KaMook loose, and then everyone else goes away."

"What do you think the chances are?" my friend asked.

"I don't know. Charlie's pretty despondent that he lost his motion in the court of appeals [asking for the immediate return of the case for trial], and Bonds is going to impress him with how stupid it is to have this case go to trial over KaMook Banks. To give the deal a chance, I'm staying clear of Charlie until we have to tie down final details with the judge. We've also enlisted support from inside enemy ranks. Bauman and Sheldahl[4] would rather be doing other things with their time."[5]

"We're on!" Bonds told me the next afternoon. "Charlie agrees," he said. "We're meeting tomorrow to hammer out the details."

I was pleased and hopeful but deflated. Emotionally and politically, a plea bargain seemed wasteful. A trial would have been a great show. I *was* planning to call Marlon Brando as a witness. And with all the material I had gathered, it would have educated people about problems in Indian country, most of which, except for the terror, had not changed since 1975.

I also expected to win. The defense had a good chance to work. Even if it did not, Charlie would never get around the technical

---

4. Another assistant U.S. Attorney newly recruited to work on the case. Barry Sheldahl was the brightest person in Turner's office and had a reputation, which he deserved, as a "straight shooter."

5. According to the federal defense bar, Bauman and Sheldahl had been spending so much time on *Loud Hawk* that local bank robbers and other criminals were getting "previously unheard of deals."

problems in his case. And even if by some miracle he managed to do so, he was so unstable he would blow, causing a mistrial for prosecutorial misconduct. There was no way we could lose.

Intellectually, however, the plea bargain was the right thing. It offered the only finality. A trial would disrupt so many lives—the defendants, their kids, and all the poor, frightened Indian witnesses we would have to drag to Portland.

That afternoon, still conflicted, I drove to the airport to meet Redner. He was returning from South Dakota, from a visit to his wife, Debbie, and her three young daughters (from her previous marriage).

"Shit!" Redner yelled, when I told him of the plea discussions. "Fuck," he added. "I still want to go to trial! You mean I have no say in this? After thirteen years, I want a jury to *know* what the government has done to me!"

"Michael Bonds called the judge and had a meeting with Charlie," one of my courthouse informants told me the next day. I pretended as if I knew and that I was not concerned.

"We've got a deal," Bonds said, when he finally called me later that afternoon.

"Wonderful!" I replied, not wanting to deflate Bonds by asking him why he had gone to the judge behind my back.

"Okay," he continued. "Dennis has to plead guilty, admit the thing. One count. Everything else gets dismissed."

"I heard you met with Redden," I said.

"Yep. He's cool. He just wants one favor. After the plea, Dennis can say whatever he wants, explain things, say he was justified, but he shouldn't say he's not guilty."

"No problem," I said. "My client's not a fool. What about the one-year bench probation?"

"Redden says he'll sentence him that day but that he can't promise probation. But then, he said there's no way he could send anyone to jail after so many years, especially when all the codefendants are dismissed."

"I told Dennis we'd have the judge locked into bench probation for a year."

"Don't worry," Bonds snapped. "Take my word for it. It's going to be bench probation for one year."

"Think we should set up another meeting and see if the judge would commit?"

"No, there's no reason to."

"What's Charlie going to say?"

"He promised to take no position. He won't say anything about sentence."

The next day, I found that what Bonds told me had not been the entire truth. Turner told me he would, in fact, make a sentencing recommendation—formal probation. He said Redden was not sure he would sentence Banks on the day of the plea. And Redden had not guaranteed bench probation. Bench probation was a legally binding promise to behave. Formal probation, the other option, required reporting to a probation officer, surprise visits, and other indignities. I called Redden's office, suggesting another meeting since I had a legal obligation to advise my client directly of the promises that the judge and prosecutor would make, not what I had learned secondhand through another lawyer with a different client.

Bonds called me that evening, drunk, his voice ranging from slurred whispers to shrieks. Then, in midsentence, he reverted to non sequiturs in murmurs, complaining.

I spoke slowly and calmly. "I need the judge's word, privately if he can't give it publicly, so that I could advise Dennis of the risks," I explained.

"Why don't you just the fuck shut up and let me take care of it," Bonds shouted back. Then, in a hush, "I can take care of Dennis. When push comes to shove, Redden is going to do what I, I, *I*, I, *me*, Michael Bonds (swallow) . . . Redden will do whatever I tell him. Absolutely. Unquestionably. Do not." His voice faded. Then, loudly, "Yes, I can warrant that to Dennis. I'll call him up and tell him that. Fine, I will do that. Listen, they got captured by this little faggot corporal in the middle of the night. Don't do anything without clearing it with me. If you want to do that, then I'm willing to go to trial."

Dennis Banks and I talked for a long time that night. Bonds had developed into our loose cannon. But he had talked Turner into settlement, and I trusted Redden, even without any commitment on his part. I simply could not imagine Redden sending Banks to jail.

"I'm sorry that there are no promises," I said, "but it's worth the risk."

"Okay," Banks agreed.

My judgment was confirmed the next day, when Redden's secretary called. "The judge wants you to know," she said, "that if anything shows up in the presentence report that makes him feel he has to give Dennis any jail time, he'll let you know beforehand, so that you can back out of the deal."

The plea was set for Monday, March 7, 1988. Everything fell into place. There was an interview with Redner in the Sunday morning (February 28) *Oregonian*. His comments, from a Saturday morning speaking engagement, were fatalistic, about people struggling in different ways. It was fortunate that the same reporter did not attend a talk Redner gave later that day. "I can't wait to go to trial and jump on Charlie Turner's chest!" Redner had shouted into a microphone. His earlier, mellower remarks were taken as a sign by the government and the judge that "the deal" was on track.

I laid low, reclaiming my more comfortable role as the voice of reason in a crazy case, rather than the out-of-town zealot. My approach—stirring things up—had worked better than I could possibly have predicted. It was now time to collect what had settled.

Turner, driven totally nuts, was giving in, thinking he had finally won after losing so many times over so many years. The millions of taxpayer dollars wasted on this case were somehow justified by a sentence more lenient than a first-time, starving shoplifter would receive in return for a magic word, "Guilty."

Let Turner rant and rave. All the defendants could now continue their lives, uninterrupted by this old prosecution. "I can finish school!" KaMook told me, at least a half dozen times, recounting all the occasions she had decided not to register because of *Loud Hawk*. Nothing could get this deal off track.

The day had started out foggy, but by the time I left Banks at the airport that afternoon, the sky was blue. Mount Hood was gleaming white with fresh snow. Our spirits were up.

Banks had flown in the night before. We talked for hours. We discussed his new projects—working with Kentucky officials against grave desecration;[6] getting new ambulances, fire trucks, and a high school building for Pine Ridge. He had just testified before a congressional committee.

We discussed the possibility of another, future Wounded Knee. "There may have to be one," he said. "The conditions are still the same," I agreed.

We discussed how we had changed over the years. Banks, who always spoke reverently about Chief Lyons of the Onondagas, said he learned how to be "a diplomat" from him. I told him of my work against anti-Semitism and lamented how the Indian community did not have the resources to monitor, program against, and respond to racism.

We also reminisced.

"I finally figured out about the blue Comet," he said. "They were friends of Annie Mae's. I even waved to them from the motor home."

"And about those two new eyewitnesses that the government hid for years—the ones that saw you," I asked. "I take it you and Anna Mae went out to eat while KaMook slept?"

"Um hum," he said.

Banks was relaxed, in good humor. His only worry, it seemed, was Redner. "How's he going to be?" Banks asked.

"He left town a few days ago for Seattle," I said. "I don't think he'll be back. Russ's last words were, 'I don't sign peace treaties.' He wouldn't believe that this one is different from the 368 others, backed by a judge who is a fan."

Others, besides Redner, did not understand. The next morning a defense committee member, a thin woman with crooked teeth, marched in front of the courthouse with a sign complaining about the plea: "Anna Mae Aquash—Not Guilty." She spoke to the television cameras. "Russell Redner has said, 'If we go to jail we'll go with our heads held high.' We were perfectly prepared."

In the courthouse lobby a small Indian guy in his twenties yelled, "Hey, Dennis, you gonna sell us out again?" Upstairs, in the same packed courtroom where the case had been dismissed

---

6. Twelve hundred Indian graves had been unearthed. Banks was helping to rebury the bones and design legislation to make grave desecration a felony.

in 1976, 1980, 1983, and 1986, Banks pleaded guilty eloquently, offering no apologies.

"In the late '60s," he said, "when we began to raise our voices about the deplorable condition of Indian people, there was some response, but it was a diplomatic response. It was a response of sympathy and never any real action to correct injustices.

"When we began to organize and demonstrate to bring about changes, we were met with a lot of force. There was, in my mind, an actual war being waged by the FBI against the American Indian Movement.

"The tactics that the FBI used on the reservation after Wounded Knee were designed to scare and terrorize Indian people. They would often come in four or five squad cars to make a single arrest. They would surround houses and knock down doors and scare the old people.

"During '73, '74, '75, a great number of American Indian Movement supporters were killed, murdered. And we had asked and demanded that the Justice Department investigate these murders, but the agents in South Dakota refused to help us. We were desperate. The Justice Department is supposed to protect Indian people, supposed to file cases against itself, the government, to protect natural resources, land and timber and water. But the only time that I ever see the Justice Department lawyers is prosecuting Indian people.

"So we took what we felt what was necessary to try and protect our people.

"At a meeting in Oglala the elders said, 'We need help. You've got to get us help.' So we came here and the help that we got, we were carrying it back to South Dakota."

Redden understood. He said Banks's words "explained," although they could not "excuse." He sentenced Dennis Banks to five years formal probation.

Privately, after the sentencing, after Banks had spoken with reporters and had been fingerprinted and processed by the probation department, Redden asked to see Banks and me in chambers. We sat at his conference table.

"I gave you formal probation so that I wouldn't embarrass Charlie, or cause him to respond," he said. "It'll be changed to nonreporting probation in a month."

"Thanks, Your Honor," Banks said. "I won't let you down."

"I know you won't, Mr. Banks," Judge Redden replied, putting his arm around my client.

Two hours later at the airport, Banks was ready to fly back to watch Tosh cheerlead at a basketball game. He stepped out of my car, slung the strap of his brown garment bag over his shoulder, and gave me a bear hug.

"Thanks," he said. "You're the best attorney I've ever had."

"Shit, Dennis," I said. "Give me thirteen years and I'll get anything right."

EPILOGUE

THE southern presidential primaries of 1988, known as Super Tuesday, were the day after the plea and sentencing. Dennis Banks was already old news.

Ken Bauman released all the "evidence" that was not associated with guns or bombs, things that had held no interest to the prosecutors or the FBI: pots and pans, old food, radio equipment, books, Brando's screenplay of *The Missouri Breaks*. The food—old peanut bags, ice cream cones, evaporated milk, Kraft Caramels—I discarded. The rest I either gave away as souvenirs or collected in Steenson's storeroom for eventual donation to skid road.

As I was throwing out the thirteen-year-old garbage, I noticed a brown paper restaurant placemat, circa 1975. It did not have an evidence label on it. The government had not intended to introduce it at trial. The placemat had a map of the United States in the center. There were different cities. Each had a date: Portland 7-16-75, Phoenix 2-1-76, San Francisco 10-1-75.

I checked it against a notebook that had a government exhibit tag. That notebook, found in the motor home, was important because it contained a troubling shopping list: "3,000 A.K.; 1,500 Ammo; 700 Auto; 1,000 Dym.; 200 fatigues [crossed out]; Ammo—308, 270, 7.5mm, 762mm, 223, 7mm, 12 gau, 30 cal., 45 auto."

It had a second list, too.

7-1-75 = Olympia
7-16-75 = Portland
10-1-75 = San Francisco
8-10-75 = Salt Lake City
8-27-75 = Helena
8-25-75 = Pocatello
9-1-75 = Casper
10-1-75 = Fort Mandan
10-15-75 = Pierre
11-1-75 = Fort Laramie
1-1-76 = Los Angeles

2-1-76 = Phoenix
4-1-76 = Fort Laramie
3-7-76 = Oklahoma City
4-18-76 = Minn./St. Paul
5-1-76 = Madison
6-4-76 = Richmond

That list, in what looked like Anna Mae Aquash's handwriting, continued for months, specifying dates and places. It had never made any sense. I had asked. None of the defendants could explain it. It was both past and prospective relative to November 14, 1975. If it were an itinerary, it put the motor home in places it had never been.

I checked. The cities and dates on the placemat matched the list in the green spiral notebook. The government had missed it.

This was evidence that at least some of the people in the motor home had an interest in the scheduled arrival of the Bicentennial Freedom Train[1] in cities around the country. Nineteenth-century trains had brought subjugation to Indian people. Maybe, as the FBI alleged in one of its 1976 press releases, the AIM group was "interested in Bicentennial activities"?

I thought back to 1980, when Agent Rubin testified about informants "A" and "B," who had told him that the group planned "to travel around the United States," an assertion that was never followed up in any other government document or testimony. If this had been a part of the plan, or part of a plan coordinated with other underground groups in 1975, why wouldn't the FBI have made the specific accusation at the time? I wondered. It was best to leave things as they were.

I returned to New York the following week. I saw Russ Redner two months later. Leonard Peltier had drafted him to head his defense committee. He had traveled to the Soviet Union. He had spoken with President Gorbachev on Peltier's behalf. He was the Indian who brought up the plight of Indian people during President Reagan's visit there.

Redner had seen Banks once. "I thanked him for taking the rap," Redner said. "There were tears in his eyes."

Redner told me that Kenny Loud Hawk's wife had given birth to his third daughter. "He was drunk at the time. Dennis found him and drove him to the hospital. But Kenny had to be escorted out by security guards. He was too intoxicated."

Months later, I spoke with Redner again. "I had a falling out with

---

1. An exhibit, celebrating the Bicentennial of the American Revolution, pulled around the country by an antique locomotive.

Leonard," he said. He had now given up politics. He was going to raise his new family. A year later, I heard that he was separated from his wife, again.

I went to hear Banks when he next spoke in New York, at Hunter College. "I learned that justice in America depends largely on the judge you get," he told his audience. Redden had terminated his probation after only four months.

After that, I did not hear from Banks much. He got quiet when he was troubled. I heard he and KaMook split up. "It was over the kids," a mutual friend told me. "KaMook wanted the kids to have a Christmas tree again. Dennis said no. But KaMook didn't want them to feel deprived."

I see Dennis now and then, when he comes to New York and when he sends me material on his project, the Sacred Run, a program designed to foster greater international respect for Indian tradition and culture through annual long-distance runs in various parts of the world. And we keep in contact through my work, as specialist on anti-Semitism for the American Jewish Committee. Anti-Semitism thrives best in climates that tolerate other prejudices as well. I try to do all I can through my work to educate people about anti-Indian prejudice. I am proud that the American Jewish Committee is increasingly reaching out to Indian country, to support Indian religious freedoms and to combat anti-Indian bigotry. Dennis once commented to me that all his lawyers over the years were Jewish. Neither of us thought that was a coincidence.

KaMook, I hear, has been working in the movie industry. I saw her name credited in the production of *Dances with Wolves*. She helped with casting. I also heard that she had gotten married to one of the actors in the film and then divorced.

This case, which affected so many people's lives, lives on today only in boxes stored in my mother's basement. For two years, to my great discomfort, one small box sat with all the other remnants of *Loud Hawk*. It contained a brown leather purse with a hair brush, a toothbrush, toothpaste, a tampon, a cake of soap wrapped in aluminum foil, a turquoise ring, and a turquoise bracelet.

The items belonged to Anna Mae Aquash, until the night she was arrested in the Oregon desert. After dozens of inquiries into Indian country, I returned the contents to Anna Mae's daughters—children she had left behind nearly twenty years before to work in Indian struggles. For all I know, Anna Mae's children may have children of their own now. I hope their lives will be more peaceful and less affected by the abrasion of prejudice than their grandmother's.

ACKNOWLEDGMENTS

AT times *United States v. Loud Hawk et al.* seemed like it was a living entity more than a case or a collection of people. In the early 1980s, I said to Dennis, "if the case makes it to its thirteenth birthday, we're going to have a bar mitzvah."

He smiled and agreed.

It fell short by eight months.

On November 14, 1988, the thirteenth anniverary of Griffith's stop, I was writing the first draft of this book in Brooklyn. My next-door neighbor, Esta Bigler, gave me the name of her rabbi, Marjorie Slome, on a yellow Post-It slip. Esta knew I was not observant.

"Esta," I said, "you've never tried to fix me up before."

"Nu?" she replied with a smile.

Fearing that it was going to be another awful blind date, I hoped that the coincidence with the case's anniversary would prove propitious.

We went on our first date the following Saturday. The second on Wednesday. The third on Friday. The fourth on Saturday. Then I moved in. In five days, we talked love. In ten days, we talked marriage. In a month we were engaged. Seven months after we met, we had a beautiful wedding. Three years later, on December 20, 1991, our son Daniel Slome Stern was born.

This book would have been markedly inferior without the miracle of Margie and Daniel in my life. To them I owe the greatest thanks and love. Margie is also an excellent editor.

Others, of course, helped too.

Candy Schulman of the New School helped me hone my nonfiction writing style, after so many years of legal prose. Suzanne Gluck from ICM offered valuable advice in trying to find a publisher for *Loud Hawk*. John Drayton, Editor-in-Chief of the University of Oklahoma Press, was there at the right time with the interest and insight to find something useful in this unusual story. And Sally Hertz helped guide me through negotiations.

I owe thanks to my mother, Gertrude Stern, whose basement is still littered with thousands of pages of *Loud Hawk*. And to her housemate, my aunt, Terry Frank, who fought to restrain her extra cleanliness gene every time I searched those papers. And to my sister, Alice, for her enthusiasm and support.

Thanks also to two veteran AIM attorneys who read the manuscript: Ken Tilsen and Dennis Roberts. Although the rest of us were horribly underpaid as appointed attorneys on *Loud Hawk*, Roberts never received a penny—in fact, he spent his own money, not only for his plane tickets but for other expenses on the case as well. Dennis Roberts and his associate Karen Spelke worked tirelessly to thwart South Dakota's efforts to extradite Banks back from California. That saga, touched on briefly in this book, deserves an entire volume.

Most important, this book could not have been written without the help of all those who played a role in *Loud Hawk*. In addition to Judges Redden and Belloni and all the prosecutors, defense lawyers, defendants, witnesses, and eastern Oregon and western Idaho officers, I thank everyone who came to defense committee meetings, handed out leaflets, collected food, researched legal issues or history, and offered investigative leads, meals, places to sleep, and encouragement. They all shared a part in the case, and thus, in this book. If I have missed any of you, I apologize for my faulty memory.

Thanks to Elliott Abramson, Esq.; Diane J. Ackerman; Dorothy N. Ackerman; Hank Adams; Leroy Adolph; Barbara Aehle; Harvey Akeson; Everett Antilla; Martina Antilla; Carol Apple; Mary Isabel Arnold-Galan; Dave Audet, Esq.; Beverly Axelrod, Esq.; Melvin Ayer; Ann Bailey; Carey E. Bailey; Michael Bailey, Esq.; Bonnie Baldwin; Chinopa Banks; "Chubbs" Banks; Dennis Banks; KaMook Banks; Mark Banks; Tasina Banks; TaTiopa Banks; Catherine Baretta; Sandra Baringer, Esq.; Mike Barnes; Rick Bass; Ken Bauman, Esq.; Sondra Beaulieu; Ellen Beckett; Clyde Bellecourt; Vernon Bellecourt; Ramona Bennett; Tony Bennett; Erin Berger; Joe Berger; Stephanie Kay Berger; Daniel Berrigan; Chivon Best; Zoe Best; Jamie Bevson; Esta Bigler, Esq.; Margaret Bird; Jim Blashfield; John Bonn; Marlon Brando; Dewey R. Brave Heart; Lehman Brightman; Trudy Mellisa Brightman; Dennis Brock; Chelsea Brown; Susan Brown; John V. Buchanan; Leonard Buckskin; Sally Burns; Cindy Butler; Dino Butler; Gillian Butler; Margaret Butler; Nilak Butler; Brad Buvinger; Bonnie Byron; LaVerna C. Castillo; Leslie Cauldron; John Chamberlin, Esq.; Carol Chappel; Gail Chehak; Lisa J. Chickadonz; John Chiquiti; Cippriano; Deanna M. Clark; Judy Clark; Ramsey Clark; Anna Coelho; Linda Coelho; Phyliss Cohen; Sherman Cohn, Esq.; Kaye Cole; Jenny Cook, Esq.; Martha

Copelman, Esq.; Judy Corona; Nancy Coupez; Constance Crooker, Esq.; Lynn Culbertson; Martina Curl; William Curl; Roberta D'Anneo; Angela Davis; Paulette F. D'Awleuil; Rev. Alan Deale; Lenny Dee; Frank Charles Dion; David Duayua; Jimmy "Jimmy Dean" Dumont; Holly Duncan; Ramona Dunston; Ray Eaglin; David Eastman; Wendy Eaton, Esq.; C. Park Eldred; Alice Ellis, Esq.; Jane Ellis; Bruce Ellison, Esq.; Rayne Engle; Arla Escontrias; Al Feder, Esq., Jane Feder; Bill Fettig; David Fine; Sharon Fireday; Ceelia Fisher; Claudia Fisher; Gloria Fisher; Jamie Fishman, Esq.; Edward Fitch, Esq.; Molly Fleming; Richard Foltin, Esq.; Ron Fontana, Esq.; Ken Ford; Sandra Ford; Pat Foster; Bill Frank, Jr.; Terry Frank; Herman Frankel, M.D.; The Honorable Kim Frankel; Ruth Frankel; Wendy Friedman; Betty Fry, Esq.; Albert Galan; Sandy Gandleman; Father John Garvey; John Clinton Geil, Esq.; Frank Giese; Anne Fagan Ginger, Esq.; Steve Goldberg, Esq.; Thomas Gonsiewski; Bob Gould; Donald K. Grant, Esq.; Trisha Gray; Toni Gregg; Dick Gregory; Susana Gren; Mary L. Gress; Jeanne Gross; Lew Gurwitz, Esq.; Kathy Haley, Esq.; Candy Hamilton; Marcia Hamley; Paul Hanson; Susan Harjo; Sasha Harmon, Esq.; Jay Harris; Jacquelin J. Haught; Tommy Hawk, Esq.; Kathleen Hawkins; Glenna Hayes; Joseph Heath, Esq.; Bernie Heller; Susan Heller; Kathleen Herron, Esq.; Deborah L. Higdon; Gail High Pine; Janet Hoffman, Esq.; Phil Hornick, Esq.; Anne Hughes; Anna Hunter; Richard Hunter; Doug Hurd; Chrystie Ingraham; Connie Isgro, Esq.; Jerry Isgro; Ken Isserlis, Esq.; Buzz Jackson; Linda Jackson; Steve Jacobsen, Esq.; Twila Jacobsen; Lorrie Renée Jackson; Robert Jackson; Chris Jennings; Vicki M. Jensen; Byron Johns; Beatrice Johnson; Margaret Johnson; The Honorable Nelly Johnson; Carol Johnston, Esq.; Kathryn Johnston, Esq.; Denise Jolley; Tammy Jolley; Theresa Jolley; Ed Jones, Esq.; Cecelia Jumping Bull; Harry Jumping Bull; Jackie Jurkins; Judith Kahn; Helga Kahr, Esq.; John Kangas; Ivan Karmel, Esq.; Greg Kaster; Dave King; Larry Kitchen; Lt. Don Kliensmith; Douglas G. Klotz; Charles B. Knight; Min Koblitz; Dr. Robert Koblitz; Steve Kosokoff; Anton Kritchmeric; William Kunstler, Esq.; Eva Kutas; Joan Laatz; Roberta Lambert; Agnes Lamont; Marty Landsberg; Fred Lane; Michael Lane; Ray Lane; Steve Law; Sheila Lea, Esq.; Wendy Lecker, Esq.; Dennis Lein; Robert Lerch, M.D.; Jane Levine, Esq.; Sidney Lezak, Esq.; Sharon Lieberman; Avery Lienova; David Lifton; David Lillig, Esq.; Myra Linares; Archie Little; Paul Lobell; Joanna Lohnes; Kathryn Logan, Esq.; The Honorable Donald Londer; David Long; Michael J. Long; Stanley Looking Elk; Jim Looking Hawk; Angel Lopez, Esq.; Cheryl Lopez; Arlette Loud Hawk; Kenny Loud Hawk; Russell Loud Hawk; Sam Loud Hawk; Stella Loud Hawk; Tony Low; Cerren Fratas

Lowe; Maurice Lucas; Oren Lyons; Juan Macias; Margie Macias; Bernard Mack; Roberto Maestas; Eloise Malek; Shirlyn A. Mart; Lisa Martens; Frank Martinez; Shelley Massman; Faith Mayhew; Al Mazokok; Barney B. McClelland; Janet McCloud; Matthew Bigler-McCorkell; Charlie McCorkell; Ron McCreary; Holly McGuigen, Esq.; Kathy McKay; Robert McKay, Esq.; Don McLeod; Michael McNeeley; Loraine McQuackey; Maggy McSwigen; Sudy Meehan; Carol Merle; Merry; Pete Mesteth; Craig Meyer; Rebecca Michael; James F. Miller; Mary Jane Miller; Dian Lynn Million; Dan Millstone, Esq.; Walter Mitchell; Parvis Moghadas; Pat Moran; Violeta Morton; Walt Mose; Ellen Moves Camp; Alice Muccio; V. Annetta Murphy; Tom Murton; Peggy Nagae, Esq.; Jonita C. Najera; Mary Nathan; Jody A. Nelson; The Honorable Fred Nichol; Bernie Nichols; Cheyene Nichols; Doreen Nepom, Esq.; The Nixon Project; Pat Noonan, Esq.; Basil C. Norris; Karen Northcott; Forrest Oglesby; Larry Olstad, Esq.; Billy J. Onihan; David Orloff; Ruth Orloff; David Osha; Romelle Pacheco; Glenna Page; Rodney Page; Kindra Parkinson; Kitsy Parkinson; Lynn Parkinson; Megan Parkinson; Father Richard Pates; Doug Patterson; Mary Pearson, Esq.; Alvina Peltier; Leonard Peltier; Lillian Peterson; Sandra Phelan; Phil Phelps; Phoenix; Tim Plenk; Julia Plummer; Sandy Polocheck; Sandy Polshinik; Herb Powless; Walley Priestley; Lorainne Queener; Madeline Queener; Steve Queener; Tom Queener; Kasia Quilinan, Esq.; Sam Rabinove, Esq.; Tom Rafael; Linda Friedman Ramirez, Esq.; Margaret Ratner, Esq.; Michael Ratner, Esq.; Virginia Raymond; Albert Red Bear, Jr.; Jackson Red Horn; Courtney Red Horse; Debbie Redner; Lena Redner; Russ Redner; Tsi-Am-Utza Redner; Roger Reeves; Forrest Rieke, Esq.; David Rice; Harper Richardson; Lan Brooks Ritz; Dennis Roberts, Esq.; Allen L. Robideau; Bob Robideau; Greg Robideau; Steve Robideau; Reyes Rodriguez; Darlene P. Rogers; Robby Romero; Bob Rose; Michael Rose, Esq.; Sally Rose; Dr. Justus Rosenberg; Don Rosenbloom; Michael Royce, Esq.; Gary Rubin; Sheila Rubin; Stuart Rush; Steve Sady, Esq.; Milt Sahme; André Saine; Anita Sanchez; Nancy Sanders; Zack Sanders; Susanne Santos; Ronald Saranich; William Savage, Esq.; Linda Sawaya; John Sayer, Esq.; Jon K. Schaefer; Ron Schiffman, Esq.; Jack Schwartz, Esq.; Emma Scott; Jack Scott; John Scott; Jonah Scott; Lydia "Louise" Scott; Lydia Scott; Mary Scott; Micki Scott; Joel Shapiro; Christopher Sharp; Jerry Sheehan; Baron Sheldahl, Esq.; Arden Shenker, Esq.; Judy Shields; Bob Shimabukuro; Kathy Shimakuruo; Phil Shinnik; Lisa Siegel; Glen Silber; Erika Silver; Donna Slepak; Marilyn Slome; Nancy Slome; Cheryl Smalley; Maralyn Smith; Norman Solomon; Karen Spelke, Esq.; Marjorie Spitz; Wendy Squires, Esq.; Susan Stanley; Mort Stavis, Esq.;

Michael Stebbins, Esq.; Amber Steenson; Josh Steenson; Mariah Steenson; River Steenson; Tom Steenson, Esq.; Beverly Stein, Esq.; Dennis Stenzel, Esq.; Alice Stern; Gertrude Stern, M.D.; Michael Stern, Esq.; Nora Stern; Seymour Stern, M.D.; Steven Stern; Don Stevens; Jane Stevens; John Stewart; Ben Stiffarm; Ida Stiffarm; Michael Stoops; Robert Stoyles, Esq.; Ray Strickland; Craig Strobel; Ida Stuntz; Steve Suagee; Shirley Suttles; Doug Swanson, Esq.; Martha Takaro, Esq.; John Talbot; John H. Talley; Tom Taylor; Maria Tenario; Ray Thomas, Esq.; Ken Thompson; Becky Tiffany; Judith Tiffany; Ken Tilson, Esq.; Rachel Tilson; Scott Tilson, Esq.; Arturo Torres; Sidney Tribell; John Trudell; Charles Turner, Esq.; Mackie Two Bulls; Eugene Uphoff, M.D.; Mrs. Eugene Uphoff; Jeniffer Vanderwall; Kris Vervaecke; Helen Von Zelenick; Alice Walker; Doris Walker, Esq.; Pat Walker; The Honorable Steve Walker; Andy Walton; Bill Walton; Martha Walton; Susan Walton; Yvonne Wanrow; Bill Wapepah; Steve Wax, Esq.; Carl Webner; Gaston Weisz; Sheri Weisz; Mike Wells; Cheryl Wesley; Fred White; Charles White Elk; Mark Whitlow, Esq.; Michele Whitneck; Susan Whitson; Camie Wiggins; Judith Wilde; Ken Williams; Ron Williams; Susan Williams; Buzz Willits; Billy W. Wilson; J. Denise Wilson; Genny Winterschied; Laurel Winterschied; Ann Witte, Esq.; Kate Wittenstein; Katy Wolk-Stanley; Robert Wollheim, Esq.; Fred Young; Pat Youngblood, Esq.; Bill Youngman, Esq.; Bill Zeller.

INDEX